THE THINKING MIND

The field of thinking has undergone a revolution in recent years, opening itself up to new perspectives and applications. The traditional focus on laboratory-based thinking has transformed as theoretical work is applied to new contexts and real-world issues. This volume presents a state-of-the-art survey of human thinking in everyday life, based around, and in tribute to, one of the field's most eminent figures: Ken Manktelow.

In this collection of cutting-edge research, Manktelow's collaborators and colleagues review a wide range of important and developing areas of inquiry. This book explores modern perspectives on a variety of traditional and contemporary topics, including Wason's reasoning tasks, logic, meta-reasoning, and the effect of environment and context on reasoning.

The Thinking Mind offers a unique combination of breadth, depth, theoretical exploration and real-world applications, making it an indispensable resource for researchers and students of human thinking.

Niall Galbraith is Senior Lecturer in the Institute of Psychology, University of Wolverhampton, UK.

Erica Lucas is Senior Lecturer and Academic Group Leader in the School of Psychology, Sport and Exercise at Staffordshire University, UK.

David E. Over is Emeritus Professor in the Department of Psychology, Durham University, UK.

THE THINKING MIND

A Festschrift for Ken Manktelow

*Edited by Niall Galbraith, Erica Lucas
and David E. Over*

Routledge
Taylor & Francis Group

LONDON AND NEW YORK

First published 2017
by Routledge
2 Park Square, Milton Park, Abingdon, Oxon OX14 4RN

and by Routledge
711 Third Avenue, New York, NY 10017

Routledge is an imprint of the Taylor & Francis Group, an informa business

© 2017 selection and editorial matter, Niall Galbraith, Erica Lucas and
David E. Over; individual chapters, the contributors

British Library Cataloguing in Publication Data
A catalogue record for this book is available from the British Library

Library of Congress Cataloging-in-Publication Data
Names: Manktelow, K. I., 1952– honoree. | Galbraith, Niall, editor. |
   Lucas, Erica, editor. | Over, D. E., 1946– editor.
Title: The thinking mind : a festschrift for Ken Manktelow / edited by
   Niall Galbraith, Erica Lucas and David Over.
Description: New York : Routledge, 2017.
Identifiers: LCCN 2016020614 | ISBN 9781138937864 (hardback :
   alk. paper) | ISBN 9781138937871 (pbk. : alk. paper) |
   ISBN 9781315676074 (ebk)
Subjects: LCSH: Reasoning (Psychology) | Thought and thinking.
Classification: LCC BF442 .T445 2017 | DDC 153.4/2—dc23
LC record available at https://lccn.loc.gov/2016020614

ISBN: 978-1-138-93786-4 (hbk)
ISBN: 978-1-138-93787-1 (pbk)
ISBN: 978-1-315-67607-4 (ebk)

Typeset in Bembo
by Apex CoVantage, LLC

CONTENTS

List of figures   *vii*
List of tables   *viii*
Contributors   *ix*
Preface   *xii*
Phil Johnson-Laird

1   A brief history of the Wason selection task   1
    Jonathan St B T Evans

2   The "defective" truth table: its past, present, and future   15
    David E. Over and Jean Baratgin

3   Pragmatic factors in Wason's 2–4–6 task: implications
    for real–world hypothesis testing   29
    Linden J. Ball and Caroline N. Wade

4   Thinking and deciding beyond the brain   40
    Frédéric Vallée-Tourangeau and Gaëlle Vallée-Tourangeau

5   Deontic reasoning and social norms: broader implications   54
    Harriet Over and David E. Over

6   Certainty and action   66
    Valerie A. Thompson

7 Belief bias, base rates and moral judgment: re-evaluating
the default interventionist dual process account 83
Stephanie Howarth and Simon Handley

8 Dual frames in causal reasoning and other types of thinking 98
*Masasi Hattori, David E. Over, Ikuko Hattori, Tatsuji Takahashi
and Jean Baratgin*

9 Reasoning in everyday life 115
Guillaume Gimenes, Valérie Pennequin and Tom Mercer

10 Moral reasoning 126
Véronique Salvano-Pardieu and Sandra Lepeltier

11 Rationality and backward induction in Centipede games 139
*Andrew M. Colman, Eva M. Krockow, Caren Frosch, and
Briony D. Pulford*

12 Scams and rationality: Dutch book arguments are not all
they are cracked up to be 151
Shira Elqayam

13 If Easterners are illogical when reasoning, then what does
this mean? 166
Hiroshi Yama

14 From reasoning and intelligence research to information
design: understanding and optimising the usability and
acceptability of schematic transit maps 178
Maxwell J. Roberts

15 How mood affects reasoning 191
Nick Perham

16 Toward a rationality quotient (RQ): the Comprehensive
Assessment of Rational Thinking (CART) 202
Keith E. Stanovich, Richard F. West, and Maggie E. Toplak

Index *223*

FIGURES

1.1	Distribution of 1,567 citations to Peter Wason	3
1.2	Distribution of 432 citations to Wason	3
1.3	Distribution of 289 papers featuring 'Wason' and 'selection task' in a topic search	4
2.1	The three levels of knowledge	24
6.1	The linear relationship between Feeling of Rightness, rethinking time and probability of changing answers	68
8.1	Rubin's vase	104
11.1	Game tree of Rosenthal's (1981) original (as yet unnamed) Centipede game	140
11.2	Game tree of Aumann's (1992) exponential Centipede game	142
11.3	The Prisoner's Dilemma game with conventional payoffs	146
12.1	Two lottery tickets reflecting the betting odds of a conjunction fallacy	154
14.1	Four matrix items typical of the sort used in intelligence tests	185
14.2	Sections of maps showing the line trajectories of an area of central London around Paddington	187

TABLES

1.1 Seminal theoretical papers featuring the Wason selection task,
with citations in Web of Science (December 2014)   4

2.1 The truth table for the material conditional, equivalent to *not-p or q*   16

2.2 The "defective," 2 × 2 de Finetti table for the indicative
conditional *if p, then q*   17

2.3 The 3 × 3 de Finetti table for *if p, then q*   18

2.4 The Jeffrey table for *if p, then q*   24

7.1 Three paradigms used to examine dual processes in reasoning 85

8.1 Characteristics of the two frames in causal reasoning   99

8.2 A 2 × 2 contingency table representing covariation information
between a candidate cause and a target effect   100

12.1 Lottery outcome of Tickets A and B for Jack   155

12.2 Lottery outcome of Tickets A and B for Jill   157

16.1 Heuristics, biases, and effects studied in the Stanovich/
West/Toplak lab   207

16.2 Framework for classifying the types of rational thinking
tasks and subtests on the CART   212

CONTRIBUTORS

Linden J. Ball
University of Central Lancashire, UK

Jean Baratgin
University of Paris VIII, France

Andrew M. Colman
University of Leicester, UK

Shira Elqayam
De Montfort University, UK

Jonathan St B T Evans
Plymouth University, UK

Caren Frosch
University of Leicester, UK

Guillaume Gimenes
University of Tours, France

Simon Handley
University of Plymouth, UK

Ikuko Hattori
Ritsumeikan University, Japan

Masasi Hattori
Ritsumeikan University, Japan

Stephanie Howarth
Plymouth University, UK

Eva M. Krockow
University of Leicester, UK

Sandra Lepeltier
University of Tours, France

Tom Mercer
University of Wolverhampton, UK

David E. Over
Durham University, UK

Harriet Over
University of York, UK

Valérie Pennequin
University of Tours, France

Nick Perham
Cardiff Metropolitan University, UK

Briony D. Pulford
University of Leicester, UK

Maxwell J. Roberts
University of Essex, UK

Véronique Salvano-Pardieu
University of Tours, France

Keith E. Stanovich
University of Toronto, Canada

Tatsuji Takahashi
Tokyo Denki University, Japan

Valerie A. Thompson
University of Saskatchewan, Canada

Maggie E. Toplak
York University, Canada

Frédéric Vallée-Tourangeau
Kingston University, UK

Gaëlle Vallée-Tourangeau
Kingston University, UK

Caroline N. Wade
Lancaster University, UK

Richard F. West
James Madison University, USA

Hiroshi Yama
Osaka City University, Japan

PREFACE

Phil Johnson-Laird

Kenneth Ian Manktelow is an outstanding investigator of human thinking and reasoning. His education in psychology was at Plymouth Polytechnic (now Plymouth University), where he was Jonathan Evans's very first PhD student. Ken won a prize for top marks in his graduating class, and so, as Jonathan reports in his chapter herein, he offered Ken a PhD place. Ken pondered the offer, and after some hesitation accepted it. The hesitation, he says, was because he'd been thrilled by a course on physiological psychology whereas he knew little about Jonathan's research. Ken's first teaching position was at Sunderland Polytechnic (now Sunderland University), and he was there for twelve years. In 1992, he moved to the University of Wolverhampton. This volume is a Festschrift to honour his life and research, on his retiring from teaching at Wolverhampton in 2014, and becoming an Emeritus Professor.

Everyone is either a horse or a muffin. So a student of personality once told me. It's true that people often concur on who is what, which one hopes attests more to their projective abilities than to the veracity of the categories. The philosopher Isaiah Berlin popularized a more useful dichotomy, applying it to well-known writers and philosophers. His guide was an ancient poet, who wrote: a fox knows many things, but a hedgehog knows one big thing. It is diverting to classify psychologists in the same way. The eminent English fox who looms over this book is Peter Wason. An exemplary hedgehog is the Swiss developmental theorist Jean Piaget. Ken himself is known for his studies of:

the selection task (which Wason invented)
practical reasoning versus epistemic reasoning
the role of utility in reasoning
the shortcomings of evolutionary psychology
reading skills in the hearing-impaired
human–computer interaction
and delusional ideas.

He's a veritable fox. And, as befits the category, he is the author of two excellent textbooks: *Reasoning and Thinking* (1999) and *Thinking and Reasoning* (2012).

Ken's multifaceted research includes three primordial studies, whose influence is detectable in the chapters in this book. They all concern the selection task. Wason's original version calls for you to test a hypothesis, such as, 'If there's an A on one side of card, then there's a 2 on the other side.' You select which cards to turn over to find out whether the hypothesis is true or false. A surprising result is that you are likely to neglect to select the card depicting a 3; yet an A on its other side would show you that the hypothesis was false. Thanks to Ken and others, we know a lot about what manipulations affect the selections people make (see Evans's chapter). Could it be that the difficulty of the task has to do with the abstract, if not artificial, nature of hypotheses about letters and numbers on cards? The first of Ken's primordial studies, published with Evans in 1979, ruled out mere abstractness as important. They used hypotheses, such as:

If I eat haddock, then I drink gin.

These contents are concrete, though reflecting a bizarre dietary preference, and they failed to improve performance. A wistful suggestion (in Gimenes, Pennequin and Mercer's chapter) is that the participants themselves should have drunk the gin, which might have had the desired effect.

The second study (published in 1990 with his lifelong collaborator David E. Over) examined the selection task in a novel version. It concerned the admonition:

If you clear up spilt blood, then you must wear rubber gloves.

This assertion is 'deontic', that is, it concerns an obligation. When participants selected evidence for who might have violated the rule, they correctly selected those who had cleared up blood, and those who had not worn rubber gloves. Evolutionary psychologists had hitherto argued that the secret to the selection task is that everyone has an innate capacity to check whether other people are cheating them. Here, however, was a case that forced them to think again (see the Over and Over chapter).

The third study (published with Over in 1991) concerned a deontic rule about what's permissible:

If you spend more than $100, then you may take a free gift.

When the participants tested whether the shop had broken this rule, they tended to select the cases in which a shopper had spent more than $100, and in which a shopper had not taken the free gift. But, when the participants tested whether a shopper had broken the rule, they tended to select the cases in which a shopper had not spent more than $100, and in which a shopper had taken the free gift. These results had consequences that resonate to this day. They demonstrated the importance of context, utilities and probabilities. The theme is taken up in Elqayam's chapter and in Salvano-Pardieu and Lepeltier's chapter. And, as Over and Over emphasize, it is a harbinger of the new paradigm in reasoning that, roughly speaking, aims to replace logic with probability.

The chapters in this book reflect many of Ken's interests, and they give readers a refreshing look at their authors' thoughts about many topics from rationality (Stanovich, West and Toplak) to map-making (Roberts). But, as is inevitable, they do not capture the man himself. The most immediate impression of him that you're likely to form is that he is a very amusing and congenial individual. He is witty, self-deprecating and insightful. Hence, we all look forward to his biography of Peter Wason, who bequeathed him the set of cards used in the original selection task. By the way, there is still no comprehensive explanation of the phenomena that the task has revealed. One difficulty is that they are not consistent from one study to another. Ken is partly to blame. His primordial study with Evans failed to replicate Wason's experiment showing that content is critical to performance. It is. But not in a way that is easy to comprehend.

In Paris, a few years ago, Ken remarked in a talk, 'There was a time when Margaret Thatcher was a rational person.' He apologized at once for introducing politics, albeit implicitly, into a scientific meeting. He had in mind the Mrs Thatcher who worked for Joe Lyons and Co. as a food scientist, and who invented a method for doubling the amount of air in ice cream. (Her finest moment, Ken implied.) It's symptomatic of his range of interests that he would know Thatcher's past.

1

A BRIEF HISTORY OF THE WASON SELECTION TASK

Jonathan St B T Evans

My talk at Ken Manktelow's Festschrift conference was titled 'Whatever happened to the selection task?'. However, some recent study of Web of Science has convinced me that my reports of its demise were somewhat exaggerated. While certainly past its prime, research on the task continues to feature in a number of recent publications, as we shall see. What the task has contributed overall to the psychology of reasoning in its 50 odd years of life is, however, quite remarkable. I offer here a brief, selective, affectionate and doubtless biased account of its history.

The selection task was first presented to an unsuspecting academic world in a book chapter. Wason (1966) reported an experiment in which the subjects, as he called them, were to decide whether a rule was true or false. The rule was 'If a card has a vowel on one side, then it has an even number on the other side'. Subjects were told that the rule applied only to four particular cards which had a letter written on one side and a number on the other. The visible sides of the cards were

E K   4   7

Wason and Johnson-Laird (1972, p. 173) later described the results as follows: 'The vast majority of subjects say either "E" and "4" or "only E". Both answers are wrong. The correct answer is "E" and "7". Any odd number on the other side of the E falsifies the rule in exactly the same way as would any vowel on the other side of the 7.' Wason (1966, p. 146) comments that 'In spite of instructions to the contrary, they [the subjects] cannot inhibit a tendency to see whether the statement is "true".' He later adds (p. 147) that 'this apparent bias towards verification' is analogous to that observed on his 2–4–6 task, discussed earlier in his chapter. In fact, there is a striking parallel between Wason's (1966) first account of the task and that of his (1960) original paper on the almost equally famous '2 4 6' problem (see Evans, 2016). In both cases a single condition is reported, without controls and comparisons, and the reader invited to wonder at the difficulty of a task which (in Wason's opinion) should be easy. Wason was wont to refer to both these problems as 'deceptively simple' and expressed wonder that anyone would call them 'deceptively difficult'. I still have not worked that one out.

The impact of Peter Wason

Wason was discharged from the army as an officer at the end of World War 2 and took up the opportunity offered to read for a university degree. However, this was in English. On graduation, he decided he wanted to be a psychologist, for reasons he never explained to me, and went to University College London (UCL) to take a second degree in psychology. He never left UCL but after obtaining his PhD moved to the linguistics department because, as he told me when supervising my own PhD, 'I refused to teach' (!). He worked most of his career as a Reader in Psycholinguistics despite concentrating the bulk of his research on the psychology of reasoning. And indeed, he did not teach, or do any administrative work so far as I can tell. His position, in effect, was that of full-time researcher.

Given this happy situation and his later fame, one might suppose him to have a prolific publication output and to feature in the world's elite journals. In fact, neither is the case. Web of Science (WoS) records just 31 journal articles published by Wason between 1953 and 1984. (There were a couple of books and a few book chapters in addition.) The bulk of these were published in British journals and not one APA publication is to be found on his list. In a modern British university, such an output would be considered modest at best, even for someone who did his share of teaching and administration. When we look at his impact, however, the picture is quite different. Because of the age of the papers it is difficult to get a fully accurate picture of his citations. For example, Web of Science shows a total of 1,576 which does not include his most cited paper, Wason (1960), or his original book chapter, (Wason, 1960), although elsewhere in the WoS database these are given at 571 and 254, respectively (the last, being a book chapter, as well as old, is almost certainly underestimated). Even on these figures, however, we can see a total citation count between 2,000 and 2,500.

What is most striking, however, is the distribution of citations to Peter Wason (Figure 1.1). Twenty years on from his last published journal article, citations of Peter Wason's work are still *increasing*.[1] The citations to his first published account of the selection task in a journal article (Wason, 1968) are shown in Figure 1.2, and they also have increased in recent years – all this despite my perception that actual studies of the task are on the decline. Identifying how many papers actually report work on the task is very difficult without reading all the citing papers. However, to get an indication, I searched for papers that give both 'Wason' and 'selection task' in their topic, with the results shown in Figure 1.3. A scan of the abstracts of the more recent ones suggests that most of these do in fact report new empirical work on the task. So the number of such studies is indeed decreasing, but not so much as I had thought.

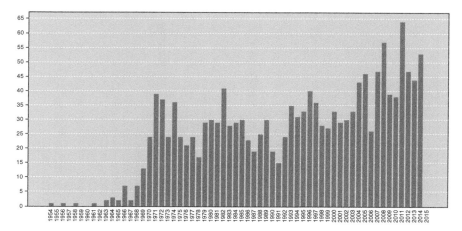

FIGURE 1.1   Distribution of 1,567 citations to Peter Wason – Web of Science, December 2014. Excludes Wason (1960) – 571 citations – and Wason (1966) – 254 citations

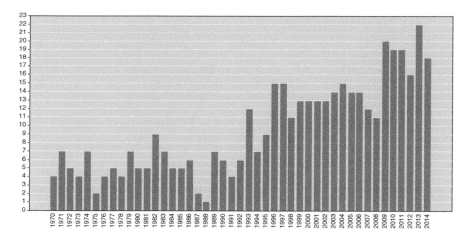

FIGURE 1.2   Distribution of 432 citations to Wason (1968) – Web of Science, December 2014

Much more interesting than this quantitative impact, however, is the influence the selection task had on the development of reasoning theory. Table 1.1 presents a highly selected list of important papers based on the selection task, together with citations rates. Each of these develops an important new theoretical perspective on the psychology of reasoning and all involve either the report of new experiments using the selection task or the extensive re-analysis of selection task data in order to support the theoretical claims made. Note that there are a number of other important papers on the selection task, some of which will be discussed later in this

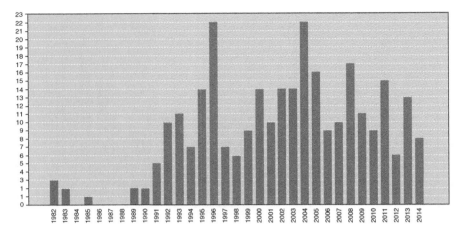

FIGURE 1.3 Distribution of 289 papers featuring 'Wason' and 'selection task' in a topic search – Web of Science, December 2014

TABLE 1.1 Seminal theoretical papers featuring the Wason selection task, with citations in Web of Science (December 2014)

Authors	Subject	WoS
Wason and Evans (1975)	Dual-process theory of reasoning	125
Cheng and Holyoak (1985)	Pragmatic reasoning schemas	624
Cosmides (1989)	Evolutionary theory of reasoning	814
Manktelow and Over (1991)	Decision theoretic treatment of reasoning	151
Oaksford and Chater (1994)	Rational analysis; Bayesian theory of reasoning	362
Sperber, Cara and Girotto (1995)	Relevance theory of reasoning	182

chapter. Table 1.1 does not include papers which simply discovered new empirical phenomena, however important, or whose main thrust was the understanding of the selection task itself. Of these kinds of papers, well-cited (100+) examples include Evans and Lynch (1973, 148 citations) – early report of 'matching bias'; Griggs and Cox (1982, 259 citations) – key experimental paper elucidating the thematic facilitation effect; Fiddick, Cosmides and Tooby (2000, 129 citations) and Gigerenzer and Hug (1992, 148 citations) both developing the evolutionary theory of reasoning.

I will discuss three phases of work on the selection task: the early work (1966–1979), the heyday (1980–1999) and the modern work of 2000 onwards.

Early work on the selection task (1966–1979)

Peter Wason was very enthused by the selection task following his 1966 book chapter and discussed it with me often during my PhD years (1969–1971) under his supervision and in the decade that followed in which we kept close contact. This was one of his most productive periods with a relative flurry of papers on the selection task published by him between 1968 and 1976, some of them in collaboration with Phil Johnson-Laird and, later, myself. It was during this period also that his influential book *Psychology of Reasoning* was published (Wason & Johnson-Laird, 1972), including several chapters on the selection task and helping to spread its fame. Even so, as Figure 1.2 shows, citations were no more respectable prior to the post-1980 heyday.

When I first joined Wason as a PhD student, he was working on the abstract version of the selection task, similar to the letters-numbers rule given earlier. He had decided by then that his subjects were incorrigibly irrational victims of 'verification bias' (later known as confirmation bias). He had shown their failures to be insensitive to a number of experimental variations such as binary materials or the use of both values on one side of the card with masks and so on. He was fascinated by their 'irreversible' thinking, quoting verbal protocols and trying to induce better performance by various therapies (Wason, 1969, is a particularly fascinating read). Two developments were, however, radically to change this picture (Wason hated split infinitives). The first was the discovery of the so-called *thematic facilitation effect*, in which the difficulty of the task apparently evaporated when realistic rather than abstract materials were used. The two early studies on this were run while I was working with him at UCL (Johnson-Laird, Legrenzi & Legrenzi, 1972; Wason & Shapiro, 1971). The second, which I discuss later, was the discovery that matching rather than verification bias explained the abstract selection patterns (Evans & Lynch, 1973).

Wason appeared disappointed when Diana Shapiro reported the first experiment to show that the difficulty of the task could be removed using realistic materials – but not for long. He soon became fascinated by how the task could be made easy in such a simple way, and the thematic facilitation effect featured strongly in the book he and Johnson-Laird were writing at the time (Wason & Johnson-Laird, 1972). The simple idea that realistic materials improve reasoning became a powerful *meme* (Dawkins, 1976) that escaped from the small reasoning field into psychology more generally. It was the thing that everyone who had never studied reasoning knew about reasoning. And like all memes, it proved very hard to recall when later research showed that this idea was oversimplified and inaccurate. (I originally wrote 'simplistic' before I remembered that Wason hated this word.[2])

On starting my lecturing career, my (equal) first PhD student was Ken Manktelow. As an undergraduate, Ken had little interest in cognitive psychology and none at all in reasoning. But he had top marks in his class, and when I offered him a PhD studentship which had dropped into my lap, he thought about it for a while and then – with some apparent reluctance – accepted. (The rest is history.) We decided to combine two hot topics on the selection task – matching bias and the thematic facilitation effect. Showing matching bias requires the introduction of negatives into the conditional statements. Suppose the standard abstract rule is

If there is an A on one side of the card, then there is a 3 on the other side of the card.

We know that people tend to choose A and 3, and Wason had originally seen this as a verification bias. He thought people were trying to confirm the rule by looking for an A and 3 combination rather than a falsifying A and not-3 combination. But suppose the statement was this:

If there is an A on one side of the card, then there is NOT a 3 on the other side of the card.

And suppose that for both statements the visible sides of the card show

A   D   3   7

If people have a verification bias, they should select A and 3 for the affirmative rule and A and 7 for the negative rule (looking for a confirming combination of A and not-3). What they actually tend to do is to choose A and 3 on both problems, the so-called matching bias effect (Evans, 1998; Evans & Lynch, 1973). This was a very difficult finding for Peter Wason and he was somewhat shocked when I first showed it to him. But he almost immediately accepted that the matching bias account must be right, and we subsequently collaborated on work to reconcile this with previous findings (Evans & Wason, 1976; Wason & Evans, 1975).

Now back to Ken Manktelow's PhD. We thought that since realistic materials remove the difficulty of the selection task, they might remove matching bias as well. So Ken ran a series of experiments comparing abstract and realistic materials and including negations in the conditional sentences. Most of his materials used food and drink problems, with statements such as

If I eat haddock, then I drink gin.

While somewhat arbitrary, these materials are definitely thematic, and because people have no preconceptions about these relations, they work fine with negations added such as

If I eat haddock, then I do not drink gin.

Participants were told that each card represented what was eaten and drunk at a particular meal and shown cards with visible words such as

Haddock   beef   gin   beer

Letter-number rules were used as abstract controls. The logic of the design was impeccable. According to the thematic facilitation meme, logical performance should have been better with thematic materials. The only problem was that these materials did not facilitate. At all. Not even a little bit. In fact, they behaved exactly the same as the abstract materials, including full matching bias effects (Manktelow & Evans, 1979).

At the time Ken was desperately disappointed with these negative results. He eventually replicated the thematic facilitation effect using materials similar to those that had succeeded for other authors, and so we realised that it was the nature of the materials that was the problem. I persuaded Ken that negative findings can be important, and so it proved. The paper we published on this (Manktelow & Evans, 1979) counts among the most cited on the task. Web of Science (December 2014) still lists 120 citations to this paper, despite its age, which compares favourably with a number of others mentioned earlier. With hindsight, this paper is one of the most important ever published on the selection task because it broke the myth of the thematic facilitation meme. It led quickly to the highly cited paper of Griggs and Cox (1982), who demonstrated the conditions under which realistic materials would and would not facilitate logical performance. More important, these two papers together laid the foundation for the heyday of the selection task to follow.

The other significant work in this early period was the collaboration of Peter Wason and myself (Wason & Evans, 1975), the only seminal paper shown in Table 1.1 to precede the heyday. I will not describe this in detail here as it has been well covered elsewhere (Evans, 2004, 2016). In essence, we showed that while people choose matching cards, they do not seem to be aware that this is what they are doing. Instead they come up with rationalisations, justifying the choices made in light of the instructions. We suggested a distinction between type 1 (unconscious) processes which led to card choices, and type 2 (conscious) processes which responded to the request to justify the choices. This paper was the foundation for later dual-process theories of reasoning, but also drew upon ideas in Wason's earlier studies of the 2–4–6 and selection tasks. For this reason, he probably has not received enough credit for his contribution to dual-process theory (see Evans, 2016).

The heyday: 1980–1999

Peter Wason had no idea that the selection task would take off in the way it did, commenting in 1975 that 'the reader might well expect some justification for yet another paper on the problem' (Wason & Evans, 1975, p. 141). Little did he know! The 1980s and 1990s were the heyday of the selection task, not only because of the number of papers published on the task, but also because the bulk of the seminal theoretical papers (Table 1.1) fall into this period. Most of this interest was focussed on realistic or thematic forms of the selection task.

Following Manktelow and Evans (1979) and Griggs and Cox (1982), it was apparent that only specific types of realistic content changed the responses dramatically from those to the abstract task, although it would take until the early 1990s for a full explanation of this to be developed, in fact by Ken Manktelow working with David E. Over (Manktelow & Over, 1990). A good example of a reliable facilitator is the drinking age problem that Griggs and Cox (1982) introduced. The problem included a brief scenario as follows:

> On this task imagine that you are a police officer on duty. It is your job to ensure that people conform to certain rules. The cards in front of you have information about four people sitting at a table. On one side of the card is a

person's age and on the other side of the card is what the person is drinking. Here is a rule: IF A PERSON IS DRINKING BEER THEN THE PERSON MUST BE OVER 19 YEARS OF AGE. Select the card or cards that you would definitely need to turn over to determine whether or not the people are violating the rule.

The cards had DRINKING A BEER, DRINKING A COKE, 16 YEARS OF AGE and 22 YEARS OF AGE written on their visible sides. People very reliably choose to investigate the beer drinkers and the underage drinkers – equivalent (or so the authors thought at the time) to choosing the correct logical answers on their abstract control task. Of course, only those two groups violate the rule and hence seem similar to cards which falsify on the standard task. The difference between violation and falsification turned out to be critical, however.

It became apparent that pragmatic factors are critical for the facilitation and that success also depends on both (a) the exact presentation of the problem and (b) the prior knowledge of the participants. For example, Pollard and Evans (1987) showed that if the problem is slightly modified so that no reference is made to being a police officer or enforcing rules, the facilitation disappears and the problem becomes as hard as an abstract one. Another apparently strong facilitator is the postal rule first used by Johnson-Laird and colleagues (1972), which relates the value of a stamp on an envelope (used in place of cards) to whether the envelope is sealed. This worked on their British participants, who all had experience of a similar rule in force in the United Kingdom at the time, but it produced no facilitation at all on an American population, who had no real life experience of such a rule (Griggs & Cox, 1982, Experiment 2). Other studies showed that the postal rule worked for Hong Kong participants, who had recent experience of a similar rule (Cheng & Holyoak, 1985), and for older UK citizens, who could remember it but not for younger ones who could not (Golding, 1981). So it seemed for a while that people were retrieving the right answers from memory. But that was not right either, as versions were found that would facilitate without any direct relevant experience (see Evans, Newstead & Byrne, 1993, for detailed review of relevant studies).

Two of the other seminal papers shown in Table 1.1 arose from attempts to understand the kinds of finding discussed earlier. The first was the pragmatic reasoning schema theory of Cheng and Holyoak (1985). They noticed that successful thematic versions of the selection task mostly involved relations of permission or obligation. They suggested that people might have pragmatic schemas, elicited by the context, which enabled them to reason effectively in particular contexts – but not by some kind of general logical reasoning ability. A permission schema would include rules such as

1   If an action is taken, then a precondition must be met.
2   If a precondition is not met, then an action may not be taken.

When a situation is recognised as one of permission, the values of 'precondition' and 'action' are instantiated in the context. For example, precondition = 'Over 19 years of age' and action = 'drinking alcoholic beverage'. By rule 1, we must check alcohol drinkers to make sure they meet the precondition of being over 19 years of age. By rule 2, we must check underage drinkers to make sure they are not drinking alcohol. Thus the schema directs people to choose the correct cards. But it will not help on a letter-number rule where there is no permission (or obligation) context.

The next paper was by Cosmides (1989) and caused something of a minor earthquake in the field when it was published. None of us (reasoning researchers) had previously heard of Leda Cosmides, knew anything much about evolutionary theory or had even considered it could be applied to reasoning tasks. This paper was very successful, however, and was one of three published on the selection task taking the evolutionary approach that achieved high citations (the others being Fiddick et al., 2000 and Gigerenzer & Hug, 1992, as mentioned earlier). They proposed an innate cognitive module for social contracts, which would trigger a search for cheaters. But Cosmides' paper was very controversial from the start, attracting many published criticisms of both theory and method. Ken, I recall, was very interested in the paper when it was published; I, on the other hand, hated the paper and hoped it would be ignored. (Instead, it became the most cited paper ever published on the task!) I was extremely sceptical of the claim it contained: essentially that evolution could account for choices on the selection task (or any other laboratory reasoning task) in a genuinely testable manner. David E. Over, a mutual collaborator of Ken and me, later edited a book on the controversy (Over, 2003). One of the reasons it was so controversial was the claim (later elaborated in collaboration with John Tooby, e.g. Cosmides & Tooby, 2000) that the mind was massively modular,[3] and that reasoning could only be domain-specific and not a general purpose system.

Both Cheng and Holyoak (1985) and Cosmides (1989) used the abstract selection task as their control task. In what remains one of my favourite papers on the task, Manktelow and Over (1991) showed that this is inappropriate because the abstract and thematic tasks are different logical problems. The abstract task is based on indicative logic which concerns what is true and false, whereas the facilitatory thematic versions involved deontic logic, which deals with what is and is not *permitted* (see also Over and Over, this volume). When 16-year-olds drink beer, they violate the drinking age rule, but they do not make it false. Such a rule cannot be true or false; it can simply be obeyed or violated. The literature to this point was almost entirely based on a confound: tasks which were both abstract and indicative were being compared with those which were thematic and also deontic. Manktelow and Over also discussed a facilitatory deontic rule 'If you clean up spilt blood, then you must wear rubber gloves' (Manktelow & Over, 1990), which Cosmides' theory of social exchange could not explain. The evolutionary camp responded not by agreeing that its theory was falsified; instead it decided a second innate reasoning module must be in play on the selection task, designed for hazards and precautions (Fiddick et al., 2000).

Two other papers mark the latter stages of the heyday. Oaksford and Chater (1994) presented a 'rational analysis' of the selection task, claiming that the usual choices were correct when viewed from the perspective of expected information gain. While also controversial at the time, the paper attracted great interest and launched a programme of rational analysis and a Bayesian theory of reasoning which has endured and prospered (Oaksford & Chater, 2007, 2010, 2013) and also forms an important foundation for the 'new paradigm' psychology of reasoning (Elqayam & Over, 2013; Evans, 2012; Manktelow, Over & Elqayam, 2011). Another paper of great originality and impact was that of Sperber and colleagues (1995), which applied the influential theory of pragmatic relevance Sperber and Wilson (1995) had devised to explicit reasoning tasks for the first time. The authors gave an alternative account of the deontic selection task Cheng and Holyoak (1985) and Cosmides (1989) offered, and it was later followed by a much lesser known but quite devastating critique of the evolutionary theory (Sperber & Girotto, 2002). Sperber and colleagues' (1995) paper was important for placing pragmatics at the forefront of reasoning research, where it has remained ever since, and is hence another foundation for the new paradigm.

More recent work (post-2000)

Over the past 15 years or so, papers have continued to appear regularly on the selection task and include significant contributions to the psychology of reasoning. But the blockbuster papers of the heyday have not been emulated. Nor, in my view, have the issues raised about the deontic selection task ever really been resolved. It is clearly beyond doubt that it is the deontic nature of the task that makes it solvable: it has something to do with the use of permissions and obligations, and to do with the prior knowledge and belief the reasoner brings to the experiment. But has it ever been resolved as to which of the pragmatic reasoning schemas, Darwinian algorithms, pragmatic relevance or decision-theoretic approaches is the best explanation of the task? Not really. It is more that a number of the big players, having made their statements, have moved on or out of the field. Of those that remain (e.g. Over, Oaksford), the decision-theoretic approach is best represented (see Over and Over, this volume).

I will mention a few selected studies of the abstract selection task in the post-2000 era. There has been a trend towards mathematical modelling of reasoning data in the past decade or so, mostly within the German universities. These studies include one major paper modelling the selection task data with large numbers of participants and considering all 16 possible combinations of card selections (Klauer, Stahl & Erdfelder, 2007). The model includes multiple parameters and sheds some light on dual-process accounts of the task. It certainly provides a powerful and unrivalled description of the data. Testing theoretical accounts can benefit from process-tracing methods, however, and one such is the eye-tracking paper of Ball, Lucas, Miles and Gale (2003), which used eye movement measurement to track attention to different cards. This paper tested predictions made by Evans (1996) based on the heuristic-analytic theory of reasoning (Evans, 1989, 2006) with improved methodology but similar findings. In the original paper, I had questioned whether card choices on the abstract selection task involved any real process of reasoning at all. A re-analysis of Ball and colleagues' data showed that reasoning is involved, at least to some extent (Evans & Ball, 2010). This supports claims based on different methods (Feeney & Handley, 2000; Handley, Feeney & Harper, 2002).

An important programme in the recent study of reasoning is that developed by Valerie A. Thompson (Thompson, 2010; Thompson, Prowse Turner & Pennycook, 2011). Thompson adopts a dual-process approach, but proposes that intervention of type 2 reasoning to override type 1 intuitions is related to intuitive 'feelings of rightness' (FOR) in the answer initially proposed by type 1 processing. She developed a two-response task in which an initial quick answer is followed by a second (which may change the first) after an unrestricted period of reflection. She also proposed that FOR is mediated by fluency – the ease with which initial answers come to mind (Thompson et al., 2011). Recently, she was able to demonstrate these effects on the abstract selection task (Thompson, Evans & Campbell, 2013). Matching cards, it appears, produce rapid and fluent intuitive responses with high feelings of rightness. Such cards are chosen more quickly and subject to less rethinking and response changes than are initial choices of mismatching cards. The selection task has also played a fringe role in other major research programmes, most notably the work on individual differences in reasoning and decision making by Keith Stanovich and Rich West (see Stanovich, 2011, for a recent review). They devoted one of their many papers to showing a relation between general intelligence and success on the abstract but not deontic version of the task (Stanovich & West, 1998), supporting their dual-process account. As in many modern studies, the interest is not in understanding the selection task per se, but rather in its use as a tool for investigating broader issues.

Conclusions

The question of most interest is not why there has been relative decline in papers on the selection task. Paradigms come and go and fashions change. The really interesting question is how it achieved greatness at all. Within the specialist thinking and reasoning community, the most popular task is conditional inference, followed by syllogistic reasoning: two methods that have never captured the imagination of non-specialists. The key to the heyday of the selection task was that it attracted interest from people who had not worked on reasoning previously (or since in some cases) and who were addressing much broader questions about human cognition. The task, of course, is richer than a standard deductive reasoning task. It involves hypothesis testing, imagination and decision making. A striking paradox, however, is that this most famous of reasoning tasks may invoke very little actual reasoning in the participants to whom it is given. At least that is what a number of the aficionados of the field believe. The ability to solve the abstract selection task is related to general intelligence, however, suggesting that the small minority who can solve it do so by reasoning (Stanovich & West, 1998). On the other hand, formal training in logical reasoning principles does not benefit performance on the task (Cheng, Holyoak, Nisbett & Oliver, 1986).

While interest in the task itself may have declined somewhat, it leaves a great legacy. Selection task papers include the first dual-process theory of reasoning which has proved increasingly popular and influential, together with broader applications of dual processes (Evans, 2008, 2010; Evans & Stanovich, 2013; Stanovich, 2004, 2011). It launched the rational analysis and Bayesian inference approach of Oaksford and Chater, was responsible for much of the current interest in pragmatic aspects of reasoning, and helped to make evolutionary theory a part of mainstream cognitive psychology. This is a quite incredible heritage and a lasting testament to the brilliance and creativity of its inventor, Peter Wason.

Notes

1 With an increased number of journals and papers being published, probably citations generally are increasing. However, the number that Wason has recently received, so long after he stopped publishing, is still remarkable.
2 Wason is my academic superego. Even today I hear him disapproving of every split infinitive and dangling preposition that escapes my fingers at the keyboard.
3 Modularity was an idea introduced by Fodor (1983), in which self-contained sections of the mind combined with a general purpose reasoning system. Massive modularity denies the latter and tries to explain all cognition in terms of modules. Fodor (e.g. 2000, 2001) was very critical of this approach.

References

Ball, L. J., Lucas, E. J., Miles, J. N.V., & Gale, A. G. (2003). Inspection times and the selection task: What do eye-movements reveal about relevance effects? *Quarterly Journal of Experimental Psychology, 56A*(6), 1053–1077.

Cheng, P. W., & Holyoak, K. J. (1985). Pragmatic reasoning schemas. *Cognitive Psychology, 17*, 391–416.

Cheng, P. W., Holyoak, K. J., Nisbett, R. E., & Oliver, L. M. (1986). Pragmatic versus syntactic approaches to training deductive reasoning. *Cognitive Psychology, 18*, 293–328.

Cosmides, L. (1989). The logic of social exchange: Has natural selection shaped how humans reason? *Cognition, 31*, 187–276.

Cosmides, L., & Tooby, J. (2000). Consider the source: The evolution of adaptations for decoupling and metarepresentation. In D. Sperber (Ed.), *Metarepresentations* (pp. 53–115). Oxford: Oxford University Press.

Dawkins, R. (1976). *The selfish gene*. Oxford: Oxford University Press.

Elqayam, S., & Over, D. E. (2013). New paradigm psychology of reasoning: An introduction to the special issue edited by Elqayam, Bonnefon, and Over. *Thinking & Reasoning, 19*(3–4), 249–265.

Evans, J. St. B.T. (1989). *Bias in human reasoning: Causes and consequences*. Brighton: Erlbaum.

Evans, J. St. B.T. (1996). Deciding before you think: Relevance and reasoning in the selection task. *British Journal of Psychology, 87*, 223–240.

Evans, J. St. B. T. (1998). Matching bias in conditional reasoning: Do we understand it after 25 years? *Thinking & Reasoning, 4*, 45–82.

Evans, J. St. B. T. (2004). History of the dual process theory of reasoning. In K. I. Manktelow & M. C. Chung (Eds.), *Psychology of reasoning: Theoretical and historical perspectives* (pp. 241–266). Hove, UK: Psychology Press.

Evans, J. St. B.T. (2006). The heuristic-analytic theory of reasoning: Extension and evaluation. *Psychonomic Bulletin and Review, 13*(3), 378–395.

Evans, J. St. B. T. (2008). Dual-processing accounts of reasoning, judgment and social cognition. *Annual Review of Psychology, 59*, 255–278.

Evans, J. St. B. T. (2010). *Thinking twice: Two minds in one brain*. Oxford: Oxford University Press.

Evans, J. St. B. T. (2012). Questions and challenges for the new psychology of reasoning. *Thinking & Reasoning, 18*, 5–31.

Evans, J. St. B. T. (Ed.). (2014). *Reasoning, rationality and dual processes: Selected works of Jonathan St B T Evans*. London: Taylor & Francis.

Evans, J. St. B. T. (2016). Reasoning, biases and dual processes: The lasting impact of Wason (1960). *Quarterly Journal of Experimental Psychology, 69*, 2076–2092.

Evans, J. St. B. T., & Ball, L. J. (2010). Do people reason on the Wason selection task?: A new look at the data of Ball et al. (2003). *Quarterly Journal of Experimental Psychology, 63*(3), 434–441.

Evans, J. St. B. T., & Lynch, J. S. (1973). Matching bias in the selection task. *British Journal of Psychology, 64*, 391–397.

Evans, J. St. B. T., Newstead, S. E., & Byrne, R. M. J. (1993). *Human reasoning: The psychology of deduction*. Hove, UK: Erlbaum.

Evans, J. St. B. T., & Stanovich, K. E. (2013). Dual process theories of higher cognition: Advancing the debate. *Perspectives on Psychological Science, 8*, 223–241.

Evans, J. St. B. T., & Wason, P. C. (1976). Rationalisation in a reasoning task. *British Journal of Psychology, 63*, 205–212.

Feeney, A., & Handley, S. J. (2000). The suppression of q card selections: Evidence for deductive inference in Wason's selection task. *Quarterly Journal of Experimental Psychology, 53A*, 1224–1243.

Fiddick, L., Cosmides, L., & Tooby, J. (2000). No interpretation without representation: The role of domain-specific representations and inferences in the Wason selection task. *Cognition, 77*, 1–79.

Fodor, J. (1983). *The modularity of mind*. Scranton, PA: Crowell.

Fodor, J. (2000). Why we are so good at catching cheaters? *Cognition, 75*, 29–32.

Fodor, J. (2001). *The mind doesn't work that way*. Cambridge, MA: MIT Press.

Gigerenzer, G., & Hug, K. (1992). Domain-specific reasoning: Social contracts, cheating and perspective change. *Cognition, 43*, 127–171.

Golding, E. (1981). *The effect of past experience on problem solving*. Paper presented at the British Psychological Society, London.

Griggs, R. A., & Cox, J. R. (1982). The elusive thematic materials effect in the Wason selection task. *British Journal of Psychology, 73*, 407–420.

Handley, S. J., Feeney, A., & Harper, C. (2002). Alternative antecedents, probabilities and the suppression of fallacies on Wason's selection task. *Quarterly Journal of Experimental Psychology, 55A*, 799–813.

Johnson-Laird, P. N., Legrenzi, P., & Legrenzi, M. S. (1972). Reasoning and a sense of reality. *British Journal of Psychology, 63*, 395–400.

Klauer, K. C., Stahl, C., & Erdfelder, E. (2007). The abstract selection task: New data and an almost comprehensive model. *Journal of Experimental Psychology: Learning, Memory and Cognition, 33*(4), 680–703.

Manktelow, K. I., & Evans, J. S. B. T. (1979). Facilitation of reasoning by realism: Effect or non-effect? *British Journal of Psychology, 70*, 477–488.

Manktelow, K. I., & Over, D. E. (1990). Deontic thought and the selection task. In K. J. Gilhooly, M. T. Keane, R. H. Logie, & G. Erdos (Eds.), *Lines of thinking. Volume 1* (pp. 153–164). Chichester: Wiley.

Manktelow, K. I., & Over, D. E. (1991). Social roles and utilities in reasoning with deontic conditionals. *Cognition, 39*, 85–105.

Manktelow, K. I., Over, D. E., & Elqayam, S. (2011). Paradigm shift: Jonathan Evans and the science of reason. In K. I. Manktelow, D. E. Over & S. Elqayam (Eds.), *The science of reason: A Festschrift for Jonathan St B T Evans* (pp. 1–16). Hove, UK: Psychology Press.

Oaksford, M., & Chater, N. (1994). A rational analysis of the selection task as optimal data selection. *Psychological Review, 101*, 608–631.

Oaksford, M., & Chater, N. (2007). *Bayesian rationality: The probabilistic approach to human reasoning*. Oxford: Oxford University Press.

Oaksford, M., & Chater, N. (Eds.). (2010). *Cognition and conditionals*. Oxford: Oxford University Press.

Oaksford, M., & Chater, N. (2013). Dynamic inference and everyday conditional reasoning in the new paradigm. *Thinking & Reasoning, 19*(3–4), 346–379.

Over, D. E. (2003). From massive modularity to metarepresentation: The evolution of higher cognition. In D. E. Over (Ed.), *Evolution and the psychology of thinking: The debate* (pp. 121–144). Hove, UK: Psychology Press.

Pollard, P., & Evans, J. S. B. T. (1987). On the relationship between content and context effects in reasoning. *American Journal of Psychology, 100*, 41–60.

Sperber, D., Cara, F., & Girotto, V. (1995). Relevance theory explains the selection task. *Cognition, 57*, 31–95.

Sperber, D., & Girotto, V. (2002). Use or misuse of the selection task? Rejoinder to Fiddick, Cosmides and Tooby. *Cognition, 85*, 277–290.

Sperber, D., & Wilson, D. (1995). *Relevance* (Second edition). Oxford: Basil Blackwell.

Stanovich, K. E. (2004). *The robot's rebellion: Finding meaning in the age of Darwin*. Chicago: University of Chicago Press.

Stanovich, K. E. (2011). *Rationality and the reflective mind*. New York: Oxford University Press.

Stanovich, K. E., & West, R. F. (1998). Cognitive ability and variation in selection task performance. *Thinking & Reasoning, 4*, 193–230.

Thompson, V. A. (2010). Towards a metacognitive dual process theory of conditional reasoning. In M. Oaksford & N. Chater (Eds.), *Cognition and conditionals: Probability and logic in human thinking* (pp. 335–354). Oxford: Oxford University Press.

Thompson, V. A., Evans, J. S. T., & Campbell, J. I. D. (2013). Matching bias on the selection task: It's fast and feels good. *Thinking & Reasoning, 19*(3–4), 431–452.

Thompson, V. A., Prowse Turner, J. A., & Pennycook, G. (2011). Intuition, reason, and metacognition. *Cognitive Psychology, 63*(3), 107–140.

Wason, P. C. (1960). On the failure to eliminate hypotheses in a conceptual task. *Quarterly Journal of Experimental Psychology, 12*, 129–140.

Wason, P. C. (1966). Reasoning. In B. M. Foss (Ed.), *New horizons in psychology I* (pp. 106–137). Harmondsworth: Penguin.

Wason, P. C. (1968). Reasoning about a rule. *Quarterly Journal of Experimental Psychology, 20*, 273–281.

Wason, P. C. (1969). Regression in reasoning? *British Journal of Psychology, 60*, 471–480.

Wason, P. C., & Evans, J. S. B. T. (1975). Dual processes in reasoning? *Cognition, 3*, 141–154.

Wason, P. C., & Johnson-Laird, P. N. (1972). *Psychology of reasoning: Structure and content*. London: Batsford.

Wason, P. C., & Shapiro, D. (1971). Natural and contrived experience in a reasoning problem. *Quarterly Journal of Experimental Psychology, 23*, 63–71.

2

THE "DEFECTIVE" TRUTH TABLE

Its past, present, and future

David E. Over and Jean Baratgin

The study of conditionals has always been a prominent part of the psychology of reasoning, as can be seen from the first introduction to the subject (Wason & Johnson-Laird, 1972) to the most recent (Manktelow, 2012), and understandably so. There is a philosophical view that a conditional, *if p, then q*, is nothing but an "inference ticket" for inferring *q* from *p* (Bennett, 2003, pp. 118–119). A conditional is seen as essentially an inference, and every inference can be expressed as a conditional. This suggestive "inference ticket" idea is far from a full theory, but conditionals and inferences are clearly so closely related that the psychology of reasoning could almost be thought of as equivalent to the psychology of conditionals. In this chapter, we will cover the discovery, by Wason (1966), of a most important fact about ordinary people's evaluations of natural language indicative conditionals. They do not classify these conditionals as only true or false, but think of them as sometimes having a third value of some kind. We will explain what has become of this finding in the contemporary psychology of reasoning, and make recommendations for how it should be developed in the future.

The table's past

It was natural for the first psychologists of reasoning to have binary and truth functional *propositional logic* in mind as the normative theory of conditional reasoning (Binet, 1902; James, 1908; Wason, 1966). It is the fundamental logic for negation, *not*, disjunction, *or*, and conjunction, *and*. It can also be used to express the simplest notion of a conditional, the *material conditional* (material implication), which is logically equivalent to *not-p or q*. This logic satisfies the *principle of bivalence* in having only two *truth values*, truth or falsity, for classifying propositions, and its compound propositions, for example, *not-p or q*, are *truth functional*: the truth value of *not-p or q* is fully determined by the truth values of its components, *p* and *q*. Truth functionality in this logic can be represented in *truth tables* (Kneale & Kneale, 1962, p. 531).

Table 2.1 is the truth table for the material conditional. As this table indicates, the material conditional has the same truth conditions as *not-p or q*: it is true when both *p* and *q* are true, false when *p* is true and *q* is false, true when *p* is false and *q* is true, and true when *p* is false and *q* is false.

The precise mathematical formulation of propositional logic was a giant step forward in the history of logic (Kneale & Kneale, 1962). But Wason (1966) found that people's truth and falsity judgments for an indicative conditional did not match the material conditional truth table, Table 2.1. What people did produce came to be known as the "defective" truth table, although Wason did not at first use "defective" for it. He concluded (p. 146) that people "assume implicitly that a conditional statement has, not two truth values, but three: true, false, and 'irrelevant.'" Wason and Johnson-Laird (1972) have the best early introduction to and theory of the "defective" truth table. They use the following example of a natural language indicative conditional:

(1)   If John loved Mary, then he married her.

Consider the four logical possibilities for this conditional of the form *if p, then q*: *p* and *q* both true, *p* true and *q* false, *p* false and *q* true, and *p* and *q* both false. If we followed Table 2.1, we would, in effect, take (1) as a material conditional and judge it true when John loved Mary and married her, false when John loved Mary and did not marry her, and true in the two cases in which John did not love Mary. However, from evidence in experiments, ordinary people would not make all of these judgments about (1). They would respond that (1) is true when John loved Mary and married her, and false when John loved Mary and did not marry her. But they would not agree that (1) is true in the last two cases, when John did not love Mary. They would say that these cases are "irrelevant" to the truth of (1) or use some other "third" term not equivalent to "true" or "false."

Wason and Johnson-Laird (1972) accounted for the three-value responses by using the distinction Quine (1952) made between the assertion of a conditional and a *conditional assertion*. A material conditional, that is, *not-p or q*, can be categorically asserted and is true, or false, in every possible state of affairs. But according to Quine and Wason and Johnson-Laird, to use a natural language indicative conditional like (1) is to make a conditional assertion, which only becomes a true or false full assertion when its antecedent is true. If the antecedent is false, the use of the conditional is *void* as an assertion and is neither true nor false. But if the antecedent

TABLE 2.1 The truth table for the material conditional, equivalent to *not-p or q*

1 = true, 0 = false

p \ q	1	0
1	1	0
0	1	1

is true, the conditional assertion becomes the categorical assertion of the consequent, and is then true or false depending on whether the consequent is true or false. The result is Table 2.2.

Viewing the use of an indicative conditional as a conditional assertion goes well with referring to this conditional as an "inference ticket." A "ticket" or "license" to infer q from p is "irrelevant" and of "void" value when p is known to be false. Both these views are closely related in turn to the positions of de Finetti (1936/1995, 1937/1964) and Ramsey (1929/1990) on indicative conditionals. They both held that an indicative conditional is "void" when its antecedent is false. It is instructive to consider Ramsey's example of two people arguing about a conditional like (1). One of these people affirms (1) and the other denies (1). They will agree that the first person has stated a truth supposing that John loved Mary and married her, and a falsehood supposing that John loved Mary but did not marry her. However, if these people in dispute find out that John did not love Mary, they will lose interest in (1) and their dispute about it: (1) will become "void." They might go on to have a dispute about the counterfactual conditional, "If John had loved Mary, then he would have married her," but this is a different kind of conditional, and the dispute about it could not be definitively settled by directly observing an actual state of affairs. Many theorists sharply distinguish between indicative conditionals and counterfactuals (Bennett, 2003; Evans & Over, 2004).

In contrast, assume that (1) is equivalent to a material conditional, with Table 2.1 as its truth table. Then (1) is true when it is a matter of fact that John did not love Mary. The first person, who affirmed (1), could claim to have asserted a truth, and it would be vain for the second person to point out that Mary hated and despised John and would never have agreed to marry him, even if he did love her and asked her. Assuming natural language indicative conditionals are material conditionals, and John did not love Mary, all other indicative conditionals with the same antecedent as (1) would also be true, for example, "If John loved Mary, then he hated her." These absurdities can be avoided by holding that to use (1) is to make a conditional assertion and not to assert a material conditional.

It is better to call Table 2.2 the *2 x 2 de Finetti table than the "defective" table*. Such a table was proposed by de Finetti (1936/1995, 1937/1964), and "defective" has an unwarranted negative connotation, which suggests that the table, or the participants who produce it, are somehow faulty or at fault. (Kneale & Kneale, 1962, pp. 135–136, were the first philosophers to use "defective" for Table 2.2, but other logicians or

TABLE 2.2 The "defective," 2×2 de Finetti table for the indicative conditional *if p, then q*

$1 =$ true, $0 =$ false, and $V =$ void

p \\ q	1	0
1	1	0
0	V	V

philosophers have not generally picked up this usage.) One way to interpret what de Finetti says about Table 2.2 is the following. When we learn *p* and *q*, we are certain that *if p, then q* holds. When we learn *p* and *not-q*, we are certain that *if p, then q* does not hold. But supposing we learn *not-p*, the indicative conditional *if p, then q* is "void." This is a kind of radical uncertainty about the conditional that cannot be definitively resolved, and we can only make a probability judgment about *if p, then q*. More generally, we can also be uncertain about *p* and *q* for epistemological reasons. This epistemological state is especially common for indicative future hypothetical conditionals:

(2)   If John falls in love with Mary, then he will marry her.

We could easily be uncertain about the antecedent or consequent of (2), and uncertain about (2) itself, and Table 2.2 is actually a sub-table of Table 2.3, which is given in de Finetti (1936/1995, 1937/1964). Table 2.3 can be appropriately called the *3 × 3 de Finetti table*. As seen in this table, an indicative conditional *if p, then q* is uncertain when *p* or *q* is uncertain and when *p* is false.

Fallacies past and present

The classical philosophers were the first to discuss whether the principle of bivalence – that every statement is true or false – always holds. They asked whether a third value is necessary in addition to truth and falsity, and started a line of research that continues to this day on three-valued and many-valued logics (Gottwald, 2015). Aristotle appeared to doubt the principle of bivalence in what he said about future contingencies (Kneale & Kneale, 1962, pp. 47–48), and his argument is relevant to the contemporary psychology of reasoning. He was puzzled by the apparent truth of two conditionals like these:

(3)   If it is true that there will be a sea battle tomorrow, then it is necessary that there will be a sea battle tomorrow.
(4)   If it is true that there will not be a sea battle tomorrow, then it is necessary that there will not be a sea battle tomorrow.

If it is true that there will be a sea battle tomorrow, we can *apparently* infer from (3) that it is necessary that there will be a sea battle tomorrow. Alternatively, if it is true

TABLE 2.3 The 3 × 3 de Finetti table for *if p, then q*

1 = true, 0 = false, and U = uncertain

	q 1	U	0
p			
1	1	U	0
U	U	U	U
0	U	U	U

that there will not be a sea battle tomorrow, we can *apparently* infer from (4) that it is necessary that there will not be a sea battle tomorrow. But logically, there will either be a sea battle tomorrow or not, and that appears to force us to the conclusion that logical determinism holds. Either it is logically necessary that there will be a sea battle tomorrow or it is logically necessary that there will not be a sea battle tomorrow, and it is not a contingent matter whether or not there will be a sea battle tomorrow. Clearly, these inferences could be repeated for every statement about the future, and the consequence would seem to be logical determinism. Whatever is going to happen might be causally necessary, but it is absurd to infer that it happens by logical necessity.

This argument to logical determinism as a conclusion contains at least one fallacy. There is a *scope ambiguity* in natural language conditionals, like (3) and (4), of the general form, *if p, then necessarily q* (see Gaskin, 1995, for this problem in Aristotle on the sea battle). The necessity operator in these conditionals can either be given wide scope, *necessarily (if p, then q)* or narrow scope, *if p, then (necessarily q)*. With wide scope *necessarily* applies to the whole conditional, and with narrow scope *necessarily* applies only to the consequent of the conditional. But as Garson (2014) says in his introduction to modal logic, "In English, 'necessarily' is an adverb, and since adverbs are usually placed near verbs, we have no natural way to indicate whether the modal operator applies to the whole conditional, or to its consequent." To indicate this, we have to apply parentheses as they are used in formal modal logic. Once we do this, we can see that the argument to logical determinism commits a *modal fallacy* by confusing the wide scope of necessity with the narrow scope (Bradley & Swartz, 1979; Swartz, 1999). Conditionals about the future in which *necessarily* has wide scope can trivially hold, for example, *necessarily (if it is true that an event will occur, then it will occur)*, but logical determinism does not follow, because the apparent inferences that lead to it fail to be valid. Logical determinism does follow when *necessarily* is given narrow scope, *if it is true that an event will occur, then (necessarily it will occur)*, but now this conditional premise is false, stating as it does that a necessary truth follows from the contingent truth.

Modal operators, like *necessarily* and *probably*, are often used in natural language conditionals, and modal fallacies can result if theorists are confused about scope. Byrne and Johnson-Laird (2010, p. 56), for instance, claim that *it is necessary that* applied to the whole conditional "is synonymous with" *it is necessary that* applied only to the consequent, that is, *it is necessary that (if p, then q)* "is synonymous with" *if p, then (it is necessary that q)*, but this is clearly a modal fallacy. We can see that by comparing *it is necessary that (if p, then p)*, which is trivial, with *if p, then (it is necessary that p)*, which is false for contingent *p* (Over, Douven, & Verbrugge, 2013; Politzer, Over, & Baratgin, 2010). Clearly, *if (it is necessary that p) then p* always holds, and supposing *if p, then (it is necessary that p)* always held as well, *p if and only if (it is necessary that p)* would follow and with it logical determinism. By committing a simple modal scope fallacy, Byrne and Johnson-Laird have implied the absurdity of logical determinism.

The explicit and implicit use of the modal *probably* to qualify conditionals is of deep interest to the contemporary psychology of reasoning, which has come to recognize that almost all everyday and scientific reasoning takes place in the context of uncertainty. There is the universal uncertainty of contingent statements about the future, but also wide uncertainty about the past and the present. The recognition of this fact has led to the development of probabilistic, and specifically Bayesian, accounts of cognition in general (Chater & Oaksford, 2008) and of reasoning in particular, in an advance that has been called a new paradigm in the psychology of reasoning (Baratgin & Politzer, 2016; Elqayam & Over, 2013; Manktelow, Over, & Elqayam, 2011; Oaksford & Chater, 2007; Over, 2009).

From the perspective of this new approach, Johnson-Laird & Byrne (1991, pp. 7, 74) took a retrograde step, after the advance of Wason and Johnson-Laird (1972), by claiming that the natural language conditional is equivalent to the material conditional, with mental models for *if p, then q* corresponding to the rows of Table 2.1 where the material conditional is true: the *p & q*, *not-p & q*, and *not-p & not-q* rows. Johnson-Laird and Byrne also made the unjustified claim that people give the "defective" truth table response because they represent only the "initial" *p & q* mental model of the material conditional (Bonnefon & Vautier, 2008). Their account implies that the supposedly "correct" (Byrne & Johnson-Laird, 2009) probability of the natural language conditional, *P(if p, then q)*, is the probability of the material conditional, *P(not-p or q)*. But this again has absurd results; for example, "If John loves Mary, then he hates her" becomes more and more probable as it becomes more and more likely that John does not love Mary (see also Bennett, 2003, Edgington, 1995, and Evans & Over, 2004, on the negative implications of claiming that the natural language conditional is equivalent to the material conditional).

The table's present

In the new paradigm, the correct analysis of the natural language indicative conditional is given by the de Finetti tables, Tables 2.2 and 2.3, and the *Ramsey test* for judging the probability of this conditional (Ramsey, 1929/1990). Using the Ramsey test (as Stalnaker, 1968, refined it), we assess the probability of "If John loves Mary, then he hates her" by hypothetically supposing that John loves Mary, making any further hypothetical changes necessary to maintain consistency in our beliefs, and judging to what extent we can be confident, under that supposition, that John hates Mary. The result of the test is that the probability of the conditional, *P(if p, then q)*, is the conditional probability of *q* given *p*, *P(q|p)*. This test has much more satisfactory results, for example, the probability of "if John loves Mary, then he hates her" is the conditional probability that John hates Mary given that he loves her, which is 0 (unless one allows the meaning of "love" to include the possibility of a "love-hate" relationship).

By the Ramsey test, an obvious or trivial truth, for example, "If John loves Mary, then he loves her," has a probability of 1, even if its antecedent is false. An assertion, categorical or conditional, can be said to be "true" in a "pleonastic" or "deflationary" use of the word that is not represented in Tables 2.1–2.3 (Bennett, 2003; Edgington, 2003; Over & Cruz, in press; Politzer et al., 2010). In this use, "true" applied to an assertion indicates that the speaker endorses it to the highest degree, or at least to a high enough degree in context. The word "true" has a wide number of uses in natural language, and it is regrettable that the psychology of reasoning has mainly used truth tables to study this word.

The identity $P(if\ p,\ then\ q) = P(q|p)$ has such profound implications for the psychology of conditional reasoning that it has simply been called *the Equation* (Edgington, 1995; Oaksford & Chater, 2007). It fits perfectly with the "inference ticket" and conditional assertion views of the indicative conditional, and the fuller explanation of *if p, then q* using the de Finetti tables and the Ramsey test. The probability of *if p, then q*, by Tables 2.2 and 2.3, is that *p & q* holds given that a non-void assertion has been made, that is, that *p* holds, and that is the probability of *q* given *p*, $P(q|p)$. The Ramsey test is used to derive $P(q|p)$, which measures the strength, or "value," of the "inference ticket" from *p* to *q*. In this account, the use of an indicative conditional is a conditional assertion that exactly parallels a conditional bet. Suppose we make a bet with someone else on (1) in the course of arguing about it. We win this bet when John loved Mary and married her, and we lose this bet when John loved Mary and did not marry her. If John did not love Mary, the bet is "void" and no one wins or loses the bet. The probability that we will win the bet is the conditional probability that John married Mary given that he loved her. This parallel relation is actually found in people's judgments about indicative conditionals and conditional bets (Baratgin, Over, & Politzer, 2013, 2014; Politzer et al., 2010).

Both the Ramsey test and the de Finetti tables are needed to give a full account of *if p, then q*, and they are closely connected in people's judgments (Evans, Handley, Neilens, & Over, 2007). It is a mistake to claim that *if p, then q* semantically means *if p, then the probability of q is high* (Goodwin, 2014). People will only assert *if p, then q* as a speech act if $P(q|p)$ is high enough in context, but that is a pragmatic matter. For example, people will not usually assert *if p, then q* if $P(q|p) = 0.5$, but that does not make *if p, then q* definitely false, and indeed by the Equation, $P(if\ p,\ then\ q) = 0.5$ in this case.

A conditional that satisfies the Equation has been called a *probability conditional* (Adams, 1998) and a *conditional event* (de Finetti, 1936/1995, 1937/1964). We will use the term "conditional event" here, as so much of what we say depends ultimately on de Finetti (see also Pfeifer & Kleiter, 2009, 2010, on conditional events). The Equation has been tested in psychological experiments as the descriptive *conditional probability hypothesis*, $P(if\ p,\ then\ q) = P(q|p)$, and highly confirmed (Baratgin et al., 2013; Cruz & Oberauer, 2014; Douven & Verbrugge, 2010; Evans et al., 2007; Evans, Handley, & Over, 2003; Fugard, Pfeifer, Mayerhofer, & Kleiter, 2011; Oberauer & Wilhelm, 2003; Over, Hadjichristidis, Evans, Handley, & Sloman, 2007; Politzer et al., 2010; Singmann, Klauer, & Over, 2014).

Some critical responses to the confirmation of the conditional probability hypothesis (Byrne & Johnson-Laird, 2010; Girotto & Johnson-Laird, 2010) are vitiated by modal fallacies (Milne, 2012; Over et al., 2013; Politzer et al., 2010). The critics claimed that people interpret the question "What is the probability of *if p, then q*?" as the question "If *p*, then what is the probability of *q*?" and that the latter question is trivially a request for the conditional probability judgment. The modal operator *probably* is supposed by the critics to attach to the consequent semantically in conditionals and to express the conditional probability as a result. But as we have pointed out earlier, conditionals with modal operators – *if p, then necessarily q* and *if p, then probably q* – have a scope ambiguity in natural language. It is a modal fallacy to give *probably* narrow scope, *if p, then (probably q)*, rather than wide scope, *probably (if p, then q)*, and then to imagine that the narrow scope reading expresses the conditional probability of *q* given *p* (Edgington, 1995; Over et al., 2013). These logically fallacious claims were made without testing how people actually interpret scope ambiguities, but experiments have confirmed that participants interpret *probably* in *if p, then probably q* as having wide scope and not narrow scope (Over et al., 2013).

Some experiments on the probability of conditionals give their participants an abstract conditional about a random item to be selected from a frequency distribution, for example, "If the chip is square, then it is black," with a display of square or circular and black or white chips (Baratgin et al., 2013; Politzer et al., 2010; note that examples like this are singular conditionals about a specific item – see Cruz & Oberauer, 2014, on general conditionals). In these experiments, participants sometimes produce the conjunctive response that $P(\text{if } p, \text{ then } q) = P(p \& q)$, but this declines, to be replaced by the conditional probability response $P(\text{if } p, \text{ then } q) = P(q \,|\, p)$, as the participants make more and more probability judgments about conditionals and so get more familiar with the task (Fugard et al., 2011).

Barrouillet and Gauffroy (2015) find that there is sometimes an interesting "defective" biconditional response, $P(\text{if } p, \text{ then } q) = P(p \& q \,|\, p \text{ or } q)$, for "causal" conditionals with artificial frequency distributions, for example, "If the lever is down, then the rabbit's cage is open," plus information on how many times the lever has been down or up and the cage open or closed. It is better to call this the *biconditional event* response (Fugard et al., 2011). The biconditional event is part of de Finetti's logical system and is true when *p & q* holds, false when *p & not-q* holds, false when *not-p & q* holds, and "void" when *not-p & not-q* holds. It is, in effect, the conjunction of two conditional events, both of which satisfy the Equation, and as such, a *biconditional event* response, when it occurs, can hardly imply a serious problem with the Equation and the conditional probability hypothesis, as Barrouillet and Gauffroy claimed (see Over & Cruz, in press).

Barrouillet and Gauffroy predict that a causal conditional, *if p, then q*, will be given a "defective" biconditional interpretation when there are few "alternatives" to *p* for causing *q*. This prediction implies that the interpretation will tend to be given when the probability of the *not-p & q* possibility, $P(\text{not-}p \& q)$, is low, since $P(\text{not-}p \& q) = P(\text{not-}p)P(q \,|\, \text{not-}p)$, and $P(q \,|\, \text{not-}p)$ will be low when there are few "alternatives" to *p* for bringing about *q*. But the probability of the biconditional event, $P(p \& q \,|\, p \text{ or } q)$, is equal to $P(p \& q)/((p \& q) + P(p \& \text{not-}q) + P(\text{not-}p \& q))$, and so clearly when $P(\text{not-}p \& q)$ is low, $P(p \& q \,|\, p \text{ or } q)$ will be close to $P(p \& q)/((p \& q) + P(p \& \text{not-}q))$, which is the same as $P(q \,|\, p)$. And again we see that Barrouillet and Gauffroy's own position implies that there is not a serious problem with the Equation and the conditional probability hypothesis (see also Barrouillet and Gauffroy, 2015, on developmental truth table studies of great interest).

Experiments on realistic conditionals, without artificial frequency distributions, provide the strongest support for the conditional probability hypothesis (Over, in press; Over & Cruz, in press). There are relevant artificial frequency distributions only in special contexts for everyday indicative conditionals, for example, in lotteries and some other types of gambling. Sometimes there are natural sample frequencies that are relevant for ordinary singular conditionals, for example, "If unemployment increases over the next year, then crime will too," but ordinary people do not often know much about these when they make a probability judgment about the conditionals. People also make probability judgments about singular conditionals for which there are no relevant sample frequencies, for example, "If global warming continues, then Hamburg will be flooded." In these cases, it is plausible that people use causal beliefs or models to make their probability judgments, and the conditional probability hypothesis is very highly confirmed for these conditionals (Over et al., 2007; Singmann et al., 2014).

The table's future

Table 2.3 is not the final stage in the development of de Finetti's theory. He held that people are not simply in a third state of "uncertainty" when they do not know for sure whether an assertion, categorical or conditional, is true or false. They have a range of degrees of belief, which they can express with graded modal operators, indicating that some possibilities are more or less probable than others, to some more or less precise degree (Baratgin & Politzer, 2016; de Finetti, 1980). Classical bivalent logic was of course perfectly acceptable for de Finetti as an axiomatic system used in mathematics, but it does not cover reasoning under uncertainty. For this reason, he went beyond bivalent classical logic to "the logic of probability" and distinguished two further levels for states of belief, the epistemic and the meta-epistemic (de Finetti, 1930, 1936/1995, 1980, 2006). At the first of these further levels, the epistemic, bivalent logic generalized to a three-valued logic, and at the next, three-valued logic is itself extended to a many-valued logic; see Figure 2.1.

Jeffrey (1991) was influenced by de Finetti and, in effect, proposed Table 2.4 as a *many-valued* extension of the de Finetti tables, Tables 2.2 and 2.3. Table 2.4 can be called the *Jeffrey table*; in it, the uncertain value U is replaced by the conditional probability itself, $P(q \,|\, p)$, which of course can be any degree of belief (Edgington, 1995; Over & Cruz, in press; Stalnaker & Jeffrey, 1994). Tables 2.2 and 2.3 have the value V or U for trivial or certain truths with false antecedents, such as *if p, then p* when p is false. But if there is a necessary or certain connection between p and q, $P(if\ p,\ then\ q)$ should be 1, and 1 will be the entry in the Jeffrey table for this conditional in the *not-p* cells. In this way, a Jeffrey table could express the pleonastic, or deflationary, use of "true." Unlike the old "defective," 2 x 2 de Finetti table, the Jeffrey table has not yet been explored by psychologists of reasoning, but this is the direction in which, we suggest (Baratgin et al., 2013), research on the "defective" truth table should develop in the future.

An event q can be:

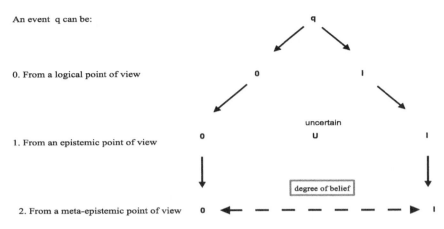

0. From a logical point of view

1. From an epistemic point of view

2. From a meta-epistemic point of view

FIGURE 2.1 The three levels of knowledge (de Finetti, 1980)

TABLE 2.4 The Jeffrey table for *if p, then q*

1 = true, 0 = false, and *P(q|p)* = the subjective conditional probability of *q* given *p*

p \ q	1	0
1	1	0
0	*P(q|p)*	*P(q|p)*

There is a row in all the truth tables we have considered in this chapter that deserves much more attention in the psychology of reasoning. It is the first row and as such hides in plain sight: the row in which *if p, then q* is shown to be true when *p & q* is true. The question is whether people generally consider the corresponding inference form valid: inferring the conclusion *if p, then q* from the premise *p & q*. We will simply call this inference form *centering* (it is often called "conjunctive sufficiency"). It might seem easy to predict that people will find it valid, because of all the evidence from truth table studies that we have referred to, from Wason (1966) on. However, centering has only recently been studied as an explicit inference, with participants being asked about inferring *if p, then q* from *p & q*. The result of these limited studies is that people do appear to find centering valid for the materials used (Cruz, Baratgin, Oaksford, & Over, 2015; Politzer & Baratgin, 2016). It is normatively valid in a wide range of logical systems for both indicative and counterfactual conditionals (Over, in press). As examples, it is valid for the material conditional, with *not-p or q* validly following from *p & q*, and for the conditional event, since *P(p & q) ≤ P(q|p)*. However, there is also a strong intuition that for a conditional *if p, then q* to be "acceptable," at least pragmatically if not semantically, there has to be a connection or relation between *p* and *q*, perhaps causal, with *p* a cause of *q*, or evidential, *p* being evidence for *q*.

The theory that this "acceptability" requirement is semantic has been called *inferentialism*, and there are arguments for it (Douven, 2015a; Krzyzanowska, Wenmackers, & Douven, 2013; Over & Cruz, in press). It implies that centering is invalid, since $p \,\&\, q$ can obviously hold when no connection of any kind exists between p and q. A conditional without such a relation between p and q has been called a *missing-link conditional* (Douven, 2015b), for example, "If John loved Mary, then global warming will continue." It may be that future research will show that people do not endorse centering for missing-link conditionals, and then inferentialism will have been supported, and a long tradition of truth table studies will have been found to have given misleading results.

Conclusion

Truth table studies have played a central part in the psychology of reasoning since Wason (1966), especially in experiments on and theories of the indicative conditional of natural language. Any account of reasoning has to have a theory of indicative conditionals at its core, and this theory must explain the truth table studies. The "defective" truth table has been there from the start, from Wason (1966). The finding that people produce a three-valued table for the indicative conditional fits perfectly with accounts of this conditional, and conditional reasoning, that go back to Ramsey and de Finetti, so much so that the "defective" truth table should be renamed the de Finetti 2 x 2 table. It is almost certain that much more remains to discover about how this table and its extensions, the 3 x 3 de Finetti table and the Jeffrey table, relate to people's probability judgments and reasoning.

Acknowledgments

This work was supported by a grant from the ANR Chorus 2011 (project BTAF-DOC). We are grateful to Nicole Cruz, Igor Douven, and Guy Politzer for comments and discussions about the content of this chapter, and to Ken Manktelow for teaching us much about its topic.

References

Adams, E. (1998). *A primer of probability logic.* Stanford, CA: CLSI Publications.

Baratgin, J., Over, D. E., & Politzer, G. (2013). Uncertainty and de Finetti tables. *Thinking & Reasoning, 19*, 308–328.

Baratgin, J., Over, D. E., & Politzer, G. (2014). New psychological paradigm for conditionals and general de Finetti tables. *Mind and Language, 29*, 73–84.

Baratgin, J., & Politzer, G. (2016). Logic, probability and inference: A methodology for a new paradigm. In L. Macchi, M. Bagassi, & R. Viale (Eds.), *Cognitive unconscious and human rationality* (pp. 119–142). Cambridge, MA: MIT Press.

Barrouillet, P., & Gauffroy, C. (2015). Probability in reasoning: A developmental test on conditionals. *Cognition, 137*, 22–39.

Bennett, J. (2003). *A philosophical guide to conditionals.* Oxford: Oxford University Press.

Binet, A. (1902). *La psychologie du raisonnement: Recherches expérimentales par l'hypnotisme*. Bibliothèque de philosophie contemporaine. Paris: Alcan.

Bonnefon, J. F., & Vautier, S. (2008). Defective truth tables and falsifying cards: Two measurement models yield no evidence of an underlying fleshing-out propensity. *Thinking & Reasoning, 14*, 231–243.

Bradley, R., & Swartz, N. (1979). *Possible worlds: An introduction to logic and its philosophy*. Indianapolis, IN: Hackett Publishing.

Byrne, R. M. J., & Johnson-Laird, P. N. (2009). "If" and the problems of conditional reasoning. *Trends in Cognitive Science, 13*, 282–287.

Byrne, R. M. J., & Johnson-Laird, P. N. (2010). Conditionals and possibilities. In M. Oaksford & N. Chater (Eds.), *Cognition and conditionals: Probability and logic in human thought* (pp. 55–68). Oxford: Oxford University Press.

Chater, N., & Oaksford, M. (Eds.). (2008). *The probabilistic mind: Prospects for Bayesian cognitive science*. Oxford: Oxford University Press.

Cruz, N., Baratgin, J., Oaksford, M., & Over, D. E. (2015). Bayesian reasoning with ifs and ands and ors. *Frontiers in Psychology, 6*, 192.

Cruz, N., & Oberauer, K. (2014). Comparing the meanings of "if " and "all." *Memory & Cognition, 42*, 1345–1356.

de Finetti, B. (1930). Fondamenti logici del ragionamento probabilistico. *Bollettino dell'Unione Matematica Italiana, 9*, 258–261.

de Finetti, B. (1936/1995). The logic of probability [translation of 1936 original]. Translated in R. B. Angell, The logic of probability. *Philosophical Studies, 77*, 181–190.

de Finetti, B. (1937/1964). Foresight: Its logical laws, its subjective sources [translation of 1937 original]. In H. E. Kyburg & H. E. Smokler (Eds.), *Studies in subjective probability* (pp. 55–118). New York: Wiley.

de Finetti, B. (1980). *Voice probabilità*. Encyclopedia (pp. 1146–1187). Cambridge: Einaudi.

de Finetti, B. (2006). *L'invenzione della verità*. Milan: Cortina.

Douven, I. (2015a). *The epistemology of indicative conditionals*. Cambridge: Cambridge University Press.

Douven, I. (2015b). How to account for the oddness of missing-link conditionals. *Synthese*. Advance online publication. DOI: 10.1007/s11229-015-0756-7.

Douven, I., & Verbrugge, S. (2010). The Adams family. *Cognition, 117*, 302–318.

Edgington, D. (1995). On conditionals. *Mind, 104*, 235–329.

Edgington, D. (2003). What if? Questions about conditionals. *Mind and Language, 18*, 380–401.

Elqayam, S., & Over, D. E. (2013). New paradigm psychology of reasoning: An introduction to the special issue edited by Elqayam, Bonnefon, & Over. *Thinking & Reasoning, 19*, 249–265.

Evans, J. St. B. T., Handley, S., Neilens, H., & Over, D. E. (2007). Thinking about conditionals: A study of individual differences. *Memory & Cognition, 35*, 1772–1784.

Evans, J. St. B. T., Handley, S. J., & Over, D. E. (2003). Conditional and conditional probability. *Journal of Experimental Psychology: Learning, Memory, and Cognition, 29*, 321–335.

Evans, J. St. B. T., & Over, D. E. (2004). *If*. Oxford: Oxford University Press.

Fugard, J. B., Pfeifer, N., Mayerhofer, B., & Kleiter, G. D. (2011). How people interpret conditionals: Shifts toward conditional event. *Journal of Experimental Psychology-Learning Memory and Cognition, 37*, 635–648.

Garson, J. (2014). Modal logic. In Edward N. Zalta (Ed.), *The Stanford encyclopedia of philosophy*. http://plato.stanford.edu/archives/sum2014/entries/logic-modal/.

Gaskin, R. (1995). *The sea battle and the master argument: Aristotle and Diodorus Cronus on the metaphysics of the future*. Berlin: Walter de Gruyter.

Girotto, V., & Johnson-Laird, P. N. (2010). Conditionals and probability. In M. Oaksford & N. Chater (Eds.), *Cognition and conditionals: Probability and logic in human thought* (pp. 103–115). Oxford: Oxford University Press.

Goodwin, G. P. (2014). Is the basic conditional probabilistic? *Journal of Experimental Psychology: General, 143*, 1214–1241.

Gottwald, S. (2015), Many-valued logic. In Edward N. Zalta (Ed.), *The Stanford encyclopedia of philosophy*. http://plato.stanford.edu/archives/spr2015/entries/logic-many-valued/.

James, W. (1908). *Text-book of psychology, briefer course.* London: McMillan.

Jeffrey, R. C. (1991). Matter of fact conditionals. *Aristotelian Society Supplementary, 65*, 161–183.

Johnson-Laird, P. N. and Byrne, R. M. J. (1991). *Deduction.* Hillsdale, NJ: Lawrence Erlbaum.

Kneale, W., & Kneale, M. (1962). *The development of logic.* Oxford: Oxford University Press.

Krzyzanowska, K., Wenmackers, S., & Douven, I. (2013). Inferential conditionals and evidentiality. *Journal of Logic, Language and Information, 22*(3), 315–334.

Manktelow, K. I. (2012). *Thinking and reasoning.* Hove, UK: Psychology Press.

Manktelow, K. I., Over, D. E., & Elqayam, S. (2011). Paradigm shift: Jonathan Evans and the science of reason. In K. I. Manktelow, D. E. Over, & S. Elqayam (Eds.), *The science of reason: A Festschrift for Jonathan St B T Evans* (pp. 1–16). Hove, UK: Psychology Press.

Milne, P. (2012). Indicative conditionals, conditional probabilities, and the "defective truth-table": A request for more experiments, *Thinking & Reasoning, 18*, 196–224.

Oaksford, M., & Chater, N. (2007). *Bayesian rationality: The probabilistic approach to human reasoning.* Oxford: Oxford University Press.

Oberauer, K., & Wilhelm, O. (2003). The meaning(s) of conditionals: Conditional probabilities, mental models and personal utilities. *Journal of Experimental Psychology: Learning Memory and Cognition, 29*, 680–693.

Over, D. E. (2009). New paradigm psychology of reasoning. *Thinking & Reasoning, 15*, 431–438.

Over, D. E. (in press). Causation and the probability of causal conditionals. In Michael Waldmann (Ed.), *The Oxford handbook of causal reasoning.* Oxford: Oxford University Press.

Over, D. E., & Cruz, N. (in press). Probabilistic accounts of conditional reasoning. In Linden J. Ball & Valerie A. Thompson (Eds.), *International handbook of thinking and reasoning.* Hove, UK: Psychology Press.

Over, D. E., Douven, I., & Verbrugge, S. (2013). Scope ambiguities and conditionals. *Thinking & Reasoning, 19*, 284–307.

Over, D. E., Hadjichristidis, C., Evans, J. St. B. T., Handley, S. J., & Sloman, S. A. (2007). The probability of causal conditionals. *Cognitive Psychology, 54*, 62–97.

Pfeifer, N., & Kleiter, G. D. (2009). Framing human inference by coherence based probability logic. *Journal of Applied Logic, 7*, 206–217.

Pfeifer, N., & Kleiter, G. D. (2010). The conditional in mental probability logic. In M. Oaksford & N. Chater (Eds.), *Cognition and conditionals: Probability and logic in human thinking* (pp. 153–173). Oxford: Oxford University Press.

Politzer, G., & Baratgin, J. (2016). Deductive schemas with uncertain premises using qualitative probability expressions. *Thinking & Reasoning, 22*(1), 78–98.

Politzer, G., Over, D. E., & Baratgin, J. (2010). Betting on conditionals. *Thinking & Reasoning, 16*, 172–197.

Quine, W. V. O. (1952). *Methods of logic.* London: Routledge.

Ramsey, F. P. (1929/1990). General propositions and causality. In D. H. Mellor (Ed.), *Philosophical papers* (pp. 145–163). Cambridge: Cambridge University Press.

Singmann, H., Klauer, K. C., & Over, D. E. (2014). New normative standards of conditional reasoning and the dual-source model. *Frontiers in Psychology, 5*, 316.

Stalnaker, R. (1968). A theory of conditionals. In N. Rescher (Ed.), *Studies in logical theory* (pp. 98–112). Oxford: Blackwell.

Stalnaker, R., & Jeffrey, R. (1994). Conditionals as random variables. In E. Eells & B. Skyrms (Eds.), *Probability and conditionals* (pp. 31–46). Cambridge: Cambridge University Press.

Swartz, N. (1999). "The" modal fallacy. www.sfu.ca/philosophy/swartz/modal_fallacy.htm.

Wason, P. (1966). Reasoning. In B. M. Foss (Ed.), *New horizons in psychology I* (pp. 106–137). Harmondsworth: Penguin.

Wason, P., & Johnson-Laird, P. N. (1972). *Psychology of reasoning: Structure and content*. London: Batsford.

3

PRAGMATIC FACTORS IN WASON'S 2–4–6 TASK

Implications for real-world hypothesis testing

Linden J. Ball and Caroline N. Wade

Introduction

In 1960 Peter Wason published a short paper reporting a single study investigating people's inductive reasoning and concept learning with his newly developed '2–4–6 task'. Wason's primary interest in developing this task was to ascertain whether people could discover that a concept is necessary rather than merely sufficient. In this task the experimenter explains to the participant that he has in mind a rule with regard to number triples made up of three integers. The rule is that these integers must be in ascending order of magnitude, but, crucially, the participant doesn't know what this rule is and therefore has to try to discover it. As a starting point the participant is given an example triple, '2–4–6', which she is told conforms to the rule. The participant is then requested to generate her own triples, with feedback being given in each case as to whether the triple conforms to the experimenter's rule. In Wason's (1960) study participants could write down each triple along with their reasons for their choice of numbers and the feedback received. Participants were also reminded that their task was not simply to find numbers that conformed to the rule but to discover the rule itself. Only when they were highly confident that they had discovered the rule were they asked to tell the experimenter what it was. If participants announced an incorrect rule (which was commonplace), they were invited to continue with more testing and could make further announcements. The experiment continued until correct rule announcement or the session reached 45 minutes (or the participants gave up).

Wason's (1960) paper has become one of the most highly cited articles in the *Quarterly Journal of Experimental Psychology*. In reflecting on the lasting impact of Wason's article, Evans (2014) views the reported research as significant for at least three reasons. First, Evans notes that Wason's (1960) paper was his earliest foray into the topic of reasoning (having previously published on psycholinguistics) and involved him making strong claims for bias and irrationality during a period dominated by rationalist researchers (e.g. Henle, 1962; Inhelder & Piaget, 1958), who assumed that people were good logical reasoners. As Evans explains, Wason's paper set in motion the study of cognitive biases in thinking and reasoning a decade ahead of the 'heuristics and biases' programme established in the domain of human judgement (e.g. Tversky & Kahneman, 1974). Second, Evans affirms that the 2–4–6 task is ingenious, both in its conceptualisation and in its capacity to give rise to apparent error and bias in intelligent participants. Third, Evans contends that Wason's work on the 2–4–6 task, together with his later studies with his four-card selection task, led to foundational developments of the 'dual process' theory of reasoning, which now dominates theorising in this area.

In the present chapter we primarily focus on the potential role 'pragmatic' factors play in determining performance of Wason's 2–4–6 task. Pragmatics is a subfield of linguistics that focuses on how *context* contributes to meaning. Key concerns include: (1) the 'performative' function of utterances in communication, where utterances take the form of 'speech acts' such as promising, warning or requesting (e.g. Bach, 2006); and (2) the conversational implications associated with utterances, that is, the meaning suggested by utterances beyond that which is directly expressed or entailed (e.g. Grice, 1989). Of particular note in pragmatic theorising is Sperber and Wilson's (1986) 'communicative principle of relevance', which states that by the very act of making an utterance a speaker is conveying to a listener that what is being said is worth listening to (i.e. that the utterance will provide 'cognitive effects' in terms of conveying meaning worthy of the processing effort required to derive that meaning). We return later to a detailed consideration of the potential role of *relevance* in people's inductive reasoning with the 2–4–6 task. Suffice it to say that much of our ensuing discussion is predicated on the assumption that the very presentation by the experimenter of the 2–4–6 exemplar conveys a strong presumption of the relevance of the directly perceivable properties of this seed triple, which in turn has major consequences for how people then tackle the task.

The remainder of this chapter is structured as follows. First, we present an overview of Wason's (1960) classic findings with the 2–4–6 task that have since been replicated many times. We also summarise Wason's initial theoretical claims regarding participants' behaviour on the task and review subsequent theorising that has disputed aspects of Wason's original conceptual analysis. Next, we present a summary of important studies that have shown enhanced performance on the 2–4–6 task, some of which, we suggest, support a role for pragmatic factors in hindering or facilitating task success. Finally, we summarise new experiments that we have conducted, including ones that directly manipulated the perceived relevance of the 2–4–6 exemplar. We propose that the resulting findings corroborate the way in which pragmatic factors are central to understanding success and failure on the 2–4–6 task.

Space considerations preclude presentation of an in-depth review of the many findings and conceptual ideas arising from studies of the 2–4–6 task and its variants. For the reader interested in such an encompassing review we advocate Chapter 7 of Manktelow (2012).[1] We also recommend Evans' (2014) article, which presents a state-of-the-art assessment of the broader impact of Wason's (1960) paper on theoretical developments relating to thinking biases, rationality and dual-process accounts of reasoning.

Wason's (1960) observations and claims relating to the 2–4–6 task

Wason (1960) observed that of the 29 participants attempting his 2–4–6 task, just 6 (21%) announced the correct rule at the first attempt, 10 at the second, 4 at the third and 1 after a fifth attempt. Wason viewed this poor performance as a direct consequence of participants' pursuit of 'enumerative' (or positive) tests to check that a triple was compatible with a current hypothesis about the to-be-discovered rule. Remember that in Wason's study participants wrote down the reasons for their triple choices, such as testing 10–12–14 on the assumption that the rule is 'ascending with equal intervals'. In contrast to what seemed to be an abundance of such enumerative testing, Wason observed relatively few 'eliminative' (or negative) tests aimed at determining if a triple was incompatible with a current hypothesis (e.g. testing 10–12–23 for the same hypothesis 'ascending with equal intervals'). Eliminative tests are critical for enabling the disconfirmation of a mistaken hypothesis since receiving feedback that 10–12–23 fits the experimenter's rule indicates that 'ascending with equal intervals' is incorrect. In support of an association between task success and eliminative testing Wason showed that those announcing the correct rule on their first or second attempts also tended to be those generating more eliminative tests. Wason also observed that many incorrect rule announcements were more restricted versions of the to-be-discovered rule (e.g. 'numbers increasing by two'; 'numbers increasing with equal intervals'), with repeated enumerative testing reinforcing beliefs in the correctness of such overly restricted hypotheses.

Evans (2014) notes that although Wason's (1960) paper is often cited as a seminal source of evidence for 'confirmation bias' in human reasoning (i.e. an attitude or disposition toward confirmatory testing), the term does not appear in the paper, nor does the synonymous term 'verification bias' as subsequently used by Wason and Johnson-Laird (1972) and Wason (1966). Evans (2014) also explains how research reported by Wetherick (1962) presented a persuasive challenge to the credibility of a confirmation bias as a cause of failure on the 2–4–6 task. Wetherick's key insight was that an enumerative test is not necessarily a 'confirmatory' test since for some rules an enumerative test will readily lead to disconfirmation of a current hypothesis. For example, an enumerative test such as 10–12–14 on the assumption that the rule is 'ascending with equal intervals' could disconfirm this hypothesis if the experimenter's rule is 'numbers less than ten ascending with equal intervals'. Wetherick's (1962) important ideas were subsequently formalised and corroborated by Klayman and Ha (1987, 1989). They proposed that the application of a 'positive test strategy' will frequently be successful for eliminating hypotheses (e.g. in science), but that the strategy causes profound difficulties with the 2–4–6 task because the very general nature of the to-be-discovered rule in this particular case means that positive tests cannot disconfirm the participant's current hypothesis.

Nowadays it is generally accepted that people's application of a positive test strategy is an important aspect of their difficulties on the 2–4–6 task and that a confirmation bias account is untenable. Oaksford and Chater (1994) note, however, that a positive test strategy cannot explain *all* findings, including Wason's (1960) observation that the task tends *eventually* to be solved after repeated attempts at rule announcement. Oaksford and Chater argue that to advance theorising on this issue, researchers need to consider the mechanisms that underpin participants' generation of *new* hypotheses based on the feedback received. Their proposal for such a mechanism draws on Farris and Revlin's (1989) suggestion that people who solve the task are using a 'counterfactual strategy', whereby they construct and test hypotheses that are *oppositional* to the one being considered. Recent empirical evidence provides good support for counterfactual processes being linked to success on the 2–4–6 task and variants of it (e.g. Gale & Ball, 2006, 2009, 2012).

Cognitive and pragmatic factors that facilitate performance on the 2–4–6 task

Since Wason's (1960) study numerous attempts have been made to uncover manipulations that facilitate performance on the 2–4–6 task, particularly through efforts to increase eliminative testing via instructions and exposure to different kinds of test triples. Most studies have had little success (e.g. Gorman & Gorman, 1984; Kareev & Halberstadt, 1993; Kareev, Halberstadt & Shafir, 1993). This is perhaps not so surprising given the pervasiveness of a positive test strategy in human reasoning (cf. Evans, 1989) and the fact that the nature of the 2–4–6 task renders it impossible for positive testing to elicit disconfirming evidence about current hypotheses. However, one striking facilitatory manipulation has been identified, which involves the use of so-called dual-goal (DG) instructions (Tweney et al., 1980). These require participants to discover *two* complementary rules that the experimenter has in mind, one called DAX, the other called MED. Participants are given 2–4–6 as an example of DAX and are then asked to generate triples that are classified as either conforming to the DAX rule ('any ascending sequence') or the MED rule (i.e. all triples that are not DAX).[2] Using these instructions success rates for initial DAX rule announcements are typically greater than 60% (e.g. Gale & Ball, 2006; Vallée-Tourangeau, Austin & Rankin, 1995; Wharton, Cheng & Wickens, 1993).

Numerous accounts of the DG facilitation effect have emerged, and how best to explain the phenomenon remains uncertain. Although we do not have space to review these competing accounts, it nevertheless seems that a key aspect of the facilitation derives from the way in which positive tests of the MED hypothesis are effectively negative tests of the DAX hypothesis; as such, they benefit participants' understanding of the overly restrictive nature of their current DAX hypotheses. This account again draws on the primacy of a positive test strategy in hypothesis testing (Klayman & Ha, 1987, 1989), although recent research by Gale and Ball

(2006, 2009) also emphasises the critical role 'descending' triples (e.g. '6–4–2') play in the DG facilitation effect, with descending-triple generation being the main predictor of success. Gale and Ball suggest that descending triples provide useful 'contrast-class cues' that make salient the way in which key DAX and MED triples fall along a descending/ascending dimension. Indeed, when Gale and Ball (2012) manipulated the availability of contrast-class cues within a DG study, they showed major benefits arising from the direct provision of an example MED triple with descending properties. The presentation of such a MED triple effectively changes the pragmatic context associated with the DG paradigm in ways that emphasise the relevance of 'descendingness' for the MED rule, and thereby the relevance of 'ascendingness' for the DAX rule.

A few other manipulations also facilitate performance on versions of the 2–4–6 task, some of which implicate cognitive factors in failed task performance, whilst others speak to pragmatic effects. Vallée-Tourangeau and Payton (2008), for example, found facilitation when presenting participants with graphical representations of generated triples, suggesting that working-memory limitations contribute to task difficulty. More recently, Vallée-Tourangeau (2012) reported research addressing the pragmatics of the 2–4–6 task in terms of participants' goals and the *utilities* associated with particular triple tests. In his ingenious study, Vallée-Tourangeau manipulated the pay-offs associated with testing critical, eliminative triples such as '2–4–11' so as to increase their perceived utility for attaining task goals. In the presence of these pragmatic cues participants were more likely to generate triples in which numbers ascended with unequal intervals, subsequently benefiting from the disconfirmatory evidence that these triples provided for overly narrow hypotheses.

Further evidence for a pragmatic origin for difficulties in the 2–4–6 paradigm derives from a study reported by Van der Henst and colleagues (2002). In motivating their study, the authors questioned whether the standard task instructions are 'conversationally misleading' inasmuch as they *overemphasise* the relevance of the 2–4–6 exemplar. In essence, the argument is that the experimenter, by presenting a single, very specific triple as an example of his rule, appears to be conveying the message that this triple has all the key properties that are relevant to the to-be-discovered rule. Is there any surprise, then, that participants are drawn towards basing initial hypotheses around the parameters established by this exemplar triple[3] such that they end up exploring a narrow range of hypotheses?

To obtain empirical support for their proposals, Van der Henst and colleagues (2002) reasoned that if a 2–4–6 paradigm could be established that *eliminated* the apparent relevance of the 2–4–6 example, then participants should explore a broader space of hypotheses and test a wider range of triples, which would benefit rule discovery. To undermine the perceived relevance of the presented 2–4–6 triple, Van der Henst and colleagues developed a computer-based 'jackpot machine' that generated triples involving three randomly selected numbers. After five trials in which the participants operated the jackpot to generate triples they were given standard rule-discovery instructions and had one further opportunity to trigger the jackpot, at which point they were told whether the obtained triple was compatible with the to-be-discovered rule. However, unbeknownst to the participant, the jackpot had been rigged so as always to present the 2–4–6 triple on this final trial. Of course, from the participant's perspective, the salient properties of the 2–4–6 triple were simply a chance occurrence, and even if this triple did suggest specific hypotheses, the participant could not consider these to be ones that the experimenter wanted them to entertain. After encountering the 2–4–6 triple, participants completed the rule-discovery task in the normal manner, self-generating further triples (not using the machine), with the experimenter providing feedback as to whether each triple fitted the rule.

Van der Henst and colleagues predicted that in the condition where participants believed that the 2–4–6 exemplar had been produced by a random process they should rely much less on the salient properties of the triple and should perform better than in the standard paradigm, where the triple is intentionally chosen by the experimenter. This is exactly what was observed, with participants performing far more successfully in terms of initial rule announcements in the jackpot condition (55% correct) compared to the standard condition (24% correct). It was also found that the mean number of rules that needed to be announced to reach a correct solution was lower in the jackpot condition (1.59) than in the standard condition (2.38). Other interesting findings were that participants in the jackpot condition explored a greater variety of triples than participants in the standard condition, who focused more on triples exhibiting the salient properties of the 2–4–6 exemplar (cf. Cherubini et al., 2005). In sum, Van der Henst and colleagues (2002) suggest that their evidence provides good grounds for the view that 'when participants are not misled they are not so bad after all.' In other words, in the standard 2–4–6 task participants are being misdirected because they rationally consider that the givens of the problem are fundamentally relevant to solving the task.

Replication of Van der Henst and colleagues (2002)

Van der Henst and colleagues' (2002) findings provide seemingly good support for the view that pragmatic factors significantly impact performance on the 2–4–6 task. Given the importance of these observations we decided to run a replication study to generalise the results whilst also addressing methodological aspects of their study. In particular, Van der Henst and colleagues failed to report the composition of the five pre-exposure triples or whether these differed across participants, merely stating that these triples involved random numbers. Vallée-Tourangeau and Krüsi Penney (2005) note similar methodological concerns and wonder whether participants may have inadvertently been pre-exposed to crucially significant triples such as ones where numbers ascend with unequal intervals.

To address these issues, we developed a jackpot machine (in our case a stand-alone device), which we pre-programmed so that it always generated the following example triples: 28–70–42; 41–56–70; 18–18–27; 14–01–06; 23–86–86. Participants in the jackpot condition were initially shown the machine and informed that it produced triples made up of randomly selected numbers in the range 1–99.

They were invited to press the start button to see how the machine worked and repeated this action five times so as to trigger the presentation of the example triples. Participants were next presented with task instructions that involved triggering the machine a further time to receive the 'randomly' generated 2–4–6 triple, which they were told fitted the to-be-discovered rule. Participants were then invited to self-generate up to 20 triples to try to discover the experimenter's rule, writing down each triple and the resulting feedback. Participants were allowed one opportunity to announce the rule when they were very confident they knew it. We included a further manipulation in that one group of participants (N = 20) undertook the jackpot condition with the 2–4–6 exemplar appearing at the start of the instructions (cf. the normal paradigm), whilst another group (N = 20) undertook the jackpot condition with the 2–4–6 exemplar appearing at the end of the instructions. We also included a control condition (the standard 2–4–6 task).

Like Van der Henst and colleagues (2002), we observed a significant enhancement in people's successful initial rule announcement in the two jackpot conditions (60% and 65% solvers in the 'exemplar early' and 'exemplar late' conditions) compared to 20% solvers in the standard task. Further analyses showed that compared to the control condition both jackpot conditions significantly increased: (1) the variety of triple types generated; (2) the number of descending triples generated (e.g. '6–4–2'); and (3) the likelihood of generating at least one descending triple and at least one triple that ascended with unequal intervals (e.g. '2–5–13'). In addition, logistic regression indicated that the best predictor of task success was the production of at least one descending triple.

These findings suggest that in the standard 2–4–6 task the perceived relevance of the proprieties of the 2–4–6 exemplar undermines people's ability to engage in effective inductive reasoning. Once this relevance effect is undermined it seems that people can engage in a creative search of the triple space that leads to successful rule discovery. Before drawing this conclusion, however, we note one further criticism lodged against the original Van der Henst and colleagues (2002) study by Vallée-Tourangeau and Krüsi Penney (2005), which also raises questions regarding the interpretation of our own replication. Vallée-Tourangeau and Krüsi Penney mention the possibility that pre-exposure to a multiplicity of triple types might simply seed in participants 'a taste for exploration . . . for the formulation of unusual or creative number sequences'. Such creative generation of triples – which does indeed appear to arise in the jackpot conditions in our study – may thence promote rule discovery merely as a consequence of the informative feedback elicited.

This critique gives rise to the important question of what, exactly, is helpful about the jackpot condition. One possibility is that the mere exposure to five different triples in addition to the 2–4–6 exemplar serves to reduce the relevance of the 2–4–6 exemplar and primes the existence of various triple types, thereby inducing a broader search of the triple space. The alternative possibility is that the hint that the 2–4–6 exemplar has been produced by a random process is critical to a broader search of the triple space given that the salient properties of the exemplar are not seen as *uniquely* relevant to the to-be-discovered rule. We refer to these accounts as the 'mere exposure' and 'random process' explanations and note that both have their origin in the *dilution* of the perceived relevance of the 2–4–6 exemplar. Determining which account is correct, however, is not possible on the basis of Van der Henst and colleagues' (2002) study or our own replication since the random process manipulation is completely confounded with the mere exposure manipulation (we owe this important observation to Vallée-Tourangeau & Krüsi Penney, 2005).

What is needed, then, is a replication study that involves giving identical triple pre-exposure to both control and experimental participants whilst manipulating the random process element across conditions. We therefore conducted a follow-up experiment implementing the necessary design to unconfound the mere exposure and random process accounts of the relevance effect in the jackpot conditions. We established three conditions as follows: (1) a random process condition (N = 20), which was identical to the late-exemplar jackpot condition in the previous study; (2) a mere exposure condition (N = 20), which used the jackpot machine to present the same example triples whilst at no point mentioning the random selection of numbers; and (3) a standard control condition (N = 20). These latter two conditions also involved late exposure of the 2–4–6 exemplar. Results indicated significantly higher rates of solvers in the random process condition (60%) and the mere exposure condition (55%) relative to the control condition (20%). Further analyses showed that the key differences in increased triple variety arose in the mere exposure versus the control condition, whilst logistic regression indicated that the production of at least one descending triple was the best predictor of successful rule discovery.

In sum, it appears that the critical factor that promotes success in Van der Henst and colleagues' jackpot paradigm is participants' mere exposure to a range of different example triples. As noted, we still claim that this is a *relevance* effect, albeit one that derives from diluting the salience of the properties associated with the 2–4–6 exemplar and priming awareness of the variety of triples that are available for testing, which in turn promotes a creative exploration of the triple space. Following through the logic of this account to its natural end-point leads to an obvious question: What if an experimental manipulation was implemented that removed any possibility of the participant ascribing *relevance* to a presented triple? One way to achieve such a manipulation would be to run the standard Wason rule-discovery paradigm whilst asking participants to generate their own starting triple – rather than presenting the 2–4–6 exemplar. We ran such an experiment (N = 30 in both the standard condition and the 'self-generation' condition), with participants being requested to test up to 20 triples before announcing their best guess at the rule. Since participants were generating their own starting triple, then they could not be influenced by potentially misleading relevance cues deriving from the experimenter. In this self-generation condition 64% of participants stated the correct rule on their first announcement versus 23% in the standard control condition, representing a striking facilitation effect in the absence of relevance cues relating to the 2–4–6 exemplar.

Conclusions

Substantial evidence indicates that cognitive factors promote key difficulties with effective rule discovery on Wason's 2–4–6 task. In particular, people's dominant use of a 'positive test strategy' (Klayman & Ha, 1987, 1989), whereby they generate new number triples that match their current, overly restrictive hypotheses, seems to lead to conceptual dead-ends and a failure to discover the more general 'ascending numbers' rule. At the same time, it is clear that the adoption of a positive test strategy cannot provide a complete account of task difficulty given that some people can announce the correct rule on their first attempt, whilst a majority can discover the rule after repeated attempts. Here we concur with others (e.g., Cherubini et al., 2005; Van der Henst et al. 2002) who have proposed that pragmatic factors are important in understanding people's difficulties with the 2–4–6 paradigm. Indeed, we argue that relevance cues that focus participants' attention on the presented 2–4–6 exemplar lead, unsurprisingly, to a fixation on its salient properties, whereas cues that focus attention on a wider breadth of triple types can foster task success by engendering a more creative exploration of the triple space. As a critical test of this pragmatic account of failure on the 2–4–6 task we have shown how entirely removing the presentation of the 2–4–6 exemplar (and thence the presence of relevance cues to the significance of this triple) can promote high rates of task success. Overall, we conclude that the well-established 2–4–6 paradigm essentially sets people up to fail by the very nature of the pragmatic cues provided, leading to a gross underestimation of people's true capacity to engage in effective hypothesis testing and rule discovery. As such, we contend that the 2–4–6 task may well be a poor paradigm for understanding the nature of real-world inductive reasoning and concept learning that arises in everyday life as well as in discipline-specific contexts linked to domain expertise.

Notes

1 The first author knows from many conversations with Ken Manktelow that he has long been fascinated by Wason's various tasks given the important role they have played as 'tools' for studying and understanding human reasoning. Although we are not aware of Ken having conducted empirical research on Wason's 2–4–6 task, we contend that the chapter that we refer to here in his 2012 monograph on thinking and reasoning is certainly one of the most eloquent and integrative reviews of the 2–4–6 literature that has been written. We ourselves turned to this chapter for wisdom on numerous occasions when drafting our contribution to the current volume.

2 Subsequent studies have shown that strict complementarity for the DAX and MED rules is not a critical aspect of the beneficial effect of dual-goal instructions (e.g. Gale & Ball, 2009; Vallée-Tourangeau et al., 1995).

3 Indeed, subsequent research by Cherubini, Castelvecchio, and Cherubini (2005) supports Van der Henst and colleagues' (2002) supposition that participants ascribe a particularly high value to the given example triple in terms of its 'information relevance'. In their study Cherubini and colleagues varied the types and number of *perceivable relationships* in example triples. For example, a triple such as 2–4–6 involves various relationships between numbers, including that they are all even, ascending and increasing by two. Using various exemplar triples, Cherubini and colleagues demonstrated that participants derive initial hypotheses that maintain the maximum amount of information that is salient in the relational regularities within the exemplar.

References

Bach, K. (2006). Speech acts and pragmatics. In M. Devitt & R. Hanley (Eds.), *The Blackwell guide to the philosophy of language* (pp. 147–167). Oxford, UK: Blackwell Publishing.

Cherubini, P., Castelvecchio, E., & Cherubini, A. M. (2005). Generation of hypotheses in Wason's 2–4–6 task: An information theory approach. *Quarterly Journal of Experimental Psychology, 58A*, 309–332.

Evans, J. St. B. T. (1989). *Bias in human reasoning: Causes and consequences*. Hove, UK: Erlbaum.

Evans, J. St. B. T. (2014). Reasoning, biases and dual processes: The lasting impact of Wason (1960). *Quarterly Journal of Experimental Psychology.* Advance online publication. DOI:10.1080/17470218.2014.914547.

Farris, H. H., & Revlin, R. (1989). Sensible reasoning in two tasks: Rule discovery and hypothesis evaluation. *Memory & Cognition, 17*, 221–232.

Gale, M., & Ball, L. J. (2006). Dual-goal facilitation in Wason's 2–4–6 task: What mediates successful rule discovery? *Quarterly Journal of Experimental Psychology, 59*, 873–885.

Gale, M., & Ball, L. J. (2009). Exploring the determinants of dual goal facilitation in a rule discovery task. *Thinking & Reasoning, 15*, 294–315.

Gale, M., & Ball, L. J. (2012). Contrast class cues and performance facilitation in a hypothesis-testing task: Evidence for an iterative counterfactual model. *Memory & Cognition, 40*, 408–419.

Gorman, M. E., & Gorman, M. E. (1984). Comparison of disconfirmatory, confirmatory and control strategies on Wason's 2–4–6 task. *Quarterly Journal of Experimental Psychology, 36A*, 629–648.

Grice, H. P. (1989). *Studies in the way of words*. Cambridge, MA: Harvard University Press.

Henle, M. (1962). On the relation between logic and thinking. *Psychological Review, 69*, 366–378.

Inhelder, B., & Piaget, J. (1958). *The growth of logical thinking*. New York: Basic Books.

Kareev, Y., & Halberstadt, N. (1993). Evaluating negative tests and refutations in a rule discovery task. *Quarterly Journal of Experimental Psychology, 46A*, 715–727.

Kareev, Y., Halberstadt, K., & Shafir, D. (1993). Improving performance and increasing the use of non-positive testing in a rule-discovery task. *Quarterly Journal of Experimental Psychology, 46A*, 729–742.

Klayman, J., & Ha, Y.-W. (1987). Confirmation, disconfirmation, and information in hypothesis testing. *Psychological Review, 94*, 211–228.

Klayman, J., & Ha, Y.-W. (1989). Hypothesis testing in rule discovery: Strategy, structure and content. *Journal of Experimental Psychology: Learning, Memory & Cognition, 15*, 596–604.

Manktelow, K. (2012). *Thinking and reasoning: An introduction to the psychology of reason, judgment and decision making*. Hove, UK: Psychology Press.

Oaksford, M., & Chater, N. (1994). Another look at eliminative and enumerative behaviour in a conceptual task. *European Journal of Cognitive Psychology, 6*, 149–169.

Sperber, D., & Wilson, D. (1986). *Relevance: Communication and cognition* (Second edition). Oxford, UK: Blackwell Publishing.

Tversky, A., & Kahneman, D. (1974). Judgement under uncertainty: Heuristics and biases. *Science, 185*, 1124–1131.

Tweney, R. D., Doherty, M. E., Warner, W. J., Pliske, D. B., Mynatt, C. R., Gross, K. A., & Arkkelin, D. L. (1980). Strategies of rule discovery in an inference task. *Quarterly Journal of Experimental Psychology, 32*, 109–123.

Vallée-Tourangeau, F. (2012). Utilities in the 2–4–6 task. *Experimental Psychology, 59*, 265–271.

Vallée-Tourangeau, F., Austin, N. G., & Rankin, S. (1995). Inducing a rule in Wason's 2–4–6 task: A test of the information-quantity and goal-complementarity hypotheses. *Quarterly Journal of Experimental Psychology, 48A*, 895–914.

Vallée-Tourangeau, F., & Krüsi Penney, A. (2005). The impact of external representation in a rule discovery task. *European Journal of Cognitive Psychology, 17,* 820–834.

Vallée-Tourangeau, F., & Payton, T. (2008). Graphical representation fosters discovery in the 2–4–6 task. *Quarterly Journal of Experimental Psychology, 61,* 625–640.

Van der Henst, J. B., Rossi, S., & Schroyens, W. (2002). When participants are not misled they are not so bad after all: A pragmatic analysis of a rule discovery task. In W. D. Gray & C. Schunn (Eds.), *Proceedings of the 24th annual conference of the Cognitive Science Society* (pp. 902–907). Mahwah, NJ: Erlbaum.

Wason, P. C. (1960). On the failure to eliminate hypotheses in a conceptual task. *Quarterly Journal of Experimental Psychology, 12,* 129–140.

Wason, P. C. (1966). Reasoning. In B. M. Foss (Ed.), *New horizons in psychology I* (pp. 106–137). Harmondsworth: Penguin.

Wason, P. C., & Johnson-Laird, P. N. (1972). *Psychology of reasoning: Structure and content.* London: Batsford.

Wetherick, N. E. (1962). Eliminative and enumerative behaviour in a conceptual task. *Quarterly Journal of Experimental Psychology, 14,* 129–140.

Wharton, C. M., Cheng, P. W., & Wickens, T. D. (1993). Hypothesis-testing strategies: Why two goals are better than one. *Quarterly Journal of Experimental Psychology, 46A,* 743–758.

4

THINKING AND DECIDING BEYOND THE BRAIN

*Frédéric Vallée-Tourangeau and
Gaëlle Vallée-Tourangeau*

Thinking and deciding beyond the brain

Manktelow and Over's (1991) elegant demonstration of how utilities associated with different perspectives predict and explain systematic patterns of card choices in deontic versions of Wason's (1968) card selection task was a source of inspiration for many. At the time of its publication, one of us (FVT) started working on another of Wason's tasks, the so-called 2–4–6 task, exploring why so few participants performed well at the task and how the context of reasoning could be modified to encourage more creativity, diligence and better inductive reasoning. Our work soon led us to explore the role of utilities in this hypothesis-testing task, and then how utilities also play an important role in people's ability to gauge the diagnostic value of new information in so-called pseudodiagnostic reasoning tasks.

The 2–4–6 task

In the classic hypothesis-testing task Wason (1960) designed, participants are invited to discover a rule that governs how three numbers are put together. Participants generate new sequences of three numbers, which the experimenter classifies as conforming or not to the rule. Participants are instructed to test new sequences until they feel confident they know the answer. Critically, they are also informed that the sequence '2–4–6' conforms to the rule. However, the rule to be discovered is 'any increasing sequence', and hence the initial example suggests an arithmetic specificity that is not reflected in the correct rule. Typically, participants don't fare well at this task. Approximately 20% announce the correct rule; they test few sequences before announcing their answer and these number triples conform to some form of arithmetic progression similar to the one implied by the test example (e.g. Evans, 2014; Vallée-Tourangeau & Payton, 2008). Ignoring debates surrounding the appropriate normative perspective from which to interpret performance, explanations of performance initially focused on thinking dispositions and cognitive capacity. Wason (1960, p. 139) wrote:

> (T)he readiness (as opposed to the capacity) to think and argue rationally in an unsystematized area of knowledge is presumably related to other factors besides intelligence, in so far as it implies a disposition to refute, rather than indicate assertions, and to tolerate the disenchantment of negative instances. And certainly, these qualities are no less important for thinking in general than the more obvious cognitive functions associated with purely deductive thinking.[1]

The exact mix of disposition and capacity in reasoning performance has remained a major preoccupation (e.g. Stanovich & West, 2000). Such a focus on the individual reflects an implicit commitment to 'methodological individualism': seeking to understand thinking in terms of the features of the individual (see Malafouris, 2013, p. 25; Vallée-Tourangeau, 2014). This commitment naturally deflects attention away from the context of reasoning. Yet context is intrinsic to performance: the conversational context may shape reasoning through shared rules of conversational inferences (Hilton, 1995); the informational context may shape performance depending on how information is structured and formatted (Gigerenzer & Hoffrage, 1995). More generally, we would argue, reasoners are embedded in a system defined by internal constraints (e.g. conversational rules, processing and computational abilities, personal utilities etc.) as well as external constraints (e.g. physical, social and cultural action possibilities or affordances, Hollan, Hutchins & Kirsh, 2000; G. Vallée-Tourangeau, Abadie & Vallée-Tourangeau, 2015).

Participants' hypothesis testing behaviour is substantially transformed in the dual-goal version of the 2–4–6 task, where positive instances are labeled 'Dax', negative ones 'Med' and participants are instructed to discover two rules, one for Dax instances, and one for Med instances (see Tweney et al., 1980 for the original paper on the Dax-Med manipulation, a manipulation Wason himself incidentally suggested; see p. 119; Vallée-Tourangeau, Austin & Rankin, 1995). This change in the framing of the task results in a substantial increase in diligence – participants produce more sequences before announcing their rule – and creativity – participants produce a more varied set of sequences. As a consequence, participants are much more likely to discover the ascending sequence or Dax rule. Thus, whatever dispositions or capacities, the typically indolent and prosaic reasoner that Wason's original experimental procedure reveals can be transformed into a creative and industrious thinker, able to overcome the inferential challenge designed by the 2–4–6 task.

Borrowing directly from Manktelow and Over (1991), we conjectured that it might be possible to manipulate the value or utility of certain number sequences, thus transforming 'the unsystematized area of knowledge' into one where test sequences meant something defined with respect to goals that reasoners valued, and thus transforming the exercise of generating new sequences as a pragmatic one with utilities attached to certain tests. In Vallée-Tourangeau and New (1998) participants are invited to adopt the role of a health official that either sought to eradicate a scourge of rats or, in another condition, save elephant calves. In the Plague condition, participants read:

> The plague sewer rats have invaded a major city. This breed of rats has developed immunity to all commercially available brands of rat poison. Health officials fear an outbreak of the plague if these rats are not exterminated. Chemists at a local university have isolated three chemical elements, call them P, Q, R, which when combined together kill the rats. Preliminary tests have shown that the following combination killed a captured sewer rat: P = 2, Q = 4, R = 6. Your task is to test new combinations in any quantity to discover the general rule that determines which combinations of the chemical elements are lethal for the sewer rats.

Participants in this condition are thus encouraged to test positive sequences, that is sequences that receive the feedback RAT KILLED. In the Vaccine condition, the production of negative sequences, that is sequences that did not follow the rule for which 2–4–6 was an instance, had a greater utility for the reasoner than positive sequences. Participants read the following instructions:

> The terraglia parasite has infested most of the elephant calves in their natural habitat. The parasite causes fatal heart disease before the animals reach maturity. Researchers working on a treatment have identified three chemicals, call them P, Q, R, which when combined together destroy the parasite, but which in most tests kill the calf as well. Researchers believe that there exist combinations of chemicals whose interactions should be lethal only to the parasite and not the elephant. Preliminary tests have shown that the following combination is lethal to both: P = 2, Q = 4, R = 6. Your task is to test new combinations of the chemicals in any quantity you choose in order to discover the general rule that determines which combinations of chemical elements are lethal for the calves.

Thus participants in this condition were particularly interested in the feedback CALF SURVIVED, rather than CALF KILLED. Participants in both conditions proceeded to produce new sequences of chemical combinations, akin to Wason triples, for which they received feedback, and did so until they were confident of knowing the rule that killed the sewer rats (in the Plague scenario) or elephant calves (in the Vaccine scenario). The relative utility of different types of triples – increasing sequences were valued in the Plague condition, non-increasing sequences were valued in the Vaccine condition – had a systematic impact on the participants' hypothesis testing behaviour. Participants in the Vaccine condition worked longer at the task, produced more non-ascending sequences, and were more likely to discover the 'any ascending sequence' rule than participants in the Plague condition. Thinking dispositions and cognitive capacities no doubt varied considerably within and across conditions. However, since participants were randomly allocated to one of the two conditions, these individual differences cannot explain the significant difference in rule discovery success. Rather, hypothesis-testing behaviour was primarily determined by the cost-benefit structure configured by the utilities ascribed to different types of triples. When participants valued non-ascending triples, they were more likely to seek them (see also Vallée-Tourangeau, 2012a), and in the process to better understand the key contrast feature (Gale & Ball, 2009) that captures the difference between positive and negative sequences: positive sequences go up.

Pseudodiagnostic reasoning

Evaluating the diagnosticity of new information, or its relevance in the process of adjudicating competing hypotheses, involves determining its likelihood of being observed not only given a target hypothesis under consideration, but also its likelihood given an alternative hypothesis. Imagine a manager who interviews two candidates for a sales assistant position. She considers Ms A. and Ms B. The manager leans towards Ms A. and discovers that she successfully completed 70% of her sales transactions in the last month in her previous position. To determine the importance and information value of this new evidence, the manager needs to examine the sales performance of Ms B. However, research suggests that the manager's search for information will be driven by a need for evidence confirming the hypothesis she is entertaining. Thus, if, at this point, the manager believes Ms A. *is* the best candidate, she would naturally seek more information about Ms A rather than checking Ms B's sale performance. Yet, without establishing the sales performance of Ms B, the diagnostic value of Ms A's sales performance is undetermined, and hence cannot judiciously inform the decision-making process.

More generally, the diagnosticity of a datum D for a given hypothesis X (H_x) is defined in terms of the ratio of the probability that D is observed given that H_x is true, $P(D \mid H_x)$, and the probability that D is observed given that an alternative hypothesis Y is true, $P(D \mid H_y)$. Hence, diagnosticity can only be assessed from the perspective of *multiple* hypotheses. The likelihood ratio in Bayes's Theorem is the normative metric of the diagnosticity of information (Doherty, Mynatt, Tweney & Schiavo, 1979). Early research examining how people gather information in order to make inferences suggested they did not fully appreciate that diagnosticity is defined in terms relative to at least two hypotheses, not just one (Beyth-Marom & Fischhoff, 1983; Doherty et al. 1979; Kern & Doherty, 1982). For example, Beyth-Marom and Fischhoff (1983, Experiment 1) told participants that an individual possessed a distinguishing feature and asked them what information they deemed relevant to determine whether that individual was a member of Group A. Nearly 90% of their participants indicated that it was relevant to know $P(D \mid \text{group A})$, but of those 'only' 50% deemed it important to know the probability that this information would also be observed given membership in a different group, or $P(D \mid \text{group B})$. Yet both probabilities must be examined in order to gauge the diagnosticity of the distinguishing feature.

An important characteristic that seems to determine whether people will make diagnostic search choices is the goal of the task. Mynatt, Doherty and Dragan (1993) distinguished between *inference* and *action* problems. The group membership example discussed earlier represents an inference problem. In that scenario, the protagonists belong to one of two possible groups, and the goal is to determine whether the person belongs to Group A or B. In effect the problem is a categorisation inference, and in principle the categorisation can be true or false. In contrast, an action problem is one where hypotheses represent two courses of action. One might be better than the other, but the decision cannot in principle be evaluated in terms of whether one action is true and the other false. Mynatt and colleagues asked participants to imagine *buying* a car, considering car X or car Y, and told them they were 'concerned about (. . .) petrol consumption and mechanical reliability' (p. 768). Participants were then given the same anchoring piece of information ('65% of car Xs do over 25 mpg') and were asked to choose one among three pieces of information in order to help them decide which car to buy: (i) the percentage of car Ys that do over 25 mpg. [Diagnostic, $P(D_1 | H_Y)$]; (ii) the percentage of car Xs that have had no major mechanical problems for the first two years of ownership. [Pseudodiagnostic, $P(D_2 | H_X)$]; the percentage of car Ys that have had no major mechanical problems for the first two years of ownership. [Switching, $P(D_2 | H_Y)$].

Fifty-two percent of the participants chose the piece of information that could determine the petrol consumption of car Ys (the diagnostic choice) and 41% chose the piece of information that could determine the mechanical reliability of car Xs (a pseudodiagnostic choice). To explain the high proportion of diagnostic choices in action problems, Mynatt and colleagues propose that the choice among the three alternatives is determined by the datum which bears more utility for each individual participant: 'Precisely how many subjects will select (the diagnostic choice) will depend on the content of a given problem and subjects' *idiosyncratic* utility function and decision strategies' (pp. 765–766, emphasis added). On this account, those who consider petrol consumption more important than mechanical reliability would be motivated to establish the petrol consumption of car Ys and hence choose the diagnostic option. In contrast, those who are more concerned about mechanical reliability should seek information about car Xs' mechanical reliability, a pseudodiagnostic choice. The authors, however, did not manipulate explicitly the perceived utilities of the two dimensions characterising each alternative (e.g. petrol consumption and mechanical reliability in the car scenario).

Vallée-Tourangeau and Villejoubert (2010) tested the hypothesis that the diagnostic value of new information in evaluating two competing courses of action is determined by the relevance of the data presented. Participants were asked to imagine they were the director of a large zoo and that they had set up a programme aiming to promote reproduction in captivity of African elephants, a species at risk of extinction. Their calves, however, were facing a severe health issue. They were informed of the presence of a parasite whose eggs could lodge in the calves' aortic artery, causing strokes and killing the calves if left untreated, threatening the success of the reproduction programme. The zoo's chief veterinary suggested using one of two treatments to save the calves: treatment A or treatment B. Participants were then told about the mortality rate of calves treated with treatment A and that both treatments could also potentially cause infertility in calves. Participants were told treatment A could cause the death of 80% of the calves. Before making their choice, however, they were allowed to consult one additional piece of information among three alternatives: they could choose to consult the mortality rate of calves treated with treatment B (a diagnostic choice). They could also choose to learn more about treatment A and ask to consult the percentage of infertile calves among those treated with treatment A (a pseudodiagnostic choice). Finally, they could choose to learn about the rate of infertility observed in calves treated with treatment B.

Independent ratings of utility confirmed that people were more concerned about mortality rates (D_1) than about infertility rates (D_2). We thus conjectured that diagnostic choices would be observed because people believe D_1 to be more relevant than D_2 in choosing a course of action. Indeed, 70% of the participants made a diagnostic choice, opting to get information about the mortality rate of Treatment B, while only 10% made a pseudodiagnostic choice, in this instance seeking to know the rate of infertility (and 20% made an irrelevant choice). These results confirmed that participants are strongly drawn to check the diagnostic value of new information, when that information bears the highest relevance for the decision. Thus the diagnostic assessment of new information is determined by the reasoner's goal (see also Villejoubert & Vallée-Tourangeau, 2012).

The essence of thinking

Reasoners' performance on these hypothesis-testing tasks can be predicted by a consideration of the pragmatic goals they seek to achieve. The nature of their thinking dispositions or their cognitive capacities do little to help us explain hypothesis-testing behaviour in these contexts. We recognise, though, that the original Wason 2–4–6 procedure or the initial methodology employed to explore pseudodiagnostic reasoning are designed to examine reasoning in 'an unsystematized area of knowledge', that is the context of reasoning is barren – devoid of meaning or pragmatic relevance – purposefully, so as to offer a platform from which to observe thinking in its purest essence, unsullied by beliefs and goals. We don't mean to articulate a facile ecological validity argument: we believe in the importance of laboratory work. However, in designing a laboratory preparation to investigate a natural phenomenon, it is important to question the pertinence of measuring reasoning in a semantic and pragmatic vacuum of the kind that is very rarely encountered outside the laboratory. We would argue that it is much more fruitful to explore the conditions under which people test hypotheses and make inferences that are better aligned with canons of rationality, than to focus on thinking dispositions and cognitive capacities as an explanation of reasoning performance. For one, interventions designed to improve the quality of thinking are often met with mitigated success. For example, Heijltjes, van Gog, Leppink and Paas (2014) report that instructions and training to improve critical thinking work best with concrete practice; it's not sufficient to tell people to be more open minded. In the 2–4–6 task, instructional manipulations designed to encourage participants to seek disconfirmation of their hypothesis does not improve rule discovery (Tweney et al., 1980). In turn, efforts to train working memory can lead to improvements in working memory capacity, but these don't translate to improvements in fluid intelligence (Harrison, Hambrick, Redick, & Engle, 2013). But, as illustrated in the preceding section, radical changes in thinking performance are possible when the context of reasoning highlights the pragmatic relevance of the task. A focus on dispositions and capacities implicitly strengthens a commitment to methodological individualism which narrows the nature of the proposed explanations and starves ingenuity to design new experimental procedures to unveil a broader range of performance in reasoning tasks. Thinking is the product of the interface between the reasoner and a context. The interface configures a system that is not simply reducible to its components such that the reasoner can be studied independently. Thus, ignoring the context does not simply factor out a component of that interface, it sheds an unrepresentative and perhaps even misleading light on thinking.

Embrained bodies interacting in and with the world

Thus far we have examined the context of reasoning in terms of the framing of traditional reasoning tasks: changes to the framing in terms of the reasoner's goals substantially influence reasoning performance. In our work on problem solving (e.g. Steffensen, Vallée-Tourangeau & Vallée-Tourangeau, 2016) and Bayesian reasoning (G. Vallée-Tourangeau et al., 2015), we've broadened our characterisation of the context of reasoning by casting reasoners as embodied agents embedded in a physical environment that can be modified to support and guide thinking. Thus we engineer thinking tasks where interactivity couples an agent to a physical environment. The physical presentation of a problem matters, of course (Duncker, 1945; Weller, Villejoubert & Vallée-Tourangeau, 2011), and the exact nature of the artefacts – with their physical constraints and affordances, especially if those map onto the rules and features of a problem (e.g. Zhang & Norman, 1994) – can exert a significant influence on problem-solving performance. For example, in a transformation problem such as the river-crossing problem, participants who work on the problem with physical artefacts corresponding to the scenario protagonists and a raft moved over a board representing the river and the river banks generate more moves, and generate moves more quickly, than participants who solve the problem in a less interactive environment (Guthrie, Vallée-Tourangeau, Vallée-Tourangeau & Howard, 2015; Vallée-Tourangeau, Guthrie & Villejoubert, 2013). However, thinking with artifacts can transform thinking not simply because the problem is more concrete, but because participants can interact with a physically modifiable presentation of the problem. Interactivity produces a dynamic agent-environment system. Changes in the problem presentation cue and drive the allocation of attentional resources (Kirsh, 2014) and the retrieval of long-term memory knowledge (Vallée-Tourangeau, 2013), and prompt new actions that result in changes in the problem presentation. A dynamic problem presentation and shifting action affordances guide and constrain the evolution of the agent-environment system along a contingent path (Vallée-Tourangeau & Vallée-Tourangeau, 2014).

Mental arithmetic

Interactivity benefits the process of solving transformation or analytic problems as well as insight problems. As briefly outlined earlier, interactivity prompts a substantially different way of working on the river-crossing problem – a transformation problem: when the cost of making a move (O'Hara & Payne, 1998) is low, involving little planning or mental effort, participants engage with the physical model of the problem using moves as epistemic actions (Kirsh & Maglio, 1994), and make more moves in solving the problem, as well as select the moves quicker than in a low-interactivity version of the same problem.

Mental arithmetic is a type of transformation problem in that operators are applied to transform an initial problem presentation through a series of intermediate states until the solution is derived. In our experiments we ask participants to add series of (typically) single-digit numbers in a low-interactivity condition with their hands flat on a tabletop or in a high-interactivity condition where the same problems are given as a set of numbered tokens which can be manipulated in calculating the sum. Performance is measured in terms of calculation error as well as efficiency, which we operationalise as the proportion of correct answers over the proportion of time the participant invested in calculating the sums out of the maximum time the slowest participants take to do so. We also profile participants in terms of maths anxiety (as assessed with the scale developed by Hunt, Clark-Carter & Sheffield, 2011) and working memory (as measured with a computation span test adapted from Ashcraft & Kirk, 2001). Unsurprisingly, high interactivity fosters better performance in terms of accuracy, calculation error and efficiency (Vallée-Tourangeau, 2012). Interactivity does not simply augment working memory storage; rather, the opportunity to modify the problem presentation dynamically over time provides a physical environment that facilitates the creation and recognition of a great number of congenial groupings which in turn transform participants' ability to deploy arithmetic skills and knowledge (Vallée-Tourangeau, 2013). Perhaps more important are the individual differences that predict performance in the low- and high-interactivity contexts. Thus, in the low-interactivity condition, maths anxiety is a strong positive predictor of absolute calculation error, but explains no variance in calculation error in the high-interactivity condition (Allen & Vallée-Tourangeau, 2015; Vallée-Tourangeau, Sirota & Villejoubert, 2013). In turn, working memory capacity is a strong negative predictor of calculation error – that is, the higher the working memory capacity the lower the calculation error – but this relationship is typically observed in the low interactivity context, not when participants can manipulate tokens in calculating the sums (Guthrie, Harris & Vallée-Tourangeau, 2015; Vallée-Tourangeau et al., 2013). Thus traditional measures of individual differences predict thinking performance but only in a reasoning context that limits or eliminates interactivity.

Insight problem solving

Our work on insight problem solving adopts a similar methodology (e.g. Weller et al., 2011), with the exception that now participants work on a problem for which there is no readily retrievable operator that can transform the initial problem presentation into a goal state; participants experience an impasse, which some can't overcome. The solution to the problem requires a reinterpretation of a key assumption. The type and degree of interactivity are manipulated experimentally, and participants are video recorded. Participants are also profiled in terms of thinking dispositions and capacities. Recently, we examined performance on the so-called 17 animals problem (Vallée-Tourangeau, Steffensen, Vallée-Tourangeau & Sirota, in press, Experiment 1): how to place 17 animals in four enclosures such that there is odd number in each (adapted from Metcalfe & Wiebe, 1987; a 'pure' insight problem according to Weisberg, 1995). The problem masquerades as an arithmetic one, but clearly one odd number cannot be split into four odd ones; rather the solution involves overlapping enclosures and placing some of the animals in the resulting intersections. During the experimental procedure participants completed the Actively Open-minded Test (Haran, Ritov & Mellers, 2013) and working memory span tasks. Participants were initially presented the problem for a three-minute period during which they were invited to sketch an answer on paper. None could, that is every participants labored on an arithmetic solution during this initial phase, all experiencing an impasse. After a 25-minute interval (during which they completed one of the two span tests), the sample was split into two groups. In the first, the model-building group, participants were given pipe cleaner pieces of various lengths and 17 animal figurines and asked to build a model of the solution. In a second group, the tablet group, participants sketched a solution using an electronic tablet and a stylus. Both groups were given 10 minutes to solve the problem. Forty-four percent of the participants built a solution involving overlapping sets; none solved the problem in the tablet condition. Video analysis revealed that participants' focus in the model-building group was primarily on the shape and positioning of the enclosures. In turn, sketches on the tablet revealed that once the enclosures were drawn, they were rarely re-drawn. The shape and position of the enclosures became static features of the problem over which participants exerted quixotic efforts to distribute the 17 animals in a manner that solved the problem. Participants in the tablet condition were fixated on an arithmetic solution whereas those in the model-building condition were more likely to enact a solution involving overlapping sets (see Steffensen et al., 2016, for a detailed analysis of one participant's trajectory to the solution).

Since participants were randomly allocated to the two groups, no differences in AOT and working memory span scores were predicted, and none were observed. Of greater interest, solvers and non-solvers within the model-building group did not differ either: mean AOT score for solvers was 34.2 (SD = 4.98) and it was 30.5 (SD = 5.61) for non-solvers; mean operation span score was 51.5 (SD = 7.5) and 53.5 (SD = 10.4) for solvers and non-solvers, respectively. Thus thinking dispositions and cognitive capacities did not predict the participants' ability to solve the problem.

Interactivity elevates and transforms thinking as traditionally measured using experimental procedures that either limit or eliminate participants' ability or opportunity to manipulate a physical problem presentation. The contingent nature of the problem-solving path is what determines success at the task, not thinking dispositions or cognitive capacities. These findings cast a different light on much recent work aimed at determining the degree to which working memory (and its conjectured components) contributes to insight problem solving (e.g. Chuderski, 2014; Gilhooly & Fioratou, 2009), work that proceeds with a methodology that ignores the role of interactivity in problem solving. The agent–environment system evolves along a certain itinerary towards a solution (Ingold, 2010). The likelihood of arriving at a solution is not predictable, a priori, from measures of thinking dispositions or working memory capacity.

Concluding remarks

Manktelow and Over (1991) inspired us to examine the pragmatic context of reasoning, that reasoning serves goals relevant to agents and actors. As a result, reasoning is sometimes aligned with an abstract normative metric, sometimes not, but always faithful to the goals a reasoner wishes to achieve. An important consequence of this powerful demonstration of the influence of contextual pragmatics is that an explanation of logical reasoning is much more likely to be unveiled by identifying the goals subserving thinking rather than the thinking dispositions and capacities of the reasoner. The random allocation of participants to the four experimental conditions of Manktelow and Over's (1991) third experiment (see p. 98) ensured that dispositions and capacities were randomly distributed across the conditions. The clear and predicted pattern of card selection had absolutely nothing to do with participants' open-mindedness, working memory capacity or IQ.

There is tremendous heuristic value in exploring contextual determinants of reasoning. For one, it forces researchers to rethink accepted, at times fossilised, experimental procedures as offering a representative window onto thinking (this is in part a feature of paradigmatic research that degenerates a little under the pressure of publishing and modern academia). Efforts to craft new experimental procedures unveil a broader range of thinking performance. Applications and intervention possibilities are also more easily discerned by starting with the context of reasoning rather than the nature of the reasoning agent. This is especially true in light of the mitigated success of interventions geared to improve cognitive capacities or sharpen critical thinking skills. A schoolteacher does not design lesson plans for the minority who score highest on aptitude tests. Rather she is avid for ideas on how to communicate information and design better discovery activities to ensure that the majority of her pupils achieve learning objectives (Allen & Vallée-Tourangeau, 2015).

Our work on problem solving encouraged us to analyse the context of reasoning in terms of the artifacts that populate a physical space and that correspond to the elements of a model of the problem. People think by interacting with the model. As participants manipulate the model, changing how the elements are physically configured, some actions are planned, others less so. By that we mean that not all changes to the physical presentation of the problem follow what Ingold (2010) refers to as a hylomorphic model of creativity, that is the implementation (or imposition!) of a pre-determined plan onto the material world. Rather, some of these changes may be the product of perception-action loops unmediated by higher-order cognition (see Figure 9 in G. Vallée-Tourangeau et al., 2015). The shifting topography of affordances cue different actions as the model is modified. The exact nature of the agent-environment system at a given point in time is contingent on the singular evolution of the system up to that point. To adapt Gould (1989), rewinding the tape at a previous point in time does not guarantee the same problem-solving itinerary (although across participants there might be convergent commonalities especially with relatively simple insight problems as domesticated under laboratory conditions).

As our research efforts increasingly focused on interactivity, we have come to view thinking as first order *actions*. The verbal protocol recorded by the cognitive psychologist is a second order narrative of the enacted changes to the physical model of the problem. Clearly the process of verbalising is a form of thinking, and can alter thinking by self-cueing hitherto invisible avenues of deliberation. But, we would argue, verbal protocols are a retrospective narration of an agent acting in and on the world. Experimental procedures that encourage interactivity with a model of the problem, such as the ones we illustrated in this chapter, produce substantially different thinking performance in a wide range of problems and tasks: river-crossing problems (Guthrie et al., 2015), Luchins's water jar (mental set is defused with interactivity; Vallée-Tourangeau, Euden & Hearn, 2011), mental arithmetic (Vallée-Tourangeau, 2013), Bayesian reasoning (G.Vallée-Tourangeau et al.,2015), and insight problem solving (F. Vallée-Tourangeau et al., in press; Weller et al., 2011). Engineering interactive thinking environments unveils a broader range of perceptual, action and cognitive processes than those implicated in the solving of textbook problems in traditional low-interactive or non-interactive procedures. These processes are more representative of those that take place outside the cognitive psychologist's laboratory as people solve problems in the world. Interactive thinking environments motivate detailed qualitative analyses of behaviour to identify precisely the important cognitive events enacted during problem solving (Steffensen, 2013; Steffensen et al., 2016). The emerging theoretical framework draws inspiration from recent work in cognitive archeology, especially from the theory of material engagement (Malafouris, 2010, 2013) that forces a rethink of the nature of cognition, agency and intentionality. These are cast as emergent properties of the interaction with material objects. We believe that a systemic perspective on problem solving and a focus on how interactivity shapes the agent-environment coupling throw a number of fascinating ontological gauntlets. For one, we would argue that a problem representation reflects a meshwork of internal cognitive elements and physical features of the world. The traditional – AI validated – conception of a 'mental' representation needs to be substantially modified or abandoned to capture the stuff of representation distributed across the organism and the world in which it is embedded. In turn, the internalist nature of executive functions, typically outlined in models of working memory (Coolidge, Wynn & Overmann, 2012) is also called into question if attention allocation mechanisms and long-term knowledge retrieval processes are in part elicited and guided by the dynamic configuration of the agent–environment system.

Note

1 Twenty-five years later, Baron (1985) would offer a similar distinction (e.g. p. 15).

References

Allen, M., & Vallée-Tourangeau, F. (2015). Interactivity defuses the impact of maths anxiety in primary school children. *International Journal of Science and Mathematics Education*, forthcoming. Advance online publication. DOI: 10.1007/s10763-015-9659-9.

Ashcraft, M. H., & Kirk, E. P. (2001). The relationships among working memory, math anxiety, and performance. *Journal of Experimental Psychology: General, 130*, 224–237.

Baron, J. (1985). *Rationality and intelligence*. Cambridge: Cambridge University Press.

Beyth-Marom, R., & Fischhoff, B. (1983). Diagnosticity and pseudo-diagnosticity. *Journal of Personality and Social Psychology, 45*, 1185–1195.

Chuderski, A. (2014). How well can storage capacity, executive control, and fluid reasoning explain insight problem solving? *Intelligence, 46*, 258–270.

Coolidge, F. L., Wynn, T., & Overmann, K. A. (2012). The evolution of working memory. In T. P. Alloway & R. G. Alloway (Eds.), *Working memory: The connected intelligence* (pp. 37–60). New York: Psychology Press.

Doherty, M. E., Mynatt, C. R., Tweney, R. D., & Schiavo, M. D. (1979). Pseudodiagnosticity. *Acta Psychologica, 43*, 111–121.

Duncker, K. (1945). On problem solving. *Psychological Monographs, 58*(5), i–113.

Evans, J. St. B. T. (2014). Reasoning, biases and dual processes: The lasting impact of Wason (1960). *Quarterly Journal of Experimental Psychology*. Advance online publication. DOI:10.1080/17470218.2014.914547.

Gale, M., & Ball, L. J. (2009). Exploring the determinants of dual goal facilitation in a rule discovery task. *Thinking & Reasoning, 15*, 294–315.

Gigerenzer, G., & Hoffrage, U. (1995). How to improve Bayesian reasoning without instruction: Frequency formats. *Psychological Review, 102*, 684–704.

Gilhooly, K. J., & Fioratou, E. (2009). Executive functions in insight versus non-insight problem solving: An individual differences approach. *Thinking & Reasoning, 15*, 355–376.

Gould, S. J. (1989). *Wonderful life: The Burgess Shale and the nature of history*. New York: Norton.

Guthrie, L. G., Harris, C., & Vallée-Tourangeau, F. (2015). Interactivity, expertise and individual differences in mental arithmetic. In D. C. Noelle, R. Dale, A. S. Warlaumont, J. Yoshimi, T. Matlock, C. D. Jennings, & P. P. Maglio (Eds.), *Proceedings of the Thirty-seventh Annual Conference of the Cognitive Science Society* (pp. 842–847). Austin, TX: Cognitive Science Society.

Guthrie, L. G., Vallée-Tourangeau, F., Vallée-Tourangeau, G., & Howard, C. (2015). Learning and interactivity in a transformation problem. *Memory and Cognition, 43*, 723–735.

Haran, U., Ritov, I., & Mellers, B. A. (2013). The role of actively open-minded thinking in information acquisition, accuracy, and calibration. *Judgment and Decision Making, 8*, 188–201.

Harrison, T. L., Shipstead, Z., Hicks, K. L., Hambrick, D. Z., Rednick, T. S., & Engle, R. W. (2013). Working memory training may increase working memory capacity but not fluid intelligence. *Psychological Science, 24*, 2409–2419.

Heijltjes, A., van Gog, T., Leppink, J., & Paas, F. (2014). Improving critical thinking: Effects of dispositions and instructions on economics students' reasoning skills. *Learning and Instruction, 29*, 31–42.

Hilton, D. J. (1995). The social context of reasoning: Conversational inference and rational judgment. *Psychological Bulletin, 118*, 248–271.

Hollan, J., Hutchins, E., & Kirsh, D. (2000). Distributed cognition: Toward a new foundation for human computer interaction research. *ACM Transactions on Computer-Human Interaction, 7*, 174–196.

Hunt, T. E., Clark-Carter, D., & Sheffield, D. (2011) The development and part validation of a UK scale for mathematics anxiety. *Journal of Psychoeducational Assessment, 29*, 455–466.

Ingold, T. (2010). The textility of making. *Cambridge Journal of Economics, 34*, 91–102.

Kirsh, D. (2014). The importance of chance and interactivity in creativity. *Pragmatics and Cognition, 22*, 5–26.

Kirsh D., & Maglio P. (1994). On distinguishing epistemic from pragmatic actions. *Cognitive Science, 18*, 513–549.

Kern, L., & Doherty, M. E. (1982). 'Pseudodiagnosticity' in an idealized medical problem-solving environment. *Journal of Medical Education, 57*, 100–104.

Malafouris, L. (2010). Knapping intentions and the marks of the mental. In L. Malafouris & C. Renfrew (Eds.), *The cognitive life of things: Recasting the boundaries of the mind* (pp. 13–22). Cambridge: McDonald Institute Monographs.

Malafouris, L. (2013). *How things shape the mind: A theory of material engagement.* London: MIT Press.

Manktelow, K. I., & Over, D. E. (1991). Social roles and utilities in reasoning with deontic conditionals. *Cognition, 39*, 85–105.

Metcalfe, J., & Wiebe, D. (1987). Intuition in insight and noninsight problem solving. *Memory & Cognition, 15*, 238–246.

Mynatt, C. R., Doherty, M. E., & Dragan, W. (1993). Information relevance, working memory, and the consideration of alternatives. *Quarterly Journal of Experimental Psychology, 46A*, 759–778.

O'Hara, K. P., & Payne, S. J. (1998). The effects of operator implementation cost on planfulness of problem solving and learning. *Cognitive Psychology, 35*, 34–70.

Stanovich, K. E., & West, R. F. (2000). Advancing the rationality debate. *Behavioral and Brain Sciences, 23*, 701–717.

Steffensen, S. V. (2013). Human interactivity: Problem-solving, solution probing and verbal patterns in the wild. In S. J. Cowley & F. Vallée-Tourangeau (Eds.), *Cognition beyond the brain: Computation, interactivity and human artifice* (pp. 195–221). London: Springer-Verlag.

Steffensen, S. V., Vallée-Tourangeau, F., & Vallée-Tourangeau, G. (2016). Cognitive events in a problem-solving task: Qualitative methods for investigating interactivity in the 17 animals problem. *Journal of Cognitive Psychology, 28*(1), 79–105.

Tweney, R. D., Doherty, M. E., Worner, W. J., Pliske, D. B., Mynatt, C. R., Gross, K. A., & Arkkelin, D. L. (1980). Strategies of rule discovery in an inference task. *Quarterly Journal of Experimental Psychology, 32*, 109–123.

Vallée-Tourangeau, F. (2012a). Utilities in the 2–4–6 task. *Experimental Psychology, 59*, 265–271.

Vallée-Tourangeau, F. (2012b). Mental arithmetic efficiency: Interactivity and individual differences. In N. Miyake, D. Peebles & R. P. Cooper (Eds.), *Proceedings of the thirty-fourth annual conference of the Cognitive Science Society* (pp. 1060–1065). Austin, TX: Cognitive Science Society.

Vallée-Tourangeau, F. (2013). Interactivity, efficiency, and individual differences in mental arithmetic. *Experimental Psychology, 60*, 302–311.

Vallée-Tourangeau, F. (2014). Insight, materiality and interactivity. *Pragmatics and Cognition, 22*, 27–44.

Vallée-Tourangeau, F., Austin, N. G., & Rankin, S. (1995). Inducing a rule in Wason's 2–4–6 task: A test of the information-quantity and goal-complementarity hypotheses. *Quarterly Journal of Experimental Psychology, 48A*, 895–914.

Vallée-Tourangeau, F., Euden, G., & Hearn, V. (2011). Einstellung defused: Interactivity and mental set. *Quarterly Journal of Experimental Psychology, 64*, 1889–1895.

Vallée-Tourangeau, F., & New, M. (1998). Rational hypothesis-testing strategies in a rule discovery task. In M. A. Gernbascher & S. J. Derry (Eds.), *Proceedings of the twentieth annual conference of the Cognitive Science Society* (pp. 1079–1083). Mahwah, NJ: Erlbaum.

Vallée-Tourangeau, F., & Payton, T. (2008). Graphical representation fosters discovery in the 2–4–6 task. *Quarterly Journal of Experimental Psychology, 61*, 625–640.

Vallée-Tourangeau, F., Sirota, M., & Villejoubert, G. (2013). Reducing the impact of math anxiety on mental arithmetic: The importance of distributed cognition. In M. Knauff, M. Pauen, N. Sebanz, & I. Wachsmuth (Eds.), *Proceedings of the thirty-fifth annual conference of the Cognitive Science Society* (pp. 3615–3620). Austin, TX: Cognitive Science Society.

Vallée-Tourangeau, F., Steffensen, S. V., Vallée-Tourangeau, G., & Sirota, M. (2016). Insight with hands and things. *Acta Psychologica, 170*, 195–205.

Vallée-Tourangeau, F., & Villejoubert, G. (2010). Information relevance in pseudodiagnostic reasoning. In S. Ohlsson & R. Catrambone (Eds.), *Proceedings of the thirty-second annual conference of the Cognitive Science Society* (pp. 1172–1177). Austin, TX: Cognitive Science Society.

Vallée-Tourangeau, G., Abadie, M., & Vallée-Tourangeau, F. (2015). Interactivity fosters Bayesian reasoning without instruction. *Journal of Experimental Psychology: General, 144*, 581–603.

Vallée-Tourangeau, G., & Vallée-Tourangeau, F. (2014). The spatio-temporal dynamics of systemic thinking. *Cybernetics and Human Knowing, 21*, 113–127.

Villejoubert, G., & Vallée-Tourangeau, F. (2011). Constructing preferences in the physical world: A distributed-cognition perspective on preferences and risky choices. *Frontiers in Psychology, 2*.

Villejoubert, G., & Vallée-Tourangeau, F. (2012). Relevance-driven information search in 'pseudodiagnostic' reasoning. *Quarterly Journal of Experimental Psychology, 65*, 541–552.

Wason, P. C. (1960). On the failure to eliminate hypotheses in a conceptual task. *Quarterly Journal of Experimental Psychology, 12*, 129–140.

Wason. P.C. (1968). Reasoning about a rule. *Quarterly Journal of Experimental Psychology, 20*, 273–281.

Weisberg, R. W. (1995). Prolegomena to theories of insight in problem solving: A taxonomy of problems. In R. J. Sternberg & J. E. Davidson (Eds.), *The nature of insight* (pp. 157–196). Cambridge MA: MIT Press.

Weller, A., Villejoubert, G., & Vallée-Tourangeau, F. (2011). Interactive insight problem solving. *Thinking & Reasoning, 17*, 429–439.

Zhang, J., & Norman, D. A. (1994). Representations in distributed cognitive tasks. *Cognitive Science, 18*, 87–122.

5

DEONTIC REASONING AND SOCIAL NORMS

Broader implications

Harriet Over and David E. Over

We can see how much the psychology of reasoning has changed in the past 40 years by comparing the classic introduction to the field, Wason and Johnson-Laird (1972), with the now standard introduction, Manktelow (2012). Wason and Johnson-Laird focus on the traditional topics first studied by Aristotle and the Stoic philosophers, primarily syllogisms and the indicative conditional (Kneale & Kneale, 1962). The emphasis was on how logical reasoning takes place with factual statements, which have the purpose of describing the world as it is. Wason and Johnson-Laird did not include anything explicit on the topic of our chapter, *deontic* reasoning about human actions, about what people 'must', 'should' or 'may' do to change the world. Manktelow (2012), in contrast, explains the great significance of deontic reasoning and its central position in the new paradigm of the psychology of reasoning, which is Bayesian in its concern with subjective probability and utility judgments (Elqayam & Over, 2013; Oaksford & Chater, 2007). The point of deontic reasoning is to go beyond judgments about what the world is probably like to inferences that will guide human action and behaviour in the achievement of goals, which have utility in the technical sense. It establishes prudential rules, regulations, laws, moral doctrines and broadly social norms, and then uses these as normative premises for inferences about which actions to perform.

The study of deontic inference has the potential to connect the psychology of reasoning to other fields in psychology and related disciplines. It has clear connections to social psychological research on norm following, conformity, persuasion and social influence. Children grow up in societies in which they learn, as a matter of primary importance, how they ought to behave and what they are permitted to do, and hence developmental psychologists are interested in deontic thought and normative behaviour (Cummins, 1996, 2013; Harris & Nuñez, 1996; Rakoczy & Schmidt, 2013). The question of what guides human behaviour is also a central focus of applied researchers interested in how positive social behaviours can be encouraged (Cialdini, Reno & Kallgren, 1990). The new paradigm thus offers researchers in the psychology of reasoning a valuable opportunity to engage with other areas of psychology. It is no coincidence that this volume, compiled in honour of Manktelow, contains so many chapters which focus on thinking in everyday life.

We begin our review with a brief historical sketch, outlining how reasoning researchers came to recognise the importance of deontic reasoning. We will then discuss how deontic conclusions are inferred, not from probable descriptions of the world alone, but also from human preferences. Throughout our theoretical review, we emphasise the importance of fostering connections between the psychology of reasoning and other areas of psychology.

Indicative and deontic reasoning: a historical sketch

As Manktelow (2012) makes clear, psychologists of reasoning did not initially recognise the importance of deontic reasoning. At first, in fact, they took no notice of its existence. Wason and Johnson-Laird (1972) could not have predicted that the study of deontic thought would be forced on the psychology of reasoning by the investigation of the deceptively simple experiment that came to be known as the *Wason selection task* (Evans, this volume; Manktelow, 2012; Wason, 1966), which they implicitly assumed could only be about indicative conditionals. Nor could they have predicted how deeply studying deontic reasoning would affect the psychology of reasoning as a whole.

Wason and Johnson-Laird (1972, pp. 172–173) introduced the selection task in the following way. Four cards are placed on a table, and participants are told that each of these cards has a letter on one side and a number on the other side. With the four cards flat on the table, they can only see these symbols:

E K 4 7

They are then given a 'rule', of the form *if p, then q*, referring to only these four cards:

(1) If a card has a vowel on one side, then it has an even number on the other side.

Participants are instructed, 'Your task is to name those cards, and only those cards, which need to be turned over to determine whether the rule is true or false.' Wason and Johnson-Laird reported that the vast majority of participants in an experiment on this task chose the E and 4 cards or just the E card, and argued that these answers were 'wrong'. The 'correct' response was to choose the E and 7 cards. Most people realise that turning over the E card will show whether there is an even number on the other side, but they fail to see that turning over the 7 card could reveal a falsifying instance of (1), a card with a vowel on one side but an odd number, 7, on the other side. This finding appeared to support the general conclusion that people do not seek evidence that has the potential to falsify their beliefs or even a hypothesis that they are supposedly investigating.

Much research of great value has been done on this task, trying to discover why people give the answers they do, and how they can be helped to the 'correct' answer (Evans & Over, 2004; Manktelow, 2012). But Wason and Johnson-Laird (1972, pp. 191–192) described another version of the task that is directly relevant to our topic (Johnson-Laird, Legrenzi & Legrenzi, 1972). They called this a 'realistic' and 'concrete' version of the task and used this conditional as *if p, then q*:

(2) If a letter is sealed, then it has a 5d stamp on it.

The background context to (2) is that, until 1969, the British Post Office had a surcharge on sealed letters. The participants in this realistic task were asked to imagine that they were Post Office workers whose job was to discover whether (2) had been 'violated'. The participants could now see only one side of four realistic envelopes, with the seal on one side and the stamp on the other. One envelope was shown as sealed, one as unsealed, one had a 5*d* stamp on it, and one had a low-value 4*d* stamp on it. These envelopes thus corresponded, respectively, to the E, K, 4 and 7 cards for (1). But in this realistic experiment on (2), almost all of the participants gave the right answer of selecting the sealed envelope, which is here the *p* card, and the envelope with the 4*d* stamp on it, which is now the *not-q* card. Only these envelopes could reveal a violation of (2): a sealed envelope with the low-value stamp on it.

Wason and Johnson-Laird attributed this striking change in responses to the way the postal task 'simulates exactly as real life activity' (p. 192). But other, deeper, differences between the card and postal tasks have been found to be more important (Evans & Over, 2004; Manktelow, 2012). More specifically the two examples, (1) and (2), differ in their logical form (Manktelow & Over, 1991; and see McNamara, 2010, on the special characteristics of deontic logic). The indicative conditional (1) is used to try to describe a factual relation between vowels and even numbers. It is factually true or false and is asserted for the epistemic purpose of describing the world. It is not a 'rule' in the standard sense of a guide to behaviour, which might be followed by one group of people as a social norm but not another, like left-hand driving for cars found in some countries but not others. On the other hand, (2) is a rule in this proper sense. Rules like this often contain an explicit *deontic modal* in the consequent, about what 'must' or 'should' be done under the condition of the antecedent, in this case to qualify for privacy in a sealed letter. A deontic conditional explicitly contains, or like (2) is implicitly interpreted with, a deontic modal. A selection task referring to such a conditional can be called a *deontic selection task*. It should be contrasted with an *indicative selection task* like that based on (1).

Other differences appear between indicative and deontic selection tasks. Participants in a deontic task are generally asked to choose items that can reveal whether a rule is *violated*, and not whether an indicative conditional is true or false. In the postal task Wason and Johnson-Laird described, a sealed letter (the *p* state) with a low-value stamp (the *not-q* state) on it does not falsify (2). In this violating case, (2) as a rule to be followed is not in any sense 'false', but remains in force as a regulation, and the person who has violated it, posting the offending letter, suffers some penalty, perhaps an extra charge for delivering the letter. In the experimental task, the participants imagine themselves to be Post Office workers with the job of checking for violations of (2) as a Post Office rule and implicit deontic conditional, and there are other, presupposed Post Office norms with explicit or implicit deontic modals, about how they should do their job and what will happen, in the way of penalties, if they do not.

Cheng and Holyoak (1985) were the first psychologists to recognise the deontic nature of selection tasks based on conditionals like (2), using the term *deontic* for the first time in connection with these tasks, and they tried to explain them using what they called 'pragmatic reasoning schemas', which were production rules that contained deontic modals. For example, one of their schemas was, 'If an action is to be taken, then the precondition must be satisfied.' In the postal task, the action is sealing a letter, and the precondition that 'must' be taken is putting a high-value stamp on the envelope. Cheng and Holyoak supported their account with informative experiments about regulations, but their production rules are themselves deontic conditionals, and their account contains a degree of circularity. They were vague about where the deontic modals come from in the first place.

Johnson-Laird and Byrne (2002) followed Cheng and Holyoak in distinguishing between indicative and deontic conditionals, and they tried to give an account of deontic reasoning by postulating that there are mental models of 'deontic possibilities'. For a deontic conditional of the form *if p, then q is obligated*, people are supposed to have mental models indicating that *p & q*, *not-p & q* and *not-p & not-q* are 'deontic possibilities', with *p & not-q* implicitly thought of as the 'deontic impossibility'. Clearly, this account is tightly circular. Ordinary people's understanding of the natural-language words for obligation and permission, 'must', 'may' and related terms, can hardly be explained by labelling theoretical 'mental models' as 'deontic', which is a technical term derived from a Greek word and initially used only by sophisticated logicians and philosophers (McNamara, 2010). Any theory of deontic reasoning must be related to and supplemented by other areas of psychology: judgment and decision making, and developmental, evolutionary and social psychology.

Inferring 'ought' from 'is'

Deontic reasoning cannot be fully explained by using the deontic modals alone, and certainly not by labelling some hypothetical mental representations as 'deontic'. Given these problems with previous accounts, we may ask whether it is possible for scientists to give an account of deontic reasoning at all.

Hume (2000/1739–1740) famously argued against trying to derive 'ought' judgments from 'is' statements, or in other words, deontic judgments from factual statements alone (see also Elqayam & Evans, 2011). We can use the selection task to make Hume's point. A deontic selection task, like (2), is essentially different from an indicative, factual selection task, like (1). Deontic tasks cannot be reduced to or derived from indicative tasks. The rules in the deontic tasks are for guiding human behaviour and are not attempts to state matters of fact.

However, Hume's argument for this conclusion does not imply that scientists are unable to investigate and theorise about the origin and nature of deontic, normative and moral judgments, and study how people make inferences to conclusions containing the deontic modals. To continue with the selection task as an example, a deontic selection task cannot be reduced to an indicative task just about describing the world, for example a relation between letters and numbers on cards as stated by (1). A deontic task is about benefits and costs, or more technically, expected subjective utility. For the deontic task based on (2), the relevant benefit is the privacy of a sealed letter, and the relevant cost is a stamp that has a higher price in money.

There are branches of psychology that study people's judgments about benefits and costs, most notably judgment and decision making, but also evolutionary and social psychology. There are benefits that can increase reproductive success, and costs that can diminish it, and many benefits and costs arise in social contexts, such as enhanced or reduced reputation (Engelmann, Over, Herrmann & Tomasello, 2013). Deontic judgments cannot be reduced to factual assertion about the world because, for the former, agents must make subjective judgments about their preferences, about what they see subjectively as benefits and costs.

Hume (2000/1739–1740) himself pointed out how quickly and readily people do infer 'ought' from 'is'. But even Hume might have been surprised at the early age at which this appears to happen. In a recent study of social norms, Schmidt, Rakoczy and Tomasello (2011) taught 3-year-old children how a novel game is played, for example how to 'dax' (see also Rakoczy, Warneken & Tomasello, 2008). After the children had been shown what it was to 'dax', a puppet announced his intention to 'dax' but performed an inappropriate action. The children protested the puppet's violation in normative language using deontic modals, saying things like, 'You must do this.' They did this even though the experimenter had not used normative language herself when teaching the children the game. The children had inferred how the game 'ought' to be played from a simple demonstration of how the game was played in this social setting. Further research has shown that, from early in development, children create social norms themselves in social settings, generating rules about how games ought and ought not to be played (Göckeritz, Schmidt & Tomasello, 2014). In our view, these children were not fallaciously inferring an 'ought' from an 'is' alone. Rather, implicit benefits and costs underlay these children's games. The potential benefits are those that come from cooperative behaviour in a social group, and the potential costs are those of being outside, or even excluded from, the social group (Over & Carpenter, 2009).

Elqayam, Thompson, Wilkinson, Evans & Over (2015) study how adults infer 'ought' from 'is'. Adults do this quickly and readily, confirming Hume's observation. Elqayam and colleagues use the following example (from Evans, Neilens, Handley & Over, 2008):

(3) If you pull the dog's tail again, then he will bite you.

The speech act of the indicative conditional (3) is that of a warning, which of course takes place in a cooperative social setting. Because (3) links an antecedent (pulling the dog's tail) to a consequent that has 'negative' utility (in this case the cost of being bitten), (3) can also be classified as a type of *utility conditional* (Bonnefon & Sloman, 2013). In the account of Elqayam and colleagues, people interpret (3) as making a causal connection between the action of pulling the dog's tail and the effect of getting bitten. The cost of the effect is thereby transferred to the action, and people will infer, introducing a deontic modal and so a norm, that the action of pulling the dog's tail 'should not' be taken. Elqayam and colleagues present a series of experiments that confirm this account. Here again we see that inferences to deontic and normative conclusions are based on 'is' statements about the world, *plus* human judgments about benefits and costs.

Deontic rules and costs and benefits

Cosmides (1989) was the first researcher to try to explain the deontic selection task with a theory about benefits and costs in social groups. Her account was grounded in evolutionary psychology, and she supported it with her own versions of the Wason selection task. In one of her examples, participants were given this conditional about an imaginary social group:

(4) If a man eats cassava root, then he has a tattoo on his face.

As usual in a selection task, there were four cards, with information on whether a man had eaten cassava root on one side, and whether he had a tattoo on the other side. The participants could of course see only one side of these cards, so that there was, again as usual, for (4) as *if p, then q,* a *p* card, a *not-p* card, a *q* card and a *not-q* card. In one condition, using a deontic version of the task, Cosmides presented (4) as a *social contract* in the social group. A social contract is a kind of deontic rule requiring a cost be paid if a benefit is received. In this example, the benefit is eating the desirable cassava root, which is restricted to married men in the group as a social norm, and the cost is getting a tattoo, which by another social norm is the sign of getting married. In another condition, using an indicative version of the task, she simply presented (4) as an indicative conditional attempting to describe a factual relation between cassava root eating and tattoos in the social group. She found that participants were more likely to choose the combination of the *p* card, showing that cassava root was eaten, and the *not-q* card, showing that there was no tattoo, in the deontic version of the task than in the indicative version of the task.

Cosmides tried to explain this difference between the deontic and indicative tasks by postulating that the former is about looking for cheaters. People who take a benefit in a social contract but do not pay the associated cost are *cheaters*. To be cheated is to suffer a cost that can negatively affect reproductive success, and so it is vital to discover cheaters and exclude them from further exchanges. For a more realistic example, consider a hunter under primitive conditions who has been unsuccessful one day, but is given food by others in the group. They will then expect him to share food with them on another occasion when he has been successful. If he does not, the resulting social disapproval will be disadvantageous to him and negatively affect his reproductive success. Such reciprocal relations are the basis of many social norms, and the ultimate justification of many laws and regulations. The post rule (2) and the task that goes with it can be analysed in this way. For the benefit of privacy in a letter, a person posting it is expected to pay the cost of a high-value stamp. The postal workers who check for violations of (2), which are cases of cheating, also have social contracts. To get the benefit of their wage, they are expected to pay the cost of working to find any such cases of cheating, and if they do not do this effectively, they are cheating themselves.

Cosmides argued that, thanks to natural selection, people have what she termed a Darwinian algorithm in a domain-specific module in their minds for analysing the benefit/cost structure of social exchanges and for detecting cheaters on social contracts. She predicted that people would choose the *p* and *not-q* cards, looking for violators of *if p, then q*, when this conditional expressed a social contract and these cards could reveal the existence of a cheater. She seemed to imply that there could be no other explanation of the selection of the *p* and *not-q* cards in a selection task.

However, this implication was shown to be false by Manktelow and Over (1990), who created a selection task using the deontic conditional, 'If you clear up spilt blood, then you must wear rubber gloves,' with cards showing on one side whether there was clearing up of spilt blood, and on the other side, whether rubber gloves were worn. Most participants selected the 'spilt blood cleared up' (*p*) card and the 'rubber gloves not worn' (*not-q*) cards. These participants could not be looking for cheaters. Clearing up spilt blood with bare hands endangers oneself and does not cheat anyone.

In reply, Cosmides and her collaborators went on to postulate the existence of yet another Darwinian algorithm and domain-specific module in the mind for making inferences about possible hazards (Fiddick, Cosmides & Tooby, 2000). Being unable to recognise potential hazards – poisonous plants, sources of infection and dangerous animals – can obviously severely limit reproductive success, and being able to do this and take appropriate avoidance action can obviously be beneficial in this way. The domain-specific module for dealing with hazards is held to be distinct from that for social exchanges and identifying cheaters, and in fact, Cosmides and her followers argue that the mind has no general, content-independent ability for deontic reasoning, and still less for reasoning even more generally. They claim that the mind only has separate modules for inferences about specific contents, such as social exchanges and hazards.

Cosmides and her followers took a significant step with their analysis of the costs and benefits of conforming to and violating deontic conditionals, and grounding this analysis in an evolutionary framework. They did not use the deontic modals, or 'deontic' applied to mental models, as unexplained primitive terms in their theory, and they did not try to derive deontic thought from descriptive statements alone, but rather from people's subjective judgments about expected benefits and costs. Furthermore, her theory began to connect the psychology of reasoning to other areas of psychology. Indeed, her work on cheater detection is regularly cited in other fields.

An apparent weakness of this approach is that instances of cheating are so diverse that it is not clear how a single module could deal with them. To try and resolve this concern, Cosmides (1989, p. 196) conceded that the algorithms in her supposedly domain-specific module for social exchanges had to be 'item-independent', able to process any items of exchange as long as the individual perceived them as benefits and costs. This position apparently allows her to explain how there can be social exchanges of, say, poison dart frogs in one society, in a Brazilian rainforest, and scientific data on gravitational perturbations in another, among academics. An individual in the one group gets the benefit of poison darts made from the frogs' skin, and an individual in the other group gets the benefit of advancing astronomical knowledge from the data on the perturbations. A 'cheater' takes the frogs, or the data, without giving anything in return at any point. However, we argue that a 'module' that could identify such a general range of 'benefits', abstractly defined, would be domain-general and have the capacity, or at least be an aspect of the capacity, for general deontic reasoning. (See Over, 2003, for papers for and against Cosmides' account of deontic reasoning and the more general application of evolutionary psychology to the psychology of reasoning.)

People can generate highly individual deontic statements for their own purely subjective reasons and guidance when nothing as serious as cheating or a hazard is in question, but where we see some 'benefit' or 'cost', in the general sense, for ourselves. We might think to ourselves that, if we make risotto for dinner, then we should use Arborio rice. Risotto for dinner without Arborio rice is neither cheating nor a hazard. We might prefer Arborio rice, if it is not too expensive or hard to get, simply because we like its taste and texture. Of course, a desire for foods high in calories has some general evolutionary explanation, but that alone cannot account for our specific deontic conditional, which derives from our individual preference for Arborio rice over some other variety of rice, all else being equal. For the great variety of human deontic judgments and reasoning, there has to be a general capacity for balancing benefits and costs.

A Bayesian approach

Manktelow and Over (1991) argued that the foundation of deontic reasoning lies in human decision making (see also Evans & Over, 2004, and Over, Manktelow & Hadjichristidis, 2004). This can be about the benefits and costs of social exchanges and cheating, or the dangers of hazards, but of course about much else as well. To simplify, people will conclude in decision making about two options, that they 'should' take one action rather than another when they prefer the former to the latter. People select the cards in a deontic selection task that maximise their expected utility, and this decision-theoretic account of these tasks can be placed in a decision-making and Bayesian account of human reasoning in general (Oaksford & Chater, 2007). What is characteristic of deontic thought is its dependence, not just on probability judgments about matters of fact, but also on utility judgments about benefits and costs.

Some of our decisions are based on personal taste, like a preference for white wine over red wine. More typically, deontic reasoning takes place within social contexts. It is often pointed out that humans are obligate cooperative foragers. Unlike many extant primates, humans rely on cooperation to secure sufficient resources for survival (Tomasello, Melis, Tennie, Wyman, & Herrmann, 2012). Deontic reasoning usually occurs within this context of social interaction and collaboration. For example, some people may reason that they ought to share the berries they have gathered because their social group shunned them in the past when they kept all the berries for themselves. Other people may infer that they ought to share their knowledge of where to find the best game with their hunting partners because this increases the chances of a successful hunt (which benefits them personally as well as their social group). Again, the 'ought' in these examples comes from a decision to avoid a cost or obtain a benefit, but within the context of collaboration, and these 'benefits' and 'costs' can have almost any content.

Within such a context, a tendency to enforce social norms on others can also develop. For example, a person may say that a group member 'ought' to forage by the river because, if they do not, they will not find sufficient berries to share with the group. To the extent that others' welfare is important to us (because we rely on them as cooperative partners), we can also analyse costs and benefits as they apply to others. For example, we might advise a cooperative partner of a particular course of action which, in the short term, benefits only them. From an evolutionary perspective, we do this because, ultimately, their survival is beneficial to us.

Tomasello and Schmidt (2012) have argued that norm enforcement emerges from collaborative agreements. In situations where we all agree, at least implicitly, to collaborate, we can hold you accountable if you defect. This claim is closely related to the concept of shared intentionality (Tomasello, Carpenter, Call, Behne, & Moll, 2005). When children join a social group, they agree, at least implicitly, to uphold the norms of the group. This agreement implies enforcing those norms on other members of the group (Tomasello & Schmidt, 2012). In our account, however, such implicit agreements are not strictly necessary for norm enforcement to emerge. An analysis of costs and benefits is at the heart of norm enforcement, although this analysis can be affected and reinforced by implicit or explicit agreements.

Broader implications of the Bayesian approach

A significant advantage of the Bayesian perspective is that it opens up the possibility of a more flexible perspective on reasoning in general and deontic reasoning in particular, and leaves space for a more nuanced and genuinely developmental account of human reasoning and decision making. Cosmides, in contrast, argued that the entire architecture of human reasoning, including deontic reasoning, is innately specified and narrowly modular in nature. Her position leaves little room for subtle developmental change and cross-cultural differences in reasoning. Inspired by the Bayesian account, we may start to ask about the origins of our preferences and our judgments of costs and benefits. Some personal preferences, for example for foods high in fat or sugar, may have innate roots and be reinforced by early experience, but we can still learn later in life to enjoy a 'Mediterranean' diet low in fat and sugar. Some social preferences may also have an innate basis, for example a preference for social connection with others (Baumeister & Leary, 1995; Over, in press). Experimental research has shown that young children, but not chimpanzees, prefer to cooperate with others than to work alone (Rekers, Haun & Tomasello, 2011). This preference for social contact, inclusion and cooperation could explain why children learn deontic rules and norms so readily, as in the 'dax' game we described earlier, and it may be so deep within us that we cannot learn to enjoy ostracism by our social group any more than being burnt at the stake by them (Williams, 2007). Other preferences, however, can be learned, through interaction with the environment or social training, giving scope for cross-cultural and individual differences in the decisions human beings make. Even highly abstract scientific preferences can be learned over time, for example for double-blind studies of new medical drugs. It is hard to see how domain-specific modules alone can explain these developments. The origins of our preferences, and of our ability to infer costs and benefits, remain important questions for future research.

Concluding thoughts

The psychology of reasoning has come a long way since Wason and Johnson-Laird (1972), as Manktelow (2012) explains. Nothing better illustrates the change in the field than the study of deontic reasoning. Wason and Johnson-Laird did not even recognise it as a type of reasoning, but it is present in all areas of human thought and action. It is found even in the most abstract scientific disciplines, in which norms exist for how scientific theories 'should' be formulated and tested in experiments. From early in development, humans readily infer 'ought' from 'is'. In the new Bayesian perspective in the psychology of reasoning, these deontic judgments are derived from inferences about costs and benefits. This account explains why people form and enforce social norms and so has broad implications for developmental, evolutionary and social psychology.

Acknowledgment

We are very grateful to Ken Manktelow for many inspiring discussions about deontic reasoning.

References

Baumeister, R. F., & Leary, M. R. (1995). The need to belong: Desire for interpersonal attachments as a fundamental human motivation. *Psychological Bulletin, 117*, 497–529.

Bonnefon, J. F., & Sloman, S. A. (2013). The causal structure of utility conditionals. *Cognitive Science, 37*, 193–209.

Cheng, P. N., & Holyoak, K. J. (1985). Pragmatic reasoning schemas. *Cognitive Psychology, 17*, 391–416.

Cialdini, R. B., Reno, R. R., & Kallgren, C. A. (1990). A focus theory of normative conduct: Recycling the concept of norms to reduce littering in public places. *Journal of Personality and Social Psychology, 58*, 1015–1026.

Cosmides, L. (1989). The logic of social exchange: Has natural selection shaped how humans reason? *Cognition, 31,* 187–276.

Cummins, D. D. (1996). Evidence of deontic reasoning in 3- and 4-year-old children. *Memory & Cognition, 24,* 823–829.

Cummins, D. D. (2013). Deontic and epistemic reasoning in children revisited: Comment on Dack and Astington. *Journal of Experimental Child Psychology, 116,* 762–769.

Elqayam, S., & Evans, J. St. B. T. (2011). Subtracting 'ought' from 'is': Descriptivism versus normativism in the study of human thinking. *Behavioral and Brain Sciences, 34,* 233–248.

Elqayam, S., & Over, D. E. (2013). New paradigm psychology of reasoning: An introduction to the special issue edited by Elqayam, Bonnefon, & Over. *Thinking & Reasoning, 19,* 249–265.

Elqayam, S., Thompson, V., Wilkinson, M., Evans, Jonathan St. B. T., & Over, D. E. (in press). Deontic introduction: A theory of inference from is to ought. *Journal of Experimental Psychology: Learning, Memory, and Cognition, 41,* 1516–1532.

Engelmann, J. M., Over, H., Herrmann, E., & Tomasello, M. (2013). Young children care more about their reputations with ingroup members and potential reciprocators. *Developmental Science, 16,* 952–95.

Evans, J. St. B. T. (2010). *Thinking twice: Two minds in one brain.* Oxford: Oxford University Press.

Evans, J. St. B. T., Neilens, H., Handley, S. J., & Over, D. E. (2008). When can we say 'if'? *Cognition, 108,* 100–116.

Evans, J. St. B. T., & Over, D. E. (2004). *If.* Oxford: Oxford University Press.

Evans, J. St. B. T., & Stanovich, K. E. (2013). Dual process theories of higher cognition: Advancing the debate. *Perspectives on Psychological Science, 8,* 223–241.

Fiddick, L., Cosmides, L., & Tooby, J. (2000). No interpretation without representation: The role of domain-specific representations and inferences in the Wason selection task. *Cognition, 77,* 1–79.

Göckeritz, S., Schmidt, M. F. H., & Tomasello, M. (2014). Young children's creation and transmission of social norms. *Cognitive Development, 30,* 81–95.

Harris, P., & Nuñez, M. (1996). Understanding of permission rules by preschool children. *Child Development, 67,* 1572–1591.

Hume, D. (2000). *A treatise on human nature* (Original publication date 1739–1740). Oxford: Clarendon Press.

Johnson-Laird, P. N., & Byrne, R. M. J. (2002). Conditionals: A theory of meaning, pragmatics and inference. *Psychological Review, 109,* 646–678.

Johnson-Laird, P. N., Legrenzi, P., & Legrenzi, M. S. (1972). Reasoning and a sense of reality. *British Journal of Psychology, 63,* 395–400.

Kneale, W., & Kneale, M. (1962). *The development of logic.* Oxford: Oxford University Press.

Manktelow, K. I. (2012). *Thinking and reasoning.* Hove, UK: Psychology Press.

Manktelow, K. I., & Over, D. E. (1990). Deontic thought and the selection task. In K. J. Gilhooly, M. T. G. Keane, R. H. Logie & G. Erdos (Eds.) *Lines of thinking: Reflections on the psychology of thought* (pp. 153–164). Chichester, UK: John Wiley & Sons.

Manktelow, K. I., & Over, D. E. (1991). Social roles and utilities in reasoning with deontic conditionals. *Cognition, 39,* 85–105.

Manktelow, K. I., & Over, D. E. (1995). Deontic reasoning. In S. E. Newstead & J. St. B. T. Evans (Eds.), *Perspectives on thinking and reasoning: Essays in honour of Peter Wason* (pp. 91–114). Hillsdale, NJ: Erlbaum.

McNamara, P. (2010). Deontic logic. In E. N. Zalta (Ed.), *Stanford encyclopedia of philosophy* (Summer 2010 edition). Stanford, CA: Stanford University. http://plato.stanford.edu/archives/sum2010/entries/logic-deontic/.

Oaksford, M., & Chater, N. (2007). *Bayesian rationality: The probabilistic approach to human reasoning*. Oxford: Oxford University Press.

Over, D. E. (Ed.). (2003). *Evolution and the psychology of thinking: The debate*. Hove, UK: Psychology Press.

Over, D. E., Manktelow, K. I., & Hadjichristidis, C. (2004). Conditions for the acceptance of deontic conditionals. *Canadian Journal of Experimental Psychology, 58*, 96–105.

Over, H. (2016). The origins of belonging: Social motivation in young children. *Philosophical Transactions of the Royal Society B.* Philosophical Transactions of The Royal Society B Biological Sciences, 371(1686), 20150072.

Over, H., & Carpenter, M. (2009). Priming third-party ostracism increases affiliative imitation in children. *Developmental Science, 12*, F1–F8.

Rakoczy, H., & Schmidt, M. F. H. (2013). The early ontogeny of social norms. *Child Development Perspectives, 7*, 17–21.

Rakoczy, H., Warneken, F., & Tomasello, M. (2008). The sources of normativity: Young children's awareness of the normative structure of games. *Developmental Psychology, 44*, 875–881.

Rekers, Y., Haun, D., & Tomasello, M. (2011). Children, but not chimpanzees, prefer to forage collaboratively. *Current Biology, 21*, 1756–1758.

Schmidt, M. F. H., Rakoczy, H., & Tomasello, M. (2011). Young children attribute normativity to novel actions without pedagogy or normative language. *Developmental Science, 14*, 530–539.

Schmidt, M. F. H., & Tomasello, M. (2012). Young children enforce social norms. *Current Directions in Psychological Science, 21*, 232–236.

Stephens, D. W., Brown, J. S., & Ydenberg, R. C. (2007). *Foraging: Behaviour and ecology*. Chicago: Chicago University Press.

Tomasello, M., Carpenter, M., Call, J., Behne, T., & Moll, H. (2005). Understanding and sharing intentions: The origins of cultural cognition. *Behavioral and Brain Sciences, 28*, 675–691.

Tomasello, M., Melis, A. P., Tennie, C., Wyman, E., & Herrmann, E. (2012). Two key steps in the evolution of human cooperation. *Current Anthropology, 53*, 673–692.

Wason, P. C. (1966). Reasoning. In B. M. Foss (Ed.). *New horizons in psychology*. Harmondsworth, UK: Penguin.

Wason, P., & Johnson-Laird, P. N. (1972). *Psychology of reasoning: Structure and content*. London: Batsford.

Williams, K. D. (2007). Ostracism. *Annual Review of Psychology, 58*, 425–452.

6

CERTAINTY AND ACTION

Valerie A. Thompson

How old am I? Will the salmon or pasta taste better? Will I see greater returns investing in the stock market or in real estate? The answer to each of these questions has two elements. The first is the content of the answer (e.g., 39, the salmon, real estate) and the second is a feeling of certainty about that answer. It is tempting to think that understanding behaviour requires understanding the former, that is, the output of our cognitive processes. However, it is the latter, namely the certainty with which a decision is reached, that determines how vigorously we pursue a course of action or whether we act at all; certainty will determine whether we stay with our initial choice or search for another, and how we present our decision to other people. Certainty, in other words, is the arbiter of action.

Metacognition, monitoring, and control

Metacognition is the study of how we monitor and control our cognitive processes. Stated like this, it seems like a very erudite pursuit: the study of self-reflection and self-knowledge. Instead, the mechanisms that monitor our cognitions are assumed to be relatively low-level, implicit processes that provide ongoing feedback on the success or failure of our cognitive activity (Koriat, 2007). An analogy might be a thermostat, which passively monitors air temperature and initiates a control process when the ambient temperature falls below a certain level. Similarly, metacognitive processes monitor mental states and initiate corrective actions (Nelson & Narens, 1990), which include re-reading a paragraph that was not well comprehended, writing down rather than attempting to remember a shopping list, deciding whether to solve a problem or look up the answer, and so forth. A large number of monitoring processes have been studied, mostly in the context of learning and memory (e.g., Dunlosky & Tauber, 2014), but also recently in the domain of reasoning and problem-solving (Ackerman & Thompson, 2014).

These go by a variety of names, depending on the cognitive activity being monitored, and include Judgments of Solvability, Judgments of Learning, Feelings of Rightness, Feelings of Knowing, and so forth. Judgments of Solvability, for example, refer to an internal assessment of whether a problem can be solved; Judgments of Learning refer to the subjective probability that one will remember a just-studied item on a subsequent test, Feelings of Rightness index the degree to which an initial problem solution is correct, and Feelings of Knowing measure the subjective probability that a currently unrecallable item is nonetheless available in memory. Although they go by different names, at the core, they all index a subjective sense of confidence or certainty. The goal of this chapter is to explore the basis and consequences of this sense of certainty.

Certainty and the allocation of cognitive resources

In our lab, we have been interested in how confidence signals whether further thought is required (Thompson, 2009; Thompson, Prowse Turner, & Pennycook, 2011). Consider the following examples: Fred and Alan are both looking for a new car. Fred has his eye on a used Toyota Camry, which gets high ratings for reliability and owner satisfaction from *Consumer Reports*. He test drives a Camry and finds it comfortable, and decides to buy it. Fred, on the other hand, is sceptical of numerical information, but decides to take the car for a test drive anyway. Although the car is comfortable, he is not convinced and decides to keep looking. Fred's information search leads to a situation of confidence, and further reflection is not required. Alan's produces a sense of uncertainty, and so he continues to search. One's degree of certainty is one of the primary cues we rely on to signal whether to be content with the current choice or to rethink it.

In the laboratory, we have demonstrated this relationship in a variety of reasoning and decision-making tasks (Thompson et al., 2011, 2013; Thompson & Johnson, 2014). Take, as an example, this variant on a classic reasoning problem, first developed by Peter Wason (1966):

> Imagine a deck of cards, each of which has a letter on one side of the card and a number on the other. Below are four cards drawn at random from the deck. Which cards do you need to turn over to determine whether the following rule is true or false?

> If there is a K on one side, then there is a 3 on the other.

> K
>
> 3
>
> D
>
> 7

The correct answer is to choose the K and 7 cards (which would show definitely that the rule was false), but most people choose the K and 3 cards instead. Our interest was not to explain people's reasoning on the task, which has been the subject of numerous investigations (see Evans, 1998, for review), but to use it as a vehicle to study monitoring and control in the context of reasoning. In our version of the task (Thompson et al., 2013), the cards were presented one at a time and participants gave two responses: an immediate, intuitive answer and an answer that they could take all the time they wanted to think about. After their intuitive answer, they were asked to rate their *Feeling of Rightness* (FOR) about that answer on a scale of 1–7, with "1" marked as "guessing" and "7" marked as "certain I am right". We were interested in the relationship between the initial feeling of rightness and two indices of analytic thought: how long people spent reconsidering their initial answer when given the opportunity and the probability that they changed their answers. The results are plotted in Figure 6.1.

As is clear, each increment on the Feeling of Rightness scale produced a sharp decline in both the amount of time rethinking an answer and the probability that the answer changed. Thus, we have found that the FOR, like many other measures of certainty, appears to exert a control function over behaviour (Ackerman & Thompson, 2014): low levels of certainty are associated with long rethinking times and more answer changes. In contrast, high levels of certainty produce very short thinking times and almost no answer changes (Thompson et al., 2011; Thompson et al., 2013; Thompson & Johnson, 2014).

This relationship also holds in other domains. In a context of learning, feelings of certainty predict how participants allocate study time and decide on learning strategies. For example, metacognitive measures of certainty predict the length of

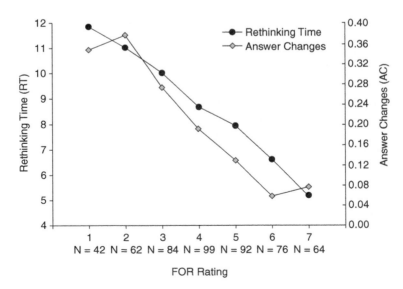

FIGURE 6.1 The linear relationship between Feeling of Rightness, rethinking time, and probability of changing answers

time spent studying an item for a subsequent recall test (e.g., Mazzoni & Cornoldi, 1993; Nelson, 1993; Son, 2004; Son & Metcalfe, 2000), the amount of time one will spend searching for an item in memory (Singer & Tiede, 2008), the decision to engage in massed or distributed practice (Benjamin & Bird, 2006; Son, 2004), and whether to derive a solution by computation or attempt to retrieve it from memory (Reder & Ritter, 1992).

In fact, so powerful is the relationship between certainty and resource allocation that it is possible to artificially manipulate people's judgments of certainty and show that this judgment nonetheless influences their subsequent behaviour. Metcalfe and Finn (2008) were interested in *Judgments of Learning*, which are taken right after an item has been studied and which reflect participants' confidence that they will be able to recall that item in a subsequent test. Each item was studied on two separate occasions. On one occasion, the item was studied only once, and on the other, it was studied three times. After study, participants indicated their judgment of learning. Key to their experiment was the observation that judgments of learning were higher if the three-repetition condition preceded the one-repetition condition than vice versa, even though learning outcomes were the same in both conditions. Thus, the order of the repetition conditions artificially affected judgments of learning. Despite that, judgments of learning continued to have a control function over the allocation of study time: when the three-repetition preceded the one-repetition condition, people were less likely to indicate a need to study the items further, consistent with their higher judgments of learning.

Indeed, confidence is the basis for action in a wide range of situations. For example, the degree of confidence one has in a conclusion predicts the likelihood of action (e.g., Berger & Mitchell, 1989; Pieters & Verplanken, 1995), as well as how committed one is to a course of action suggested by that conclusion (Adidam & Bingi, 2011); confidence in a conclusion is also a signal to other people that the conclusion is right and can be shared (Fox & Walters, 1986; Vidmar, Coleman, & Newman, 2010). A well-documented example of this concerns the testimony of eyewitnesses, whose confidence has been known to persuade investigators and jurors, despite abundant evidence that the correlation between confidence and accuracy is, at best, modest. Indeed, as reviewed later, much research shows that people's understanding of their cognitive processes is faulty, which makes them prone to mis-assessing their performance and misdirecting their cognitive resources (Bjork, Dunlosky, & Kornell, 2013).

Certainty as a goal state

Another way confidence interacts with cognition is as a goal. It is thought that people work on a task until they reach an aspirational level of confidence in the product. In other words, people are thought to set a confidence threshold and continue working until their level of confidence reaches that threshold. This model is referred to as the discrepancy reduction model (Nelson & Narens, 1990). As a consequence, for example, people will tend to allocate more time to the study of items perceived as more difficult, presumably because the more difficult items need more study for the participant to be confident in their recall (see Son & Metcalfe, 2000, for review).

Complicating this picture is the finding that aspirational levels are goal-driven, and can be adjusted to the current context. In a learning context, for example, if the goal is to learn only a subset of items or if participants are pressed for time, they direct resources selectively to easier items (Son & Metcalfe, 2000; Thiede & Dunlosky, 1999). The confidence threshold may also change as a function of elapsed time. Ackerman (2014) measured ongoing confidence every 15 seconds during a problem-solving task. Consistent with the discrepancy reduction model, answers given within a short period of time had high levels of confidence, which suggests that people set the threshold and gave answers that met that threshold. However, as time passed, people gave answers with lower and lower degrees of confidence, suggesting that they were lowering the threshold as time progressed. Thus, as time passed, people lowered their aspirations and provided answers with lower and lower degrees of confidence.

The need to meet an aspirational level of confidence may also explain people's information-gathering strategies in decision-making situations. In a typical task, people are asked to decide between a number of alternatives (e.g., about which stock to invest in) and are allowed to gather information about each of the options until they feel they have enough information to make a decision. In these situations, people often continue to gather information after the point at which they had enough information to discriminate between options (see Bröder & Newell, 2008; Hilbig, 2010, for reviews). In fact, people will pay to have that information, even if the information obtained is not helpful (Newell, Weston, & Shanks, 2003). This suggests that having additional information, even of poor quality, may help people reach the confidence threshold necessary for them to make a choice.

In the same way that additional information appears to build confidence, additional time on task also appears to increase confidence. In all of the studies that we have carried out with the two-response paradigm described earlier, we have noticed that confidence is always higher for the second response than the first, even when the second responses are no more accurate than the first ones. We have speculated that people believe that more thinking produces better decisions, and are thus more confident in decisions that take more time, even when they are not more accurate (Shynkaruk & Thompson, 2006). Thus, when allowed more time to think about an answer, confidence increases.

The calibration of confidence

In this section, I discuss evidence that addresses the issue of how accurate our confidence judgments are. Do we know when we are right? Do we have insight into the types of skills and activities that we are good at? The intuitive answer to this question might be "of course" and that "no-one knows you like you know yourself" (Zell & Krizan, 2014, p. 112). In reality, however, the accuracy of self-assessment varies widely from domain to domain, with good accuracy in some domains and very poor accuracy in others.

Discrimination or relative accuracy

Confidence can be measured in three different ways. The first is called discrimination accuracy or relative accuracy and refers to the ability of an individual to discriminate between correct and incorrect answers (Koriat, 2012). This relationship has been studied in a number of domains and the correlation between confidence and accuracy ranges from very low to moderately high.

The more optimistic research comes from the field of metamemory, which is interested in studying how well people can introspect on their memory processes. Indeed, much of the early research in this domain was concerned with explaining why people appear to have accurate introspections about current or future memory performance. As an example, consider the seminal work of Joseph Hart (1965), who asked people to answer difficult general knowledge questions such as "Who painted 'Afternoon at La Grand Jatte'?" Hart was interested in the *Tip of the Tongue* phenomenon, whereby one has a nagging sense that one knows the answer, but cannot currently recall it. On questions that participants could not answer, they were asked to indicate whether they had a feeling that they knew the answer to the question. Hart found that this *Feeling of Knowing* was related to their subsequent ability to pick out the correct answer on a recognition test: performance was better when people had a feeling of knowing than when they did not, although the accuracy of their "know" judgments was substantially higher than their "don't know" judgments. This was a remarkable finding: people who were currently unable to produce the answer to a question nonetheless appeared to know that the answer was "in there somewhere". Subsequent research demonstrated that a variety of just judgments, including confidence that one has recalled an item correctly showed above-chance correlations with accuracy (e.g., Koriat & Goldsmith, 1996).

On the more pessimistic side, despite the positive relationship between confidence and memory observed earlier, it is nonetheless the case that people can hold high degrees of confidence in false memories (things that were never experienced) and wrong memories (Roediger & McDermott, 1995). This misplaced confidence has implications for a great many fields, but has been most extensively examined in the field of eyewitness testimony, where eyewitnesses play a key role in determining the guilt or innocence of an accused person. Unlike the case for the feeling of knowing, eyewitness confidence and accuracy are not well calibrated (the correlation is about 0.3; Sporer, Penrod, Read, & Cutler, 1995), although like the feeling of knowing, the relationship is better for positive judgments (i.e., when a witness picks someone out of a lineup) than for negative ones (i.e., when they fail to select anyone; e.g., Palmer, Brewer, Weber, & Nagesh, 2013, Sporer et al., 1995). Not only is the correlation imperfect, but the general finding is that witnesses tend to be overconfident relative to their level of accuracy. Moreover, the variables that positively or negatively affect the accuracy of identification may have opposite effects on confidence judgments; for example, overconfidence is greater in difficult conditions (i.e., where there is a long delay or a short viewing time) than easier ones (Palmer et al., 2013). Similarly, eyewitness confidence is increased by repeated questioning and reinforcement, without necessarily an increase in accuracy (Wells, Olson, & Charman, 2002).

This miscalibration of confidence and accuracy has profound consequences: many cases of wrongful conviction result from mistaken eyewitness investigation (Wells & Quinlivan, 2009). Wells and Quinlivan also review archival evidence showing that eyewitnesses pick out the wrong suspect from a lineup about 30% of the time. The fact that these mistakes may be made with confidence has further implications, because other people's confidence is a signal to us that they know what they are talking about (see Sporer et al., 1995, for review): Confident people are more likely to be believed than less confidence ones, and this includes eyewitnesses.

Consequences of misplaced confidence are not limited to memory; they apply also to skilled behaviour, such as medical diagnosis. Podbregar and colleagues examined the medical records of patients who died in the ICU and who were subsequently subject to post-mortem examination (Podbregar, Voga, Krivec, Skale, Parežnik, & Gabršček, 2001). They were interested in whether the post-mortem confirmed the original diagnosis of the attending physician and whether errors were more common when the diagnosis was offered with low confidence (as evidenced, for example, by the presence of question marks). They found fatal diagnostic errors in about 10% of the cases they examined; the rate of error did not vary as a function of whether the original diagnosis was confidently or less confidently expressed.

Finally, we have also done some preliminary investigations into the correlation between accuracy and confidence on various reasoning tasks. On these tasks, reasoners are presented with a set of premises (e.g., if someone is brandup, then they glep; this person gleps) and are asked to figure out what follows logically from them. On easy tasks, as in the preceding example, the correlation between confidence and accuracy is modest (Markovits, Thompson, & Brisson, 2015; Thompson et al., 2011); but on more difficult reasoning tasks, the correlation is close to zero (Prowse Turner & Thompson, 2009; Shynkaruk & Thompson, 2006).

Discrimination

A second measure, sometimes referred to as *discrimination*, refers to the degree to which people's predictions discriminate those who perform well and poorly (Dunning & Helzer, 2014). In a variety of different domains, people turn out to be only modestly accurate at assessing their performance against objective criteria, such as test performance or supervisor evaluations. In a meta-synthesis of 22 meta-analyses that studied the relationship between self- and objective assessments in domains such as academic ability, medical skills, vocational skills, and sports skills, Zell and Krizan (2014) found the average correlation between self- and objective assessments to be about 0.30. The correlation was somewhat larger for simple than complex tasks, for familiar rather than unfamiliar environments, and when performance was measured objectively rather than subjectively. In all cases, however, the correlations were modest, and not much greater than 0.30.

Once again, the consequences of this miscalibration can be profound. Students who misestimate their academic ability may not allocate their study time efficiently (Dunlosky & Rawson, 2012) and may choose to enter careers or pursue majors not well suited to their abilities (Zell & Krizan, 2014). Teachers, doctors, and other professionals who misestimate their abilities may fail to take the appropriate remedial action or may spend unnecessary time reevaluating their choices. In the workplace, overconfidence may lead both employees and leaders to think they are pursuing successful strategies, when, in fact the strategies may be detrimental to the company (Dunning, Heath, & Suls, 2004). People also tend to be unrealistically optimistic about their health and their ability to diagnose their ailments, with predictably poor outcomes (Dunning et al., 2004). A well-studied example of miscalibration is the planning fallacy, which refers to a systematic tendency to underestimate the time needed to complete a task (Buehler, Griffin, & Ross, 1994), with the obvious consequence that one is often scrambling to meet (or miss) a deadline.

Bias and calibration

A third measure is called *bias* (Dunning & Helzer, 2014) or *calibration* (Koriat, 2012) and refers to the difference between a person's performance and his or her estimate of that performance. An example of this is the overconfidence described earlier for eyewitnesses: people are more confident than they are accurate, a phenomenon observed in many other domains (Dunning & Helzer, 2014). We have observed this phenomenon in a number of reasoning studies: when asked to judge the correctness of their answers, people tend to use the high end of the scale, even when performance is very close to chance (Shynkaruk & Thompson, 2006; Thompson et al., 2011, 2013). Similarly, when asked how many of the preceding problems were answered correctly, people overestimated their performance (Prowse Turner & Thompson, 2009; Shynkaruk & Thompson, 2006). One reason for this might be that the reasoning problems we used seemed simpler than they were, so that people thought the difficult problems were actually easy, which might be corrected by training. To test this, we gave people extensive training in how to solve logical reasoning problems and looked at their discrimination and calibration (Prowse Turner & Thompson, 2009). We found that training did not affect discrimination accuracy – it remained close to zero for both trained and untrained participants. The trained participants *appeared* to be better calibrated, in that the difference between their estimated and observed performance was small than their untrained counterparts. However, closer examination showed that this was misleading: overall levels of confidence were similar in the two groups, but the training procedure increased accuracy and thus reduced the appearance of bias.

Cues to confidence

Given the obvious benefit of accurate self-assessment, why are discrimination and calibration poor? The answer is not fully understood, but researchers hypothesise that a mixture of motivational factors and feedback may be at work (see Dunning et al., 2004; Zell & Krizan, 2014, for reviews). For example, people may be motivated to see themselves in a positive light, or may misinterpret encouragement as positive feedback. Feedback may also be lacking or not well calibrated to performance (Kahneman & Klein, 2009). Another reason might be that people lack the skills to assess how well they are doing; lacking skill in a domain means one both performs poorly in that domain and lacks the skills needed to determine performance has been poor (Dunning et al., 2004). In addition, people's attention tends to focus on the occurrence, rather than the absence of events (Hearst, 1991), so that they are unaware of their errors of omission, that is, times in which one missed an opportunity for action or failed to find relevant information (Dunning et al., 2004). Thus, self-assessments are based on irrelevant or misleading cues, rather than on actual information about performance.

The same is true of relative accuracy. That is, the reason that confidence can be poorly correlated with accuracy is that confidence judgments are inferential in nature and are based on subjective experiences associated with producing an answer. A case in point is fluency, which is the ease with which an answer comes to mind, and which is a ubiquitous cue to confidence. Answers that come to mind fluently tend to engender a feeling of confidence in the answer, regardless of whether the answer is a memory retrieval (Costermans, Lories, & Ansay, 1992; Kelley & Lindsay, 1993; Robinson, Johnson, & Herndon, 1997) or the answer to a reasoning problem (Thompson et al., 2011; Thompson, Evans, & Campbell, 2013), and regardless of whether the answer is right or wrong (Ackerman & Zalmanov, 2012). Generally speaking, answers that are easy or familiar come to mind easily (and are thus rightly held with confidence; Ackerman & Koriat, 2011), but sometimes, so do answers that are erroneous. Indeed, fluent processing can produce an illusion that an item has been previously experienced, regardless of whether it has or not (e.g., Jacoby, Kelley, & Dywan, 1989; Whittlesea, Jacoby, & Girard, 1990). Thus, relying on fluency as a cue will often result in well-calibrated confidence judgments (Koriat, 2012), but can also produce a strong sense of confidence in incorrect answers.

In other domains, fluency can be a very misleading cue. Many so-called reasoning biases are thought to arise from autonomous processes that deliver an intuitive answer quickly to mind (Stanovich, 2009). You may or may not have encountered this intriguing little problem (Frederick, 2005):

> If it takes 5 machines 5 minutes to make 5 widgets, how long will it take 100 machines to make 100 widgets?

A large majority of people give the incorrect answer as "100" (the correct answer is 5). The answer "100" is intuitive, compelling, and comes to mind quickly, even amongst those who answer correctly (Mata, Ferreira, & Sherman, 2013). Advertisers take advantage of this intuitive mode of decision making. We use price to estimate the value of consumer goods: shirts that are marketed for $20 may be perceived as "cheap"; the same shirts marked down from $40 are bargains. In other cases, answers that come quickly to mind may be based on stereotypes or easily accessed memories (Kahneman, 2003). As an example, many people believe that crime rates, especially the rates of violent crimes, are increasing. In fact, in most Western nations, crime rates are at historically low levels. Most people, however, do not have access to that statistical information, but instead only have access to information from news reports, which provide compelling and memorable images of crime, creating the sense that crime is everywhere. The literature documents dozens of such reasoning biases. The point is that they are created by processes that tend to be fast and because they are fast, they arrive with a strong sense of confidence (Thompson et al., 2011, 2013), which, as described earlier, may be the clue that further thinking is not required. Thus, reliance on fluency may be part of why people stick with answers based on these heuristic processes and do not pause to rethink them, even when rethinking is warranted.

Similar illusions arise during learning (Kornell, Rhodes, Castel, & Tauber, 2011). In that study, students learned a list of words for a future test. Some of the words were presented in large font, making them easy to read. Independently of that, the students were told that they would have the opportunity to study some of the items again. After studying each item, students made Judgments of Learning about how likely they were to recall the items on the subsequent test. Not surprising, repetition, but not font size was related to actual test performance. Somewhat surprising, students' judgments of learning showed the opposite pattern: they were higher for items presented in large font and did not vary with future study opportunities.

Fluency is such an ubiquitous cue to confidence that it may also contribute to misunderstanding the effectiveness of various strategies (Bjork et al., 2013). For example, many students believe that repeated study benefits learning. That is true to an extent, but study repetitions are especially beneficial when they are spaced out, rather than bunched together. Nonetheless, students overwhelmingly believe that the "bunched together" approach is better, even when they show superior results with the spacing paradigm (Kornell, 2009). Bjork and colleagues (2013) speculated that fluency is the culprit: when items are studied in close proximity, the study is fluent – items that have just been studied come easily to mind. In contrast, by spacing them out, one decreases the fluency with which they come to mind, reducing the perceived (but not the actual) efficacy of this strategy.

Another cue to confidence is familiarity. People are more confident in memory retrievals in a domain that they are familiar with (Costermans et al., 1992) or when familiar cues are used to elicit a memory (Reder & Ritter, 1992; Schunn, Reder, Nhouyvanisvong, Richards, & Stroffolino, 1997; Vernon & Usher, 2003). A similar phenomenon occurs in reasoning. Markovits and colleagues (Markovits et al., 2015) asked participants to draw inferences about familiar (e.g., if a person meditates, they will feel rested) and unfamiliar (e.g., if a person glebs, then they are brandup) premises. Participants were more confident in their answers to the familiar items, even when they did not differ in terms of accuracy. As with fluency, familiarity may frequently be an accurate cue to confidence because, after all, we do know more about familiar than unfamiliar domains; however, as was the case with fluency, we unwittingly generalize our reliance on familiarity, which may result in misplaced confidence.

Other cues to confidence are the amount and consistency of information available. As described earlier with the stock market task, people continue to gather additional information to guide their decision making, even when that information is not useful. Presumably, they do this in order to increase their degree of confidence in their decision. Early findings in the metamemory literature support the conclusion that confidence rises with the amount of information available (Koriat, 1993): specifically, Feeling of Knowing judgments increased with the amount of partial information about the target that was recalled, even if that information was inaccurate. Thus, the volume rather than the accuracy of information available was the cue to certainty. This relationship holds true for externally provided, as well as internally generated information (Gill, Swann, & Silvera, 1998). In that study, participants were asked to form impressions of people seen in a videotape (e.g., of their kindness and intelligence). During the clip, they saw varying amounts of relevant (e.g., volunteers for charity) and pseudo-relevant (e.g., enjoys movies) information; more information, even information that was not directly relevant to the judgment in question, increased confidence in the accuracy of that judgment.

Recently, Koriat (2012) has proposed an updated version of the accessibility model. In this model, confidence is derived from both the amount, but more important, the consistency of the information that was searched as part of the decision-making process. Information may include explicit reasons to choose one alternative over another, but also a number of cues that may not be part of the explicit decision process, such as associations, hunches, and images. These cues create a "gist" recollection of the decision-making process that serves as the basis of confidence in the decision: confidence is assumed to increase as a function of the consistency amongst the cues. For example, when deciding between two options, such as which of two cars to buy, one might explicitly focus on cues such as price, gas mileage, and reliability. Confidence in the decision depends on the degree to which these, and other, possibly implicit, cues (e.g., how the car looks and feels, general impressions of the salesman and car brand, etc.) cohere around one option or the other.

Consistent with this model, reasoning problems that give rise to two conflicting answers are solved with less confidence than problems that give rise to a single solution (De Neys, Cromheeke, & Osman, 2011; Thompson & Johnson, 2014). Consider this problem, which is a variant on Tversky and Kahneman's (1973) lawyer and engineer problem.

In a study 1,000 people were tested. Among the participants were 5 engineers and 995 lawyers. Jack is a randomly chosen participant of this study. Jack is

36 years old. He is not married and is somewhat introverted. He likes to spend his free time reading science fiction and writing computer programs. What is the probability that Jack is an engineer? _____

People are presented with two pieces of information, the base-rate probability of belonging to each category and a description of a randomly sampled person. The numbers can be fixed so that they give rise to a different answer than the description, or so that the two pieces of information suggest the same answer (e.g., 995 engineers and 5 lawyers). Confidence is reliably lower for the conflict than the non-conflict version of the problems (Thompson et al., 2011), a finding that also generalizes to other types of problems (Thompson & Johnson, 2014).

To summarize, confidence judgments are inferentially derived from cues that reflect the subjective experiences of processing items: whether the items are fluent or familiar, how much information one has, how coherent that information is, and so forth. The degree to which confidence tracks the accuracy or quality of performance depends, therefore, on the degree to which the cues to confidence also reflect accuracy of performance (Koriat, 2007). In many situations, these cues are well calibrated. As earlier, items that come to mind easily are likely to be easy to learn; we know more about domains we are familiar with than unfamiliar ones; we are better off having information on which to base our decisions than trying to decide without. The difficulty is that the reliance on those cues does not appear to be limited to the contexts in which they are well calibrated. Thus, people continue to rely on fluency even when it is not diagnostic of difficulty, familiarity when it does not facilitate performance, and sheer volume of information even when it is not entirely relevant to the decision at hand.

For that reason, the analogy to confidence as a thermostat needs to be revised. Thermostats work by monitoring directly the quantity of interest, namely air temperature. Confidence, in contrast, is inferential and thus better likened to a speedometer. Speedometers track an indirect measure of speed: they measure tire rotations, which is a proxy for, rather than direct measurement of, speed (Bjork et al., 2013).

Certainty, fluency, and rationality

In this chapter, I have presented evidence to show the importance of metacognitive processes to the monitoring and control of reasoning behaviour. In this section, I consider the relevance of this evidence to the rationality debate that has been going in psychology and other disciplines for decades (see Manktelow, 2012, for an overview). In other words, are our metacognitive processes agents of rationality or a cause of poor decisions? It is clear that the cues that underlie many metacognitive judgments may, sometimes, produce faulty outputs, as, for example, when a strong FOR signals that analysis is not required, when, in fact, the situation at hand would benefit from further deliberation. As discussed earlier, many of the so-called biases in reasoning may arise precisely because of failures such as this. On the other hand, it is highly controversial to make judgments about rationality based on the failure to implement rules of probability or logic in laboratory reasoning tasks (Elqayam & Evans, 2011).

A more important issue is whether reliance on familiarity, fluency, and so forth as cues to feelings of rightness or confidence prevents people from making optimal (or even satisfactory) decisions in their lives; equally, do metacognitive monitoring failures prevent people from reaching their goals (rationality1; Evans & Over, 1996)? We know, for example, that whilst it can lead us astray, fluency is often a reliable cue to difficulty and that children learn to exploit that regularity as they develop (Koriat & Ackerman, 2010). Nonetheless, the evidence reviewed earlier suggests, like autonomous processes, fluency gives rise to judgments of confidence whenever the triggering conditions are present in the environment and regardless of whether the cue is reliable in the current context (see Stanovich, 2004, for a discussion of autonomy). In other words, fluency is likely to be a ubiquitous cue (Hertwig, Herzog, Schooler, & Reimer, 2008), and as such, it is reasonable to assume that the instances of poor decision making that we see in personal, professional, and public contexts likely have a metacognitive component. To the extent that those decisions are inconsistent with the reasoner's goals and/or produce suboptimal outcomes that additional thought could have bettered, it seems likely that metacognitive processes contribute to instances of suboptimal rationality.

There is, however, some irony in the proposition that implicit, affect-driven cues such as fluency (Koriat, 2007; Topolinski, 2014) are the gatekeepers for analytic modes of thinking. That is, analytic thinking may be engaged in response to a weak FOR without any explicit evaluation of that feeling (Thompson, 2009). Consequently, analytic thinking, which is the centerpiece of many theories of rationality, may be initiated without the explicit intention of the reasoner. In this respect, analytic processes share important features with implicit ones, namely that they may be triggered automatically (Thompson, 2013). Even if one were prepared to accept that argument, one may object and point out that an important difference between autonomous and deliberate processes is that the latter may be terminated or redirected in a goal-driven way. Nonetheless, given the control functions of metacognitive processes in strategy selection and terminating thinking described earlier, it is possible that most of the control over analytic thought is exercised by implicit processes (see also Kahneman, 2011, for a discussion of implicit cognition).

Conclusions

In conclusion, we do not have privileged access to truth: just certainty. That is, we can never know for sure that we are right or wrong about something; the only guidepost we have is our subjective feeling of confidence. That is (short of looking up the answer), we do not, in fact, ever know whether our knowledge is correct, that we have remembered truly versus falsely, or that we have adequately understood a situation. All we have available to make this judgment of correctness is our subjective degree of confidence in a given belief, memory, or decision.

Confidence, in other words, is the barometer by which we determine whether we know, remember, or understand something. Sadly, however, confidence is often determined by factors that are unrelated to the accuracy of our cognitive processes, leading us to hold high levels of confidence when it is unwarranted to do so, which, in turn, misdirects us to act (or fail to act) in the most efficacious manner.

References

Ackerman, R. (2014). The diminishing criterion model for metacognitive regulation of time investment. *Journal of Experimental Psychology: General, 143*(3), 1349.

Ackerman, R., & Koriat, A. (2011). Response latency as a predictor of the accuracy of children's reports. *Journal of Experimental Psychology: Applied, 17*(4), 406–417.

Ackerman, R., & Thompson, V. A. (2014). Meta-Reasoning. In A. Feeney & V. A. Thompson (Eds.). *Reasoning as memory*. Psychology Press: Hove, UK.

Ackerman, R., & Zalmanov, H. (2012). The persistence of the fluency–confidence association in problem solving. *Psychonomic Bulletin & Review, 19*(6), 1189–1192.

Adidam, P. T., & Bingi, R. P. (2011). The importance of decision confidence to strategy outcomes. *Journal of Applied Business Research (JABR), 16*(2).

Benjamin, A. S., & Bird, R. D. (2006). Metacognitive control of the spacing of study repetitions. *Journal of Memory and Language, 55*, 126–137.

Berger, I. E., & Mitchell, A. A. (1989). The effect of advertising on attitude accessibility, attitude confidence, and the attitude–behavior relationship. *Journal of Consumer Research*, 269–279.

Bjork, R. A., Dunlosky, J., & Kornell, N. (2013). Self-regulated learning: Beliefs, techniques, and illusions. *Annual Review of Psychology, 64*, 417–444.

Bröder, A., & Newell, B. R. (2008). Challenging some common beliefs: Empirical work within the adaptive toolbox metaphor. *Judgment and Decision Making, 3*(3), 205–214.

Buehler, R., Griffin, D., & Ross, M. (1994). Exploring the "planning fallacy": Why people underestimate their task completion times. *Journal of Personality and Social Psychology, 67*(3), 366.

Burton, R. A. (2008). *On being certain: Believing you are right even when you're not*. New York: St. Martin's Griffin.

Costermans, J., Lories, G., & Ansay, C. (1992). Confidence level and feeling of knowing in question answering: The weight of inferential processes. *Journal of Experimental Psychology: Learning, Memory, and Cognition, 18*(1), 142–150.

De Neys, W., Cromheeke, S., & Osman, M. (2011). Biased but in doubt: Conflict and decision confidence. *PloS One, 6*(1), e15954.

Dunlosky, J., & Rawson, K. A. (2012). Overconfidence produces underachievement: Inaccurate self-evaluations undermine students' learning and retention. *Learning and Instruction, 22*(4), 271–280.

Dunlosky, J., & Tauber, S. K. (2014). Understanding people's metacognitive judgments: An isomechanism framework and its implications for applied and theoretical research. In T. Perfect & D. S. Lindsay (Eds.), *Handbook of applied memory* (pp. 444–464). Thousand Oaks, CA: Sage.

Dunning, D., Heath, C., & Suls, J. M. (2004). Flawed self-assessment. *Psychological Science in the Public Interest, 5*(3), 69–106.

Dunning, D., & Helzer, E. G. (2014). Beyond the correlation coefficient in studies of self-assessment accuracy commentary on Zell & Krizan (2014). *Perspectives on Psychological Science, 9*(2), 126–130.

Elqayam, S., & Evans, J. St. B. T. (2011). Subtracting "ought" from "is": Descriptivism vs normativism in the study of human thinking. *Behavioral and Brain Sciences, 34,* 233–290.

Evans, J. St. B. T. (1998). Matching bias in conditional reasoning: Do we understand it after 25 years? *Thinking & Reasoning, 4*(1), 45–110.

Evans, J. St. B. T., & Over, D. E. (1996). *Rationality and reasoning.* Hove, UK: Psychology Press.

Fox, S. G., & Walters, H. A. (1986). The impact of general versus specific expert testimony and eyewitness confidence upon mock juror judgment. *Law and Human Behavior, 10*(3), 215.

Frederick, S. (2005). Cognitive reflection and decision making. *Journal of Economic Perspectives, 19*(4), 25–42.

Gill, M. J., Swann, W. B., Jr., & Silvera, D. H. (1998). On the genesis of confidence. *Journal of Personality and Social Psychology, 75,* 1101–1114.

Hart, J. T. (1965). Memory and the feeling-of-knowing experience. *Journal of Educational Psychology, 56*(4), 208.

Hearst, E. (1991). Psychology and nothing. *American Scientist, 79,* 432–443.

Hertwig, R., Herzog, S. M., Schooler, L. J., & Reimer, T. (2008). Fluency heuristic: A model of how the mind exploits a by-product of information retrieval. *Journal of Experimental Psychology: Learning, Memory, and Cognition, 34,* 1191–1206.

Hilbig, B. E. (2010). Reconsidering "evidence" for fast-and-frugal heuristics. *Psychonomic Bulletin & Review, 17*(6), 923–930.

Jacoby, L. L., Kelley, C. M., & Dywan, J. (1989). Memory attributions. In H. L. Roediger III & F. I. M. Craik (Eds.), *Varieties of memory and consciousness: Essays in honour of Endel Tulving* (pp. 391–422). Hillsdale, NJ: Erlbaum.

Kahneman, D. (2003). A perspective on judgment and choice: Mapping bounded rationality. *American Psychologist, 58,* 697–720.

Kahneman, D., & Klein, G. (2009). Conditions for intuitive expertise: A failure to disagree. *American Psychologist, 64*(6), 515.

Kelley, C. M., & Lindsay, D. S. (1993). Remembering mistaken for knowing: Ease of retrieval as a basis for confidence in answers to general knowledge questions. *Journal of Memory and Language, 32,* 1–24.

Koriat, A. (1993). How do we know that we know? The accessibility model of the feeling of knowing. *Psychological Review, 100*(4), 609–639.

Koriat, A. (2007). Metacognition and consciousness. In P. D. Zelazo, M. Moscovitch, & E. Thompson (Eds.), *The Cambridge handbook of consciousness* (pp. 289–326). New York: Cambridge University Press.

Koriat, A. (2012). The self-consistency model of subjective confidence. *Psychological Review, 119*(1), 80.

Koriat, A., & Ackerman, R. (2010). Choice latency as a cue for children's subjective confidence in the correctness of their answers. *Developmental Science, 13,* 441–453.

Koriat, A., & Goldsmith, M. (1996). Monitoring and control processes in the strategic regulation of memory accuracy. *Psychological Review, 103*(3), 490–517.

Kornell, N. (2009). Optimising learning using flashcards: Spacing is more effective than cramming. *Applied Cognitive Psychology, 23*(9), 1297–1317.

Kornell, N., Rhodes, M. G., Castel, A. D., & Tauber, S. K. (2011). The ease-of-processing heuristic and the stability bias. *Psychological Science, 22*(6), 787–794.

Manktelow, K. (2012). *Thinking and reasoning: An introduction to the psychology of reason, judgment, and decision making.* Hove, UK: Psychology Press.

Markovits, H., Thompson, V. A., & Brisson, J. (2015). Metacognition and abstract reasoning. *Memory & Cognition, 43*(4), 681–693.

Mata, A., Ferreira, M. B., & Sherman, S. J. (2013). The metacognitive advantage of deliberative thinkers: A dual-process perspective on overconfidence. *Journal of Personality and Social Psychology, 105*(3), 353.

Mazzoni, G., & Cornoldi, C. (1993). Strategies in study time allocation: Why is study time sometimes not effective? *Journal of Experimental Psychology: General, 122,* 47–60.

Metcalfe, J., & Finn, B. (2008). Evidence that judgments of learning are causally related to study choice. *Psychonomic Bulletin & Review, 15*(1), 174–179.

Nelson, T. O. (1993). Judgments of learning and the allocation of study time. *Journal of Experimental Psychology: General, 122,* 269–273.

Nelson, T. O., & Narens, L. (1990). Metamemory: A theoretical framework and new findings. *The Psychology of Learning and Motivation, 26,* 125–141.

Newell, B. R., Weston, N. J., & Shanks, D. R. (2003). Empirical tests of a fast and frugal heuristic: Not everyone "takes-the-best." *Organizational Behavior and Human Decision Processes, 91,* 82–96.

Palmer, M. A., Brewer, N., Weber, N., & Nagesh, A. (2013). The confidence–accuracy relationship for eyewitness identification decisions: Effects of exposure duration, retention interval, and divided attention. *Journal of Experimental Psychology: Applied, 19*(1), 55.

Pieters, R. G., & Verplanken, B. (1995). Intention behaviour consistency: Effects of consideration set size, involvement and need for cognition. *European Journal of Social Psychology, 25*(5), 531–543.

Podbregar, M., Voga, G., Krivec, B., Skale, R., Parežnik, R., & Gabršček, L. (2001). Should we confirm our clinical diagnostic certainty by autopsies? *Intensive Care Medicine, 27*(11), 1750–1755.

Prowse Turner, J. A., & Thompson, V. A. (2009). The role of training, alternative models, and logical necessity in determining confidence in syllogistic reasoning. *Thinking & Reasoning, 15*(1), 69–100.

Reder, L. M., & Ritter, F. E. (1992). What determines initial feeling of knowing? Familiarity with question terms, not with the answer. *Journal of Experimental Psychology: Learning, Memory, and Cognition, 18*(3), 435–451.

Robinson, M. D., Johnson, J. T., & Herndon, F. (1997). Reaction time and assessments of cognitive effort as predictors of eyewitness memory accuracy and confidence. *Journal of Applied Psychology, 82,* 416–425.

Roediger, H. L., & McDermott, K. B. (1995). Creating false memories: Remembering words not presented in lists. *Journal of Experimental Psychology: Learning, Memory, and Cognition, 21*(4), 803.

Schunn, C. D., Reder, L. M., Nhouyvanisvong, A., Richards, D. R., & Stroffolino, P. J. (1997). To calculate or not to calculate: A source activation confusion model of problem familiarity's role in strategy selection. *Journal of Experimental Psychology: Learning, Memory, and Cognition, 23,* 3–29.

Shynkaruk, J. M., & Thompson, V. A. (2006). Confidence and accuracy in deductive reasoning. *Memory & Cognition, 34*(3), 619–632.

Singer, M., & Tiede, H. L. (2008). Feeling of knowing and duration of unsuccessful memory search. *Memory & Cognition, 36,* 588–597.

Son, L. K. (2004). Spacing one's study: Evidence for a metacognitive control strategy. *Journal of Experimental Psychology: Learning, Memory, and Cognition, 30*(3), 601.

Son, L. K., & Metcalfe, J. (2000). Metacognitive and control strategies in study-time allocation. *Journal of experimental psychology. Learning, Memory, and Cognition, 26*(1), 204–221.

Sporer, S. L., Penrod, S., Read, D., & Cutler, B. (1995). Choosing, confidence, and accuracy: A meta-analysis of the confidence–accuracy relation in eyewitness identification studies. *Psychological Bulletin, 118*(3), 315.

Stanovich, K. E. (2004). *The robot's rebellion: Finding meaning in the age of Darwin.* Chicago: Chicago University Press.

Stanovich, K. E. (2009). Distinguishing the reflective, algorithmic, and autonomous minds: Is it time for a tri-process theory? In J. Evans & K. Frankish (Eds.), *In two minds: Dual processes and beyond* (pp. 55–88). Oxford, UK: Oxford University Press.

Thiede, K. W., & Dunlosky, J. (1999). Toward a general model of self-regulated study: An analysis of selection of items for study and self-paced study time. *Journal of Experimental Psychology: Learning, Memory, and Cognition, 25,* 1024–1037.

Thompson, V. A. (2009). Dual-process theories: A metacognitive perspective. In J. Evans & K. Frankish (Eds.), *In two minds: Dual processes and beyond* (pp. 171–195). Oxford, UK: Oxford University Press.

Thompson, V. A. (2013). Why it matters: The implications of autonomous processes for dual process theories – Commentary on Evans & Stanovich (2013). *Perspectives on Psychological Science, 8,* 253–256.

Thompson, V. A., Evans, J. St. B. T., & Campbell, J. I. (2013). Matching bias on the selection task: It's fast and feels good. *Thinking & Reasoning, 19*(3–4).

Thompson, V. A., & Johnson, S. C. (2014). Conflict, metacognition, and analytic thinking. *Thinking & Reasoning, 20*(2), 215–244.

Thompson, V. A., Turner, J. A. P., & Pennycook, G. (2011). Intuition, reason, and metacognition. *Cognitive Psychology, 63*(3), 107–140.

Thompson, V. A., Turner, J. A. P., Pennycook, G., Ball, L. J., Brack, H., Ophir, Y., & Ackerman, R. (2013). The role of answer fluency and perceptual fluency as metacognitive cues for initiating analytic thinking. *Cognition, 128,* 237–251.

Topolinski, S. (2014). Intuition: Introducing affect into cognition. In A. Feeney & V. A. Thompson (Eds.), *Reasoning as memory.* Hove, UK: Psychology Press.

Tversky, A., & Kahneman, D. (1973). Availability: A heuristic for judging frequency and probability. *Cognitive Psychology, 5*(2), 207–232.

Vernon, D., & Usher, M. (2003). Dynamics of metacognitive judgments: Pre-and postretrieval mechanisms. *Journal of Experimental Psychology: Learning, Memory, and Cognition, 29*(3), 339–346.

Vidmar, N., Coleman Jr., J. E., & Newman, T. A. (2010). Rethinking reliance on eyewitness confidence. *Judicature, 94,* 16.

Wason P. C. (1966). Reasoning. In B. M. Foss (Ed.), *New horizons in psychology.* Harmondsworth, England: Penguin.

Wells, G. L., Olson, E. A., & Charman, S. D. (2002). The confidence of eyewitnesses in their identifications from lineups. *Current Directions in Psychological Science, 11*(5), 151–154.

Wells, G. L., & Quinlivan, D. S. (2009). Suggestive eyewitness identification procedures and the Supreme Court's reliability test in light of eyewitness science: 30 years later. *Law and Human Behavior, 33*(1), 1.

Whittlesea, B. W. A., Jacoby, L. L., & Girard, K. (1990). Illusions of immediate memory: Evidence of an attributional basis for feelings of familiarity and perceptual quality. *Journal of Memory and Language, 29*(6), 716–732.

Zell, E., & Krizan, Z. (2014). Do people have insight into their abilities? A metasynthesis. *Perspectives on Psychological Science, 9*(2), 111–125.

7

BELIEF BIAS, BASE RATES AND MORAL JUDGMENT

Re-evaluating the default interventionist dual process account

Stephanie Howarth and Simon Handley

Introduction

Dual process theory (DPT) is a theoretical framework commonly associated with the field of reasoning and decision making which proposes that thinking is characterised by the action of two systems with distinctive cognitive processes. These processes can be classified as Type 1 (T1): fast, automatic, unconscious and effortless by nature, and Type 2 (T2): slow, controlled, conscious, effortful and demanding of working memory (WM) (Evans, 2009). T1 processes depend on context for the production of intuitive conclusions whilst T2 processes are context independent and can deliver judgments that are sensitive to logical structure using explicit information only (Stanovich & West, 2000). These processes are thought to play a significant role in guiding everyday reasoning, judgment and decision making, with responses reflecting the extent to which they draw upon T1 or T2 processes. Whilst often T1 processes will deliver judgments that draw upon relevant knowledge and provide a useful guide to action, on occasions T1 and T2 processes will suggest differing responses (Evans & Stanovich, 2013). The focus of this chapter is on just these types of situation, where a conflict occurs between competing responses. We will examine the extent to which studies of conflict resolution provide support for dual process theories and suggest that, contrary to the claims of these accounts, many of the paradigmatic cases of conflict cited in support of DPTs actually provide very weak evidence indeed.

This chapter is organised in the following way. We first consider three phenomena that are cited as evidence of dual processes in operation, each example drawn from a distinct literature on reasoning and judgment. We then go on to briefly review the experimental evidence for Default Interventionist (DI) dual process accounts of reasoning and judgment drawing on the three key paradigms introduced in the previous section. In the next section we consider recent evidence which suggests that conflict detection on these tasks is automatic, a set of findings that has been interpreted as showing that reasoners have an intuitive sensitivity to some aspects of logical or normative structure. Finally we consider more recent research which shows, contrary to the claims of DPTs, that evidence drawn from each paradigm does not clearly support the claimed distinction between T1 and T2 responding.

Three classic dual process paradigms

A classic example of the requirement to resolve conflict between competing responses arises in the study of belief bias (see Table 7.1). On certain problems the believability of the conclusion conflicts with its logical status (see, for example, Sá, West & Stanovich, 1999). Consider, for example, the following argument:

> *All plants need water*
> *Roses need water*
> *Therefore, roses are plants.*

In this case the invalid conclusion is often endorsed because it is consistent with what is true in the world (Evans, Barston & Pollard, 1983). However, if the content of the argument is changed to the following;

> *All plants need water*
> *Humans need water*
> *Therefore, humans are plants.*

Belief in the conclusion is no longer in conflict with its logical status, making the conclusion easier to reject (Evans et al., 1983). These examples help to illustrate the impact beliefs can have over the ability to evaluate the validity of an argument.

The tendency to defer to beliefs in making judgments is not confined to logical reasoning but is also shown in tasks that require judgments of posterior probability based on problems in which statistical base rates are presented together with diagnostic information. To illustrate consider the second problem detailed in Table 7.1 (De Neys & Glumicic, 2008). This problem provides two conflicting pieces of information, a base rate which suggests that Jake is more likely to be a nurse than a doctor and a description which suggests instead that Jake is more likely to be a doctor rather than a nurse. According to DPTs, T1 processes support an intuitive response based on the description, whereas effortful T2 processing is required to resist this intuition and give a response based on the base rates.

The final example we are concerned with in this chapter involves making choices linked to moral principles. The 'Footbridge' problem (Thomson, 1976) is a classic moral dilemma in which a conflict exists between a judgment based on utilitarian or consequentialist principles and one based on moral rules or deontological considerations (see Table 7.1). In general the decision to act, whereby one

TABLE 7.1 Three paradigms used to examine dual processes in reasoning

---

Belief bias task:
All living things need water
Roses need water
Therefore, roses are living things
1. The conclusion is valid*
2. The conclusion is invalid

Base-rate neglect task:
In a study 1,000 people were tested. Among the participants were 995 nurses and 5
  doctors. Pat is a randomly chosen participant of this study.
Pat is 34 years old and lives in a beautiful home in a posh suburb. Pat is well spoken and
  very interested in politics and invests a lot of time in his or her career.
Which of the following is more likely?
1. Pat is a nurse
2. Pat is a doctor*

Footbridge Problem:
There is a runaway trolley on the railway tracks heading towards five people tied up and
  unable to get away. You are on a footbridge over the tracks standing next to a large man.
  The only way to save the five people is to push the man off the bridge, onto the tracks
  and into the path of the trolley.
Do you:
1. Do nothing, and the trolley kills the five people on the track*
2. Push the man off the footbridge and onto the track, killing one person and saving five

---

Note: The T1 default response is indicated by an asterisk*; the remaining response is assumed to be effortful and based on T2 processes.

has to push a large man off a footbridge in order to save five people, is rated as much lower in acceptability than in similar problems where there is less personal engagement with the action (Greene, Nystrom, Engell, Darley, & Cohen, 2004; Greene, Sommerville, Nystrom, Darley, & Cohen, 2001). According to deontological moral theories, individuals perceive some acts as intrinsically wrong, violating moral standards, such as 'do not kill an innocent person.' However, according to utilitarian or consequentialist moral philosophy, the judgment of what is morally right or wrong also depends on the overall consequences (killing one to save many). Responding to problems of this kind similarly reflects a conflict between an intuitive, rapidly available response based on moral standards and emotion and a reflective, effortful response drawing on numerical comparison and utilitarian considerations (Greene, Morelli, Lowenberg, Nystrom, & Cohen, 2008; Suter & Hertwig, 2011).

These three distinct judgment tasks have been interpreted within a common framework. In each case, T1 processes are assumed to rapidly deliver a default response based on underlying beliefs. These beliefs are considered to elicit an emotional response that guides judgments (see for example, Morsanyi & Handley, 2012). In each case it is assumed that the T1 response precedes T2 processing because it is quick and effortless. This contrasts with T2 processing, which is slower due to its reliance on working memory (WM) and executive processing (see, for example, Evans, 2010; Kahneman, 2011). In all three types of problem the T2 response draws upon structural features of the problem, whether this relates to logical validity (as with the belief bias task), population distributions (as in the base rate task) or number of lives saved (as in the footbridge dilemma). We will refer to this type of model as *default interventionist* (DI), and this type of dual process account will be the main focus in the remainder of this chapter (Evans, 2003, 2007, 2010).

Default interventionist accounts

The default interventionist DPT Evans (2008) describes, defines T1 processes as generating default, automatically cued responses (Evans, 2006). These default responses precede T2 processing and can be resisted or intervened in by the more deliberative T2 level of processing, if and when conflict between the two responses is detected. In order to produce an alternative response, cognitive effort and WM resources are required to inhibit the T1 output (Handley, Capon, Beveridge, Dennis & Evans, 2004). However, overriding a T1 response would also depend on adequate cognitive ability, the application of relevant instructions and having sufficient time available for more reflective thinking (Evans & Curtis-Holmes, 2005). Consequently, the initial intuitive response to a problem is often accepted (Stanovich, 2009).

A key prediction of this account concerns the time course of processing, given that responses based on beliefs are assumed to be available before a logical output has time to complete. Evans and Curtis-Holmes (2005) tested this notion with a syllogistic reasoning task carried out under limited time and demonstrated that increased time pressure increased belief-based reasoning. This finding is consistent with the view that belief-based responses are available early and are therefore more frequent when time limits are imposed. Related findings have been reported in relation to moral judgment whereby deontological responses dominate under conditions of limited time (Suter & Hertwig, 2011). Similarly, conditions which have the effect of limiting the availability of WM resources, such as the use of secondary tasks, have been shown to increase the belief bias effect (De Neys, 2006; Quayle & Ball, 2000) and reduce rates of utilitarian moral judgment (Greene et al., 2008).

De Neys (2006) has argued that it is not that individuals differ in their motivation to reason logically, more that those with greater available cognitive resources are more successful at completing the analytic process required to do so. In other words, sometimes the requirement to engage in effortful processing is merely too great if there is a lack of sufficient resources available (Quayle & Ball, 2000).

The data interpreted as support of the DI account are not exclusively experimental; individual differences research has found converging evidence. For example, Stanovich (1999) has argued that T2 processing is associated with measures of general intelligence involved in the ability to decontextualise and decouple reasoning from beliefs. In support of this view both abstract deductive reasoning and the ability to resist belief bias correlates with WM, intelligence and certain cognitive styles (Macpherson & Stanovich, 2007; Stanovich & West, 1997). People with greater working memory capacity (WMC) are more proficient in logical reasoning for both spatial and syllogistic problems (Capon, Handley & Dennis, 2003) and specific cases of conditional reasoning (Barrouillet & Lecas, 1999; Markovits, Doyon & Simoneau, 2002).

Stanovich and West (2008) have argued that tasks such as the base rate and belief bias task, where normative accuracy shows an association with cognitive ability, involve some type of inhibition and/or sustained cognitive decoupling; the central feature of T2 processing necessary for hypothetical thinking (Evans, 2007). Similarly, Toplak, West and Stanovich (2011, 2014) showed that cognitive style (as measured by the Cognitive Reflection Task) is a predictor of an individual's tendency to default to T1 processing (cognitive miserliness). In other words, the better the ability or willingness to engage in T2 analytical processes, the better the chance at overriding an incorrect default response. Furthermore, several studies on individual differences in moral judgment have demonstrated associations between utilitarian (T2) judgments and higher levels of cognitive reflection (Hardman, 2008), WM (Moore, Clark & Kane, 2008) and measures of 'need for cognition' (Bartels, 2008).

An alternative individual differences approach is to study the development of cognitive processing across the life span. Kokis and colleagues (2002) tested normally developing children aged 10 through 13 on a range of heuristics and biases tasks and demonstrated increased normative responding as children aged. Studying an age range of 12 to 65+ years, De Neys and Van Gelder (2009) found a curvilinear effect of age on belief bias, where younger children and older adults make more errors when belief and logic conflict. De Neys and Van Gelder concluded that inhibition plays a key role when dealing with conflict in reasoning and decision making. Interestingly, developmental patterns of performance on moral dilemmas, such as the footbridge problem, which demands personal involvement in action, show little variation with age. Younger children (3, 4 and 5 years old) show remarkably similar patterns of response to adults (Pellizzoni, Siegal & Surian, 2010).

Finally, the neuropsychological literature has also offered support for the DI DPT; Tsujii and Watanabe (2009) used near-infrared spectroscopy (NIRS) and an attention-demanding concurrent task to show that those with enhanced activation in the right inferior frontal cortex (IFC) performed better on incongruent reasoning trials when a conflict arose between a logical and a belief-based response. This implicates the IFC as having an important role in the inhibition of default responses, explaining why a secondary load that impairs IFC activation leads to increases in belief bias. This research implies that distinct brain areas are required for belief-based and logic-based reasoning, which is consistent with the DI dual process account (Evans & Stanovich, 2013). Furthermore, studies have shown that patients with damage to the ventromedial prefrontal cortex (VMPC), an area of the brain linked to the generation of emotions, tend to make more utilitarian judgments on personal moral dilemmas (Koenigs et al., 2007), and deontic responses elicit increased activity in brain areas associated with emotion and social cognition (Greene et al., 2001, 2004).

The evidence presented in this section is supportive of dual processing; more specifically the studies sit well with a default processing account where belief-based responding is driven by implicit T1 processes and the inhibition of such responses in favour of ones based on structural problem features requiring explicit T2 processing. Nevertheless, despite the seemingly large body of research in support of the DI account, more recent research suggests that reasoning based on problem structure can be accomplished with relatively little effort whilst reasoning on the basis of beliefs may not be as fast and automatic as these accounts claim (Handley, Newstead & Trippas, 2011; Howarth, Handley & Walsh, 2015).

Re-evaluating the evidence

In the previous section links were made between T2 processing and cognitive development, WM, cognitive style and cognitive ability. In addition, associations were made between T2 processing and effortful reasoning across three prototypical DP paradigms, namely, the Belief-Bias Effect, Base-Rate Neglect and Moral Judgment. According to the account, if a conflict between T1 and T2 responses is detected, then with sufficient effort (T2 processing) the T1 response can be inhibited in favour of one based on structural processing. An important question raised concerns conflict detection; specifically how can conflict first be detected if T2 processing does not occur until after a T1–T2 conflict is identified? In this section we consider recent research which provides evidence that conflict can be detected automatically and rapidly. This suggests that T1 and T2 processes are triggered simultaneously rather than serially as most DI dual process models claim. This in turn indicates that responses based on structural problem features can be generated through T1 processing. We will review recent evidence consistent with this view. We then go on to consider recent research which suggests that across all three of our selected paradigms, responses associated with T2 processing may be accomplished with very little reasoning at all.

Conflict detection

A question that has received increasing attention in the recent literature concerns the extent to which reasoners are aware when there is a conflict between two competing responses on reasoning tasks. De Neys (2012) reviews a broad range of evidence across a number of domains which suggests that this is the case and holds even for participants who end up giving a biased response. For example, Stupple and Ball (2008), using inspection-time analysis, showed that conflict problems lead to increased processing latencies relative to non-conflict problems. Ball, Philips, Wade and Quayle (2006) showed, with eye-tracking techniques, that people spend longer inspecting the problem premises on conflict trials compared to no-conflict trials, offering an explanation which assumes that concurrent outputs from both T1 and T2 processes are available, with the latter requiring more time to resolve.

De Neys and Glumicic (2008) showed that people took longer to process conflict base-rate problems even though verbal protocols indicated that they were explicitly unaware of any conflict. Furthermore, when participants gave a response based on the description rather than the base rate, evidence suggested (through retrieval of base-rate information) that base rates had also been thoroughly processed. De Neys and Glumicic claim that implicit conflict detection not only suggests intuitive awareness of the base rates, but is consistent with parallel processing of the description and the base rate information. This view is consistent with recent research that monitored electroencephalography (EEG) activity whilst participants solved relational reasoning problems. Banks and Hope (2014) showed that P3 latencies (determined by the allocation of attentional resources when WM is updated) were equivalent for belief and logic responses, indicating that they both influence reasoning at the same time and relatively early.

Similarly, using physiological measures, De Neys, Moyens and Vansteenwegen (2010) confirmed the effortlessness of conflict detection present with syllogisms. They used skin conductance responses (SCRs) to show autonomic arousal with inconsistent conflict problems implying a 'gut' feeling of incorrectness. Gangemi, Bourgeois-Gironde and Mancini (2014) refer to this gut feeling as Feeling of Error (FOE), explained as the detection of the conflict between an intuitively incorrect and normatively correct answer to a problem. Gangemi and colleagues used the bat-and-ball problem drawn from the Cognitive Reflection Task (Frederick, 2005) and a non-conflict version of the same task to examine the FOE on both generation and evaluation versions of the task. They found that those who failed at the task experienced more FOE, suggesting that it is a reliable signal that errors are present and assume that it results from the detection of conflict impacting reasoning performance.

These behavioural findings have been supported using Functional Magnetic Resonance Imaging (fMRI). De Neys, Vartanian and Goel (2008) showed that the anterior cingulate cortex (ACC), which is claimed to mediate conflict detection during thinking, was much more activated on base-rate conflict problems than on no-conflict problems. A similar finding has been reported in relation to moral judgment (Greene et al., 2004), and in both cases activation of ACC was independent of the final response generated by participants.

The research appears to suggest that even if detection is not explicitly reported (e.g., De Neys & Glumicic, 2008) and judgments are often consistent with beliefs, people do appear to sense their inaccuracies. Additionally, the findings are consistent with the notion that structural processing (e.g. processing of a problem's logical, numerical or probabilistic structure) occurs at the same time as the processing of specific knowledge (e.g. beliefs or stereotypes), which is at odds with standard DI accounts and supports the idea that the processing of a problem's underlying structure can be achieved both quickly and intuitively.

Intuitive sensitivity to logical structure

As we have seen, traditional DI accounts assume that belief-based responses are generated rapidly, whereas responses that draw upon problem structure depend on more effortful processing. Research on conflict detection suggests that reasoners pick up on structural features very rapidly and are sensitive to situations where a response based on these features conflicts with a belief-based response. This is consistent with a model in which both types of response are processed in parallel rather than serially as the DI account would claim. Perhaps, however, the *generation* of a logical or probabilistically appropriate response to these tasks does indeed depend on T2 processing. It is quite possible that T2 intervention is required to fully process and validate a response of this kind. Certainly De Neys (2014) has argued that although reasoners can detect conflict automatically, the belief-based response is regularly given because it is highly salient; resisting this response depends on T2 intervention.

Assuming that this interpretation is the correct one, default interventionism should be able to make very clear predictions regarding responding on our three tasks. One would expect, for example, that if participants were asked to evaluate the believability of a presented conclusion to a logical argument, then this should be accomplished relatively quickly and be less prone to errors than judgments about a conclusion's validity. This follows on the assumption that belief-based responses are available by default and are highly salient. More specifically, the presence of a conflict between conclusion believability and its logical status should have more of an impact on validity judgments than on believability judgments, as generating a logical response should require intervention on the more salient belief-based response that is available earlier. Handley, Newstead and Trippas (2011) tested these predictions in a series of studies in which participants were presented with simple propositional arguments (conditionals and disjunctions) in which the logical validity and believability of the presented conclusion was manipulated. Participants were instructed to judge its believability or validity. Contrary to the predictions of the DI account, reasoners made more errors and took longer on belief judgments than logic judgments. In addition, conflict had a greater impact on judgments of belief than judgments of validity. These findings are the opposite of the predictions attributed to the DI account.

In a similar way, Pennycook, Trippas, Handley and Thompson (2014) employed base-rate problems of the kind shown in Table 7.1 and instructed participants to respond with reference to the base rate information (ignoring background knowledge) or on the basis of the description (ignoring the statistical information). In line with previous studies, participants were unable to ignore the description when asked to respond on the basis of the base rates. Most interesting, however, they were equally unable to ignore the base rates when asked to respond uniquely on the basis of the description. There was also no difference in response times between the two instructional conditions. These findings suggest that base rate information and knowledge based on social stereotypes are activated in parallel and consequently interfere with one another. The authors argued that both depend on T1, rather than T2, processing.

Philosophers Dubljević and Racine (2014) have recently made similar claims regarding the intuitive basis of utilitarian moral judgments (see also Białek, Terbeck & Handley, 2014). They propose a new model of moral judgments focused on three major types of conflicting intuitions; based on a) Deeds, b) Agent and c) Consequences. In particular, they claim that moral situations elicit intuitions about the act itself (do not kill another human being) and intuitions about the agents involved in the dilemma, as well as intuitions about the consequences (the number of people who will be killed). The authors argue that specific cues in the moral situation will trigger specific intuitive mechanisms, focusing on the act, the consequences or the agent. According to this view, both deontological and utilitarian responses arise from intuitive or T1 processing. This view is consistent with recent research that has examined the temporal dynamics of moral decision making (Koop, 2013). Standard DI approaches assume that moral decisions are the result of a pre-potent emotional response which can be overridden with deliberative effort. Koop (2013) argued that if a pre-potent response was elicited and then resisted, one would expect to observe online preference reversals. Koop employed mouse-tracking methodology that has been successfully used to identify preference reversals in other domains, and tested whether any evidence existed for initial movement towards the deontological response prior to a utilitarian response being provided. Across two experiments there was no indication of any preference reversals or modifications in mouse trajectory irrespective of the response generated. These findings were interpreted as indicating that both responses are initiated rapidly and in parallel.

The idea that utilitarian judgments do not require deliberative processing is also consistent with recent research that examined the impact of alcohol on moral judgment (Duke & Bègue, 2015). Alcohol intoxication has been linked to increased emotional reactivity (Euser & Franken, 2012) and impaired higher-order cognition (Giancola, 2000), which, according to DI accounts, should lead to increased deontological (non-utilitarian) processing. Duke and Bègue (2015) evaluated the association between the acute effects of alcohol and responses to the footbridge problem. They found that increased levels of intoxication were in fact linked to increased utilitarian decision making. They suggested that decreased harm aversion may be a strong predictor of utilitarian inclination in the footbridge dilemma rather than the capacity to engage a T2 processing system. These findings are consistent with other research revealing that chronic alcohol dependence can also lead to preferences towards utilitarian judgment (Khemiri, Guterstam, Franck, & Jayaram-Lindström, 2012). Most recently, the idea that utilitarian judgments on personal dilemmas reflect impartial concern for the greater good has itself been questioned. Kahane and colleagues (2015) showed that utilitarian responses were in fact closely linked to a generally immoral outlook in relation to ethics in business, sub-clinical psychopathy and less, rather than more, identification with humanity as whole. These findings suggest that utilitarian judgment on classic moral judgment tasks does not arise out of increased cognitive effort, but is rather linked to a range of amoral personality characteristics. Thus, it may well be the case that judgments on these tasks are driven intuitively as a result of underlying dispositional factors.

There is also increasing evidence that responding on the basis of the normative or logical structure of a judgment problem is not necessarily associated with greater availability of cognitive resource, a key index of T2 processing. On the contrary, amongst pre-adolescent children, biased responding on reasoning and judgment tasks is more, rather than less, common in participants who score higher on measures of WM (Morsanyi & Handley, 2008). On moral reasoning tasks there is no evidence of increased rates of utilitarian responding as children grow older; an observation one would expect if utilitarian responding is heavily dependent on cognitive resources (Pellizzoni et al., 2010). The idea that utilitarian judgment is linked to higher WMC is also undermined by recent individual differences research. Moore and colleagues (2008) examined the relationship between WMC and responses to a range of moral dilemmas in which personal involvement in action, inevitability of death and personal risk to the subject were manipulated. Although participants higher in WMC showed a greater tendency to endorse killing if death was inevitable, no evidence was found that higher WMC was associated with an increased tendency to give utilitarian judgments on personal dilemmas. This does not support the idea that executive control must override default emotional responses in order to endorse provocative resolutions to moral dilemmas. Interesting, higher WMC was linked to a higher level of consistency of responding across different moral judgment tasks. This relationship is similar to that reported in research on abstract versions of Wason's selection task, where consistency of card selections across multiple variants of the task, rather than normative accuracy, has been linked to higher cognitive capacity (Newstead et al., 2004). This suggests that cognitive capacity indexes the extent to which reasoners can identify underlying structural commonalities across similar tasks rather than the capacity to override intuitive responses.

The idea that responses on judgment tasks commonly assumed to involve T2 processing can in fact be accomplished rapidly without recourse to effortful processing is not a new claim. It has been noted for many years that logical inferences are drawn routinely in text comprehension even when they are not required to maintain coherence. For example, Rader and Sloutsky (2002) presented participants with short stories with embedded conditional Modus Ponens (MP) arguments, for example, *if the weather is nice, then Ed takes a walk; the weather was nice*, and participants had to decide if a particular word had appeared within the story. The findings indicated that participants were more likely to falsely identify that the conclusion had been presented, suggesting that the MP inference was drawn automatically and that participants mistakenly thought it was presented in the text. This suggests that logical MP inferences can be drawn without awareness at the comprehension stage, which is a rapid, automatic T1 process. These findings have been extended to problems based on Affirmation of the Consequent and to other propositional arguments (also see Lea, O'Brien, Fisch, Noveck & Braine, 1990; Leo & Greene, 2008; Reverberi, Pischedda, Burigo & Cherubini, 2012).

Summary and conclusions

In this chapter we have reviewed recent evidence which suggests that judgments typically associated with T2 processes can be accomplished with relatively little effort. Reasoners appear sensitive to the underlying structure of judgment problems and consequently show evidence of conflict detection early on, indicating an intuitive sensitivity to these features. Indeed, on simple reasoning tasks logical judgments take less time to accomplish and result in fewer errors than similar judgments regarding the believability of a given conclusion. This suggests that belief judgments require additional effort, perhaps because an intuitive logical response must be inhibited prior to generating a belief-based one. These findings are contrary to a standard DI interpretation of belief bias, and instead suggest that on certain problems, it is a logical response that is available by default, and this must be inhibited in favour of a belief-based one. Of course the direction and extent of interference between belief-based and logical responses is likely to depend on the complexity of the logical reasoning task, an observation that underpins a new parallel processing model of belief bias (see Handley & Trippas, 2015).

On base rate tasks where conflict takes place between the description and the statistics, participants are unable to generate responses based on the description without interference from the base rate, and the level of interference is similar to that observed between the description and base rates when participants are asked to base their judgment on the statistics. Once again this is inconsistent with the idea that a response based on representativeness is generated by default and that a normative response that draws appropriately on statistical information depends on T2 intervention. In this case the findings are consistent with a T1/T1 conflict, a claim supported by the observation that degree of interference is unaffected by a speeded task (Pennycook et al., 2014).

The third paradigm we considered in this chapter was moral reasoning and the claim that deontological judgments on dilemmas that involve personal action are generated by default and require intervention for a utilitarian response to be generated. Once again, recent evidence has begun to undermine the DI interpretation of this task also. There is limited evidence that WMC is linked to higher rates of utilitarian responding and process-tracing methods do not demonstrate the type of preference reversals one would expect to observe if a proponent response was initiated and then countermanded. One of the most compelling pieces of evidence in favour of the DI account of this task is the claim that utilitarian responses take reliably longer than deontological ones on personal dilemmas (see, for example, Greene et al., 2001). Crucially, however, it has been shown that the time difference observed in previous research is an artefact of a couple of extreme items included in the original research (McGuire, Langdon, Coltheart & Mackenzie, 2009). The emerging view is that these dilemmas cue competing intuitions and judgment choice may be determined by dispositional factors rather than reliance on automatic or effortful processing.

The aim of this chapter was to challenge DI accounts of performance on three very distinct judgment tasks which have been claimed to provide strong support for this approach. We hope to have shown through our review of recent evidence that these tasks do not provide the sort of robust support that has previously been claimed. On the contrary our analysis suggests that any attempt to apply a generic dual process framework across the range of paradigms that we have considered is misguided and that dual process theorists will need to carefully reconsider their analysis of some of the most classic tasks within the literature.

References

Ball, L. J., Philips, P., Wade, C. N., & Quayle, J. D. (2006). Effects of belief and logic on syllogistic reasoning: eye-movement evidence for selective processing models. *Experimental Psychology, 53*(1), 77–86.

Banks, A. P., & Hope, C. (2014). Heuristic and analytic processes in reasoning: An event-related potential study of belief bias. *Psychophysiology, 51*(3), 290–297.

Barrouillet, P., & Lecas, J.-F. (1999). Mental models in conditional reasoning and working memory. *Thinking & Reasoning, 5*(4), 289–302.

Bartels, D. M. (2008). Principled moral sentiment and the flexibility of moral judgment and decision making. *Cognition, 108*(2), 381–417.

Białek, M., Terbeck, S., & Handley, S. J. (2014). Cognitive psychological support for the ADC model of moral judgment. *AJOB Neuroscience, 5*(4), 21–23.

Capon, A., Handley, S., & Dennis, I. (2003). Working memory and reasoning: An individual differences perspective. *Thinking & Reasoning, 9*(3), 203–244.

De Neys, W. (2006). Dual processing in reasoning – two systems but one reasoner. *Psychological Science, 17*(5), 428–433.

De Neys, W. (2012). Bias and conflict: A case for logical intuitions. *Perspectives on Psychological Science, 7*(1), 28–38.

De Neys, W. (2014). Conflict detection, dual processes, and logical intuitions: Some clarifications. *Thinking & Reasoning, 20*, 169–187.

De Neys, W., & Glumicic, T. (2008). Conflict monitoring in dual process theories of thinking. *Cognition, 106*(3), 1248–1299.

De Neys, W., Moyens, E., & Vansteenwegen, D. (2010). Feeling we're biased: Autonomic arousal and reasoning conflict. *Cognitive, Affective, & Behavioral Neuroscience, 10*(2), 208–216.

De Neys, W., & Van Gelder, E. (2009). Logic and belief across the lifespan: The rise and fall of belief inhibition during syllogistic reasoning. *Developmental Science, 12*(1), 123–130.

De Neys, W. D., Vartanian, O., & Goel, V. (2008). Smarter than we think: When our brains detect that we are biased. *Psychological Science, 19*(5), 483–489.

Dubljević, V., & Racine, E. (2014). The ADC of moral judgment: Opening the black box of moral intuitions with heuristics about agents, deeds, and consequences. *AJOB Neuroscience, 5*(4), 3–20.

Duke, A. A., & Bègue, L. (2015). The drunk utilitarian: Blood alcohol concentration predicts utilitarian responses in moral dilemmas. *Cognition, 134*, 121–127.

Euser, A. S., & Franken, I. H. (2012). Alcohol affects the emotional modulation of cognitive control: An event-related brain potential study. *Psychopharmacology, 222*(3), 459–476.

Evans, J. St. B. T. (2003). In two minds: Dual-process accounts of reasoning. *Trends in Cognitive Sciences, 7*(10), 454–459.

Evans, J. St. B. T. (2006). The heuristic-analytic theory of reasoning: Extension and evaluation. *Psychonomic Bulletin & Review, 13*(3), 378–395.

Evans, J. St. B. T. (2007). *Hypothetical thinking: Dual processes in reasoning and judgement.* Hove, UK: Psychology Press.

Evans, J. St. B. T. (2008). Dual-processing accounts of reasoning, judgment, and social cognition. *Annual Review of Psychology, 59*, 255–278.

Evans, J. St. B. T. (2009). How many dual-process theories do we need? One, two, or many? In K. Frankish (Ed.), *In two minds: Dual processes and beyond* (pp. 33–54). New York: Oxford University Press.

Evans, J. St. B. T. (2010). *Thinking twice: Two minds in one brain.* Oxford: Oxford University Press.

Evans, J. St. B. T., Barston, J. L., & Pollard, P. (1983). On the conflict between logic and belief in syllogistic reasoning. *Memory & Cognition, 11*(3), 295–306.

Evans, J. St. B. T., & Curtis-Holmes, J. (2005). Rapid responding increases belief bias: Evidence for the dual-process theory of reasoning. *Thinking & Reasoning, 11*(4), 382–389.

Evans, J. St. B. T., & Stanovich, K. E. (2013). Dual-process theories of higher cognition: Advancing the debate. *Perspectives on Psychological Science, 8*(3), 223–241.

Frederick, S. (2005). Cognitive reflection and decision making. *The Journal of Economic Perspectives, 19*(4), 25–42.

Gangemi, A., Bourgeois-Gironde, S., & Mancini, F. (2014). Feelings of error in reasoning – in search of a phenomenon. *Thinking & Reasoning*, 1–14.

Giancola, P. R. (2000). Executive functioning: A conceptual framework for alcohol-related aggression. *Experimental and Clinical Psychopharmacology, 8*(4), 576.

Greene, J. D., Morelli, S. A., Lowenberg, K., Nystrom, L. E., & Cohen, J. D. (2008). Cognitive load selectively interferes with utilitarian moral judgment. *Cognition, 107*(3), 1144–1154.

Greene, J. D., Nystrom, L. E., Engell, A. D., Darley, J. M., & Cohen, J. D. (2004). The neural bases of cognitive conflict and control in moral judgment. *Neuron, 44*(2), 389–400.

Greene, J. D., Sommerville, R. B., Nystrom, L. E., Darley, J. M., & Cohen, J. D. (2001). An fMRI investigation of emotional engagement in moral judgment. *Science, 293*(5537), 2105–2108.

Handley, S. J., Capon, A., Beveridge, M., Dennis, I., & Evans, J. (2004). Working memory, inhibitory control and the development of children's reasoning. *Thinking & Reasoning, 10*(2), 175–195.

Handley, S. J., Newstead, S. E., & Trippas, D. (2011). Logic, beliefs, and instruction: A test of the default interventionist account of belief bias. *Journal of Experimental Psychology: Learning, Memory, and Cognition, 37*(1), 28–34.

Handley, S. J., & Trippas, D. (2015). Dual processes and the interplay between knowledge and structure: A new parallel processing model. *Psychology of Learning and Motivation, 62*, 33–58.

Hardman, D. (2008). *Moral dilemmas: Who makes utilitarian choices?* Unpublished manuscript. School of Psychology, London Metropolitan University, London, UK.

Howarth, S., Handley, S. J., & Walsh, C. (2016). The logic-bias effect: The role of effortful processing in the resolution of belief–logic conflict. *Memory & cognition, 44(2)*, 330–349.

Kahane, G., Everett, J. A., Earp, B. D., Farias, M., & Savulescu, J. (2015). 'Utilitarian' judgments in sacrificial moral dilemmas do not reflect impartial concern for the greater good. *Memory & cognition, 44*(2), 330-349.

Kahneman, D. (2011). *Thinking, fast and slow*. Macmillan, New York, NY.

Khemiri, L., Guterstam, J., Franck, J., & Jayaram-Lindström, N. (2012). Alcohol dependence associated with increased utilitarian moral judgment: A case control study. *PloS One, 7*(6), e39882.

Koenigs, M., Young, L., Adolphs, R., Tranel, D., Cushman, F., Hauser, M., & Damasio, A. (2007). Damage to the prefrontal cortex increases utilitarian moral judgements. *Nature, 446*(7138), 908–911.

Kokis, J. V., Macpherson, R., Toplak, M. E., West, R. F., & Stanovich, K. E. (2002). Heuristic and analytic processing: Age trends and associations with cognitive ability and cognitive styles. *Journal of Experimental Child Psychology, 83*(1), 26–52.

Koop, G. J. (2013). An assessment of the temporal dynamics of moral decisions. *Judgment and Decision Making, 8*(5), 527–539.

Lea, R. B., O'Brien, D. P., Fisch, S. M., Noveck, I. A., & Braine, M. D. (1990). Predicting propositional logic inferences in text comprehension. *Journal of Memory and Language, 29*(3), 361–387.

Leo, P. D., & Greene, A. J. (2008). Is awareness necessary for true inference? *Memory & Cognition, 36*(6), 1079–1086.

Macpherson, R., & Stanovich, K. E. (2007). Cognitive ability, thinking dispositions, and instructional set as predictors of critical thinking. *Learning and Individual Differences, 17*(2), 115–127.

Markovits, H., Doyon, C., & Simoneau, M. (2002). Individual differences in working memory and conditional reasoning with concrete and abstract content. *Thinking & Reasoning, 8*(2), 97–107.

McGuire, J., Langdon, R., Coltheart, M., & Mackenzie, C. (2009). A reanalysis of the personal/impersonal distinction in moral psychology research. *Journal of Experimental Social Psychology, 45*(3), 577–580.

Moore, A. B., Clark, B. A., & Kane, M. J. (2008). Who shalt not kill? Individual differences in working memory capacity, executive control, and moral judgment. *Psychological Science, 19*(6), 549–557.

Morsanyi, K., & Handley, S. J. (2008). How smart do you need to be to get it wrong? The role of cognitive capacity in the development of heuristic-based judgment. *Journal of Experimental Child Psychology, 99*(1), 18–36.

Morsanyi, K., & Handley, S. J. (2012). Logic feels so good – I like it! Evidence for intuitive detection of logicality in syllogistic reasoning. *Journal of Experimental Psychology: Learning, Memory, and Cognition, 38*(3), 596–616.

Newstead, S. E., Handley, S. J., Harley, C., Wright, H., & Farrelly, D. (2004). Individual differences in deductive reasoning. *Quarterly Journal of Experimental Psychology Section A, 57*(1), 33–60.

Pellizzoni, S., Siegal, M., & Surian, L. (2010). The contact principle and utilitarian moral judgments in young children. *Developmental Science, 13*(2), 265–270.

Pennycook, G., Trippas, D., Handley, S. J., & Thompson, V. A. (2014). Base rates: Both neglected and intuitive. *Journal of Experimental Psychology: Learning, Memory, and Cognition, 40*(2), 544.

Quayle, J. D., & Ball, L. J. (2000). Working memory, metacognitive uncertainty, and belief bias in syllogistic reasoning. *The Quarterly Journal of Experimental Psychology: Section A, 53*(4), 1202–1223.

Rader, A. W., & Sloutsky, V. M. (2002). Processing of logically valid and logically invalid conditional inferences in discourse comprehension. *Journal of Experimental Psychology: Learning, Memory, and Cognition, 28*(1), 59–68.

Reverberi, C., Pischedda, D., Burigo, M., & Cherubini, P. (2012). Deduction without awareness. *Acta Psychologica, 139*(1), 244–253.

Sá, W. C., West, R. F., & Stanovich, K. E. (1999). The domain specificity and generality of belief bias: Searching for a generalizable critical thinking skill. *Journal of Educational Psychology, 91*(3), 497–510.

Stanovich, K. E. (1999). *Who is rational?: Studies of individual differences in reasoning*. Mahwah, NJ: Erlbaum.

Stanovich, K. E. (2009). Distinguishing the reflective, algorithmic, and autonomous minds: Is it time for a tri-process theory? In J. St. B. Evans & K. Frankis (Eds.), *In two minds: Dual processes and beyond* (pp. 55–88). Oxford: Oxford University Press.

Stanovich, K. E., & West, R. F. (1997). Reasoning independently of prior belief and individual differences in actively open-minded thinking. *Journal of Educational Psychology, 89*, 342–357.

Stanovich, K. E., & West, R. F. (2000). Individual differences in reasoning: Implications for the rationality debate? *Behavioral and Brain Sciences, 23*(5), 645–665.

Stanovich, K. E., & West, R. F. (2008). On the relative independence of thinking biases and cognitive ability. *Journal of Personality and Social Psychology, 94*(4), 672–695.

Stupple, E. J., & Ball, L. J. (2008). Belief–logic conflict resolution in syllogistic reasoning: Inspection-time evidence for a parallel-process model. *Thinking & Reasoning, 14*(2), 168–181.

Suter, R. S., & Hertwig, R. (2011). Time and moral judgment. *Cognition, 119*(3), 454–458.

Thomson, J. J. (1976). Killing, letting die, and the trolley problem. *The Monist, 59*(2), 204–217.

Toplak, M. E., West, R. F., & Stanovich, K. E. (2011). The Cognitive Reflection Test as a predictor of performance on heuristics-and-biases tasks. *Memory & Cognition, 39*(7), 1275–1289.

Toplak, M. E., West, R. F., & Stanovich, K. E. (2014). Assessing miserly information processing: An expansion of the Cognitive Reflection Test. *Thinking & Reasoning, 20*(2), 147–168.

Tsujii, T., & Watanabe, S. (2009). Neural correlates of dual-task effect on belief-bias syllogistic reasoning: A near-infrared spectroscopy study. *Brain Research, 1287*, 118–125.

8

DUAL FRAMES IN CAUSAL REASONING AND OTHER TYPES OF THINKING

Masasi Hattori, David E. Over, Ikuko Hattori, Tatsuji Takahashi and Jean Baratgin

Introduction

Manktelow (2012, p. 89) discusses an intriguing poster he once saw on a local bus that made a causal claim. It read, 'FACT: Cigarettes and alcohol are the biggest cause of death by fire in the home.' He rightly remarks that it is not easy to pin down this claim. Causal reasoning is indispensable to living beings: we would soon die without it. But we will argue that, to be clear about causation, we must make a distinction between two types of causal induction. We can try to identify quickly and efficiently the causal, or at least relevant, factors for preventing death in our homes. Looking at some data, local health officials might swiftly detect that cigarette smoking and alcohol are such factors for death in the home and produce a poster with that information on it. But other, more scientific researchers might want deeper knowledge about how to predict and control a type of event, like death in the home, and would aim to distinguish between correlation and causation. With deeper research, they might, for example, be able to set limits to alcohol consumption, above which the danger greatly increases that it will cause people to make serious mistakes or misjudgements.

The primary claim of this chapter is that people's thinking, including causal reasoning, has two distinct processes, or ways of seeing things in the world, which we call *frames*. Among many factors that affect ways of recognising affairs in the world, causality is primary for framing, and we are starting with causal induction. People employ two types of processes for two types of causal induction: fast screening and the precise identification of a cause. People switch between two different 'perspectives', each corresponding to one of these two processes. We have labelled the first perspective as *A-frame* (A stands for attentional) and the second as *B-frame* (B stands for balanced). See Table 8.1. When perceiving causality through the A-frame, people are trying to detect a correlation between

TABLE 8.1 Characteristics of the two frames in causal reasoning

	A-frame	B-frame
Epistemic aim	Fast screening	Control
Thought style	Relevance mode	Differentiation mode
Focalisation	Positivity focus	Comparative view
Psychological symmetry	Asymmetrical	Symmetrical
Negation	Explicit (X vs. not-X)	Implicit (X vs. Y)
Cognitive process	Heuristic	Analytic
D-cell	Disregard	Respect
Base rate	Rare	Not rare
Causality scaling	Monopolar (null/effective)	Bipolar (preventive/generative)
Invasiveness	Observation	Intervention
Activeness	Passive	Active
Commitment	Uncommitted	Committed

a potential cause (hereafter *C*) and a target effect (hereafter *E*); this is the *relevance mode*. On the other hand, the B-frame facilitates a comparative examination between cases in which *C* exists and cases in which it does not, in order to detect how the occurrence of *E* is affected by the control of *C*; this is the *differentiation mode*.

Most studies of causal induction have assumed that there is just one type of induction (or learning). This includes normative rule-based theories (e.g. Cheng, 1997; White, 2003), associative accounts (e.g. Shanks, Lopez, Darby & Dickinson, 1996; Wasserman, Kao, Van Hamme, Katagiri, & Young, 1996) and Bayesian approaches (e.g. Griffiths & Tenenbaum, 2005, 2009; Lu, Liljeholm, Cheng & Holyoak, 2008). Aside from a few exceptional cases (e.g. Hattori & Oaksford, 2007), existing research has not shown a clear awareness of the difference between the two types of causal reasoning, but we will explore the distinction here. If one wants to avoid an apparent present danger or simply predict the near future, then it is not necessary to go so far as to know the causal structure. Rather, the important thing in such a case is to identify as quickly as possible the factors related to the problematic element, for example death in the home. Whether a relevant factor is a genuine cause is not a pressing issue; the important thing is to discover the most relevant factors from a small sample. The goal of the second type of causal induction is to control the effect, for example prevent accidents from alcohol consumption. In this case, it is important to gain an understanding of the causal structure. Causality usually has many factors, so it is necessary to clarify which ones have a direct causal relationship with each other, what the direction of causal relationship is and how strong the relationship is. Previous causal induction studies have dealt with normative models based on the B-frame and have not recognised the importance of causal reasoning in the A-frame. However, the A-frame is not only relevant to causal induction; it is also deeply related to errors and biases that have been clarified in research in fields other than causal induction. This assertion represents the secondary claim of this chapter.

A-frame: diagnostic probability, *D*-cell disregard and monopolar causality

The *dual-factor heuristic* (DFH) model proposed by Hattori and Oaksford (2007) represents A-frame causal induction in the simplest possible way:

$$H = \sqrt{P(E \mid C)P(C \mid E)} = \frac{a}{\sqrt{(a+b)(a+c)}}$$

In this model, a, b, c and d represent the frequencies for combinations of occurrence/non-occurrence of C and occurrence/non-occurrence of E as defined in Table 8.2. This model is notable for its incorporation of $P(C \mid E)$ and for the fact that the d-cell is not included as a variable. The latter feature will be discussed in a later section, and we now address the former feature.

Suppose people get food poisoning at a restaurant. The first step someone would take to find out the cause of the incident would likely be to ask the victims what they ate, in order to identify the problematic food item. Such an action is nothing other than the identification of a C with high $P(C \mid E)$. If E is rare (i.e. if a *rarity assumption*, Oaksford & Chater, 1994, is established), then the $P(C \mid E)$ could be extremely useful data for screening relevant factors. In this context, a rarity assumption means that the occurrence frequency is by default assumed relatively small. For example, in a case such as 'if you turn the ignition key (C), the car will start (E),' we usually consider both events – turning the ignition key and the car starting – as having low occurrence frequencies. If one needs to specify the relevant factors quickly, as in a case of food poisoning, then it would be inappropriate to form an assumption based on the traditional normative models of causal reasoning; it may be hard to go through each food item and compare food poisoning occurrence rates in the cases where the food has been eaten and in the cases not eaten (as in the case of ΔP introduced later).

The DFH is defined as the uppermost limit of the fourfold correlation coefficient phi [φ] (one of the most popular indices of linear relationship) when the value of the d-cell is infinitely large. The d-cell with an infinite divergence has the following four implications.

(1) Rarity of causes and effects
(2) Cognitive economy
(3) Monopolar causality
(4) Asymmetry between occurrence and non-occurrence

TABLE 8.2 A 2 × 2 contingency table representing covariation information between a candidate cause and a target effect

	E	$\neg E$
C	a	b
$\neg C$	c	d

Note: C and $\neg C$ represent the occurrence and non-occurrence of a candidate cause, and E and $\neg E$ represent the occurrence and non-occurrence of a target effect, respectively.

The implication that we wish to emphasise most is the fourth, which will be discussed starting in the section *Asymmetry: focalisation and negation* to clarify the distinction between A- and B-frames. For now, we will discuss the first three. Rarity of causes and effects forms the premise for the DFH. The rarer the C and E are (i.e. the lower $P(C)$ and $P(E)$ are), the greater the relative size of d will be. Therefore, insofar as a rarity assumption is established, an assumption that d is infinite serves as an effective approximation. In other words, disregarding the d-cell thus provides, as it were, a 'corner-cutting' measure.

Cognitive economy is about the trade-off between cognitive resources and calculation accuracy. Hattori and Oaksford (2007) used a computer simulation to investigate the adaptive aspect of the d-cell disregard. Assuming rarity, it is possible to calculate, disregarding the d-cell, the correlation of two events to a certain degree of accuracy. Indeed, d-cell disregard has the advantage of easing the memory load, as there is no need to retain in memory a vast number of d-cell cases. Additionally, since there is no extra memory burden, it will be possible to divert more resources to samples of other cells, which will enable a more precise estimation. In short, rather than being simply a corner-cutting measure, the d-cell disregard may be an effective heuristic device.

Monopolar causality refers to single polarity of the scale of causation (from zero to complete effectiveness). In the relevance mode of thinking (with the A-frame), the goal is to distinguish relevant events from irrelevant ones rapidly. From this point of view, absence of relevance is the default (i.e. the default is that the two events are independent of each other), and the concern is how much covariation can be observed with this default. As will be discussed later, the A-frame, by shining the spotlight on the occurrence of an event, concerns itself with the efficient detection of correlation. Therefore, it ignores negative causality heuristically. To put it another way, the A-frame is employed when there is no urgent need to detect a negative effect. In the food poisoning example, there is an urgent need to identify the item that caused the food poisoning, but there is not much need to identify an item that raises resistance to food poisoning. In accord with the A-frame, the DFH output is monopolar since the sign of phi (φ) is determined by $(ad - bc)$ and is positive when the d-cell diverges to infinity. In other words, its concern is on whether a relationship exists between C and E and, if so, how strong this relationship is. The implication of this is that an index based on such thinking does not directly deal with preventive causes. The index does not detect whether the existence of C prevents the occurrence of E.

Some authors (e.g. Lu et al., 2008) have criticized DFH as non-normative and unable to detect preventative causes. But this criticism is beside the point. DFH is a model of the relevance mode of thinking, that is the A-frame, which is not meant to be normative, but is rather generally reliable under changing circumstances, as we discuss later.

B-frame: intervention and commitment

ΔP is probably the simplest model for expressing the B-frame. It is defined as follows.

$$\Delta P = P\left(E \mid C\right) - P\left(E \mid \neg C\right) = \frac{a}{a+b} - \frac{c}{c+d}.$$

The idea underlining this model is as follows. The occurrence rate of E when C has occurred is compared to that when C has not occurred, and if the former is higher than the latter, then the difference indicates the degree of C's capacity to control E (Jenkins & Ward, 1965). This is a model of the differentiation mode in the sense that it differentiates the occurrence rate of E when C has occurred from that when C has not occurred.[1] Since the B-frame compares the presence and absence of C, it includes in its scope the detection of situations in which the presence of C actually inhibits the occurrence of E. Thus, in contrast to the A-frame, the B-frame provides a scale of *bipolar causality* (from completely preventative to completely generative).

The aim of employing the B-frame is to control the target effect. To enable accurate control of the target effect, it is essential to understand the causal structure. An effective method for understanding the causal structure between factors is intervention in the system – one makes C occur and observes whether E occurs as a result (e.g. Spirtes, Glymour & Scheines, 2001; Steyvers, Tenenbaum, Wagenmakers & Blum, 2003). Therefore, the B-frame has a high affinity with intervention. ΔP is not necessarily premised upon intervention, but it is the easiest-to-understand index for measuring the effect of intervening on C; it expresses the difference in terms of occurrence possibility between the cases when C is instigated (intervention) and when it is not (non-intervention). However, the B-frame's process load is greater than that of the A-frame. Therefore, initiation of a B-frame process may require some degree of commitment. In other words, a precondition of the B-frame is that the person be sufficiently motivated to invest the requisite cognitive resources. This is a testable hypothesis.

Asymmetry: focalisation and negation

The reason for the A-frame disregarding the d-cell is not simply proximity premised on rarity. It is deeply related to the assumption that causal reasoning is event-driven. When one is interested in the presence or absence of causation, one will usually focus on cases in which C and/or E have occurred. If we return to the ignition key example, the phenomenon of 'not turning the ignition key and not starting the car' does correspond to the d-cell, but a situation in which 'nothing occurs' does not trigger any supposition as to the relationship between the non-cause and the non-effect. Causation for people implies that one event has caused another, where an 'event' is thought of as an actual occurrence. Thus the concept of causation has an implicit presupposition: the default is a situation in which nothing is occurring. The 'event' that makes a contrast against this background of non-occurrence is deemed to be the cause. Of course, in the strictest sense, there is no such thing, objectively, as a situation in which nothing is occurring. But subjectively, non-occurrence is the default cognitive state, and there is a psychological asymmetry between occurrence and non-occurrence.

Logically, occurrence and non-occurrence have a complementary relationship. If we represent X as a hypothetical proposition, then $\neg X$ is its logical negation.

Sometimes we can find an affirmation by substituting a Y for $\neg X$, but this is not always possible, and the relationship between an affirmation and its negation is not psychologically symmetrical. Ordinary people do not usually pay attention to what does not occur. An 'exception that proves the rule' is Sherlock Holmes, who was brilliantly not like an ordinary person in his observation about 'the dog that didn't bark', which helped him to solve a mystery that baffled everyone else. Gilbert (2006) identified a lack of attention toward non-occurring things as a cause of our *illusions of foresight*, and he discussed an interesting case concerning pigeons, as well as the results of studies by Tversky (1977) and Shafir (1993), which we will come to later. Jenkins and Sainsbury (1969, 1970) demonstrated that, in the training of pigeons, there is asymmetry between the presence and absence of a distinctive feature. Pigeons were presented with two types of key – one with a distinctive feature (e.g. a key with a dot drawn on it) and one without a distinctive feature (e.g. a key with nothing drawn on it). The study showed that discrimination learning was easier in the case where the pigeons pecked the distinctive key and received a food reward than in the case where they pecked the non-distinctive key and received a food reward. Newman, Wolff, and Hearst (1980) reported that this *feature-positive effect* can also be observed amongst university students.

The asymmetrical relationship between occurrence and non-occurrence can be equated to the perceptual phenomenon of 'figure and ground' described by Rubin (1915/1958, 1921). Generally, it is occurrence (action or affirmation) that captures the attention, while non-occurrence (non-action or negation) forms the background of occurrence. This unnoticed background phenomenon is foggy and seldom cognitively processed in any great detail. The figure and ground concept is represented symbolically in the famous Rubin's vase (Figure 8.1). Rubin (1915/1958) argued that the figure and the ground function differently from each other in the perception of shape, stating that, 'in a certain sense, the ground has no shape' (p. 194). This argument corresponds with the premise for causal reasoning, in which non-occurrence is assumed as the *cognitive default*.

A closely related point is the unfeasibility of counting the d-cell frequency. 'Turning the key' (C) and 'starting the car' (E) are actions, but 'not turning the key' ($\neg C$) and 'not starting the car' ($\neg E$) are states. A set of actions (a-cell) and a set of actions and states combined (b- and c-cells) are countable, but a set of states (d-cell) cannot be counted as in 'first state, second state and so on'. All one can really do is fix the time of observation at a certain time of a certain day or record the states that exist at certain fixed intervals along a timeline. This situation indicates that the d-cell is peculiar among the data, which forms the rational basis for assuming the d-cell to be the 'ground'.

So far, we have discussed the A-frame as a particular cognitive framework for causal induction, but it may be more appropriately regarded as a general cognitive framework for generating the asymmetry between affirmative and negative occurrences. This proposal is based on the fact that a similar structure can be found in a wide variety of areas, including reasoning, hypothesis testing, similarity, probability

FIGURE 8.1 Rubin's vase (Rubin, 1921)

judgement, preferences, theory of mind and social inference. It is unclear at present whether these areas all use the same perceptual framework, but seeking out the commonality between them will be an important first step toward constructing an integrated theoretical model. This being the case, from this point on, we will look at how various errors and biases can be reinterpreted as instances of this kind of asymmetry.

Asymmetry in deduction

The first person to examine experimentally the asymmetry between affirmation and negation was probably Wason (1959). In his pioneering experiment, in which he used as indices the reaction time and number of errors in processing sentences, Wason demonstrated that affirmative information is easier to process than negative information. It seems simple enough that, if a sentence is true, its negation is false. For example, if 'the star is yellow' is a true affirmative sentence, then its negation, 'the star is NOT yellow,' is false. Conversely, if a sentence is false, its negation is true. There are therefore 2 × 2 = 4 statements: true affirmative, false affirmative, true negative and false negative. Wason investigated differences in the relative ease of processing the information of such statements. He presented participants with an illustration showing the true 'situation'. The illustration showed a number of green, red, yellow and black stars located in various positions numbered from 1 to 4. Participants were asked to select the wording to make the sentence accurately represent the situation. The participants were provided with affirmative and negative statements. The following is an example of an affirmative statement.

$$\text{There is both } \begin{Bmatrix} \text{Yellow} \\ \text{Green} \end{Bmatrix} \text{ in 4 AND } \begin{Bmatrix} \text{Red} \\ \text{Black} \end{Bmatrix} \text{ in 3.}$$

The following is an example of a negative statement.

$$\text{There is NOT both } \begin{Bmatrix} \text{Yellow} \\ \text{Green} \end{Bmatrix} \text{ in 4 AND } \begin{Bmatrix} \text{Red} \\ \text{Black} \end{Bmatrix} \text{ in 3.}$$

In the experiment, the mean reaction time was quickest with true affirmative statements, followed in order by false affirmatives, true negatives and false negative statements. The results thus revealed that affirmative information requires less cognitive load than negative information, and in our view, this experiment clarified the asymmetry between affirmation and negation.

In the year following this experiment, Wason (1960) reported confirmation bias in his 2–4–6 task, which accentuates the asymmetry between affirmative and negative information. People tend to seek confirmation of their own hypothesis by finding instances that support it and to avoid falsification of it through the use of contradicting instances. Our attention is captured by a hypothesis supported by positive instances, and affirmative feedback about these instances. The falsity of a hypothesis and negative instances are consigned to the background. The affirmative aspects of hypotheses and their instances are the 'figure', and the negative aspects of hypotheses and instances are the 'ground'. Of particular interest is the fact that positive feedback for a positive test (Klayman & Ha, 1987) has different psychological implications than negative feedback for a negative test. Both are the cases of confirmation, but the former is 'figure' confirmation and, as such, captures attention and becomes the target of bias, while the latter is the 'ground' confirmation and, as such, does not capture attention.

The asymmetry of confirmation is laid bare by Hempel's (1945) famous ravens paradox. Here the hypothesis of interest is that 'all ravens are black' (H_1), which will be confirmed by the existence of a black raven. Similarly, the hypothesis that 'everything that is not black is not a raven' (H_2) is confirmed by the existence of an object that is not black and is not a raven, for example a white shoe or red umbrella. But these two hypotheses are logically equivalent to each other, Hempel argued, by contraposition in classical logic, and he concluded that hypothesis H_1 will be equally confirmed by a white shoe and a red umbrella. The following two thinking approaches resolve this apparent paradox, and they both can be related to the concept of 'figure and ground'.

The first approach resolves the paradox through a Bayesian model. In this model, hypothesis testing is regarded as a comparison of likelihood between competitive models (McKenzie & Mikkelsen, 2000; Oaksford & Chater, 2007). If a black raven (D) is observed, this could mean two things. It could mean that hypothesis H_1 is true and that the observation of D is supporting evidence of the hypothesis. At the same time, it could also mean that D is observed by chance in spite of the falsity of H_1 (e.g. raven and blackness are independent of each other [H_0]). If the probabilities of ravens and of black things are both small, then the former (i.e. H_1 is true) is much more likely to be the case because it is improbable that D is observed by chance in such a case. In this context, the probability of ravens (or black things) refers to the probability that, if you randomly pick out a thing, it will be a raven (or a black thing). This world contains a vast diversity of things, so the probabilities of ravens and black things are very small; in other words, ravens and black things have *rarity*. For hypothesis H_1, the expected information gain of D will be much higher than that of, say, an observed white shoe. In other words, the observation of D will raise the certainty factor of the hypothesis, whereas the observation of a white shoe would hardly raise it at all. Discovering a black raven would have considerable significance, but discovering a white shoe would have negligible significance. 'Things that have rarity' (ravens and black things) are the 'figure', while everything that is not raven or black is the 'ground'.

The second approach is based on recent psychological studies of the indicative conditional of natural language. This research has supported the hypothesis that this conditional, *if p, then q*, is a *probability conditional*, or *conditional event*, and not the material conditional of classical logic (Baratgin, Over & Politzer, 2013, 2014; Baratgin & Politzer, 2016; Evans & Over, 2004; Over & Baratgin; 2016, this volume; Politzer & Baratgin, 2016). The probability of the probability conditional, $P(if\ p, then\ q)$, is the conditional probability $P(q|p)$, which is not the same as $P(not\text{-}p|not\text{-}q)$, and so contraposition fails for the probability conditional: *if p, then q* is not logically equivalent to *if not-q, then not-p*. For a particular object, the probability of 'if raven (R), then black (B)' is equal to $P(B|R)$, the probability that the object is black given that it is a raven. This can be determined by finding the proportion of black ravens out of all ravens, which can be very different from the proportion of non-ravens among non-black objects, $P(\neg R|\neg B)$ (Fitelson & Hawthorne, 2009). White shoes and red umbrellas are totally irrelevant here; we must investigate the ravens themselves. As long as we do not investigate ravens, either by searching out every single one or by using a sample, we will not be able to obtain the data on the relevant probability. Thus, the precondition (raven) and the post-condition (black thing) are the 'figure', and everything else is the 'ground'.

Asymmetry in attributes

Until now, we have discussed the logical affirmation and negation of events or things themselves, but similar arguments can be made with regard to the characteristics associated with things (i.e. attributes). A target event or thing has innumerable attributes, but an attribute that captures attention is given weight in processing. As a result, the same target object can have different cognitive processing in different contexts. For example, Levin (1987) reported that ground beef labelled '75% lean' was rated more positively on scales for 'high quality–low quality' and 'greaseless–greasy' compared to ground beef labelled '25% fat'. With lean as the 'figure' and fat as the 'ground', the affirmative attribution of lean is emphasised. Conversely, if fat is viewed as the 'figure', it will be the negative attribution of fat that is emphasised. In a similar vein, Sanford, Fay, Stewart and Moxey (2002) reported that yoghurt bearing the indication '25% fat' will be judged as less healthy than yoghurt bearing the indication '75% fat free'.

Judgements about similarity and preference are also influenced to a great extent by focalisation, viewpoint, situation and context. The concept of similarity was critically examined by the philosopher Goodman (1972). Goodman cited eight viewpoints, the most important of which concerns focalisation. Goodman illustrated his point using an allegory of baggage at an airport checking station (p. 445). Onlookers may focus on shape, size, colour and material; the pilot will be concerned with weight and the passengers with destination and ownership. Consequently, which baggage appears similar depends on the context of the judgement and on who is making the comparison. In short, 'circumstances alter similarities.' Therefore, Goodman argues, inasmuch as the concept of similarity does not provide a place for context, it has no use as a tool for philosophical analysis.

Tversky (1977) discussed the same issue, and it was he who constructed one of the most influential models of similarity. In Tversky's model, similarity judgements are based on features, and by this model, similarities and differences do not complement one another. Usually, the more similar *A* and *B* are, the greater their ratings of 'similarity' are. One would expect that their ratings of 'difference' would, conversely, be lower and that adding the two together would result in a fixed figure (such as 100), but Tversky demonstrated that this is not always the case. If the objects being compared are well known, they will have many common and distinctive features. If the objects are not so well known, then they will have few common and distinctive features. It is common features that capture the attention in similarity judgements, and distinctive features that capture attention in difference judgements. Therefore, one can expect that, if the items compared are a *prominent pair* (a pair of items that are well known), they are more likely to be judged as similar to each other – and also different from each other – than if they were a *non-prominent pair*. In Tversky's (1977) study, half of the participants (i.e. a *similarity* group) were presented with two pairs of countries (a total of four countries) and asked to judge which of the two pairs were more *similar* to each other. The rest of the participants (i.e. a *difference* group) were given the same stimulus material but asked to judge which pair were more *different* from each other. In both the similarity group and the difference group, around 70% of the participants from Israeli colleges selected 'West Germany – East Germany' as opposed to 'Ceylon – Nepal'. Thus, 'West Germany – East Germany' were judged as similar, and they were also judged as different. The same results have been obtained for other prominent pairs.

Similarity judgements are not the only factor influencing the way an object's attributes are processed. Shafir (1993) observed the same phenomenon in decision making. He found that an *enriched* option (an option with more positive and negative features) is more likely to be targeted for both selection and rejection than an *impoverished* option (an option with moderate features). Participants were asked to imagine that they were serving on the jury of an only-child sole-custody case. They were presented with the profiles of two parents and were asked to answer the questions, 'To which parent would you award sole custody of the child?' and 'Which parent would you deny sole custody of the child?' The results showed that the parent representing the enriched option was more likely to be targeted in both questions. When selecting which option to 'choose', attention is drawn to positive features, which form a basis for choosing; when rejecting something, attention is drawn to negative features, which form a basis for rejecting.

Asymmetry in meta-representation

The asymmetry between affirmation and negation is also recognised in higher-order inference (i.e. belief about belief). Birch and Bloom (2003) demonstrated that asymmetry bias traces back to the preschool psychological state in a modified version of the Smarties task (Perner, Leekam & Wimmer, 1987). They presented 3-, 4- and 5-year-old children with two sets of toys, each with an object inside. The children were told that one of the toys was familiar to a puppet introduced to the children as the experimenter's friend, and that the other was unfamiliar to the puppet. The children were shown the toy contents half of the time and not shown the toy contents the other half (i.e. puppet's familiarity/unfamiliarity with toy × child's knowledge/ignorance of contents). The children were asked to judge whether the puppet would know what was in the toys, to test their ability to infer the belief of another 'mind' accurately. The 3- and 4-year-old children, when they knew the contents, tended to assume that the puppet would also know them, regardless of whether the puppet was familiar with the toy. When they did not know the contents, they tended to assume correctly that the puppet would know if it was familiar with the toy, and these children were unlikely to assume incorrectly that the puppet would know if it was not familiar with the toy. Thus, preschool children assume that the things they know are also known by others, but on the other hand, they do not assume that the things they do *not* know are also *not* known by others.

These results are said to be evidence of what is called the *curse of knowledge*. The curse of knowledge was originally proposed in the field of economics and can be described as follows: 'Better-informed agents are unable to ignore private information even when it is in their interest to do so; more information is not always better' (Camerer, Loewenstein & Weber, 1989, p. 1232). The inability of children aged 3 or under to solve false belief tasks is indicative of their tendency to assume that the things they know are known by others even if there is no way that others could know them. All the way back to Piaget, such a tendency has traditionally been understood as *egocentrism*, but it is gradually becoming clear that children are equally poor at recalling their own past psychological states (Gopnik & Astington, 1988), and that adults also have difficulties at inferring the psychological states of others and their own past psychological states (Birch & Bloom, 2007). Based on these findings, Birch and Bloom (2003) provided the curse of knowledge explanation of this phenomenon.

The curse of knowledge is a better explanation than egocentrism in two respects. First, it can account for the asymmetry in the study's results. The study found that the children 'were biased by their knowledge when attempting to appreciate the perspective of someone more ignorant than themselves, but were not biased by their ignorance when attempting to appreciate the perspective of someone more knowledgeable than themselves' (Birch & Bloom, 2003, p. 285). Egocentrism alone cannot account for this finding. Second, the difficulty of inferring someone else's beliefs, a 'theory of mind' problem (Premack & Woodruff, 1978), can be understood comprehensively on the same level as various other (adult) cognitive biases, including social cognition. Birch and Bloom cited a number of biases related to the curse of knowledge, including the *hindsight bias* (Fischhoff, 1975), the *spotlight effect* (Gilovich, Medvec & Savitsky, 2000), the *illusion of transparency* (Gilovich, Savitsky & Medvec, 1998), and the *false consensus effect* (Ross, Greene & House, 1977).

It is possible that at least some of these belief-related biases could be understood integrally through the same cognitive framework – namely, higher-order frames. Our attention is drawn to the things that we know and believe, whereas we tend not to focus on things that we do not know or believe. Beliefs (including false beliefs) are often the 'figure', but non-beliefs cannot easily become the 'figure'. A belief can be represented as a second-order predicate, for example, 'John believes X is at Y': Believe (*John*, Exist(X, Y)). There are also nested beliefs, also described as second-order beliefs, such as 'Mary believes John believes it is here.' Just as there are higher-order beliefs, it is conceivable that there are also higher-order frames, and that it is from these higher-order frames that the asymmetry between affirmation and negation is generated. There will be much value in empirically verifying whether the phenomenon occurs in other biases Birch and Bloom cited, such as hindsight bias. This bias refers to the tendency to look back upon an event that has occurred and assume that the event was a natural, expected result. When something occurs (e.g. someone dies), people often feel like they predicted the event (i.e. death) would occur all along. However, when nothing occurs, they do not get the equivalent feeling – they do not feel that they predicted all along that nothing would occur. Thus, asymmetry exists between positive and negative beliefs. It can be argued, therefore, that the curse of knowledge is a product of asymmetric higher-order frames. This is a hypothesis that is sufficiently testable.

Trade-offs and frame-switching

We have seen how the A-frame is related to various biases. If these biases are to be considered robust, it follows that they must have some kind of epistemological utility in the A-frame. The most likely candidate is cognitive load reduction. We already explained cognitive load reduction in relation to the DFH case. Another important point is that cognitive load may be related to the structure by which the A-frame resolves the *frame problem* (McCarthy & Hayes, 1969; Pylyshyn, 1987).

The frame problem is fundamentally important and as yet unresolved in artificial intelligence (AI) studies. It concerns the fundamental difficulty of an agent with finite processing capacity with problems in a complex environment. The initial worry was that, if the agent in such an environment carries out some action or if something external to the agent occurs, a vast number of circumstances remain unaffected, but to give an account of every one of these circumstances would entail an explosion in computations and the amount of data. So far AIs are not as capable of disregarding irrelevant (or less important) information as human beings, for the AIs work exclusively in a B-frame mode. In this sense, studying the dual frames in higher cognition could contribute to intelligent machine developments.

The A-frame, of course, is not omnipotent. It is heuristic and, under certain conditions, will fail to perform. Sometimes 'the dog that didn't bark' is significant! The various cognitive biases we have explored in this chapter are examples of such failures. Given that the A-frame is one perspective, someone who wants to reduce biases may pose a question: 'Can the biases be reduced by changing the perspective?' A suggestion for answering this question can be found in the results of the experiment introduced in the *Asymmetry in deduction* section on the 2–4–6 task. Tweney and colleagues (1980, Experiment 4) discovered that modifying the form of the questions dramatically improved correct answer rates. In a modified version of the 2–4–6 task called the DAX-MED version, triples are assigned to one of two complementary categories: DAX ('three ascending numbers') or MED (other combination). In this version, the feedback the participants received about each triple was not whether the triple conforms to the rule (affirmation vs. negation) but rather one of two alternatives: whether it is categorised as DAX or MED. The correct answer rate in this version was four times higher than in the initial study (60% vs. 15%). The same finding has been obtained in a number of other studies (e.g. Tukey, 1986; Wetherick, 1962; Wharton, Cheng & Wickens, 1993). This task is a dual-goal task, and goal complementarity has been suggested as the key reason for the results (Gale & Ball, 2006). The implication of the results is that it is possible for A-frame use to be diminished by some factors. The frame one employs when categorising objects (e.g. triples) depends on whether one sees them as either X (e.g. ascending numbers) or *not-X* (e.g. others) or complementary alternatives (e.g. DAX vs. MED). This hypothesis is also testable.

Conclusion

In this chapter, we have proposed a theoretical foundation for a distinction between what we have called A/B-frames. Beginning with the relatively low-level cognitive function of visual perception, we went on to an examination of higher-order cognitive functions – like deduction, induction, judgement, decision making and problem solving – and then of particular phenomena covered by social cognition and cognitive development. Whether all of these phenomena are truly founded on a common cognitive mechanism must await the findings of future research. The significance of the framework proposed here must also be judged by the impact of its explanations and the extent to which it expands research, generating testable hypotheses. It is necessary to verify the claim that this diversity of phenomena shares commonality. We must see whether it is possible to predict that what holds for one phenomenon will also be true for as-yet-undiscovered aspects of another phenomenon. For example, Birch and Bloom (2004) proposed inhibitory control as the neural basis for the asymmetry in the curse of knowledge, but we should go beyond false belief tasks and consider visual tasks and the illusion of transparency, to determine whether they have the same neural basis. But most of all, it is necessary to verify empirically the psychological reality of A/B-frames.

Acknowledgment

This study was supported by JSPS-ANR CHORUS Program J121000148 and JSPS KAKENHI Grant 15H02717.

Note

1 The normative model most often proposed in research to date is the differentiation mode model. For example, there is a model that takes into consideration the role of alternative cause with regard to ΔP (Cheng, 1997; Lu et al., 2008); a model that incorporates weighting parameters into ΔP (Anderson & Sheu, 1995; Rescorla & Wagner, 1972; Wasserman, Elek, Chatlosh, & Baker, 1993); and a causal support model, which differentiates between the presence and absence of a causal relationship between the candidate cause and the target effect (Griffith & Tenenbaum, 2005). The present study does not attempt to compare these models. Instead, it focuses on the ΔP model as it is the simplest and most well known in our view.

References

Anderson, J. R., & Sheu, C.-F. (1995). Causal inferences as perceptual judgements. *Memory & Cognition, 23*, 510–524.

Baratgin, J., Over, D. E., & Politzer, G. (2013). Uncertainty and de Finetti tables. *Thinking & Reasoning, 19*, 308–328.

Baratgin, J., Over, D. E., & Politzer, G. (2014). New psychological paradigm for conditionals and general de Finetti tables. *Mind and Language, 29*, 73–84.

Baratgin, J., & Politzer, G. (2016). Logic, probability and inference: A methodology for a new paradigm. In L. Macchi, M. Bagassi & R. Viale (Eds.), *Cognitive unconscious and human rationality* (pp. 119–142). Cambridge, MA: MIT Press.

Birch, S. A. J., & Bloom, P. (2003). Children are cursed: An asymmetric bias in mental-state attribution. *Psychological Science, 14*, 283–286.

Birch, S. A. J., & Bloom, P. (2004). Understanding children's and adults' limitations in mental state reasoning. *Trends in Cognitive Sciences, 8*, 255–260.

Birch, S. A. J., & Bloom, P. (2007). The curse of knowledge in reasoning about false beliefs. *Psychological Science, 18*, 382–386.

Camerer, C. F., Loewenstein, G., & Weber, M. (1989). The curse of knowledge in economic settings: An experimental analysis. *Journal of Political Economy, 97*, 1232–1254.

Cheng, P. W. (1997). From covariation to causation: A causal power theory. *Psychological Review, 104*, 367–405.

Evans, J. St. B. T., & Over, D. E. (2004). *If.* New York: Oxford University Press.

Fischhoff, B. (1975). Hindsight is not equal to foresight: The effect of outcome knowledge on judgement under uncertainty. *Journal of Experimental Psychology: Human Perception and Performance, 1*, 288–299.

Fitelson, B., & Hawthorne, J. (2009). How Bayesian confirmation theory handles the paradox of the ravens. In E. Eells & J. Fetzer (Eds.), *The place of probability in science* (pp. 247–275). Netherlands: Springer.

Gale, M., & Ball, L. J. (2006). Dual-goal facilitation in Wason's 2–4–6 task: What mediates successful rule discovery? *The Quarterly Journal of Experimental Psychology, 59*, 873–885.

Gilbert, D. T. (2006). *Stumbling on happiness.* London: Harper Perennial.

Gilovich, T., Medvec, V. H., & Savitsky, K. (2000). The spotlight effect in social judgement: An egocentric bias in estimates of the salience of one's own actions and appearance. *Journal of Personality and Social Psychology, 78*, 211–222.

Gilovich, T., Savitsky, K., & Medvec, V. H. (1998). The illusion of transparency: Biased assessments of other's ability to read one's emotional states. *Journal of Personality and Social Psychology, 75*, 332–346.

Goodman, N. (1972). *Problems and projects.* Indianapolis, IN: Bobbs-Merrill.

Gopnik, A., & Astington, J. W. (1988). Children's understanding of representational change and its relation to the understanding of false belief and the appearance-reality distinction. *Child Development, 59*, 26–37.

Griffiths, T. L., & Tenenbaum, J. B. (2005). Structure and strength in causal induction. *Cognitive Psychology, 51*, 334–384.

Griffiths, T. L., & Tenenbaum, J. B. (2009). Theory-based causal induction. *Psychological Review, 116*, 661–716.

Hattori, M., & Oaksford, M. (2007). Adaptive non-interventional heuristics for covariation detection in causal induction: Model comparison and rational analysis. *Cognitive Science, 31*, 765–814.

Hempel, C. G. (1945). Studies in the logic of confirmation (I.). *Mind, 54*, 1–26.

Jenkins, H. M., & Sainsbury, R. S. (1969). The development of stimulus control through differential reinforcement. In N. J. Mackintosh & W. K. Honig (Eds.), *Fundamental issues in associative learning* (pp. 123–161). Halifax, Nova Scotia, Canada: Dalhousie University Press.

Jenkins, H. M., & Sainsbury, R. S. (1970). Discrimination learning with the distinctive feature on positive or negative trials. In D. I. Mostofsky (Ed.), *Attention: Contemporary theory and analysis* (pp. 239–273). New York: Appleton-Century-Crofts.

Jenkins, H. M., & Ward, W. C. (1965). Judgement of contingency between responses and outcomes. *Psychological Monographs: General and Applied, 79*, 1–17. (Whole No. 594).

Klayman, J., & Ha, Y.-W. (1987). Confirmation, disconfirmation, and information in hypothesis testing. *Psychological Review, 94*, 211–228.

Levin, I. P. (1987). Associative effects of information framing. *Bulletin of the Psychonomic Society, 25*, 85–86.

Lu, H., Yuille, A. L., Liljeholm, M., Cheng, P. W., & Holyoak, K. J. (2008). Bayesian generic priors for causal learning. *Psychological Review, 115*, 955–984.

Manktelow, K. I. (2012). *Thinking and reasoning.* Hove, UK: Psychology Press.

McCarthy, J., & Hayes, P. (1969). Some philosophical problems from the standpoint of the artificial intelligence. In B. Meltzer & D. Michie (Eds.), *Machine intelligence* (Vol. 4, pp. 463–502). Edinburgh, UK: Edinburgh University Press.

McKenzie, C. R. M., & Mikkelsen, L. A. (2000). The psychological side of Hempel's paradox of confirmation. *Psychonomic Bulletin & Review, 7*, 360–366.

Newman, J. P., Wolff, W. T., & Hearst, E. (1980). The feature-positive effect in adult human subjects. *Journal of Experimental Psychology: Human Learning and Memory, 6*, 630–650.

Oaksford, M., & Chater, N. (1994). A rational analysis of the selection task as optimal data selection. *Psychological Review, 101*, 608–631.

Oaksford, M., & Chater, N. (2007). *Bayesian rationality: The probabilistic approach to human reasoning*. Oxford: Oxford University Press.

Over, D. E., & Baratgin, J. (2016). The 'defective' truth table: Its past, present, and future. In E. Lucas, N. Galbraith & D. E. Over. (Eds.), *The thinking mind: The use of thinking in everyday life*. Hove, UK: Psychology Press.

Perner, J., Leekam, S. R., & Wimmer, H. (1987). Three-year-olds' difficulty with false belief: The case for a conceptual deficit. *British Journal of Developmental Psychology, 5*, 125–137.

Politzer, G., & Baratgin, J. (2016). Deductive schemas with uncertain premises using qualitative probability expressions. *Thinking & Reasoning, 22*, 78–98.

Premack, D., & Woodruff, G. (1978). Does the chimpanzee have a theory of mind? *Behavioural and Brain Sciences, 1*, 515–526.

Pylyshyn, Z. W. (1987). *Robot's dilemma: The frame problem in artificial intelligence*. Norwood, NJ: Ablex.

Rescorla, R. A., & Wagner, A. R. (1972). A theory of Pavlovian conditioning: Variations in the effectiveness of reinforcement and nonreinforcement. In A. H. Black & W. F. Prokasy (Eds.), *Classical conditioning II: Current research and theory* (pp. 64–99). New York: Appleton-Century-Crofts.

Ross, L., Greene, D., & House, P. (1977). The 'false consensus effect': An egocentric bias in social perception and attribution processes. *Journal of Experimental Social Psychology, 13*, 279–301.

Rubin, E. (1915/1958). Figure and ground. In D. C. Beardslee & M. Wertheimer (Eds.), *Readings in perception* (pp. 194–203). Princeton, NJ: D. Van Nostrand. English translation of key sections from Rubin's dissertation.

Rubin, E. (1921). *Visuell wahrgenommene Figuren: Studien in psychologischer analyse [Visually perceived figures: Studies in psychological analysis]*. Kobenhavn: Gyldendalske Boghandel.

Sanford, A. J., Fay, N., Stewart, A., & Moxey, L. (2002). Perspective in statements of quantity, with implications for consumer psychology. *Psychological Science, 13*, 130–134.

Shafir, E. (1993). Choosing versus rejecting: Why some options are both better and worse than others. *Memory & Cognition, 21*, 546–556.

Shanks, D. R., Lopez, F. J., Darby, R. J., & Dickinson, A. (1996). Distinguishing associative and probabilistic contrast theories of human contingency judgment. In D. R. Shanks, K. Holyoak & D. L. Medin (Eds.), *Causal learning* (pp. 265–311). San Diego, CA: Academic Press.

Spirtes, P., Glymour, C., & Scheines, R. (2001). *Causation, prediction, and search* (Second edition). New York: Springer.

Steyvers, M., Tenenbaum, J. B., Wagenmakers, E.-J., & Blum, B. (2003). Inferring causal networks from observations and interventions. *Cognitive Science, 27*, 453–489.

Tukey, D. D. (1986). A philosophical and empirical analysis of subjects' modes of inquiry in Wason's 2–4–6 task. *The Quarterly Journal of Experimental Psychology A: Human Experimental Psychology, 38*, 5–33.

Tversky, A. (1977). Features of similarity. *Psychological Review, 84*, 327–352.

Tweney, R. D., Doherty, M. E., Worner, W. J., Pliske, D. B., Mynatt, C. R., Gross, K. A., et al. (1980). Strategies of rule discovery in an inference task. *The Quarterly Journal of Experimental Psychology, 32*, 109–123.

Wason, P. C. (1959). The processing of positive and negative information. *The Quarterly Journal of Experimental Psychology, 11*, 92–107.

Wason, P. C. (1960). On the failure to eliminate hypotheses in a conceptual task. *The Quarterly Journal of Experimental Psychology, 12*, 129–140.

Wasserman, E. A., Elek, S. M., Chatlosh, D. L., & Baker, A. G. (1993). Rating causal relations: Role of probability in judgements of response-outcome contingency. *Journal of Experimental Psychology: Learning, Memory, and Cognition, 19*, 174–188.

Wasserman, E. A., Kao, S.-F., Van Hamme, L. J., Katagiri, M., & Young, M. E. (1996). Causation and association. In D. R. Shanks, K. Holyoak, & D. L. Medin (Eds.), *Causal learning* (pp. 207–264). San Diego, CA: Academic Press.

Wetherick, N. E. (1962). Eliminative and enumerative behaviour in a conceptual task. *Quarterly Journal of Experimental Psychology, 14*, 246–249.

Wharton, C. M., Cheng, P. W., & Wickens, T. D. (1993). Hypothesis-testing strategies: Why two goals are better than one. *The Quarterly Journal of Experimental Psychology A: Human Experimental Psychology, 46A*, 743–758.

White, P. A. (2003). Making causal judgments from the proportion of confirming instances: The pCI rule. *Journal of Experimental Psychology: Learning, Memory, and Cognition, 29*, 710–727.

9

REASONING IN EVERYDAY LIFE

Guillaume Gimenes, Valérie Pennequin and Tom Mercer

Wason's task: from the lab to real life

"*If p, then q.*" Ken Manktelow dedicated his scientific career to *P*s and *Q*s, and it is obvious that once you have read this book, you'll be quite familiar with reasoning concepts. As a result, you should be able to avoid reasoning biases. But will you? If we asked you to solve logical problems after reading this book, would you get them right every time? And would you be a better "thinker" after reading all of the work published by Ken Manktelow (e.g. Manktelow, 2012), Peter Wason (e.g. Wason, 1968), Philip Johnson-Laird (e.g. Johnson-Laird, 2006) and Jonathan Evans (e.g. Evans, 1989)?

We think the answer is "No," because people often seem to lack logic in everyday reasoning tasks. Humans are not logical machines, so we make numerous errors and are vulnerable to reasoning biases (Evans, 1989; Evans, Newstead & Byrne, 1993; Tversky & Kahneman, 1983). Being "illogical" and committing errors when making everyday choices is normal. These mistakes are adaptive for the situation, otherwise they would not exist. The aim of this chapter is to address how cognition in everyday life may differ from cognition within the psychological laboratory, and we will also examine how we can adapt reasoning to our environment.

Formal classical reasoning is a slow process, and most of the time our conclusions and actions need to be rapid. Therefore, classical formal logic is not ideally suited to daily life, as many situations do not give us access to quantitative data and we have to reason about ill-defined problems. Thus, it is more important for people to reason quickly with imperfect information in ill-defined situations, so priority is given to efficiency over accuracy. For example, in the Wason selection task (Wason, 1968, 1977), four cards (such as A, D, 4 and 7) are presented to the participants and their task is to decide which card(s) must be turned over to test the following rule: "If there is an 'A' on one side of the card, then there is a '4' on the other side." Logically, only the first (A) and fourth (7) cards must be turned over to test the truth of the rule, as the D and 4 cards do not allow valid conclusions to be drawn. However, most people are not logical and choose A and 4, possibly because these cards match the terms of the rule (the "matching bias", Evans & Lynch, 1973) or because people attempt to "prove" rather than disprove the rule (the "confirmation bias", Johnson-Laird & Wason, 1970).

Yet we may not be as inefficient in different contexts, as in real life we rarely deal with reasoning about letters and numbers. In everyday situations, these sentences often involve social contracts and results are likely to be better than with abstract cards (Cosmides, 1989). For example, if someone cheats in situations in which cooperation is expected, it's important that this person is detected. To illustrate this, Gigerenzer and Hug (1992) developed a version of Wason's selection task in the form of a social contract, and participants had to detect cheaters. One of the rules participants had to test was "*If a tennis player wins a game, then he will have to pay for drinks for the others.*" Participants had to check whether any of four players at the restaurant violated the rule, as there were suspicions of cheating. The four cards presented to participants were "won the game", "did not win the game", "paid for a round of drinks" and "did not pay for a round of drinks".

So, which card would you pick to verify the rule? According to logical laws, the correct answer is to turn over cards 1 (Modus Ponens) and 4 (Modus Tollens). Contrary to the choices made with the abstract task, which are rather bad, people often made the correct choice. In this situation, it would seem rather illogical to choose "paid for the drinks", as that would imply that somebody who pays for beers is considered a cheater! And the same applies for the second card. In this context, 89% of participants made the correct choices. You may think that these results are due to the familiarity of the situation, rather than social contracts. But this notion of a detection of "cheaters" seems to be universal, as it is a very common problem in all cultures. Sugiyama, Tooby and Cosmides (2002) supported this idea by showing the same patterns of results on very isolated Amazonian people, as well as American students.

Reasoning and problems in everyday life

Many circumstances exist in which people, friends or politicians commonly use logical arguments to support their opinions. Who hasn't heard promises made by politicians? For instance, you may have heard things like, "If you want fewer taxes, then you know what to do: vote for me!" This implies the pretty simple Modus Ponens that as you want fewer taxes (p), you'll vote for the politician (q). Modus Ponens is simple and leads to a firm conclusion. The same approach is used when people defend themselves with arguments using this type of sentence: "If I really was homophobic, I would not have gay friends," leading to sentences such as "and I have gay friends, so you can't say I'm homophobic." This premise corresponds to the proposition "not q". Denying the consequent, or "Modus Tollens", is a rule of inference used frequently because it allows us to draw conclusions with certainty.

However, politicians can also exploit biases to convince other people, including the frequently observed phenomenon known as the confirmation bias (see Poletiek,

2001, for a review). This involves using an example to confirm a hypothesis, rather than looking for a counter-example to refute it. Imagine a situation in which a politician wants to get rid of violence in major cities and promotes more police and security: "The remedy to crime is to have more police." What will you do to verify this statement? You'll add more police and cameras, right? Yet this kind of reasoning demonstrates a bias because it involves trying to confirm the premise, instead of refuting it. In Wason's selection task, this bias prevents people from turning over the card with a 4, which is the counter-example, and instead pick the card with a 7, which confirms the rule. However, in formal logic it is impossible to confirm a hypothesis. Even if we observe several examples like "it worked in other cities, so it will work in this one," we will never be able to demonstrate that a hypothesis is true. But would a politician really say, "To prove me right, vote for my opponent who wants to have less police and more parks"? Yet logically speaking, this would be the only way of avoiding the confirmation bias. So, logic does not stand in this situation. But why are people so keen to confirm hypotheses? It may be because it is better to believe in a hypothesis with a risk of being wrong, rather than doubting everything. Another reason is that people put efficiency before accuracy. When something works, you get nothing trying to prove that your hypothesis is wrong. In other terms, "you never change a winning team," even if you don't know why the team wins.

Additionally, in many situations we don't have all the elements needed to be entirely logical. Problems are rarely presented as perfectly as "if p, then q", and so we must make choices pragmatically, using hidden premises and imperfect information. Let's take an example using Modus Ponens reasoning. Here is the first premise: "If William works hard, he will obtain his PhD." The second premise is: "William works hard." By deduction, the logical conclusion should therefore be: "William will obtain his doctorate." However, if we add a third premise, which was hidden from the first one, "Lately, William has difficulty concentrating," most people will conclude that William will not get his PhD. Even though the original conclusion that William will obtain his PhD was logical, the hidden information makes it invalid. The first conclusion could be revised due to this new information. Many of our daily reasoning processes are similar to this case and are based on numerous hidden premises and imperfect details.

Another aspect to take into account is the use of fallacies to protect ourselves. Occasionally, thinking before trying to do something might make people think: "It seems impossible." So is it better to calculate our chances of succeeding or not? Sometimes being biased lets us continue forward, rather than thinking and stopping. For example, in daily life we often estimate the probability that an event will occur. People have a tendency to overestimate the probability that two events will occur at the same time, compared to the probability of each event occurring separately: this is a bias known as the conjunction fallacy (Tversky & Kahneman, 1983). It consists of overestimating the probability of two events occurring together, allowing us to remain motivated and thus pursue our actions.

For instance, when the first author was a psychology student, all of the undergraduates on the course were told, "So, about 60% of you will pass in the second year, and then 70% will pass in the third year," and the majority was happy with these statistics (who said psychologists are bad with math?). Without calculating, many students thought that the average percentage that would be together in the third year could be around 60%. This might have been due to the conjunction fallacy. The actual probability that these two events will occur together is 42% (0.60 × 0.70 = 0.42). We can see that despite a high probability of each event occurring separately, the probability that they will occur together is rather low. If students did not make the conjunction fallacy, they would calculate having less than one chance in two of going into the third year. But by making the error, perhaps it was easier to remain motivated. Without this bias, people would not take on certain projects or would be quicker to give up. Thus, the conjunction fallacy is adaptive because it protects us from inactivity.

Indeed, there are many biases that protect people from doubt and loss of motivation, and consequently from inaction (see the work of Tversky & Kahneman, 1983, on biases). They lead to a risk of error in our conclusions, but also allow us to be reactive and effective. All individuals are susceptible to these biases, but some are more susceptible than others. The capacity for logic can be considered as a continuum, from very susceptible to biases, to not susceptible. In certain cases, biases can lead to maladjustment. But at other times, they do have an adaptive role.

Wisdom vs. logic

As we have seen in the preceding sections, we do not think "logically" in every situation. In fact, we use our life knowledge, we infer what other people think and want, and we try to minimise doubt within situations. However, sometimes our actions are "logical" solely in terms of the social context. The standard reasoning measures badly reflect how we resolve social problems (Sternberg, 1999) and decision-making in everyday life (Stanovich, 2009). Some authors, such as Grossmann, Na, Varnum, Kitayama and Nisbett (2013), studied a specific kind of reasoning: "wisdom". This reasoning is pragmatic, rather than abstract, and is based on life experiences and set within social contexts. Wise strategies are described as prosocial and they help to solve important problems in daily life. Specifically, six aspects have been considered in Grossman and colleagues' (2010, 2013) studies: 1) perspective shifting from one's own point of view to the point of view of people involved in the conflict; 2) recognition of the likelihood of change; 3) prediction flexibility, as indicated by multiple possible predictions concerning how the conflict might unfold; 4) recognition of uncertainty and the limits of knowledge; 5) searching for conflict resolution; and 6) searching for a compromise. Studies show that in line with folk psychology, and the traditional proverb "with age comes wisdom," this "wisdom reasoning" increases as we age (Grossmann et al., 2010; Worthy, Gorlick, Pacheco, Schnyer, & Maddox, 2011). Indeed, older individuals tend to change their priorities towards interpersonal goals and develop better emotional skills (Charles & Carstensen, 2010; Grossmann et al., 2013). Specifically, older people (60–90 years of age) show greater skill at solving social problems than younger participants aged 25–40 and 41–59. Hoppmann, Coats and Blanchard-Fields (2008) highlight the importance of considering the aims young and old people pursue when explaining the performance differences in solving daily problems. For example, if a family meeting has to be adjourned, the decision of whether to postpone or cancel it may be different between a grandmother and her granddaughter. The grandmother might deploy cognitive efforts to plan this meeting again at another time, as she pursues an aim of maintaining intergenerational relations. However, her granddaughter may not try to reschedule this reunion as family may be less important in comparison to her other personal aims. The results of Hoppmann and colleagues' (2008) research showed that the goals a person selects during daily problem solving must be considered in order to understand the different strategies chosen by people of different ages.

Everyday problems also differ from abstract problems by the fact that they are "open". That is, they have no correct or incorrect solutions. Instead, there may be several possible ways of solving the problem, which are difficult to rank in order of relevance. Similarly, one approach to tackling the problem might be suitable for one person, but less appropriate for someone else. A solution can also be considered appropriate within one specific context, but less so in others. The relevance of the solution is judged according to the data from the problem, but it also depends on motivations, emotions, the feasibility of the solution and its impact on the world and others. Here is an example scenario of an everyday problem proposed by Crawford and Channon (2002, pp. 13–14).

"Anne is in her office when Tony comes in. She asks how he is, and he says he is alright, but tired. She agrees that he looks tired, and asks what the matter is. He has new neighbours who moved into the flat above his a couple of weeks ago. They are nice people, but they own dogs and keep them in their kitchen at night, which is directly above Tony's bedroom. All night, and every night since they moved in, the dogs jump around and bark. He finds it impossible to get to sleep. He says he has had a word with the neighbours, and although they were very reasonable, they said they had nowhere else to put the dogs as it is a block of flats."

Participants rated the degree of awkwardness in the situation for both Tony and themselves (had they been placed in the same situation). They then had to provide as many solutions to the problem as possible in 2 minutes. After this, they chose the optimal solution for Tony from those they had proposed. The authors also asked the participants to determine the solution they would have used. This offered a way of assessing the appropriateness of the solution that had been chosen for someone else. Next, the participants assessed the satisfaction rating of the optimal solution for Tony and themselves on a scale from 0 to 100. Additionally, they ranked five alternatives the experimenter had given in order of relevance. The quality of the solutions was judged on three criteria: whether they showed an adequate appreciation of the problem, whether they were socially appropriate and whether they provided effective practical means of resolving the problem. Examples of solutions included negotiating with the neighbours, complaining (to the owner or to the police) and making life changes for Tony (moving or wearing earplugs). There were also some extreme ideas (kill the dogs) and irrelevant or incomplete solutions ("People should not have a dog in an apartment."). Each of these solution types was listed according to their social adjustment and their relevance in effectively solving the problem. Crawford and Channon's (2002) results showed that people aged between 60 and 80 generated fewer solutions than young people (aged 19–37), but they were of better quality. Older people also tended to be more satisfied with their solutions than younger individuals. This shows a greater confidence in the judgments of older people, which is quite justified by the greater quality of their proposed solutions.

The smaller number of solutions the older individuals generated was not simply due to the speed at which information was processed. It is more likely that older people use different strategies to generate solutions: they would only select and verbalise the high-quality solutions, unlike younger people, who tended to verbalise all of the solutions that came to mind, without sorting them by quality. Additionally, the age groups did not differ in their judgments about the appropriateness of alternatives: they were similar in their assessment of feasibility, relevance and prosocial side solutions (their own solutions or alternative proposed solutions).

These results can be linked with the greater experience and increased knowledge that is obtained as people age. Experience confers a benefit to elderly subjects in solving everyday problems, but this is not the case for more abstract tasks (whether "executive" or reasoning). Crawford and Channon (2002) also asked participants to complete a number of executive tasks, involving working memory, inhibition, mental flexibility and abstract reasoning (Raven matrices). Their results were consistent with the literature, as they showed evidence of declining performance on the executive tasks and abstract reasoning with advancing age. However, during a verbal fluency task, older adults generated as many words as young people in less than 2 minutes. Additionally, significant correlations between a number of executive actions and resolutions of the daily performance problems in the elderly testify that these executive functions are needed to solve complex daily problems. In conclusion, daily problems might not be resolved solely with logic but also according to past experience and what people expect to give to others.

The body and the mind

When we are confronted by a problem, we mostly think that its resolution has its source from the brain, with the solution being given by the body (via the voice, a gesture etc.). In fact, we act as if the problem entered directly and perfectly into our brain, so that to solve it we only have to use reasoning. Yet we often forget that stimuli have to pass through the body, which might have an effect. The last section of this chapter concerns cognition through perception, bodily state and environment: the effect of grounded cognition.

What is "grounded cognition"? According to Barsalou (1999), grounded cognition is a theory which proposes that modal simulations, bodily states and situated action underlie cognition. In other words, cognition is rooted in the relation between our body, the environment and our brain, and not just in our brain alone. Grounded cognition is not a new concept in psychology and it has taken a variety of forms (see Barsalou, 2008, for a review). However, it has mainly been revived by Barsalou, whose studies tried to show how cognition is affected by perception (from all our senses), actions, body movements, gestures, environments and everything that makes our cognition grounded to the real world. Initially, few studies were published on this subject, but over the past few years the topic has grown exponentially and it is now a major and exciting subject. As a consequence, grounded cognition leads new research within all of the disciplines related to psychology.

So how can grounded cognition influence reasoning? Several studies have examined the subject, and marketing researchers have also expressed an interest in testing the theory. Indeed, the purpose of these marketing studies is to influence choices by activating unconscious triggers that lead to favourable representations of a product. This may subsequently make buyers purchase a product. This could, for instance, involve renaming an object to make it more appealing, or changing another aspect to make it more desirable (for reviews, see Krishna, 2012; Krishna & Schwarz, 2014).

As an example of the way in which grounded cognition can influence your behaviour and decisions, imagine that you are shopping and aiming to buy a sieve. As you put your products into your shopping trolley with your right hand (as with 90% of the population, you are probably right handed), imagine that you are multitasking and talking to your mechanic on your phone, using your left hand. After turning in the shop, you are finally facing the shelf of sieves. On what criterion will you make your decision? On Price? Colour? Texture? Or the fact that some sieves have their handles on the left, whereas others have them on the right? This last remark is not as superficial as you may think, as it has been shown to influence decision making. Ping, Dhillon and Beilock (2009) demonstrated that when right-handed participants were asked to choose between two objects presented in front of them, and to put one of these objects into a box as quickly as possible, they were more likely to choose the one they could quickly handle: that is the one with the handle on the right. The same effect might occur if you wanted to do your shopping quickly and get products into your trolley. In fact, this was demonstrated by Eelen in her doctoral work, as Ping and colleagues' results were replicated in a shopping condition.

In 2013, Eelen, Dewitte and Warlop further established that when choosing between different items, different variables can moderate the impact of the position of the object on the product evaluation (choice and attractiveness). Three aspects were considered in this moderation: the flexibility of handedness (whether as a right hander you use your left hand or not), the induction of right- or left-handed action (if you answer with your left or right hand) and the cognitive load (if you have to memorise numbers while performing the task). Interesting, they demonstrated that each one of these variables interfered with the evaluation. However, in a context where cognitive load was high, being a quasi-exclusively right-handed person led participants to preferentially choose objects with the handles on the right. Yet when the context was undemanding, it was the people who used their left hand who selected the objects with the handle on the right. In both of these situations, motor fluency (preferentially choosing an object in accordance with whether it can be interacted with) influenced the choice and decision of the participants. The authors discussed their results as if rigid right-handers do not consider attention to detail as they will use their right hand anyway. Nonetheless, in a context when choice is harder to make (high cognitive load), they will choose the easiest option. On the other hand (figuratively and literally), "flexible right handers" pay more attention to details and plan their actions. In consequence, they choose objects whose orientation corresponds to the hand they use for the action. But when decision making was more difficult (because of a high cognitive load), they chose either one or the other, as they use both of their hands.

Still, whilst grounded cognition can influence everyday decisions when shopping, can it really affect symbolic reasoning? Whilst it might seem unlikely, there is a growing literature surrounding this subject. Studies have demonstrated that grounded cognition can influence mathematical performance. For example, algebraic reasoning, considered as purely symbolic reasoning, is influenced by the way it is written (see Landy, Allen & Zednik, 2014, for a review). Imagine being asked to solve the simple operation: "six times two plus eight". In this specific order, it's hard to imagine answering anything other than 20. Still, the response might be different if the operation had been phrased in another order, such as "eight plus six times two". In this order, would you still say 20 or would you say 28? Mathematical symbols operate in a different order, so even if eight is said first, you have to multiply two and six before making the addition. However, even if you know this rule, if the person stating the operation pauses before saying "times two", you might say 28.

Landy and Goldstone (2007) used the same reasoning with the writing of calculi in the form $a + b \star c + d = d + c \star b + a$, manipulating the validity (e.g. inverting c and d after =) and spaces between the letters and mathematical symbols. They then asked participants whether they were consistent with mathematical norms. The participants were more inclined to make errors when the spacing was discordant with the mathematical rules, as if deleting spaces bound together parts of the calculi: $a+b \star c+d$ seems different from $a+b\star c+d$, although it's exactly the same thing. Moreover, the authors demonstrated that this effect was resistant to trial-by-trial feedback processes. In other words, the visual cues were treated so automatically that even with feedback participants did not consider them as invalid.

As a final demonstration of the effect of your body position on reasoning, we will ask you to sit correctly on your chair while you read the end of this chapter. This should help you understand the next study and be "stable" in your judgment. The last study to be discussed reveals that being in an imbalanced position activates metaphoric concepts associated with balance, as in several linguistic expressions such as "balancing a checkbook" or "balancing an equation". These could influence your reasoning. Larson and Billetera (2013) discovered this effect while working on compromised choice linked to physical balance. The aim of their study was to test whether online shoppers were more likely to choose a compromised option when the concept of "balance" was activated via perception, imagination or metaphors.

Larson and Billetera (2013) asked their participants to choose between three products according to two factors: for example, three computers according to the processor speed (respectively low, medium and high) and the quality of the graphic card (respectively high, medium and low). In this example, the second product was a compromise as both the processor and graphics card were medium. In six experiments, the choices were made while the concept of balance was manipulated in different conditions: leaning on a chair; playing video games involving physical balance; standing on one foot; mental simulation involving imbalance (walking across a balance beam); presenting words such as "wobbly" by supraliminal priming; or through the use of metaphors (describing "out of balance" life experiences). In every case, and most interesting for physical sensations, the conditions activated the nonphysical concepts of balance in consumer decisions. Compared to a control group, participants who had the concept of balance activated (either physically or mentally) most likely chose the balanced condition and so the compromise option. Physical experiences influence choices and how we reason.

As we saw in this last part, studies on grounded cognition demonstrate various effects of how our perceptions or physical conditions influence our reasoning. Nevertheless, is it possible that deontic reasoning might be affected by body states too? To the best of our knowledge this question is still to be explored, however, since body states interfere with decision making, mathematics and other abstract domains, it seems plausible that it might also influence reasoning. In fact, in 1979, Ken Manktelow and Jonathans Evans tried to demonstrate whether concrete sentences could help reasoning, with sentences such as "If I eat macaroni, then I do not drink champagne." But the concrete information did not help. Yet with what we now know about grounded cognition, we might think of new experiments to improve these results. For example, perhaps if Ken Manktelow had made his participants drink gin or champagne during the experiment (eating macaroni is just not fun enough in a psychology experiment), the results might have been very different. In fact, drinking alcohol might have helped his participants to behave more logically.

References

Barsalou, L.W. (1999). Perceptual symbol systems. *Behavioral and Brain Sciences*, *22*, 577–660.

Barsalou, L.W. (2008). Grounded cognition. *Annual Review of Psychology*, *59*(1), 617–645.

Charles, S., & Carstensen, L. L. (2010). Social and emotional aging. *Annual Review of Psychology*, *61*, 383–409.

Cosmides, L. (1989). The logic of social exchange: Has natural selection shaped how humans reason? Studies with the Wason selection task. *Cognition*, *31*(3), 187–276.

Crawford, S., & Channon, S. (2002). Dissociation between performance on abstract tests of executive function and problem solving in real-life-type situations in normal aging. *Aging & Mental Health*, *6*(1), 12–21.

Eelen, J., Dewitte, S., & Warlop, L. (2013). Situated embodied cognition: Monitoring orientation cues affects product evaluation and choice. *Journal of Consumer Psychology (Elsevier Science)*, *23*(4), 424–433.

Evans, J. St. B. T. (1989). *Bias in human reasoning: Causes and consequences* (Vol. ix). Hillsdale, NJ: Erlbaum.

Evans, J. St. B. T., & Lynch, J. S. (1973). Matching bias in the selection task. *British Journal of Psychology*, *64*(3), 391–397.

Evans, J. St. B. T., Newstead, S. E., & Byrne, R. M. J. (1993). *Human reasoning: The psychology of deduction*. Hove, UK: Psychology Press.

Gigerenzer, G., & Hug, K. (1992). Domain-specific reasoning: Social contracts, cheating, and perspective change. *Cognition*, *43*(2), 127–171.

Grossmann, I., Na, J., Varnum, M. E. W., Kitayama, S., & Nisbett, R. E. (2013). A route to well-being: Intelligence vs. wise reasoning. *Journal of Experimental Psychology. General*, *142*(3), 944–953.

Grossmann, I., Na, J., Varnum, M. E. W., Park, D. C., Kitayama, S., & Nisbett, R. E. (2010). Reasoning about social conflicts improves into old age. *Proceedings of the National Academy of Sciences*, *107*(16), 7246–7250.

Hoppmann, C. A., Coats, A. H., & Blanchard-Fields, F. (2008). Goals and everyday problem solving: Examining the link between age-related goals and problem-solving strategy use. *Aging, Neuropsychology, and Cognition*, *15*(4), 401–423.

Johnson-Laird, P. N. (2006). *How we reason* (Vol. x). New York: Oxford University Press.

Johnson-Laird, P. N., & Wason, P. C. (1970). A theoretical analysis of insight into a reasoning task. *Cognitive Psychology*, *1*(2), 134–148.

Krishna, A. (2012). An integrative review of sensory marketing: Engaging the senses to affect perception, judgment and behavior. *Journal of Consumer Psychology*, *22*(3), 332–351.

Krishna, A., & Schwarz, N. (2014). Sensory marketing, embodiment, and grounded cognition: A review and introduction. *Journal of Consumer Psychology*, *24*(2), 159–168.

Landy, D., Allen, C., & Zednik, C. (2014). A perceptual account of symbolic reasoning. *Frontiers in Psychology*, *5*, 275.

Landy, D., & Goldstone, R. L. (2007). How abstract is symbolic thought? *Journal of Experimental Psychology. Learning, Memory & Cognition*, *33*(4), 720–733.

Larson, J. S., & Billetera, D. M. (2013). Consumer behavior in "equilibrium": How experiencing physical balance increases compromise choice. *Journal of Marketing Research (JMR)*, *50*(4), 535–547.

Manktelow, K. (2012). *Thinking and reasoning: An introduction to the psychology of reason, judgment and decision making*. Hove, UK: Psychology Press.

Manktelow, K. I., & Evans, J. St. B. T. (1979). Facilitation of reasoning by realism: Effect or non-effect? *British Journal of Psychology*, *70*(4), 477–488.

Ping, R. M., Dhillon, S., & Beilock, S. L. (2009). Reach for what you like: The body's role in shaping preferences. *Emotion Review*, *1*(2), 140–150.

Poletiek, F. H. (2001). *Hypothesis-testing behaviour* (Vol. x). New York: Psychology Press.

Stanovich, K. E. (2009). *What intelligence tests miss: The psychology of rational thought* (Vol. xv). New Haven, CT: Yale University Press.

Sternberg, R. J. (1999). The theory of successful intelligence. *Review of General Psychology*, *3*(4), 292–316.

Sugiyama, L. S., Tooby, J., & Cosmides, L. (2002). Cross-cultural evidence of cognitive adaptations for social exchange among the Shiwiar of Ecuadorian Amazonia. *Proceedings of the National Academy of Sciences*, *99*(17), 11537–11542.

Tversky, D., & Kahneman, D. (1983). Extensional versus intuitive reasoning: The conjunction fallacy in probability judgment, *90*(4) *Psychological Review*, *90*, 293–315.

Wason, P. C. (1968). Reasoning about a rule. *Quarterly Journal of Experimental Psychology*, *20*(3), 273–281.

Wason, P. C. (1977). Self-contradictions. In P. N. Johnson-Laird & P. C. Wason (Eds.), *Thinking: Readings in cognitive science* (pp. 114–128). Cambridge: Cambridge University Press.

Worthy, D. A., Gorlick, M. A., Pacheco, J. L., Schnyer, D. M., & Maddox, W. T. (2011). With age comes wisdom: Decision making in younger and older adults. *Psychological Science*, *22*(11), 1375–1380.

10

MORAL REASONING

Véronique Salvano-Pardieu and Sandra Lepeltier

Social interaction and moral development

Social interactions with others play a crucial role in child development. Through social interactions, children begin to establish a sense of "self" and to learn what others expect from them. When playing with others, children learn appropriate social behaviors, such as sharing, cooperating, and respecting the property of others. Social interactions in the early years enhance not only cognitive development but also moral reasoning, perspective taking of others and prosocial behaviors.

Piaget's theory

In studying moral reasoning through rule games with children, Piaget (1932) distinguished three stages in children's awareness of rules related to their age: "premoral judgement" (up to 4–5 y/o, rules cannot be understood); "moral realism" (from 5 to 10 y/o, rules are seen as coming from a higher authority and cannot be changed); and a "moral subjectivism"; (after 10 years old, rules are seen as mutually agreed by the players, and can be changed through mutual consent). Cognitive development leads to the decline of egocentrism and the growth of taking others' perspective. Consequently, the unilateral respect of the higher authority (usually an adult) evolves into an agreement in which equality between peers and an autonomous morality of reciprocity prevail. Going further in the study of moral reasoning, Piaget asked children to judge, in a story, the behaviour of a person according to his intent and the consequence of his action. Children had to give a verbal explanation of their judgement. Piaget's results show that before 10 years old children judge on the basis of consequence rather than on the basis of intent because consequence is objective and does not require taking others' perspective. On the contrary, less egocentric older children take the perspective of others into account and judge according to the subjective intent of the actor. However, Piaget's method has been criticised. Karniol (1978), for instance, has shown that children as young as 5 years old can judge on the basis of intent if intentional actions are explicitly contrasted with accidental actions with equal consequences. More recently, Cushman, Shek-etoff, Wharton, & Carey (2013) have shown that when children are between 4 and 8 years old, their moral judgements become increasingly intent focused. However, their judgement development differs for accidental harm with bad consequence and for attempted harm with benign consequence. In the first situation, children tend to punish the action while they do not in the second. Therefore, during child-hood the decisive element in the moral judgement process shifts from consequence to intent.

Kohlberg's theory

According to Kohlberg (1964, 1976), see also Kohlberg and Kramer (1969), who took over Piaget's studies, the development of moral reasoning can be classified in three levels each containing two stages.

1   The "pre-conventional morality" level. At this level the morality of an action is judged by its direct outcome and external consequence. It is similar to Piaget's moral realism. Moral development is only concerned with the self in an ego-centric way.
2   The "conventional morality" level. This level is similar to Piaget's "moral sub-jectivism". People judge the morality of actions in a conventional way by comparing them with society's views and expectations. They obey rules and follow society's norms, judging as right what conforms to social rules and as wrong what does not.
3   The "post-conventional morality" level. At this level people accept social rules because they accept the general moral principles underlying these rules. Their own ethical principles include life, liberty and justice as unalterable human rights. Therefore, social rules should not be obeyed when they do not respect human rights. Ultimately, moral reasoning is based on the principles of justice, truth and right. As the subject grows from childhood to adulthood, he passes through the different moral stages by according ever more importance to the underlying principles of moral reasoning. Whilst this theory presents an inter-esting understanding of moral reasoning processes, a substantial number of criticisms were issued, the most important one by Carol Gilligan.

Gilligan: moral reasoning and gender

According to Gilligan (1982), the sequence of stages Kohlberg described reflects only the development of male morality, as the participants were all males. Gilligan (1982) thinks moral reasoning differs according to the gender of the participants. She suggests a "female psychology" differs from a "male psychology". In her study, she interviewed 29 women aged between 15 and 33 years old who were attending abortion and pregnancy counselling services. The real-life dilemma of these women was either to have an abortion or to carry on with the pregnancy. Gilligan's results were not congruent with the judgement universally applicable in Kohlberg's last stages. She defined Kohlberg's male judgement process as "justice orientation" because it relies on the human principles of justice, truth and right. Her results show that women focus more on "responsibility" than on "justice". Women made rational, context-dependent judgements that were more concerned with the impact of their behaviour on people's feelings. Contrary to the "male characteristic", which puts principles before people, the "female characteristic" will tend to put people before principle. Gilligan suggests an alternative feminine ethical handling of care and responsibility, a kind of "care orientation" as it is more representative of women's moral reasoning than a "justice orientation". In 1988, Carol Gilligan's further investigations on moral development studied the distinction between justice and care perspectives in the moral development of men and women. This new result showed that both orientations (justice and care) were used by men and women, but care-focus dilemmas were mostly used by women whilst justice-focus dilemmas were mostly used by men. According to Gilligan (1988), both moral orientations stem from different moral structures, causing a gender-determined prevalence for one moral judgement orientation.

Moral judgement

Moreover, some criticisms (Levine, 1976) concerning the usage of long fictive dilemmas and verbal explanation in the experiments were made to the previously mentioned authors. According to Hommers and Lee (2010) and Hommers, Lewand and Ehrmann (2012), Anderson's methodology avoids these issues.

Anderson's social information integration theory

According to Anderson (1981, 1996, 2008, 2013, 2014), a judgement is a decision process based on the combination of data, which can be analysed with a method because each piece of information is given a specific value. Judgement activity follows specific rules. The knowledge of these rules paves the way to a better understanding of the reasoning mechanisms behind moral judgement. Within moral judgement research, the judgement of blame has been the most frequently studied topic, that is evaluating what is known of the consequences of a negative act and of the intent behind it. Indeed, in the judgement of blame, people judge an action by weighing different factors such as the consequence of the action and the actor's level of intent. The algebraic structure of a judgement depends on how people combine these two factors, and the rules of judgement they use, that is the importance they give to each of these factors. When two factors: "bad" intent and "adverse" consequence are combined with their two possible outcomes (with–without), one obtains four possibilities: with intent–with consequence, with intent–without consequence, without intent-with consequence and without intent-without consequence. According to Anderson, three kinds of algebraic structures can be observed (a) mono-factorial: only one factor is taken into account; (b) additive: the importance given to each factor is not modulated according to the other; and (c) multiplicative: the importance given to one factor varies according to the other factor.

A common rule that Surber (1977) observed abides by the following function: Blame $= f$ (w intent $+ w'$ Consequence/ $w + w'$). Where w and w' are weights given by the person to the factors of intent and consequence. This rule is valid only if Intent > 0. While this function remains unchanged during the subject's life span, the weight given to each factor varies with age (Przygotzki & Mullet, 1997). Children give more importance to the consequence factor and less importance to the intent factor than teenagers, young adults and elderly adults. Teenagers and adults give more importance to the intention and less to the consequence. While children develop an additive algebraic structure, the algebraic structure of teenagers and adults is usually multiplicative. However, in addition to the ageing process, others factors affect moral judgement.

Factors affecting moral judgement

Some studies have found that in moral judgement situations involving children, to whom praise or blame has to be assigned, the age of the actor does affect the judgement. For example, leniency arises when judging younger actors who deliberately misbehave (Salvano-Pardieu, Fontaine, Bouazzaoui & Florer, 2009). Analysing teachers' representation of sanction with Anderson's method, Salvano-Pardieu and colleagues (2009) showed that the age of the child, his familial situation and his behaviour affect the teachers' degree of sanction. Two points were clearly observed: all teachers sanction a discipline problem more severely than a schoolwork problem, and teachers in primary school are more lenient with their pupils than teachers in secondary school. In addition, unlike teachers in secondary school, primary school-teachers took into account the familial situation of their pupils and punished less severely the disruptive behaviour and the recidivism of a pupil when he was facing familial difficulties such as the divorce of his parents. In addition, Salvano-Pardieu and colleagues (2009) showed that age and experience of the teachers affected their judgement of sanction. Indeed, the oldest and most experienced teachers were also the most lenient with their pupils and the youngest teachers, who had less than 5 years of teaching experience, the most severe. This result, congruent with previous findings, shows that although moral stage does not evolve anymore during adulthood, the weight given to the factors involved in the moral judgement continues to change with the ageing process. Finally, this result does not corroborate Gilligan's theory. No difference in the blame judgement of men and women was observed.

While adults judge less severely younger actors who deliberately misbehave (Salvano-Pardieu et al., 2009), the opposite is observed with children who have to assign blame to an aggressor (Fontaine, Salvano-Pardieu, Crouzet & Pulford, 2002).

These authors studied the judgement of blame of brutalised and non-brutalised boys from 8 to 13 years old. These boys had to judge in different situations of social interaction the behaviour of an aggressor facing a victim. Different factors were analysed: the nature of the violence (verbal vs. physical), the motive of the aggressor (with vs. without), the presence of the consequence (with vs. without), the age of the aggressor (adult vs. child) and the proximity between the aggressor and the victim (family vs. strangers). The results show that when children have to assign blame, the age of the perpetrator is taken into account if a motive triggered his action. In this case, adults are judged more leniently than children. In addition, brutalised boys, unlike other children, judge more leniently the aggressor even if he has no motive to aggress the child when he is a family member of the victim. This effect observed only with abused children suggests these children reproduce the moral schemes of their parents and judge violent acts as less reprehensible, especially when they come from a relative. When it comes to judging violent acts, abused children present a similar moral algebra than typical children except when the violence comes from a relative, in which case they are more lenient.

While these studies highlight factors affecting moral judgement and its development with typical individuals, they do not inform us on the underlying cognitive structures: their role or their resistance to the ageing process and mental disorders.

The structure of the moral judgement

How people combine intent and consequence is only one aspect of the structure of moral judgement. Judging an action based on social interaction implies understanding the actor's and the victim's thoughts and being aware of the social rules in order to decide if this action is acceptable.

The ability to judge whether a situation or an action is acceptable in a specific context and whether to blame the actor seems to be linked to deontic reasoning. In "deontic" reasoning people understand and judge according to the principles ruling their social lives (Manktelow & Over, 1991). In this type of reasoning, the subject adopts a violation detection strategy (Cummins, 1996). He has to assess if a rule has been violated and, if so, detect which one has been violated. According to Cummins (1996), deontic reasoning is the most basic form of reasoning. People must be aware of social rules before they can apply violation detection and blame the actor. When the subject issues a judgement about the morality of an action and the blame to apportion to the actor, he must be able to use deontic reasoning to decide whether the action is tolerated in social life and whether the actor is blameworthy. In the judgement of blame the person apportioning blame has to determine: (1) whether social rules permitted the action; (2) whether the actor deliberately perpetrated the action; and (3) whether the consequence of this action is serious. This cognitive ability rises at about 2–3 years old.

The second ability, "perspective taking", can be quantified as the effectiveness with which we can reason about others' beliefs and intentions. The capacity to engage in perspective-taking abilities comes usually later (around 4–5 years old) than deontic reasoning. One can appreciate which actions are allowed or forbidden and in what circumstances without awareness of the actor's motivation or intention. The ability to issue a judgement of blame is at first linked with deontic reasoning. If deontic reasoning alone was involved in the judgement of blame, blame would be apportioned always the same according to the consequence for each violated rule. On the contrary, we observed that in many circumstances apportioning blame is modulated by the intent of the actor, the seriousness of his action and the seriousness of the possible consequence. This suggests that the sanction is modulated according to the intentions of the actor; therefore, judging an action requires the Theory of Mind, ToM (i.e. the ability to understand the thoughts, beliefs and mental states of the others) and taking the perspective of others. Indeed, to define the most appropriate sanction, the person judging has to take the two following factors into account: the perpetrator's bad intention or his absence of bad intention, and the seriousness of an adverse consequence or possible adverse consequence. This suggests that those two cognitive abilities – deontic reasoning (linked with violation detection strategy) and taking others' perspective (linked with ToM) – are involved in moral judgement. Different studies have analysed moral judgement to better understand underlying mechanisms and cognitive processes involved in it. The following studies explore the structure of moral judgement with different populations either with or without mental disorders and at different levels of development.

Moral judgement in Alzheimer's patients

In order to better understand how the cognitive process involved in moral judgement is affected by ageing, Fontaine, Salvano-Pardieu, Renoux and Pulford (2004) have compared blame judgement of patients with Alzheimer's disease (AD) with their typical counterparts.

These authors have shown that moral judgement of AD populations differs from the moral judgement of the typical population. They suggest that at least two structures are involved in moral judgement: one that remains stable throughout the illness while the other is affected and ceases to operate. Indeed, Fontaine and colleagues (2004) observed in early-stage Alzheimer's patients that their judgement of blame was affected by the deterioration of their ability to take others' perspective, a recognised Alzheimer's symptom. By contrast, the cognitive ability of these patients to understand what is allowed and to judge according to social rules and deontic reasoning (Manktelow, 1999; Manktelow & Over, 1991) remains preserved. Using Anderson's methodology, the authors asked participants to judge the actor's behaviour in 12 vignettes describing situations of social interaction between two protagonists. Each vignette contained: (a) the degree of intent of the actor (intent vs. no intent) and (b) the presence of the consequences of the act (consequence vs. no consequence). In addition, three different levels of seriousness (low, medium, high) were displayed through the story: a) the "Push" story illustrated the low level of consequence (the victim falls on the floor because of a push which causes his nose to bleed) b) the "Burn" story illustrated the medium level of consequence (the victim's hands are burned by a hot skillet) and c) the "Shot" story illustrated the high level of consequence (the shot wounds the victim's leg deeply). Simple and concrete descriptions of daily life events that are easy to understand and memorise were chosen for this experiment. Under each text was a 25 cm response scale with two extremes: "no blame" as the left anchor and "very severe blame" as the right anchor. Participants had to put a cross on this scale to record the degree of blame they apportioned to the perpetrator.

The results showed that Alzheimer's patients and a control group issued identical judgements when both intent and consequence were observed. But when consequence was absent, the two groups apportioned blame differently. Indeed, when the aggressor acts deliberately with a bad intent but no negative outcome is observed (i.e. without harm to the victim), the seriousness of the potential damage to the victim does not influence the Alzheimer's patients' judging process. They apportion equal blame to an aggressor failing to burn his victim with a hot skillet and an aggressor failing to shoot her. According to Fontaine and colleagues (2004), this difference between the moral algebra (i.e. the combination of intent and consequence) of both groups is supporting evidence that both deontic reasoning and perspective-taking ability are involved in moral judgement. Deontic reasoning operates in the judgement of stories, which display either deliberate intent and adverse consequence or accidental action without consequence. For those stories knowledge of social rules and precepts is sufficient to judge the situation: deliberately harmful actions resulting in an adverse consequence require blame and accidental actions without consequence do not require blame. This principle, learned in early life, is the basis of social rules. On the other hand, when bad intent is present and consequence absent, an accurate judgement process requires imagining the aggressor's harmful aim and the possible damages attached to it, that is to say perspective-taking ability. When the action is accidental but results in a bad consequence, perspective taking is also necessary to understand the actor did not act on purpose even though adverse consequence is observed.

Teenagers with Autism Spectrum Disorder (ASD)

Fontaine and colleagues' (2004) assumption that at least two different cognitive structures are involved in moral judgement, one based on deontic reasoning and social rules and the other on taking others' perspective, was confirmed by a recent study with Autism Spectrum Disorder (ASD) and typical teenagers. In this study, using the same Anderson's method as Fontaine and colleagues (2004), Salvano-Pardieu and colleagues (2015) have analysed the judgement of blame of 13-year-old adolescents. The participants had to apportion blame to the perpetrator in the case of 12 vignettes describing social interactions between two protagonists, the behavior of the actor according to his intent (deliberately harmful vs. accidental), the presence of an adverse outcome (with vs. without) and the seriousness of this outcome (low, medium and high). The level of seriousness was displayed through the story: the low-level "Push" described a push the consequence of which was a bruised knee, the medium-level "Punch" a punch which resulted in a broken nose and the high-level "Knife" a stab which saw the victim injured with a stabbed leg. Four vignettes were set up for each story: 1) Deliberate action with an adverse consequence, 2) Deliberate action without consequence, 3) Accidental action with an adverse consequence and 4) Accidental action without consequence.

If a part of the blame judgement relies on deontic reasoning and perspective-taking ability, then participants impaired in perspective-taking ability such as those with ASD should give significantly less weight to intent and significantly more weight to consequence than typical teenagers. Indeed, judging the intent of the actor requires perspective-taking ability, especially if the negative intent does not induce an adverse consequence. On the other hand, judging the consequence does not require perspective taking, consequence being an objective and visible fact. The results revealed that adolescents with and without ASD judged intent and consequence in a very different manner. While both groups were able to judge an action by taking into account the actor's intention and the action's consequence, thus corroborating previous results (Grant, Boucher, Riggs & Grayson, 2005; Rogé & Mullet, 2011), it was clearly observed that the ASD teenagers gave less importance to the intent factor than the typically developed teenagers. They took into account bad intent only if the adverse consequence was observed. In the other situations – bad intent without adverse consequence or accidental action with adverse consequence – they did not judge the action on the basis of intent but on the basis of consequence. In addition, ASD teenagers considered intent and consequence as two independent factors; they did not combine intent and consequence in a multiplicative algebra as typical adolescents and adults did. On the contrary, their moral algebra was additive and similar to that of young children under 10 years old. Unlike adolescents with autism, typical teenagers judged on the basis of the actor's intention rather than the action's outcome and could combine intent and consequence in a multiplicative moral algebra as already proven by many studies (Moran et al., 2011; Przygotzki & Mullet, 1997; Rogé & Mullet, 2011; Turiel, 1998). Salvano-Pardieu and colleagues (2015) have also observed that typical teenagers increase the severity of their blame with the seriousness of the adverse outcome: the higher the seriousness of the outcome, the higher the blame. This difference between the three levels of seriousness of the outcome is not observed with the ASD group, who judges with the same severity the two highest levels of seriousness. This result is congruent with previous research (Zalla, Barlassina, Buon & Leboyer, 2011), which demonstrated that adults with high-functioning autism (HFA) or ASD failed to distinguish between moral transgressions with different levels of seriousness. Adolescents with autism can judge an action by taking into account the intention of the actor and the consequence of the action, but impairment in perspective taking seems to hold them to the typical moral algebra of younger and still egocentric children relying on an additive consequence-focused pattern as well as an inaccurate representation of the consequence's seriousness. This inaccurate representation of the consequence's seriousness could explain the misunderstanding of certain social situations and the dangers attached to them.

This difference in the moral algebra between ASD and typical teenagers supports the suggestion of Fontaine and colleagues (2004) that at least two different cognitive structures are involved in moral judgement: one based on deontic reasoning and the other on perspective taking. Deontic reasoning seems to be preserved in adolescents with ASD, which explains their ability to perceive what is allowed in a given social context. They consequently can judge deliberate actions with adverse consequence and accidental actions without consequence in the same way as typical adolescent or adults. By contrast, their impairment in perspective taking prevents them from understanding the victim's perspective and therefore judging an action according to the perpetrator's intent. In this case deliberate harmful actions not followed by an adverse consequence are not judged while accidental actions followed by an adverse consequence are severely judged.

These last studies highlight the role of perspective taking in the judgement of blame and its evolution with the different stages of development. This cognitive ability allows individuals to understand the motives of an actor and determine if his action is perpetrated deliberately or accidentally and adjust their answer to this social situation. However, in certain cases a deliberately harmful act leading to an adverse outcome can be understood and partly excused because of mitigating circumstances. In this situation, one can empathise with the aggressor and reduce the blame. This ability to take mitigating circumstances into account could be related to the ability to judge on the basis of intent. Indeed, understanding the motive of an aggressor and his justification is based on perspective taking of others. The following study (Lepeltier, Salvano-Pardieu, Combalbert Kilpatrick and Fontaine 2015) investigated the role of extenuating circumstances in the judgement of blame at different stages of development.

Moral judgement and extenuating circumstances

The concept of extenuating or mitigating circumstances appeared in studies on moral judgement presenting two factors: motive of the aggressor (with vs. without) and outcome of this aggression (with vs. without). According to Fontaine and colleagues (2002), the motive underlying the aggression would mitigate and reduce the severity of blame attached to the aggressor. For example, insulting someone with a motive (good reason) was judged more leniently than insulting someone without motive, that is for personal gain (bad reason). So some information could mitigate and reduce the sanction given to the aggressor, and this mitigating skill appears at 5 years old. Indeed, Rule and Duker (1973), Rule, Nesdale, and McAra (1974) and Keltikangas-Järvinen and Lindeman (1997) showed that 5-year-old boys and girls can distinguish a perpetrator's underlying motivations, especially when consequences are minor. Martin and Ross (1996) confirmed this result. In studying conflicts between siblings and reactions of their parents, these authors pointed out that some circumstances could mitigate a sanction (i.e. provocation, accidental harm, consent of the victim), and 5-year-old children understood these circumstances. In 1982, Darley and Zanna worked on accepting excuses and showed that if the aggression was an emotional response to a provocation, the sanction was reduced. However, developmental and ageing processes affect the importance given to the extenuating circumstances (Darley, Klosson & Zanna, 1978). From these studies, some authors conducted research on different types of situations and presented different factors in order to determine which one could be considered an extenuating circumstance in the judgement of blame. According to Fincham and Roberts (1985), the age of the aggressor (the perpetrator is a child) and mental disease (the perpetrator is schizophrenic) are considered mitigating circumstances. Indeed, blame assigned to a child was lower than blame assigned to a mentally disturbed person, and blame assigned in this last case was lower than blame assigned to a typical adult. Finally, Bègue and Subra (2008) highlighted the effect of alcohol as a mitigating circumstance. Most of these studies analysed extenuating circumstances with a focus on the victim's behaviour (i.e. provocation or self-defence).

Extenuating circumstances attached to the aggressor's motive had already been highlighted in Fontaine and colleagues' (2002) research on brutalised children's moral judgement. To better understand how the ageing process affects the ability to take mitigating circumstances into account, Lepeltier and colleagues (2015) have studied extenuating circumstances in the judgement of blame of children, adolescent and young adults, using Anderson's theory and methodology as in previous studies (Fontaine et al., 2002, 2004; Salvano-Pardieu et al., 2009, 2015). In this study 16 vignettes were used, describing short social interactions between a perpetrator and a victim. Three different factors were analysed: a) the behaviour of the aggressor according to three levels of extenuating circumstances (no extenuating circumstances, the aggressor has been insulted, the aggressor has been slapped), b) the presence of an adverse outcome (with vs. without) and c) the level of seriousness of the outcome (low vs. medium). As in Salvano-Pardieu and colleagues (2015), these levels of seriousness were depicted through stories: "Push" and "Punch".

Results show that children, teenagers and adults consider extenuating circumstances differently. Children take extenuating circumstances into account only when an adverse consequence is observed. In this situation, they judge more leniently an aggressor who has been slapped or insulted and much more harshly an aggressor without any extenuating circumstances. This result, congruent with previous results, confirms that children under 10 judge the motive of the aggressor and the extenuating circumstances on the basis of the outcome more than the intent of the aggressor. A different moral algebra is observed with adolescents; they consider an insult a greater offense than a slap and judge more leniently an aggressor who was insulted than an aggressor who was slapped. In addition, they always take the extenuating circumstances into account and judge less severely an aggressor with extenuating circumstances, whatever the outcome of his action. This also confirms previous results observed with adolescents (Darley et al., 1978; Salvano-Pardieu et al., 2015), who give more importance to the intent of the perpetrator than to the outcome of his action when judging. According to Lepeltier and colleagues (2015), adolescents' judgement would be influenced by their specific relationships with their peers and their higher sensitivity to others. At this level of development, the importance of social links with peers would explain why teenagers excuse aggressive behaviours and systematically take extenuating circumstances into account when apportioning blame. This context-dependent judgement, more concerned with the impact of behaviour on people's feelings than the strict application of social rules, could correspond to a care orientation (Gilligan, 1982, 1988).

Finally, adults judge less severely an aggressor who has been insulted whereas they judge with the same severity an aggressor who has been slapped and an aggressor without extenuating circumstances. However, unlike with children, this difference is observed only in the absence of adverse consequence. If the action has consequences, extenuating circumstances are not taken into account in the judgement. This could reflect the internalisation of a social rule observed at the conventional level (Kohlberg, 1976). At this level, hitting somebody else is no longer acceptable because the priority is to keep social relationships unbroken and respect social rules. Unlike with adolescents, this absence of mitigating circumstances in adults' judgement of blame and the importance given to social rules could reflect a justice orientation (Gilligan, 1982, 1988).

Conclusion

When comparing these studies on moral judgement, it seems that the ability to judge on the basis of extenuating circumstances and on the basis of intent refers to different cognitive structures. While moral judgement shifts from the objective outcomes to the subjective intent of the actor, and judging on the basis of intent develops ever more from childhood to adulthood, taking into account extenuating circumstances does not follow this evolution. Children are cognitively able to take extenuating circumstances into account, but not as much as adolescents, who are much more sensitive to the motive of the perpetrator than to social rules. The importance of rules for children and social relationships for adults reflects a justice orientation, which means they reduce a punishment only in particular conditions, while the importance of relationships with peers and the care orientation of adolescents make them take extenuating circumstances into account whatever the situation.

Furthermore, the development of moral algebras is not equivalent. While moral algebras of intentions and consequences switch from an additive structure to a multiplicative structure as a person develops, this pattern is no longer observed with extenuating circumstances and consequences. These studies pave the way to a better understanding of the cognitive structures underlying moral judgement. Identifying those cognitive structures and their way of operating will enable us to deliver help to patients with mental health problems and to offer them more independence in their social life.

References

Anderson, N. H. (1981). *Foundations of information integration theory*. New York: Academic Press.
Anderson, N. H. (1996). *A functional theory of cognition*. Mahwah, NJ: Erlbaum.

Anderson, N. H. (2008). *Unified social cognition (Vol. x)*. New York: Psychology Press.

Anderson, N. H. (2013). Unified psychology based on three laws of information integration. *Review of General Psychology, 17*(2), 125–132.

Anderson, N. H. (2014). *Contributions to information integration theory: Volume 1: Cognition*. Hove, UK: Psychology Press.

Bègue, L., & Subra, B. (2008). Alcohol and aggression: Perspectives on controlled and uncontrolled social information processing. *Social and Personality Psychology Compass, 2*(1), 511–538.

Cummins, D. D. (1996). Evidence for the innateness of deontic reasoning. *Mind and Language, 11*, 160–190.

Cushman, F., Sheketoff, R., Wharton, S., & Carey, S. (2013). The development of intent-based moral judgment. *Cognition, 127*(1), 6–21.

Darley, J. M., Klosson, E. C., & Zanna, M. P. (1978). Intentions and their contexts in the moral judgments of children and adults. *Child Development, 49*(1), 66.

Darley, J. M., & Zanna, M. P. (1982). Making moral judgments. *American Scientist, 70*(5), 515–521.

Fincham, F. D., & Roberts, C. (1985). Intervening causation and the mitigation of responsibility for harm doing: II. The role of limited mental capacities. *Journal of Experimental Social Psychology, 21*(2), 178–194.

Fontaine, R., Salvano-Pardieu, V., Crouzet, S., & Pulford, B. D. (2002). Physically abused and nonmaltreated boys' moral judgments of violence. *Child Study Journal, 32*(4), 215–230.

Fontaine, R., Salvano-Pardieu, V., Renoux, P., & Pulford, B. (2004). Judgment of blame in Alzheimer's disease sufferers. *Aging, Neuropsychology and Cognition, 11*(4), 379–394.

Gilligan, C. (1982). *In a different voice: Psychological theory and women's development* (Vol. XXX). Cambridge, MA: Harvard University Press.

Gilligan, C. (1988). *Mapping the moral domain: A contribution of women's thinking to psychological theory and education* (Vol. 2). Cambridge, MA: Harvard University Press.

Gilligan, C., & Attanucci, J. (1988). Two moral orientations: Gender differences and similarities. *Merrill-Palmer Quarterly, 34*(3), 223–237.

Grant, C. M., Boucher, J., Riggs, K. J., & Grayson, A. (2005). Moral understanding in children with autism. *Autism, 9*(3), 317–331.

Hommers, W., & Lee, W.-Y. (2010). Unifying Kohlberg with information integration: The moral algebra of recompense and of Kohlbergian moral informers. *Psicológica, 31*(3), 689–706.

Hommers, W., Lewand, M., & Ehrmann, D. (2012). Testing the moral algebra of two Kohlbergian informers. *Psicologica, 33*(3), 515–532.

Karniol, R. (1978). Children's use of intention cues in evaluating behaviour. *Psychological Bulletin, 85*, 76–85.

Keltikangas-Järvinen, L., & Lindeman, M. (1997). Evaluation of theft, lying, and fighting in adolescence. *Journal of Youth and Adolescence, 26*(4), 467–483.

Kohlberg, L. (1964). Development of moral character and moral ideology. In L. W. Hoffman & M. L. Hoffman (Eds.). (1964). *Review of child development research*. New York: Russell Sage Foundation.

Kohlberg, L. (1976). Moral stages and moralization: The cognitive-developmental approach. In T. Lickona (Ed.). *Moral Development and Behavior: Theory, Research, and Social Issues*. New York: Holt, Rinehart and Winston.

Kohlberg, L. (1984). *The psychology of moral development: The nature and validity of moral stages*. New York: Harper & Row.

Kohlberg, L., & Kramer, R. (1969). Continuities and discontinuities in childhood and adult moral development. *Human development, 12*, 93–120.

Lepeltier, S., Salvano-Pardieu, V., Combalbert, N., Kilpatrick, S., & Fontaine, R. (Manuscript under review). Extenuating circumstances in judgment of blame of typical children, adolescents and young adults. *Cognitive Development*.

Levine, C. (1976). Role-taking standpoint and adolescent usage of Kohlberg's conventional stages of moral reasoning. *Journal of Personality and Social Psychology, 34*(1), 41–46.

Manktelow, K. (1999). *Reasoning and thinking*. Hove, UK: Psychology Press.

Manktelow, K. I., & Over, D. E. (1991). Social roles and utilities in reasoning with deontic conditionals. *Cognition, 39*, 85–105.

Martin, J. L., & Ross, H. S. (1996). Do mitigating circumstances influence family reactions to physical aggression? *Child Development, 67*(4), 1455–1466.

Moran, J. M., Young, L. L., Saxe, R., Lee, S. M., O'Young, D., Mavros, P. L., & Gabrieli, J. D. (2011). Impaired theory of mind for moral judgment in high-functioning autism. *Proceedings of the National Academy of Sciences of the United State of America, PNAS, 108*(7), 2688–2692.

Piaget, J. (1932). *Le jugement moral chez l'enfant*. Paris: Presses universitaires de France.

Przygotzki, N., & Mullet, E. (1997). Moral judgment and aging. *Revue Européenne de Psychologie Appliquée, 47*, 15–21.

Rogé, B., & Mullet, E. (2011). Moral judgment among children, adolescents and adults with autism. *Autism, 15*, 702–712.

Rule, B. G., & Duker, P. (1973). Effects of intentions and consequences on children's evaluations of aggressors. *Journal of Personality and Social Psychology, 27*(2), 184.

Rule, B. G., Nesdale, A. R., & McAra, M. J. (1974). Children's reactions to information about the intentions underlying an aggressive act. *Child Development, 45*, 794–798.

Salvano-Pardieu, V., Blanc, R., Combalbert, N., Pierratte, A., Lepeltier, S., Manktelow, K., Gimenes, G., Barthelemy, C., Maintier, C., & Fontaine, R. (Manuscript under review). Judgement of blame in teenagers with Asperger's syndrome. *Thinking and Reasoning*. (in revision)

Salvano-Pardieu, V., Fontaine, R., Bouazzaoui, B., & Florer, F. (2009). Teacher's judgement of sanction in disciplinary and teaching practice. *Teaching and Teacher Education, 25*, 1–11.

Surber, C. F. (1977). Developmental processes in social inference: Averaging of intentions and consequences in moral judgement. *Developmental Psychology, 13*, 654–665.

Turiel, E. (1998). The development of morality. In W. Damon (Series Ed.) & N. Eisenberg (Volume Ed.), *Handbook of child psychology* (Vol. 3, Fifth edition, pp 863–932). New York: Wiley.

Zalla, T., Barlassina, L., Buon, M., & Leboyer, M. (2011). Moral judgment in adults with autism spectrum disorders. *Cognition, 121*(1), 115–126.

11

RATIONALITY AND BACKWARD INDUCTION IN CENTIPEDE GAMES

Andrew M. Colman, Eva M. Krockow, Caren Frosch, and Briony D. Pulford

Among all the thousands of strategic games discovered and investigated since the early development of game theory in the 1920s, especially after the publication of von Neumann and Morgenstern's (1944) landmark book *Games and Economic Behavior*, the Centipede game stands out as perhaps the most perplexing and paradoxical of them all. Rosenthal (1981) introduced it as an incidental comment (pp. 96–97) in a discussion of an entirely different game (the Chain-Store game). Binmore (1987) first named the Centipede game in print after the passing resemblance of its game tree to a multi-legged insect, as can be seen in Figure 11.1, where Rosenthal's original version of the game is depicted.

The rules of the game are simple. Starting at the left, Player A makes the initial move at the first numbered *decision node* by choosing either STOP or GO. Choosing STOP causes the game to end at that point (the label attached to this option gives a big clue), and choosing GO leads to the second numbered decision node, where Player B chooses between STOP and GO. Play continues in this fashion, with Players A and B taking turns choosing moves until one of them chooses STOP. If neither player chooses STOP at any of the 10 decision nodes, then the game ends naturally after the final node. The numbers in the *terminal nodes* at the feet of the Centipede and on its antenna protruding to the right are the payoffs to the players when the game ends, either because one of them chooses STOP or because the game reaches its natural end. Following the normal convention in game theory, the first payoff in each terminal node is for Player A and the second for Player B. Hence, if Player A chooses STOP at the first decision node, then each player receives a zero payoff; if Player A chooses GO at the first decision node and Player B chooses STOP at the second, then Player A loses one unit of payoff and Player B gains three units; and so on. Formally, the payoffs are measured in units of von Neumann–Morgenstern *utilities*, and these reflect the players' true preferences, incorporating all their tastes and predilections, selfish or altruistic motives, and so

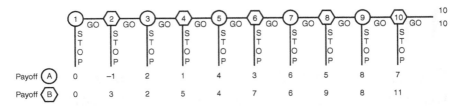

FIGURE 11.1   Game tree of Rosenthal's (1981) original (as yet unnamed) Centipede game

on, because they are defined in terms of the players' choices. But it is simpler to think of the payoffs as monetary units such as pounds sterling, euros, or dollars, and this is harmless enough for most purposes.

Rosenthal's original version in Figure 11.1 is a linear Centipede game, because the sum of payoffs to the player pair increases linearly across successive terminal nodes: the sums are 0, 2, 4, 6, . . ., 20, increasing by exactly two units from one terminal node to the next. A STOP move brings the game to an end without affecting the payoffs; a GO move alters the payoffs that the players have accumulated up to that point, invariably imposing a cost c (one unit in this particular version of the game) on the player who chooses it and conferring a benefit b (three units in this case) on the co-player. A GO move is altruistic inasmuch as it benefits another individual at some cost to the player who chooses it (a standard definition of altruism); but it is conventional to identify GO moves with cooperation and STOP moves with defection, because repeated GO moves benefit the player pair, whereas a STOP move provides a short-term selfish advantage to the individual player who chooses it. The number of decision nodes is arbitrary, and adding further legs to the Centipede does not affect any of its key strategic properties.

The fact that the payoffs shown in the terminal nodes increase as the game progresses is not because the cost and benefit parameters c and b change (they remain fixed) but merely because payoffs accumulate if both players keep choosing GO moves – a point mathematically challenged reviewers and editors sometimes struggle to grasp. A linear Centipede game always has fixed c and b, with $c \le b$, and it provides a simple model of repeated interactions between two individuals with alternating opportunities for reciprocal altruism and continual temptations for unilateral defection. An everyday example that we have frequently used is a reciprocally cooperative relationship between two university researchers who take turns reviewing and providing feedback on each other's manuscripts and grant applications, each reviewing task imposing a small cost on the reviewer but providing a larger benefit to the recipient. It is not difficult to see that everyday professional, economic, and social life involves numerous interactions with the general strategic structure of the linear Centipede game.

What, then, is so perplexing and paradoxical about this game? The answer emerges from a *backward induction* argument, so called because of its resemblance to mathematical induction, one of the standard techniques for proving theorems. The argument appears to establish that there should be no cooperation, and that a rational Player A should defect at the first decision node, yielding zero payoffs to both players. To reach this conclusion, the argument begins by assuming that the 10th decision node has been reached, where Player B faces the final decision in the game. Player B must choose between defecting and earning a payoff of 11 or cooperating and receiving a payoff of 10 when the game terminates naturally. To specify rational choice in this (or any) game, we usually base our deductions on standard game-theoretic *common knowledge and rationality* assumptions:

1   Rationality assumption: Both players are instrumentally rational in the sense that they have unlimited cognitive capacities and, whenever faced with a choice between two options with known payoffs, they invariably choose the one yielding the higher individual payoff to themselves;
2   Knowledge assumption: Both players know the rules of the game and the players' preferences, represented by the payoffs shown in the game tree;
3   Common knowledge assumption: Assumptions (1) and (2) are *common knowledge* in the sense that both players know them, both know that both know them, and so on ad infinitum (although only a finite number of iterations are required in a finite game, as we shall see).

Given these assumptions, at the 10th decision node, Player B will choose STOP. This follows from Assumptions 1 and 2, because STOP is the payoff-maximizing option (11 is better than 10), and Player B knows this without even considering what Player A knows. We can now deduce that Player A will defect at the immediately preceding ninth decision node, because the choice there is between defecting and earning a payoff of 8 or cooperating and earning a payoff of 7 when Player B defects on the next move. This follows from Assumptions 1 and 2, as before, plus one iteration of the common knowledge Assumption 3: Player A needs to know that Player B is instrumentally rational, otherwise Player A would not be certain that Player B would defect at the 10th decision node, if given the chance, and without this knowledge, Player A's choice at the ninth decision node would not be strictly determined. Following this line of reasoning further, it becomes clear that Player B will defect at the eighth decision node. This follows from all three common knowledge and rationality assumptions, and in this case Player B needs to know that Player A is rational and that Player A knows that Player B is rational, hence another iteration of the common knowledge Assumption 3 is required. Continuing in the same way, the backward induction argument unfolds, move by move, requiring one more iteration of common knowledge for each move, and it always leads to the conclusion that the rational move is to defect. Eventually, we arrive at the first decision node, where Player A will defect, because of Assumptions 1, 2, and nine iterations of Assumption 3. This outcome is the *subgame perfect Nash equilibrium* of the game, because it is, in effect, arrived at by the iterated elimination of weakly dominated strategies, and it is easy to prove that this ensures subgame perfection

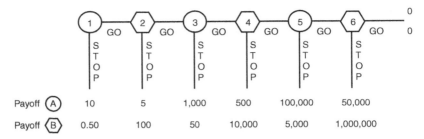

FIGURE 11.2 Game tree of Aumann's (1992) exponential Centipede game

(Osborne & Rubinstein, 1994, section 6.6.1, pp. 108–110, provide a straightforward proof). Game theorists acknowledge this as the uniquely rational outcome of this game.

The backward induction argument appears to establish that two rational players who understand the Centipede game in Figure 11.1 will earn precisely nothing from it, because Player A will defect at the first decision node. A similar conclusion applies even to exponential versions of the game, in which the sum of payoffs to the player pair is multiplied by a fixed amount at each terminal node rather than having a fixed amount added, as in a linear version. An extreme example of an exponential Centipede game, due to Aumann (1992),[1] is shown in Figure 11.2.

Note that Aumann's (1992) exponential Centipede game has zero payoffs in the final terminal node on the right; these are the payoffs that await the players if neither defects at any of the six decision nodes. This *zero-end* modification means that one of the players is virtually certain to defect at some point. The zero-end structure and the exponential form of the payoff function – payoffs mount up rapidly, increasing tenfold at each decision node, until the end – generate much more psychological pressure than Rosenthal's (1981) original version, but the logic of the game, and in particular the backward induction argument, remains the same despite these seemingly radical changes. Given the common knowledge and rationality assumptions, Player A will still defect at the first decision node, leading to the game's unique subgame perfect Nash equilibrium and yielding payoffs of 10 to A and 0.50 to Player B, although fabulous wealth is on offer if both players cooperate up to the sixth decision node.

Is the backward induction argument valid?

Can the backward induction argument possibly be valid? Instrumental rationality is defined as invariably choosing the option that maximizes one's own payoff, but backward induction leads to a solution that requires Player A to defect on the first move, and this actually *minimizes* Player A's payoff, quite literally in a standard Centipede game, and virtually in a zero-end version, where only the natural end is even worse. Game theorists acknowledge that this conclusion seems paradoxical, but the validity of the backward induction argument that underpins it has been endorsed by many authorities well qualified to make the call, including Nobel laureate, mathematician, and game theorist Robert Aumann (1995, 1998). In one of his publications, Aumann (1992) proved that even the tiniest modicum of irrationality destroys the backward induction argument and justifies cooperation, to the players' mutual benefit. If the players are in fact perfectly rational, then a *belief* that there is a miniscule probability that one of them will deviate from rationality suffices to justify cooperation. Aumann even goes as far as to suggest that it is not necessary for either of the players to actually believe that one or both of them may be the tiniest bit irrational, provided that they tacitly agree to ignore the fact that both are fully rational:

> Most of us have experienced situations where some harmful fact is perfectly well known but is studiously overlooked by everybody. In this case, the harmful fact is the players' rationality(!). More precisely, the fact itself need not be harmful, but common knowledge of it would be. The above approach enables us to understand this phenomenon within the context of the theory.
>
> *(Aumann, 1992, p. 226)*

This seems to us an artificial and unsatisfactory workaround. It is inadequate because it leaves the absurd conclusion intact when common knowledge of rationality prevails without any ifs or buts; and it seems unnecessary if the absurd conclusion does not follow from the assumptions in the first place. We wish to argue, tentatively and with due deference to many of our distinguished game-theoretical colleagues, that the conclusion does not follow, and that the backward induction argument is fatally flawed.

According to the backward induction argument, at the second decision node (Figure 11.1 or Figure 11.2), Player B will defect, in the certain knowledge that a cooperative move would be followed by Player A defecting at the third decision node. This deduction is supposed to follow from the common knowledge and rationality assumptions. But, given those assumptions, what is Player B supposed to think when choosing a move at the second decision node? If Player B has the luxury of moving at all, Player A must have cooperated at the first decision node. According to the assumptions, Player B knows that Player A is instrumentally rational and that Player A knows that Player B is also instrumentally rational and would therefore defect at the second decision node, if given the chance, yielding a smaller payoff to Player A than the payoff if Player A defects at the first decision node. These two items of knowledge seem mutually contradictory: a rational Player A would not cooperate at the first decision node, because defection would pay better (in Figure 11.1, it is obvious that 0 is better than − 1, and in Figure 11.2, that 10 is better than 5).

It seems to follow that Player B, contemplating a choice at the second decision node, is confronted with a situation that is literally impossible, given the common knowledge and rationality assumptions. Either Player A is not rational, or the payoffs are not as Player B believes them to be, or perhaps not as Player A believes them to be, or one of the players has misunderstood the rules of the game – something, at least, must have gone wrong. Furthermore, whatever it is that has gone wrong makes it impossible for Player B to predict how Player A would respond to a cooperative move. A Player A who is willing to cooperate at the first decision node may cooperate again at the third; there is simply no way of knowing, because the theory has collapsed and the principles supposedly determining Player A's actions have been invalidated. Player B simply has no rational basis for choosing a move at the second decision node, and the same applies a fortiori at later nodes.

The backward induction argument begins with a consideration of Player B's move at the final decision node, but to have arrived at that point, several moves must have occurred that are inconsistent with the common knowledge and rationality assumptions. In both Figure 11.1 and Figure 11.2, Player B still has a valid reason to defect, because defection pays better than cooperation, and the common knowledge assumption is not required at that point. But, in Figure 11.1, at the previous (penultimate) decision node, Player A cannot know that defection pays better than cooperation, because Player B's response is indeterminate. At this penultimate decision node, Player A has no basis for rational choice, because the common knowledge assumption bears the load of the whole argument, and Player A knows that it is not true, because the game could not have progressed to that point if it were true. Nothing can validly be deduced about Player A's move, and the backward induction argument therefore collapses. The same applies to Player B at Node 4 in Figure 11.2.

Aumann was not unaware of this problem, of course; rather, he carefully sidestepped it by redefining rationality according to what follows and burying the past in a manner resembling feigned dense amnesia:

> Rationality of a player at a vertex v is defined in terms of what happens at vertices after v, his payoff *if* v is reached. The idea is that when programming his automaton at v, the player does so as if v will be reached – even when he knows that it will not be! Each choice must be rational "in its own right" – a player may not rely on what happened previously to get him "off the hook."
> *(Aumann, 1995, p. 12)*

This is the crux of our disagreement. In Figure 11.1, at the ninth decision node, Player A is well and truly "off the hook" because, without ignoring the past entirely, Player A has no way of knowing what will happen after a cooperative move, and therefore no way of deciding whether STOP or GO is the payoff-maximizing move. The same dilemma confronts Player B at the fourth decision node in Figure 11.2. Centipede is a game of perfect information, and nothing in the common knowledge and rationality assumptions, nor in any commonsense interpretation of rationality, justifies a pretense by a player that what is known to have happened previously did not happen. In game theory, players are usually assumed to know the specification of the game and everything that can validly be deduced from any moves that have been made. Aumann's (1995) suggestion seems to us an inadequate and, above all, unjustified solution to the crucial problem that undermines the backward induction argument.

Experimental evidence

Whatever the rights or wrongs of the backward induction argument, human decision makers certainly do not follow its prescriptions in incentivized experimental Centipede games. Experimental players are much more cooperative, and they therefore earn much better payoffs. McKelvey and Palfrey (1992) were the first to investigate decision making in six-node exponential Centipede games with non-zero payoffs in the terminal node at the end; they found that only 0.7% of all games ended at the first decision node, and 1.4% of the games even continued until the natural end. McKelvey and Palfrey reported some learning effects – more frequent use of competitive defecting strategies – with increasing experience in repetitions of the game, but these effects were comparatively small and did not result in equilibrium play. Similar results were found in a replication study reported by Kawagoe and Takizawa (2012) and in Nagel and Tang's (1998) investigation of learning in 12-node exponential Centipede games. Even higher levels of cooperation were reported for Centipede games with linearly increasing payoff functions, like Figure 11.1 (Bornstein, Kugler, & Ziegelmeyer, 2004; Gerber & Wichardt, 2010).

These studies provide overwhelming evidence against the use of backward induction reasoning in the Centipede game, inspiring Levitt, List, and Sadoff (2011) to investigate the move choices of expert chess players (including several Grandmasters), who would arguably have greater iterated reasoning skills than the average undergraduate experimental participant. Interesting, the chess players' choices were remarkably similar to those of previous student participants and adhered to the game-theoretical solution in only 3.9% of all games. Furthermore, not a single chess player with perfect backward induction reasoning ability (as measured with the Race to 100 game, a strictly competitive game also requiring backward induction reasoning for its solution) stopped the Centipede game at the first decision node. These findings suggest that cooperation in the Centipede game cannot be accounted for merely in terms of limited cognitive abilities. Instead, experimental evidence suggests that other-regarding preferences such as concerns for the payoffs to the player pair influence the players' strategies (Pulford, Colman, Lawrence, & Krockow, 2016; Pulford, Krockow, Colman, & Lawrence, 2016).

Backward induction in the history of game theory

The first formal theorem in the history of game theory was (arguably) based on backward induction. Long before von Neumann (1928) proved his famous minimax theorem, marking the official birthday of game theory, German mathematician Ernst Zermelo (1913) proved a theorem about strictly competitive games of *perfect information* – games in which each player knows all moves made previously.

He proved that chess (or any other such game) is *strictly determined*, in the sense that there is either a guaranteed winning strategy for one of the players or guaranteed drawing strategies for both. The proof does not provide any method for actually finding the winning or drawing strategies – in the case of chess it is still not known whether White (or conceivably Black) has a winning strategy or whether both players have drawing strategies, although the latter seems most likely. Most authorities (e.g., Binmore, 1992, p. 32; Fudenberg & Tirole, 1991, p. 91) interpret Zermelo's method of proof as a form of backward induction, although some (e.g., Schwalbe & Walker, 2001) disagree. Zermelo certainly began his proof by considering terminal positions – positions from which one of the players can force a win or a draw, and he proceeded roughly as follows. There must be only a finite set of such positions, because (in chess) there are only 64 squares and, at most, 32 pieces and pawns. Assume that in all the positions that can lead immediately to those terminal positions the player whose turn it is invariably makes a best move (which must exist), and in all positions immediately preceding those, players also choose best moves. It must be possible in principle, though not in practice, to roll back through the unimaginably large game tree, specifying best moves in every position that could arise. This procedure would, in effect, construct a fully specified best-move strategy for each player, and bringing the two together would necessarily lead to a win for White, a win for Black, or a draw.

Von Neumann and Morgenstern (1944, chap. 15, pp. 112–128) surprisingly omitted to cite Zermelo's (1913) classic proof, but they included a detailed and formal discussion of backward induction in strictly competitive (two-player, zero-sum) games. Their presentation is long and abstract, and some of their mathematical notation obsolete, so that their chapter on backward induction is now largely inaccessible even to professional mathematicians.

The locus classicus of backward induction is the discussion in the standard textbook of game theory by Luce and Raiffa (1957) of finitely repeated or *finite-horizon* Prisoner's Dilemma games. We shall outline their argument using the now conventional version of the game shown in Figure 11.3. Player I chooses a strategy corresponding to a row, either *C* (cooperate) or *D* (defect), Player II independently chooses a strategy corresponding to a column (*C* or *D*), and the numbers in the cell where the two strategy choices intersect are the resulting payoffs to Players I and II respectively for that outcome of the game. From Player I's point of view, *D* is a dominant strategy, because it yields a better payoff than *C* irrespective of Player II's

II

	C	*D*
C	3, 3	0, 5
D	5, 0	1, 1

I

FIGURE 11.3 The Prisoner's Dilemma game with conventional payoffs

strategy choice (5 rather than 3 if Player II chooses *C*; and 1 rather than 0 if Player II chooses *D*); and *D* is similarly a dominant strategy for Player II. This establishes that, for a single play of this game, defection is the only rational strategy for both players, despite the fact that both are better off if both cooperate. However, in an *infinite-horizon* version, or if the game is repeated an *indefinite* number of times between the same players, then it is no longer the case that defection is uniquely rational, because there are reasons for cooperating, including signaling to the co-player a conditional willingness to cooperate by playing Tit for Tat ("I'll cooperate if you will"). However, these reasons exist only when there are further rounds to be played, because they necessarily involve making sacrifices in the short run in the hope of larger payoffs later on.

What Luce and Raiffa (1957, section 5.5, pp. 97–102) showed was that, in a finite-horizon Prisoner's Dilemma game, if both players know in advance that exactly 100 rounds (for example) are to be played, then the only rational strategy is to defect on every round. The proof begins with the last round. Here there is no reason for either player to cooperate, because there are no subsequent rounds to be taken into consideration, hence the last round is, in effect, a one-shot Prisoner's Dilemma game, and because defection is a dominant strategy for both players, the only rational choice is to defect. Therefore, on the penultimate (99th) round, there is no reason to cooperate, because the outcome of the last round is predetermined and cannot be influenced, hence the only rational choice for both players is, once again, to defect. The argument unfolds, round by round, all the way back to the beginning, where the only rational choice for both players on the first round is to defect. This appears to prove that, if the common knowledge and rationality assumptions hold, then rational players will defect on every round of a finite-horizon Prisoner's Dilemma game, but it is not vulnerable to the objection that we raised to this argument in the Centipede game.

The unexpected hanging

The unexpected hanging is a well-known paradox based on backward induction, and it bears a superficial resemblance to the Centipede game. Sentencing a man on a Friday, a judge says: "You will be hanged one afternoon next week, beginning on Sunday, but you will not know the day of your execution until the morning of that day." The prisoner reasons as follows. "I can't be hanged on Saturday, the last possible day, because by Friday night I would know that my day of execution has to be Saturday. Furthermore, I can't be hanged on Friday because, with Saturday ruled out, by Thursday night I would know that my day of execution must be Friday. Continuing in the same vein, I can exclude all the remaining days of the week. I can't be hanged on any day next week, and therefore the judge's sentence can't be carried out at all. Whoopee!"

This paradox is sometimes called the surprise examination paradox, because it can be framed as a warning by a teacher about an examination to be held the following week. It was discovered by Swedish mathematician Lennart Ekbom in 1943 or 1944, during the Second World War, when the Swedish broadcasting system announced a civil defense drill for the following week and said that no one would know in advance on which day it would take place. It was first discussed in print by O'Connor (1948), who interpreted the judge's sentence as a classic self-defeating prophecy, and for that reason considered the problem "rather frivolous." Others immediately pointed out, however, that if the hanging were to take place on Monday, for example, then it would indeed be unexpected, and hence the judge's sentence is not a self-defeating prophecy after all: it does not predict something that cannot occur.

Many philosophers have commented on the paradox, and it has generated by far the largest body of literature of any epistemic paradox. In spite of all this attention, it is clearly a falsidical paradox, and not a veridical paradox (with a true conclusion) or an antinomy (a genuine logical contradiction). The prisoner argues that there is a contradiction between the judge's statements (a) that the sentence will be carried out the following week, and (b) that the prisoner will not know the day of his execution until the morning of that day, and that either (a) or (b) must therefore be false. He then infers invalidly that (a) rather than (b) is false, and therefore that the hanging cannot take place on any day of the following week. He provides no reason why it could not be (b) that is false: he could know the day of his execution before the morning of that day. Furthermore, he assumes that if he is not hanged by Friday, then he must be hanged on Saturday, and elsewhere he (inconsistently) assumes that if he is not hanged by Friday, then Saturday will have been "ruled out"; but he cannot have it both ways.

The philosopher Quine (1953) was the first to expose the prisoner's fallacious reasoning, with the following refutation. The prisoner claims that he cannot be hanged on Saturday because he would know his day of execution by Friday night; but this is false, because if he were to be hanged on Saturday, then by his own reasoning, it would indeed come as a surprise, and the same argument extends backward to the earlier days of the week. Quine pointed out that if the judge had told the prisoner that he would be hanged *the following day* but would not know the day of his execution until the morning of that day, then it would be similarly incorrect of the prisoner to infer that he could not be hanged at all, because he could, in fact, be hanged the following day without knowing in advance that he would be hanged, because of the incoherence of the judge's sentence.

The unexpected hanging certainly involves backward induction reasoning, but its resemblance to the Centipede game is superficial. The way backward induction is applied to the Centipede game may be wrong, as we have claimed, but it is certainly not wrong for the reason that the prisoner's argument in the unexpected hanging is wrong. In particular, backward induction in the Centipede game does not reach a conclusion that could be refuted by events on the ground, as the prisoner's reasoning does.

Conclusions

Backward induction is not objectionable in itself, but it can be applied fallaciously. The way it is used in the unexpected hanging paradox seems clearly fallacious, and we have suggested that its usual application in the Centipede game may also be questionable, though for quite different reasons. If we are right, then there do not appear to be any compelling arguments against cooperation in the Centipede game, and indeed the experimental evidence confirms that intelligent human decision makers, including people capable of backward induction reasoning, almost invariably cooperate, at least for a few moves. There may be nothing strictly paradoxical about this game, although it does pose difficult strategic problems to players.

Author note

Andrew M. Colman, Eva M. Krockow, Caren Frosch, and Briony D. Pulford, School of Psychology, University of Leicester. We are grateful to the Leicester Judgment and Decision Making Endowment Fund (Grant RM43G0176) for support in the preparation of this chapter. Correspondence concerning this chapter should be addressed to Andrew M. Colman, School of Psychology, University of Leicester, Leicester LE1 7RH, United Kingdom. E-mail: amc@le.ac.uk

Note

1 Aumann (1992, p. 220) attributed this version to Megiddo (1986), but Megiddo's game does not have zeros in the final terminal node – its most original feature. One is reminded of Viennese-born Jewish violinist Fritz Kreisler (1875–1962), who frequently performed compositions that he attributed to Vivaldi and others although he had, in fact, composed them himself. We believe that Aumann introduced the zero-end Centipede game himself in 1988, at a workshop in Haifa organized by Israeli economist Joseph Greenberg.

References

Aumann, R. J. (1992). Irrationality in game theory. In P. Dasgupta, D. Gale, O. Hart, & E. Maskin (Eds.), *Economic analysis of markets and games* (pp. 214–227). Cambridge, MA: MIT Press.

Aumann, R. J. (1995). Backward induction and common knowledge of rationality. *Games and Economic Behavior, 8*, 6–19.

Aumann, R. J. (1998). On the Centipede game. *Games and Economic Behavior, 23*, 97–105.

Binmore, K. (1987). Modeling rational players: Part 1. *Economics and Philosophy, 3*, 179–214.

Binmore, K. (1992). *Fun and games: A text on game theory.* Lexington: D.C. Heath.

Bornstein, G., Kugler, T., & Ziegelmeyer, A. (2004). Individual and group decisions in the centipede game: Are groups more "rational" players? *Journal of Experimental Social Psychology, 40*, 599–605.

Fudenberg, D., & Tirole J. (1991). *Game theory.* Cambridge, MA: MIT Press.

Gerber, A., & Wichardt, P. C. (2010). Iterated reasoning and welfare-enhancing instruments in the Centipede game. *Journal of Economic Behavior & Organization, 74*, 123–136.

Kawagoe, T., & Takizawa, H. (2012). Level-*k* analysis of experimental Centipede games. *Journal of Economic Behavior & Organization, 82*, 548–566.

Levitt, S. D., List, J. A., & Sadoff, S. E. (2011). Checkmate: Exploring backward induction among chess players. *American Economic Review, 101*, 975–990.

Luce, R. D., & Raiffa, H. (1957). *Games and decisions: Introduction and critical survey.* New York: Wiley.

McKelvey, R. D., & Palfrey, T. R. (1992). An experimental study of the Centipede game. *Econometrica, 60*, 803–836.

Megiddo, N. (1986). *Remarks on bounded rationality*. Research report 5270 (54310). Yorktown Heights, NY: IBM Research Division.

Nagel, R., & Tang, F. (1998). Experimental results on the Centipede game in normal form: An investigation on learning. *Journal of Mathematical Psychology, 42*, 356–384.

O'Connor, D. J. (1948). Pragmatic paradoxes. *Mind, 57*, 358–359.

Osborne, M. J., & Rubinstein, A. (1994). *A course in game theory*. Cambridge, MA: MIT Press.

Pulford, B. D., Colman, A. M., Lawrence, C. L., & Krockow, E. M. (2016, March 24). Reasons for cooperating in repeated interactions: Social value orientations, fuzzy traces, reciprocity, and activity bias. *Decision*. Advance online publication. http://dx.doi.org/10.1037/dec0000057.

Pulford, B. D., Krockow, E. M., Colman, A. M., & Lawrence, C. L. (2016). Social value induction and cooperation in the Centipede game. *PLOS ONE, 11*(3), 1–21. e0152352.

Quine, W. V. O. (1953). On a so-called paradox. *Mind, 62*, 65–66.

Rosenthal, R. W. (1981). Games of perfect information, predatory pricing and chain-store paradox. *Journal of Economic Theory, 25*, 92–100.

Schwalbe, U., & Walker, P. (2001). Zermelo and the early history of game theory. *Games and Economic Behavior, 34*, 123–137.

von Neumann, J. (1928). Zur Theorie der Gesellschaftsspiele. *Mathematische Annalen, 100*, 295–320.

von Neumann, J., & Morgenstern, O. (1944). *Theory of games and economic behavior*. Princeton, NJ: Princeton University Press.

Zermelo, E. (1913). Über eine Anwendung der Mengenlehre auf die Theorie des Schachspiels. *Proceedings of the Fifth International Congress of Mathematicians, Cambridge, 2*, 501–504.

12

SCAMS AND RATIONALITY

Dutch book arguments are not all they are cracked up to be

Shira Elqayam

'[I]f THESE two ain't frauds, I am an idiot, that's all.'

Mark Twain, *Adventures of Huckleberry Finn*

Some years ago my husband and I considered joining a buyers' syndicate to buy a house. The offer was financially attractive, but we worried about a scam. I had just completed a master's module on the psychology of decision making, so I decided to put what I had learned to use. I opted to apply multi-attribute utility theory (MAUT), a normative model of decision making between options that differ from each other along several dimensions, or attributes (see Baron, 2008, for a review). MAUT consists of breaking down the alternatives to their constituent attributes (e.g. location, price, design), assigning a weight to each attribute according to its subjective importance, estimating its utility, then summing the weighted utilities along the list of attributes. Of course, MAUT is computationally intractable to work out in one's head, but it is perfectly manageable with the *extended mind* (Clark & Chalmers, 1998), the idea that cognitive processes extend beyond the body into the world. In this case, my extended mind consisted of pencil and paper and a pocket calculator. I sat down and drew a long list of attributes, complete with weights and utilities, then dutifully summed up the weighted utilities.

In a way, the exercise worked. It just did not work the way I had expected it to. No sooner had I completed the task and computed the scores, then I realised that I had the wrong outcome! The outcome favoured joining in, but I did not want to take the risk of falling victim to a scam, with a massive loss of money as well as loss of face, and being made to feel like an idiot to boot. The potential for financial gain, buying a house for less than its market price, was not nearly enough to offset these worries. So although MAUT certainly helped me reach a decision, it worked more along the lines of psychoanalytic therapy, allowing me to access my preconscious emotions and desires. The emotion was apprehension; the desire was to avoid loss.

In other words, I was loss averse. (In case you wonder, loss aversion triumphed: we pulled out and never bought that house.)

Loss aversion, the tendency to overweight losses (Kahneman & Tversky, 1979), is perhaps the quintessential illustration of the tension between normative and practical rationality. Expected utility theory, the normative model of decision making which specifies how we *ought* to take decisions, weighs gains and losses exactly the same. But people notoriously give losses much more weight than gains in their decision making: 'losses loom larger than gains,' as Kahneman and Tversky succinctly put it. Although loss aversion violates normative strictures, pragmatically it makes sense. We do not always live in a statistical universe – we have one-off decisions (such as buying a house) that can dramatically affect our lives, for better or worse. It makes sense to (literally) err on the side of caution.

It seems fitting, in a chapter for Ken Manktelow's Festschrift, to focus on this tension between normative and pragmatic aspects of rationality. Ken maintained active interest in this tension throughout his research career (e.g., Manktelow, 2004, 2012). He made a contribution to what was soon to become a seminal distinction between the two types of rationality (Evans, 1993; Evans & Over, 1996; Evans, Over & Manktelow, 1993): rationality$_1$, the practical or instrumental[1] type of rationality, characterised by achieving one's goals; and rationality$_2$, the normative type of rationality, characterised by conformity to a normative system. People can be rational$_1$ without being rational$_2$, argued Evans and Over, and vice versa.

Or can they? The question whether people can be pragmatically rational whilst violating normative edicts is a fraught and controversial one, going back to the dawn of normative decision theory. A long and venerable list of researchers, starting with Ramsey (1990/1926) and de Finetti (1964, 1974), and followed by contemporary contributions to the great rationality debate (e.g. Corner & Hahn, 2013; Oaksford & Chater, 1998, 2007; Stanovich, 2004, 2011a, 2011b), argued precisely the opposite: that only strict adherence to normative strictures allows one to be pragmatically rational; and that anyone diverting from these strictures puts himself or herself at pragmatic risk. The technical term much heard in this context is 'Dutch book argument(s)'. A Dutch book is a wager that inevitably leads to loss; Dutch book *argument* is the argument that violating normative rationality – specifically, probability theory – exposes the violator to a Dutch book being made against her, whereas adhering to probability theory confers immunity to Dutch books (for reviews, see Corner & Hahn, 2013; Vineberg, 2011).

The conclusion is twofold: first, that probability theory is the best normative theory because it is the only one that has pragmatic rationality lined up as well as normative rationality; and second and important, that pragmatic rationality is impossible to achieve without normative rationality. I have little quarrel with the former conclusion;[2] it is the latter that worries me. By this view, normative rationality is the origin of pragmatic rationality as well as its justification. This position seems to reduce pragmatic rationality to the normative kind, in effect killing off pragmatic rationality. This *reductionist* position seems a rather counterintuitive one to take. As my MAUT story illustrates, normative and pragmatic considerations can easily point in opposite directions.

Think of it as a clash between two types of *ought* rules (Elqayam & Evans, 2011; Evans & Elqayam, 2011). The *ought* of pragmatic rationality is directive, or instrumental: it directs us to an action. In my MAUT case, the instrumental *ought* was something along these lines:

> *Instrumental ought:* You ought to pull out to avoid losing face and money to a scam.

Pulling out was not good or bad by itself. It was simply indicated as a means to an end. It is a sort of inference we easily draw in everyday life: when participants are presented with a goal (escaping a scam, in this case) and an action leading to the goal (pulling out), they happily conclude that the agent *ought* to take the action (Elqayam, Thompson, Wilkinson, Evans & Over, 2015). In contrast, the *ought* of normative rationality specifies which thinking is good or bad, regardless of the circumstances:

> *Normative ought:* You ought to obey the dictates of probability theory.

Instrumental *oughts* are in essence descriptive, and can be easily paraphrased accordingly; for example: 'Pulling out will help you avoid a scam.' In contrast, normative oughts are evaluative. The closest paraphrase will be something like: 'Thinking in line with probability theory is good [and breaching it is bad].' *Normativism* is the position in psychology of reasoning and decision making that focuses on normative, evaluative *oughts.* In a recent critique of normativism, Jonathan Evans and I (Elqayam & Evans, 2011; Evans & Elqayam, 2011) argued against focusing on normative oughts, and normative rationality in general, in psychological science. We suggested instead a *descriptivist* stance, focusing on descriptive work – which does include instrumental rationality.

If pragmatic rationality must be reduced to normative rationality, it is difficult to see how our vision for a descriptivist psychology of higher mental processing can be achieved. My aim in this chapter, therefore, is to defend the independent nature of normative and pragmatic rationality, by critically examining the force of Dutch book arguments, especially in the context of the reductionist conclusion. The rest of this chapter is constructed as follows. I start with an explanation of the Dutch book argument and the reductionist position. I then look in critical detail at the steps necessary for Dutch book arguments to bridge between instrumental and normative rationality, reviewing several objections from the philosophical literature. The next section is devoted to psychological reasons to doubt these steps. I conclude with thoughts about the future of descriptivism.

Dutch books and Dutch book arguments

Here is an example of a Dutch book (the numbers are taken from Gilio & Over, 2012). Jack and Jill discuss their mutual friend Linda: they have not heard from Linda since they had all graduated, but now they plan to contact her again. They both believe that the probability of Linda being a banker (b) is 0.4, and the probability of Linda being a feminist banker (f&b) is 0.6. In other words, Jack and Jill commit the conjunction fallacy (Tversky & Kahneman, 1983): their subjective degree of belief that Linda is both a feminist and a banker is higher than their subjective degree of belief that Linda is a banker; P(f&b) = 0.6 > P(b) = 0.4. The technical term is *incoherence*: an agent is coherent if she obeys the probability calculus, incoherent if she violates it. Jack and Jill are both incoherent, because the probability that Linda is both a feminist *and* a banker cannot be greater than the probability that she is a banker, feminist or not.

To create a Dutch book, we first need to translate these subjective beliefs to betting odds, a move first proposed by Ramsey (1990/1926) and de Finetti (1964, 1974). That is, we assume that people would be willing to pay for a wager that promises odds that correspond to their degrees of belief (Howson & Urbach, 2006). For example, if Jack thinks that the probability of Linda being a feminist banker is 0.6, we assume that he would be willing to pay 60p for a lottery ticket which will pay him £1 if Linda actually turns out to be a feminist banker, but nothing if Linda is not a feminist banker. This is because the payoff of £1 with a probability of 0.6 is the same as the payoff of 60p with a probability of 1. Let us call this Lottery Ticket A (see Figure 12.1). Suppose Jill offers Jack this wager; in the spirit of good sportsmanship, Jack accepts. To reciprocate, Jack offers Jill another wager – Lottery Ticket B (also in Figure 12.1), for the price of 40p: he will pay Jill £1 if Linda is a banker, and nothing if she is not one. This also seems like fair odds to Jill, and she accepts.

There is nothing incongruent about either of these wagers separately: each corresponds nicely to the degree of belief it articulates, and each can therefore be easily considered fair. (Keep the latter point in mind; I will get back to it later.) Wager A corresponds to the belief that the probability of Linda being a feminist banker is 0.6; wager B corresponds to the belief that the probability of Linda being a banker is 0.4. The hitch, however, is in the combination of bets. Remember, Jill paid Jack 40p for her lottery ticket, but Jack paid Jill 60p for his, so just in terms

Lottery Ticket A (Linda is a feminist banker)

$$\boxed{\begin{array}{l}\text{£1 paid with a}\\ \text{probability of .6}\end{array}} = \boxed{\begin{array}{l}\text{60p paid with a}\\ \text{probability of 1}\end{array}} = \boxed{\text{60p}}$$

Lottery Ticket B (Linda is a banker)

$$\boxed{\begin{array}{l}\text{£1 paid with a}\\ \text{probability of .4}\end{array}} = \boxed{\begin{array}{l}\text{40p paid with a}\\ \text{probability of 1}\end{array}} = \boxed{\text{40p}}$$

FIGURE 12.1   Two lottery tickets reflecting the betting odds of a conjunction fallacy. Ticket A reflects Jack and Jill's subjective probability estimate of the conjunction; Ticket B reflects their subjective probability estimate of a single disjunct.

of the combined costs of lottery tickets Jack is 20p out of pocket before they have even begun. Of course, this is not unusual: billions of people worldwide buy lottery tickets that cost more and have even lower chances of success. For example, the odds against winning the first prize in the European lottery are given on the Euro-Millions website as 1 in 116,531,800.

In contrast to the European lottery, however, where the chances of winning are negligible but not nonexistent, the problem with the chances of Jack winning any money in our little scenario is that, well, there are none: given the combined wagers, there is no way for Jack to come out ahead. Table 12.1 presents the outcomes of the four truth-table possibilities: Linda turns out to be a feminist and a banker; Linda turns out to be a feminist but not a banker; Linda turns out not to be a feminist but to be a banker; and Linda turns out to be neither a feminist nor a banker. As the table shows, in any single one of these four possible outcomes Jack is the loser. Having placed both wagers, he cannot win. This is what a Dutch book is: a set of bets that must be lost.

More precisely, Dutch book arguments are made of two complementary statements, or theorems (Hajek, 2008a):

> *The Dutch book theorem:* If you violate probability theory, a Dutch book can be made against you.
> *The converse Dutch book theorem:* If you conform to probability theory, you are immune to a Dutch book being made against you.

In this definition, a Dutch book is a set of bets, each of which is considered fair, but which collectively guarantee loss.[3] Note that, for reasons of pragmatic rationality, both the Dutch book theorem and its converse must be the case: it is not enough that violation of the normative standard (probability calculus, in this case) guarantees a penalty. Conformity to the same normative standard should also confer immunity from that penalty, because if you are going to be penalised anyway, you might as well not bother. In other words, conforming to the probability calculus is both *necessary* and *sufficient* to avoid Dutch books. Or, more generally, normative rationality is both necessary and sufficient for pragmatic rationality.

TABLE 12.1 Lottery outcome of Tickets A and B for Jack. The accumulated bets guarantee a sure loss, no matter what Linda turns out to be.

Linda turns out to be . . .	Banker & feminist	Banker & not-feminist	Not banker & feminist	Not-banker & not-feminist
Combined costs of Tickets A (60p) and B (40p)	−0.20	−0.20	−0.20	−0.20
Payoff of Ticket A	1	0	0	0
Payoff of Ticket B	−1	−1	0	0
Total	**−0.20**	**−1.20**	**−0.20**	**−0.20**

It is easy to see why Dutch book arguments have become the gold standard for rationality among many a philosopher and psychologist. Simple and elegant, they create a strong link between compliance with the probability calculus – a widely accepted normative standard – and the straightforwardly pragmatic outcome of money loss. No one, presumably, wants to lose money, so the threat of a Dutch book is a potent one. Dutch books have become the big bad wolf of rationality: if you don't behave, a Dutch book can be made against you.

How Dutch book arguments bridge between rationality₁ and rationality₂

At this stage, you might be wondering how on earth we got from losing small sums of money to being pragmatically irrational in general. And indeed, for Dutch book arguments to provide such a useful bridge between normative compliance and pragmatic rationality, it is not enough to show that people who violate the probability calculus make themselves vulnerable to losing small bets. For Dutch book arguments to work, several steps are necessary. We need four steps:

1   *Conversion:* Transform subjective degrees of belief to betting odds
2   *Core:* Demonstrate that. . .

   a   violations of the probability calculus lead to Dutch books; and
   b   compliance with the probability calculus confers immunity to Dutch books

3   *Normative Generalisation:* Generalise from probability theory to all normative systems
4   *Pragmatic Generalisation:* Generalise from losing bets to all pragmatic contexts

Whereas the core step is easily proved, the other steps are more susceptible to criticism. Take step 3, normative generalisation: although probability theory is a powerful normative tool, it is certainly not the only one around. Alternative normative systems include binary logic, quantum statistics (Pothos & Busemeyer, 2013), inference to the best explanation (Douven, 2011) and so on. It is always possible to argue that the norm employed to judge any specific reasoning or decision-making task should be replaced – often with a different norm that makes the prevalent behaviours nicely normative (Stanovich, 1999, calls this 'alternative task construal'). It can even be argued (Elqayam & Evans, 2011) that it is just a matter of time: any reasoning or decision-making task that does not have an alternative normative explanation is due to acquire one sooner or later. Can we really generalise from probability theory to, say, Inference to the Best Explanation?

The latter point is due to Douven (2013). Inference to the Best Explanation (IBE, or abduction) is a normative system which governs the generation of explanations (for review, see Douven, 2011). You suffer insomnia and infer that the barista gave you regular coffee instead of the decaf you had asked for; you find your home door ajar and valuables strewn around, and infer that you have been burgled; your work colleague is beaming, and you infer that her promotion has finally been approved – these are all instances of IBE. In some cases it is possible to pit IBE against probability theory as conflicting normative accounts. For example, suppose you watch a conjurer flip a coin several times; you know that the coin is biased, but not how it is biased. As it turns out (Douven, 2013), IBE has the upper hand over probability theory in predicting the coin bias in a series of computer simulations. This might seem an idealised example, abstract and divorced from everyday life, but Dutch books are just as idealised (more on this shortly). And the practical implications are substantial: accurately predicting regularities in everyday events is a survival trait. The same skills that allow one to predict a coin toss, allow an expert to spot a dangerous irregularity in emergency situations and come up with the right explanation (Kahneman & Klein, 2009); for example, nurses in neonatal intensive care who can detect life-threatening infections in the infants in their case faster than the blood test results. Douven's findings challenge pragmatic generalisation as much as they challenge normative generalisation, if not more.

Even if we stick to the realm of small bets, the pragmatic generalisation step is still suspect. One of the most influential critiques of Dutch book arguments is Haíjek's (2005, 2008a, 2008b) Czech book argument. If Dutch book arguments support probabilism, the stance that subjective degrees of belief should conform to the probability calculus, then Czech book arguments undermine it. The Czech book argument turns the Dutch book argument on its head, providing an argument to the contrary: that we should *violate* the probability calculus. For every loser, there is a winner; for every Dutch book leading to inevitable loss, there is a parallel book leading to inevitable gain. Haíjek dubs these 'Czech books'. Czech books are easy to prove: just replace 'buy' with 'sell' throughout the Dutch book proof, and you have your Czech book. In fact, our betting scenario already has a Czech book built into it: our Czech book is Jill. Table 12.2 presents the payoff for Jill for each of the same four truth-table possibilities we earlier considered for Jack. For each

TABLE 12.2 Lottery outcome of Tickets A and B for Jill. The accumulated bets guarantee a sure win, no matter what Linda turns out to be.

Linda turns out to be . . .	Banker & feminist	Banker & not-feminist	Not banker & feminist	Not-banker & not-feminist
Combined costs of Tickets A (60p) and B (40p)	0.20	0.20	0.20	0.20
Payoff of Ticket A	−1	0	0	0
Payoff of Ticket B	1	1	0	0
Total	**+0.20**	**+1.20**	**+0.20**	**+0.20**

single possible outcome, Jill comes out with a gain. Jack and Jill share the same set of beliefs: they both commit the conjunction fallacy. But the outcome is very different.

The Dutch book theorem and its converse each have a Czech book parallel:

> *The Czech book theorem:* If you violate probability theory, a Czech book can be made for you.
>
> *The converse Czech book theorem:* If you conform to probability theory, a Czech book cannot be made for you.

In this context, a Czech book is set of bets, each of which is considered fair, and which collectively guarantee winning. Being incoherent (i.e. violating the probability calculus) both *allows* and *guarantees* a Czech book, just as it both allows and guarantees a Dutch book. Note that, just as we had for Dutch books, both theorems are important: It is not enough to be able to elicit a Czech book, because perhaps Czech books can be made anyway and do not depend on incoherence. For the full argument strength, it is essential that if people stick to the probability calculus, they cannot have a Czech book. This is the exact upside-down analogue of the Dutch book argument.

The significance of this Czech book argument cannot be overstated. It seems that, if we want the benevolent outcome of a Czech book, we are compelled to violate the probability calculus. We can have a Czech book if and only if we are incoherent. This leaves us between a rock and a hard place: violate the probability calculus, and a Dutch book can be made against you; conform to it, and you miss out on your chance to enjoy a Czech book. There is no more a clearly preferable pragmatic course of action, and the link between pragmatic and normative rationality is broken.

To be fair, Hájek does not leave the argument at that. He proposes an amendment to Dutch book arguments to close this particular theoretical loophole. Recall that both Dutch books and Czech books are defined as a set of bets, each of which is considered fair, but collectively guarantee a sure loss or win respectively. The key word is 'fair'. People accept fair bets, argues Hájek, but they also accept bets that are better than fair. As it turns out, if the 'fair' in the definitions is replaced with 'fair or better than fair', three of the four theorems still hold: the Dutch book theorem and its converse, and the Czech book theorem. What does not hold is the converse Czech book theorem. So conforming to the probability calculus is still *sufficient* for the revised version of Czech books, but not *necessary*. We can still enjoy a Czech book even if we conform to the probability calculus. With this amendment in place, probabilism is saved, and with it, the link between norm and praxis. We can enjoy a Czech book and avoid a Dutch book at the same time, and to do this we must be coherent – provided we also accept fair or better than fair bets.

Hájek saves probabilism, then, but at a cost (Vineberg, 2011). The beauty of Dutch book arguments is their simple down-to-earthiness: obey probability theory or else. Once gains are allowed through the back door, this simplicity is irretrievably lost.[4]

Are Dutch books psychologically plausible?

Are Dutch books merely a figment of philosophers' imagination (Douven, 2013)? Philosophers have already cast doubt on the first step, converting degrees of belief to betting odds (Eriksson & Haíjek, 2007; Howson & Urbach, 2006), for a variety of reasons. For one thing, betting odds do not exactly correspond to the probability scale, and need a mathematical adjustment to match. A somewhat more psychological argument is that, even supposing that a person agrees that a bet is fair, this does not guarantee that he would be willing to accept it: people generally prefer to bet on favourable rather than just fair odds. There is a behaviourist assumption here, that degrees of belief can only be operationalised as behavioural units such as betting, otherwise they are meaningless mentalism. Given that such assumptions are alien to contemporary cognitive psychology, it is puzzling why so many reasoning and decision-making psychologists still seem to accept Dutch book arguments at face value. I will return to this question.

Perhaps the most vulnerable link in the chain of argumentation, the conversion step and its analogues attracted plenty of criticism in the psychological literature. A similar move is done in Lewis's (1980) *principal principle*, which argues that subjective degrees of belief (*credences* is the technical term) should reflect objective probabilities (a.k.a. *chances*) where possible. The principal principle draws on the same mechanism as the conversion step of Dutch book arguments (Howson & Urbach, 2006), using betting odds as a rationale for the link from chances (objective) to credences (subjective). This has come under severe criticism as being psychologically implausible (Evans & Over, 1996), because people do not normally make one-to-one transitions from objective chance to subjective belief. On the contrary, most of us tend to be *overconfident* in our beliefs; for example, people tend to think that they are more accurate than is actually the case (Fischhoff, Slovic & Lichtenstein, 1977). Psychological implausibility aside, Evans and Over also point out that such overconfidence may well be, in some circumstances, pragmatically rational: for example, a cancer patient with overconfidence in her recovery might actually tip the scales by this belief and increase her *objective* chances of recovering from the disease.

Let me add another psychological reason to the pot, also taken from the judgement and decision-making literature: loss aversion, the tendency to overweight losses mentioned in the introduction to this chapter. More generally, the idea that betting odds can accurately represent degrees of belief is at odds with prospect theory (Kahneman & Tversky, 1979), the descriptive theory of decision making under risk (which describes how people actually make decisions, rather than how they ought to make decisions). One of its most striking features is that no linear relation exists between objective (say, monetary) gains and losses, and how much we value them subjectively. Losing £100 is not the flip side of winning £100: it hurts a lot more. Our assumption that Jack would accept the ostensibly fair bet now seems more remote: since losses loom larger than gains, he might not feel that a possible win of £1 is enough to offset a sure loss of 60p.

In the same vein, people are also *risk aversive* (Kahneman & Tversky, 1979): they tend to prefer a certain gain to an uncertain, higher one, even when their expected value is identical. In my MAUT example, I was risk averse as well as loss averse. Risk aversion should also protect Jack from accepting lottery Ticket A, as uncertain gain is pitted against certain (albeit smaller) loss. Although risk aversion violates normative decision theory, it is arguably pragmatically rational. The normative expected value, calculated by multiplying potential gains and losses by their probability, is all very well for a statistical universe, but miserably fails for one-off decisions (Evans, 2010). The statistical universe rationality is, for example, the province of insurance companies, who make a profit by selling a large number of policies. Had we lived in such a universe of multiple decisions, buying insurance would have been irrational: by expected value, we are guaranteed a loss. But we do not: we live in a world of one-off decisions. The possibility of a catastrophe such as the total loss of a car, a house severely damaged in a fire or life-threatening disease is just too terrifying. That it is a remote one is (psychologically) beside the point. This, argues Evans, is why it is perfectly rational for us to buy insurance: for one-off decisions, expected value is a poor pragmatic guide. Note that this argument undermines the pragmatic generalisation step as well as the conversion step: what does it say about a normative theory that it makes so little sense for such prevalent everyday pragmatic decision situations? The gap between normative and pragmatic rationality seems as wide as ever.

The conversion step also seems suspect from the point of view of dual process theories (Evans, 2008; Evans & Stanovich, 2013). These theories distinguish between fast, intuitive processes, and analytic, effortful ones. Remember the conjunction fallacy? Analytically, the probability that Linda is a feminist banker cannot be higher than the probability that she is a banker, but intuitively, this might feel exactly right. Probability estimates thrown up by intuitive processes might well be different from the ones generated by effortful processing. This creates a tension between dual process theory and the standard version of probability theory which goes back to De Finetti and Ramsey. To perform the transformation to betting odds, probability theory presupposes that probability judgements are stable, but with dual processing, they are anything but (Elqayam & Over, 2012). A compulsive gambler may be analytically aware that his chances of winning are remote, but intuitive overconfidence throws up a much more optimistic probability estimate. Again, conversion seems psychologically fragile.

There seems to be an irony in this. Overconfidence, loss aversion, risk aversion, probabilistic instability: far from exposing us to pragmatic irrationality, these violations of normative rules seem to safeguard us from it. We do not really need normative probability theory to avoid falling victim to unscrupulous Dutch books (such as they are). We just need to be human.[5]

Which brings us to step 4, pragmatic generalisation. Here, too, what we know of human psychology makes pragmatic generalisation less than plausible. For one thing, if I had to choose a single type of behaviour to represent all human behaviours, I am not sure that betting would be the first candidate that comes to mind.

Of course, this argument goes against Czech books as much as it goes against Dutch books: both are based on betting. One can argue,[6] however, that Dutch bookies are much more likely than Czech bookies: we live in a hostile world, and crooks ready to take advantage of us are much more likely than benevolent philanthropists ready with the next cheque. The argument has merit, but all it does is make Dutch bookies *more* likely than Czech bookies; it does not make them *likely*. Although crooks and con artists are hardly a rarity, mathematically gifted crooks are. As I am writing this, this very morning, I received an email scam of the 'stranded travel-ler' type, ostensibly from a colleague in another university. Who of us has never received phishing and scam emails? These do not require the scammers to know the probability calculus; they only need to be familiar with human gullibility. A guide booklet on avoiding scams published by the Thames Valley Police a few years ago (The Metropolitan Police Service, 2012) outlines 10 common types of fraud: every one of them involves a confidence trick, and not a single one of them involves the probability calculus. Scammers are as cognitively lazy as the next man: why think hard when a few established rules of the thumb can do the trick? Dutch bookies are possible, just not very likely.[7]

To see how this argument damages the pragmatic generalisation step, let us gen-eralise from Dutch bookies to all crooks. We can do this by replacing the term 'Dutch book' with the more general term 'scam' in the Dutch book theorems:

> *The scam theorem:* If you violate probability theory, a scam can be made against you.
> *The converse scam theorem:* If you conform to probability theory, you are immune to scams.

This scam analogue of the Dutch book theorem still holds (conversion step aside): after all, a Dutch book is a type of scam. But it is easy to see that the converse theorem no longer holds. If you conform to the probability calculus, you might be immune to Dutch books, but this will not make you immune to all scams, or even the great majority of them.

Despite their widely acknowledged weaknesses, Dutch book arguments are highly persuasive, so much so that they continue to be held almost as an article of faith amongst many a contributor to the great rationality debate. What makes Dutch book arguments so compelling? As a possible explanation, I invite you to think again about Jack and Jill. Do you not feel that Jack is more irrational than Jill? The intuition seems quite compelling – after all, he stupidly lost money. Even though Jack and Jill share the same beliefs, and the same normative violations, we are psychologically geared towards evaluating events by their outcomes (Baron & Hershey, 1988). For example, participants presented with a scenario of a surgeon deciding to operate judged the decision as good when the operation succeeded, and as bad when the operation failed, even though the a priori probability that the surgery would succeed was the same in both cases. Our susceptibility to outcome bias, combined with the idea of money loss, make Dutch book arguments into a powerful *intuition pump*. An intuition pump is a kind of rhetorical device: a thought experiment designed to persuade by pressing the right intuitive buttons (Stanovich, 2009; the term is borrowed from Dennett, 1980). Unlike other thought experiments, intuition pumps are not tools of exploration. Their function is to persuade, rather than reveal. This seems to fit Dutch book arguments to a T.

Final thoughts

We started with the veteran distinction between the pragmatic, or instrumental rationality$_1$, and the normative rationality$_2$, a distinction Ken helped define and establish. The distinction is important from the point of view of the descriptivist stance, the idea that psychology of reasoning and decision making should focus on how people behave rather than how they ought to behave. Dutch book arguments, ostensibly anchoring pragmatic rationality in a normative basis, threaten this distinction by showing that violating the probability calculus dooms the violator to losing money. However, not is all as it seems: Dutch book arguments suffer from so many weaknesses, philosophical as well as psychological, that their main function is as intuition pumps. Descriptivism seems safe for now.

If descriptivism is to go anywhere, though, it is not enough to argue against the normative *ought*: it should also account for the instrumental *ought*. Some of this work is empirical, exploring the psychological mechanisms underlying the way we generate novel norms (Elqayam et al., 2015). Human beings create new normative rules as a matter of course – think about red tape, and how it seems ever to thrive and multiply. As it turns out, the way we create normative rules (the technical term is 'deontic') is the same way we treat norms in general: sensitive to the likelihood of the outcome and its psychological value. If we know that Jack is certain to lose money if he accepts Jill's bet, we easily infer that he ought not to accept the bet. This work, too, has its roots in Ken's work: together with David Over, Ken was the first to analyse deontic thinking with decision-theoretic tools (Manktelow & Over, 1991), looking in particular at the role of utility (the technical term for psychological value).

Another theoretical development is *grounded rationality* (Elqayam, 2011, 2012). This is a contextualised view of instrumental rationality: the idea that we think and make decisions in context, and that the instrumental value of these decisions can only be gauged in context too. What is rational is what helps us achieve our goals, given who we are, what we know and what we want. Of course, we often have conflicting goals (Manktelow, 2012; Stanovich, 2008). Some of these goals might even include avoiding Dutch books.

Acknowledgments

I am grateful to Jonathan Evans, David Over and Igor Douven for critical readings and helpful comments on earlier versions of this chapter. And many heartfelt thanks go to Ken Manktelow, for friendship, collaboration and inspiration.

Notes

1 I will use the terms 'pragmatic', 'practical' and 'instrumental' interchangeably to refer to rationality$_1$.
2 On strict versus soft Bayesianism in psychology of reasoning, see Elqayam and Evans (2013).
3 This is an example of a basic Dutch book. There are also diachronic or dynamic Dutch books, in which bets are placed over time (see Vineberg, 1997, for a review). For the purposes of the current discussion, however, the basic type is sufficient.
4 The 'fair-or-better-than-fair' condition is arguably a realistic one (I owe this point to David Over): after all, people are more likely to accept favourable bets than just fair ones. The gambling industry is based on bets that are better than fair to the house (and worse than fair to the players). However, realistic is not the same as simple. 'Fair-or-better-than-fair' is disjunctive (i.e. involving an 'either-or' preposition), and disjunctions are notoriously difficult to process (Shafir, 1994).
5 This is less Panglossian (Stanovich, 1999) than it might seem. I do not argue that people are invariably rational, just that normative and pragmatic rationality are independent. True, some normative breaches are pragmatically sound, but the opposite is also true: some normatively sound behaviours are pragmatically odd. The expected value rule is a case in point: see Evans (2010, p. 87) for analysis of impractical normative compliance to this rule on *Who wants to be a millionaire?*
6 I owe this point to Jonathan Evans and Andrew Colman, who raised it in response to my talk at Ken's Festschrift workshop.
7 Another thing that makes both Dutch and Czech bookies implausible is that they need access to our degrees of belief. However, often we ourselves are not aware of the strength of our beliefs, let alone other people. I owe this point to Igor Douven.

References

Baron, J. (2008). *Thinking and deciding* (Fourth edition). Cambridge: Cambridge University Press.
Baron, J., & Hershey, J. C. (1988). Outcome bias in decision evaluation. *Journal of Personality and Social Psychology, 54*, 569–579.
Clark, A., & Chalmers, D. (1998). The extended mind. *Analysis, 58*, 7–19.
Corner, A., & Hahn, U. (2013). Normative theories of argumentation: Are some norms better than others? *Synthese, 190*, 3579–3610.
de Finetti, B. (1964). Foresight: Its logical laws, its subjective sources (original publication, 1937). In H. E. Kyburg & H. E. Smokier (Eds.), *Studies in subjective probability* (pp. 55–118). New York: Wiley.
de Finetti, B. (1974). *Probability, induction and statistics*. New York: Wiley.
Dennett, D. C. (1980). The milk of human intentionality. *Behavioral and Brain Sciences, 3*, 428–430.
Douven, I. (2011). Abduction. In E. N. Zalta (Ed.), *Stanford encyclopedia of philosophy* (Spring 2011 edition). Stanford, CA: Stanford University. *http://plato.stanford.edu/archives/ spr2011/entries/abduction/*.
Douven, I. (2013). Inference to the best explanation, Dutch books, and inaccuracy minimisation. *Philosophical Quarterly, 63*, 428–444.
Elqayam, S. (2011). Grounded rationality: A relativist framework for normative rationality. In K. I. Manktelow, D. E. Over & S. Elqayam (Eds.), *The science of reason: A Festschrift in honour of Jonathan St. B. T. Evans* (pp. 397–420). Hove, UK: Psychology Press.
Elqayam, S. (2012). Grounded rationality: Descriptivism in epistemic context. *Synthese, 189*, 39–49.

Elqayam, S., & Evans, J. St. B. T. (2011). Subtracting 'ought' from 'is': Descriptivism versus normativism in the study of human thinking. *Behavioral and Brain Sciences, 34,* 233–248.

Elqayam, S., & Evans, J. St. B. T. (2013). Rationality in the new paradigm: Strict versus soft Bayesian approaches. *Thinking and Reasoning, 19,* 453–470.

Elqayam, S., & Over, D. (2012). Probabilities, beliefs, and dual processing: The paradigm shift in the psychology of reasoning. *Mind and Society, 11,* 27–40.

Elqayam, S., Thompson, V. A., Wilkinson, M. R., Evans, J. St. B. T., & Over, D. E. (2015). Deontic introduction: A theory of inference from is to ought. *Journal of experimental psychology. Learning, Memory, and Cognition, 41,* 1516–1532.

Eriksson, L., & Hajek, A. (2007). What are degrees of belief? *Studia Logica, 86,* 183–213.

Evans, J. St. B. T. (1993). Bias and rationality. In K. I. Manktelow & D. E. Over (Eds.), *Rationality: Psychological and philosophical perspectives* (pp. 6–30). London: Routledge.

Evans, J. St. B. T. (2008). Dual-processing accounts of reasoning, judgment, and social cognition. *Annual Review of Psychology, 59,* 255–278.

Evans, J. St. B. T. (2010). *Thinking twice: Two minds in one brain.* Oxford: Oxford University Press.

Evans, J. St. B. T., & Elqayam, S. (2011). Towards a descriptivist psychology of reasoning and decision making. *Behavioral and Brain Sciences, 34,* 275–290.

Evans, J. St. B. T., & Over, D. E. (1996). *Rationality and reasoning.* Hove, UK: Psychology Press.

Evans, J. St. B. T., Over, D. E., & Manktelow, K. I. (1993). Reasoning, decision making and rationality. *Cognition, 49,* 165–187.

Evans, J. St. B. T., & Stanovich, K. E. (2013). Dual-process theories of higher cognition: Advancing the debate. *Psychological Science, 8,* 223–241.

Fischhoff, B., Slovic, P., & Lichtenstein, S. (1977). Knowing with certainty: The appropriateness of extreme confidence. *Journal of Experimental Psychology: Human Perception and Performance, 3,* 552–564.

Gilio, A., & Over, D. (2012). The psychology of inferring conditionals from disjunctions: A probabilistic study. *Journal of Mathematical Psychology, 56,* 118–131.

Hajek, A. (2005). Scotching Dutch books? *Philosophical Perspectives, 19,* 139–151.

Hajek, A. (2008a). Arguments for or against probabilism? *The British Journal for the Philosophy of Science, 59,* 793–819.

Hajek, A. (2008b). Dutch book arguments. In P. Anand, P. K. Pattanaik & C. Puppe (Eds.), *The handbook of rational and social choice: An overview of new foundations and applications.* Oxford; New York: Oxford University Press.

Howson, C., & Urbach, P. (2006). *Scientific reasoning: The Bayesian approach* (Third edition). Chicago: Open Court.

Kahneman, D., & Klein, G. (2009). Conditions for intuitive expertise: A failure to disagree. *American Psychologist, 64,* 515–526.

Kahneman, D., & Tversky, A. (1979). Prospect theory: An analysis of decision under risk. *Econometrica, 47,* 263–291.

Lewis, D. (1980). A subjectivist's guide to objective chance. In R. C. Jeffrey (Ed.), *Studies in inductive logic and probability* (pp. 263–293). Berkeley: University of California Press.

Manktelow, K. I. (2004). Reasoning and rationality: The pure and the practical. In K. I. Manktelow & M. Cheung Hang (Eds.), *Psychology of reasoning: Theoretical and historical perspectives* (pp. 157–177). Hove, UK: Psychology Press.

Manktelow, K. I. (2012). *Thinking and reasoning: Psychological perspectives on reason, judgment and decision making.* Hove, UK: Psychology Press.

Manktelow, K. I., & Over, D. E. (1991). Social roles and utilities in reasoning with deontic conditionals. *Cognition, 39,* 85–105.

The Metropolitan Police Service. (2012). The big book of little scams. Mayor's Office for Policing and Crime and the Crown.

Oaksford, M., & Chater, N. (1998). *Rationality in an uncertain world*. Hove, UK: Psychology Press.

Oaksford, M., & Chater, N. (2007). *Bayesian rationality: The probabilistic approach to human reasoning*. Oxford: Oxford University Press.

Pothos, E. M., & Busemeyer, J. R. (2013). Can quantum probability provide a new direction for cognitive modeling? *Behavioral and Brain Sciences, 36*, 255–274.

Ramsey, F. P. (1990). Truth and probability (original publication 1926). In D. H. Mellor (Ed.), *Philosophical papers* (pp. 52–94). Cambridge, UK: Cambridge University Press.

Shafir, E. (1994). Uncertainty and the difficulty of thinking through disjunctions. *Cognition, 50*, 403–430.

Stanovich, K. E. (1999). *Who is rational? Studies of individual differences in reasoning*. Mahwah, NJ: Erlbaum.

Stanovich, K. E. (2004). *The robot's rebellion: Finding meaning in the age of Darwin*. Chicago: Chicago University Press.

Stanovich, K. E. (2008). Higher order preference and the master rationality motive. *Thinking and Reasoning, 14*, 111–127.

Stanovich, K. E. (2009). *What intelligence tests miss: The psychology of rational thought*. New Haven, CT; London: Yale University Press.

Stanovich, K. E. (2011a). Normative models in psychology are here to stay. *Behavioral and Brain Sciences, 34*, 268–269.

Stanovich, K. E. (2011b). *Rationality and the reflective mind*. New York: Oxford University Press.

Tversky, A., & Kahneman, D. (1983). Extensional vs intuitive reasoning: The conjunction fallacy in probability judgment. *Psychological Review, 90*, 293–315.

Vineberg, S. (1997). Dutch books, Dutch strategies and what they show about rationality. *Philosophical Studies, 86*, 185–201.

Vineberg, S. (2011). Dutch book arguments. In E. N. Zalta (Ed.), *Stanford encyclopedia of Philosophy (Summer 2011 edition)*. Stanford, CA: Stanford University. *http://plato.stanford.edu/archives/sum2011/entries/dutch-book/*.

13

IF EASTERNERS ARE ILLOGICAL WHEN REASONING, THEN WHAT DOES THIS MEAN?

Hiroshi Yama

People's naïve theory

Many Japanese have concerns that they may be more illogical thinkers than Westerners (e.g., Nakamura, 1985). There are two possible rationales for their concern. The first and biggest one is the phantom of white supremacy and social Darwinism in the 19th century. The ground for white supremacy is the historical fact that it was neither Asian nor African countries, but Western countries that held hegemony over the world in the 19th century. Many people believed Westerners were more intelligent than other peoples (e.g., Said, 1978). Their belief was reinforced by the notion of social Darwinism. It is a general name given to various theories that apply biological concepts of natural selection and survival of the fittest to social sciences. According to this, the Western civilization and culture are the most developed through natural selection and survival of the fittest. Even though contemporary Japan is a high-tech country, many Japanese believe it was achieved by their imitation of Western industry products. They are still not confident that Easterners including Japanese are as intelligent as Westerners.

Although cultural relativists (Boas, 1911) seriously criticized white supremacy and social Darwinism, the ideas still haunt like a phantom. We regard culture as a hypothetical construct to explain people's behavior as well as to describe social patterns. Cultural relativists argued that there was not an absolute principle on which culture or civilization is advanced, and each cultural group has its own value system to determine the goals of the group members (Benedict, 1934; Boas, 1911). According to such authors, the standard of social Darwinism that Western culture is the most advanced was designed by Westerners, and hence this standard cannot be applied to other cultures. Although cultural relativism opposed the racist prejudice that Asians and Africans were inferior peoples, it has been regarded not as a scientific proposal but a political claim.

The second reason Japanese people may see themselves as less logical than West-erners is the latest results of scientific cross-cultural studies that Easterners are less likely to do rule-based thinking than Westerners (Norenzayan, Smith, Kim, & Nis-bett, 2002; Peng & Nisbett, 1999). Researchers do not argue that Easterners, includ-ing Japanese, are more illogical than Westerners in the strict sense. However, their message is not accurately transmitted to the mass media. People who read popular lay articles on these issues seem to easily maintain a belief that Easterners are illogi-cal. Later, I will introduce the results of scientific, cross-cultural studies on thinking and the explanations for the differences in thinking style, and add our latest research and interpretation in this chapter.

Easterners' dialectical reasoning

The results of cross-cultural studies that Easterners are less likely to do rule-based thinking may be scientific grounds for the aforementioned phantom. However, I will argue that they do not support the phantom. Norenzayan and colleagues (2002) conducted the first scientific cross-cultural study on reasoning. They reported that, when being asked which one of two groups a target was similar to, Americans focused more on a single property for grouping, whereas Asians did not. Americans preferred rule-based reasoning focusing on a single property that was common to both the target and the group members, whereas Koreans pre-ferred similarity-based intuitive reasoning so that the target and the group mem-bers showed family resemblance. This tendency was confirmed by their other experiment, on categorical inference. For instance, Koreans accepted the conclu-sion "all penguins have an ulnar artery" from the premise "all birds have an ulnar artery" less than Americans. Their participants were completely unfamiliar with ulnar artery, hence their cues were the terms of "bird" and "penguin." Koreans took the fact that penguins are not typical birds into consideration. Yama and col-leagues (2010) also reported Westerners' tendencies in rule-based inference. We investigated cultural differences in hindsight bias, which is the tendency of people to overestimate their ability to have predicted an outcome that could not possibly have been predicted. Choi and Nisbett (2000) had already reported that this is greater among Easterners than among Westerners. Yama and colleagues reported that that British and French people showed less hindsight bias, seemingly for their preference for rule-based thinking: they preferred not only a rule in the form of an indicative conditional, but a general rule to describe the world when estimat-ing the probability of a consequence. Yama and colleagues (2010) proposed that it was because Westerners were more likely to use a rule for the prediction without knowing the outcome.

These results may suggest that Easterners, including Japanese, are less logical thinkers than Westerners, and may revive the phantom, as they describe Easterners' thinking as just as intuitive or non-rule-based. However, some studies argue that the essence of Easterners' thinking is dialecticism. Dialecticism can be defined in different ways, but its philosophical concept is that the world consists of opposite but not necessarily opposing ideas or concepts that, when put together, either negate each other or synthesize into a whole. Peng and Nisbett (1999) had already found that the thinking style of Chinese was more dialectical than that of Americans. They conducted several cross-cultural experiments to compare Chinese with Americans. For instance, Chinese were less sensitive to and were more accepting of contradictory proverbs than Americans, with contradictions such as "too humble is half proud," for instance. Furthermore, they demonstrated that Chinese participants rated their agreement with two contradictory statements more moderately when both statements were presented together than when either was presented individually. This trend was not observed in the data of Americans. The results indicate that Chinese are more likely to take the middle way when they encounter opinions that are contradictory of each other.

Contrary to the phantom, dialectical thinking can be viewed as a higher-level style of thinking. According to Hegelians, dialecticism is defined as an inference in which a synthesis is inferred from a thesis and its antithesis. Thus dialecticism is expected to produce a higher-level conclusion where opinions contradict each other. In contrast, propositional logic does not allow contradiction. Furthermore, Piaget (1980) assumed that humans acquire a dialectical thinking style to deal with complex problems after the operational stage. In other words, dialectical thinking is also thought of as a higher level of processing within the frame of cognitive development. Riegel (1973) expanded Piaget's theory to capture human development after the peak of non-contradictory thinking in formal operations. He argued that people need mature wisdom to think dialectically, in order to solve complex problems in the real world when they become adults.

In turn, then, do Easterners have a higher-level thinking style? The answer is also no. Rather, Peng and Nisbett (1999) and Spencer-Rodgers, Williams, and Peng (2010) assumed Easterners' dialecticism to be naïve dialecticism, which represents the following three aspects.

(1) The principle of contradiction: Because of the interconnectedness of things, and the ever-changing world, paradoxes and contradictions constantly arise. Two opposing propositions may both be true, and opposites are only apparent. Consequently, people may believe that the truth is always somewhere in the middle. Hence they may take a middle way when they encounter two opposite opinions. However, the middle-way resolution is not necessarily a higher-level synthesis and in this way, naïve dialecticism is different from Hegelian dialecticism.

(2) The principle of change: The universe is in flux and is constantly changing, and so the concepts that reflect it must also be fluid. Apparent stability is a signal of likely change.

(3) The principle of holism: Nothing exists in isolation, and everything is connected to other things.

Spencer-Rodgers, Boucher, Mori, Wang, and Peng (2009) supported the claim of Peng and Nisbett (1999). They reported that Easterners have a more dialectical self-concept than Westerners. They used a questionnaire that they named the Dialectical Self Scale. It includes statements such as "When I hear two sides of an argument, I often agree with both," and thus the authors propose that it measures people's attitude toward dialectical thinking, including the tendency to agree with opposite statements. Spencer-Rodgers, Peng, Wang, and Hou (2004) also reported Easterners' tendency toward dialecticism. They found that Chinese people gave more conflicting responses in self-evaluations than Americans. For instance, Chinese respondents' self-evaluations were more likely to be both positive and negative than those of Americans.

However, the result that Easterners were more likely to take a middle way (Peng & Nisbett, 1999) has not been replicated. Mercier, Zhan, Qu, Lu, and Van der Henst (2015) conducted a replication of Peng and Nisbett (1999) with French and Chinese participants. But neither group took a middle-way resolution when confronted with a pair of contradictory statements. Van der Henst, Mercier, Yama, Kawasaki, and Adachi (2006) and Mercier, Yama, Kawasaki, Adachi, and Van der Henst (2012) found that neither French nor Japanese participants took a middle-way resolution when they received advice opposite to their own opinion. Both the French and Japanese preferred their own opinion. We proposed that the tendency not to be manipulated by others is evolutionarily adaptive and culturally universal.

Furthermore, Friedman, Chen, and Vaid (2006) did not replicate the results of Peng and Nisbett (1999) on contradictory proverbs, with Chinese and American participants. They added a question about whether each proverb was poetic, and they found that when poeticality was co-varied out, dialectical proverbs were liked better than non-dialectical proverbs across both stimulus sets by Chinese and Americans alike. When wisdom was co-varied out, the effect of dialecticality was reduced in both sets and groups. In short, Chinese preference for dialectical proverbs was overestimated compared to poetical judgment.

In order to solve the problem, Zhang, Galbraith, Yama, Wang, and Manktelow (2015) administered both the Dialectical Self Scale and an additional rating task presenting pairs of opposite opinions to Japanese, Chinese, and British high school and university students. We found that attitudes to dialectical thinking, as measured on the Dialectical Self Scale, were higher among Japanese and Chinese than among British participants. This result confirmed the claim of Spencer-Rodgers and colleagues (2009). We also found the scores of university students were higher than those of high school students. This indicates that the individual's attitude or view of the world gets more dialectical during the development of adolescence, and that this difference may reflect cognitive development in the post-operational stage (Riegel, 1973). However, this last finding runs contrary to Spencer-Rodgers and colleagues' (2010) claim that the Dialectical Self Scale measures only naïve dialecticism, which is different to the higher-level dialectic thinking supposedly found in the post-operational stage. Japanese participants also rated dialectical thinking as wiser than both Chinese and British (there was no significant difference in this judgment between Chinese students and British students). However, although the Japanese and Chinese differed from British participants on dialectical attitudes, in actual ratings of opposing statements, the Japanese tendency to think dialectically was the weakest. These results indicate that Easterners may be more dialectical in how they view the world than Westerners, whereas they are not more dialectical when they actually meet opposite opinions. Our other interesting finding was that both the Dialectical Self Scale scores and the wisdom judgment scores were higher among Japanese than among Chinese. I will discuss the differences between Japanese and Chinese in the next section.

How can Easterners' dialecticism be explained?

Westerners' analytic cognition and Easterners' holistic cognition

The contrast between Westerners' rule-based thinking and Easterners' intuitive or dialectical thinking is regarded, by Nisbett (2003; Nisbett, Peng, Choi, & Norenzayan, 2001), as a distinction between Westerners' analytic cognition and Easterners' holistic cognition. From a review of previous studies of cultural differences in cognition, Nisbett and colleagues argued that Westerners are more likely to engage in analytic cognition, whereas Easterners are more likely to engage in holistic cognition. According to Nisbett, East Asians developed an intellectual tradition emphasizing holistic, dialectical information processing, which is contrasted with the European/North American intellectual tradition, which privileges an analytical style of cognition. According to his definition, analytic cognition involves detachment of the object from its context, a tendency to focus on attributes of the object to assign it to a category, and a preference for using rules about categories to explain and predict the object's behavior. In contrast, holistic cognition has an orientation to the context or the field as a whole, attention to relationships between a focal object and the field, and a preference for explaining and predicting events on the basis of such relationships.

This distinction can be further analyzed into four dimensions. First, in the analytic style of cognition of Westerners, attention tends to be oriented to the object, whereas in the holistic style of cognition of Easterners, attention tends to be focused not only on an object itself but on the context in which the object is embedded (Masuda & Nisbett, 2001). Second, it is shown that Easterners make more situational attributions, whereas Westerners make more dispositional attributions (Morris & Peng, 1994). The third factor emphasizes the usage of rules, as mentioned in the former section. The fourth factor focuses on the perception of change (Ji, Nisbett, & Su, 2001).

According to Nisbett and colleagues (2001), Easterners' dialecticism is explained in the frame of this distinction by using the cultural value dimensions that underlie individualist culture and collectivist culture (Triandis, 1995). It is assumed that Westerners have an individualist culture while Easterners have a collectivist culture. Analytic cognition is adaptive in an individualist culture where the individual's goals are given priority over group goals. In contrast, holistic cognition is adaptive in a collectivist culture. Group goals, such as keeping group harmony, are given priority over personal goals in a collectivist culture, hence it is adaptive to pay attention not only to the object itself, but its contextual information in order to maintain the harmony of the collective. It is particularly necessary that an individual observes not only a target person but those who are related to the target person, because the relation between the target person and other group members can influence the entire harmony of this group. Furthermore, Varnum, Grossman, Kitayama, and Nisbett (2010) have proposed an explanation at an individual level: from Westerners' independent self to analytic cognition and from Easterners' interdependent self to holistic cognition. It has been proposed that Easterners have a stronger attitude toward sociability and interdependence than Westerners. Markus and Kitayama (1991) connected the distinction of individualism/collectivism to two kinds of selves respectively. They argued that Westerners have an independent self, whereas Easterners have an interdependent self. According to them, Westerners are more likely to view themselves as individualistic, egocentric, and discrete from society, whereas Easterners are more inclined to view themselves as collectivistic, socio-centric, and related to others or society.

Their explanation is compatible with the results of cultural priming (Kühnen, Hannover, & Schubert, 2001). Cultural priming is assumed to make either the independent or the interdependent self more accessible. Both selves are accessible to persons within a culture; shifts toward one or the other definition of the self can be experimentally induced by priming the corresponding cultural orientation or meaning system. Kühnen and colleagues reported that participants who were asked to point out the differences between themselves and their friends or parents (primed as the independent self) were more likely to process stimuli unaffected by the context (analytic cognition) whereas those who were asked to point out the similarities between themselves and their friends or parents (primed as the interdependent self) were more apt to engage in context-bounded thinking (holistic cognition). In short, the accessible self-construal affects the style of cognition.

Explanation based on cultural tradition

Spencer-Rodgers and colleagues (Spencer-Rodgers et al., 2004, 2009, 2010) abandon the explanation based on the individualism/collectivism distinction but emphasize the importance of cultural tradition. Spencer-Rodgers argues that the contrast between Westerners' rule-based thinking and Easterners' dialectical thinking is distinct from the other dimensions of attention, and that Easterners' dialecticism is not very strongly related to Easterners' collectivism and the interdependent self, but is related to the perception of change in the cultural tradition of Easterners. As already mentioned, Ji and colleagues (2001) proposed that Easterners believe that the universe is contradictory because it is always changing (and interesting, the Dialectical Self Scale includes the item "I am constantly changing and am different from one time to the next"). The perception of change makes it possible for Easterners to easily find the resolution of contradiction, because one opinion may be right sometimes but may be wrong at other times. In addition, a further reason Spencer-Rodgers and colleagues do not assume the relation between Easterners' dialectical thinking and their collectivist culture is that, although Latinos are assumed to have a collectivist culture, they are not dialectical (Ma-Kellams, Spencer-Rodgers, & Peng, 2011; Spencer-Rodgers et al., 2004). These results indicate that a collectivist culture or an interdependent self is not an important factor for dialectical thinking.

Spencer-Rodgers and colleagues (2010) focus on cultural tradition to explain the cultural differences. According to them, Westerners' style of thinking is affected by the philosophy of ancient Greece, whereas Easterners' style of thinking derives from the traditions of Taoism, Confucianism, and Buddhism. Easterners' naïve dialecticism, including their folk belief, is rooted in the cultural concept of *yin* (negative aspects of the universe) and *yang* (positive aspects of the universe), which is central to Taoism. It is used to describe how polar opposites or seemingly contrary forces are interconnected and interdependent in the real world. It reflects the tradition of Chinese ontology that the world is constantly changing like the changes between *yin* and *yang*, and is full of contradictions.

Easterners' folk belief is reflected in their attitude not to hasten to make final judgments as shown by a proverb: A setback may turn out to be a blessing in disguise. This proverb was provided by the famous story of *Sāi Weng's lost horse*,[1] which was in the *Huáinánzǐ*, a classic Chinese book on philosophy that blends Taoism and Confucianism. The folk belief that everything is changing is also reflected in many classic tales and essays in Japan: the absence of permanence and continuity, and the notion of impermanence. The term *impermanence* expresses the Buddhist notion that all of conditioned existence, without exception, is transient, or in a constant state of flux. This is sometimes interpreted as a caution that the individual's life is mutable, and has appeared frequently in Japanese classical literature.

> *The current of the flowing river does not cease, and yet the water is not the same water as before. The foam that floats on stagnant pools, now vanishing, now forming, never stays the same for long. So, too, it is with the people and dwellings of the world.*

This passage is in the opening paragraph of *Hōjōki*. This was written by Kamo no Chomei, who was a Japanese poet and essayist in the 13th century. His work depicts the Buddhist concept of impermanence through the description of various disasters such as earthquake, famine, whirlwind, and conflagration in Kyoto.

Difference in IQ?

One could argue that the biggest issue related to white supremacy and social Darwinism is that of IQ test scores. As mentioned in the former section, Easterners' naïve dialecticism is neither a higher-level dialecticism nor a sign of Easterners' illogicality. We need one more point to kill the phantom from the 19th century. Hence in this section, I will discuss the relation between this style of thinking and IQ, to deny the belief of Easterners' intellectual inferiority.

Before arguing the cultural differences, let me discuss IQ test scores in the frame of cognitive architecture. According to general dual process theories (e.g., Evans & Over, 1996; Stanovich, 2004), human cognitive architecture consists of the evolutionarily current, analytic system (system 2), which makes it possible to think abstractly and logically with the support of large cognitive capacity. The evolutionarily old heuristic system (system 1) is in charge of evolutionarily adaptive cognition but sometimes causes human heuristic errors. The ability of logical thinking IQ tests purport to measure (although see Stanovich, West, and Toplak's chapter in this volume for a discussion of this) is supported by the evolutionarily current analytic system. The cognitive capacity of the evolutionarily current analytic system makes it possible to suppress the drive from the evolutionarily old heuristic system. Stanovich and West (1998a, 1998b) demonstrated that the higher one's intellectual score is, the more likely one is to follow logically correct prescriptions against the cognitive biases created by the evolutionarily old system.

Lynn (2003) reported that Easterners' IQ scores are (at most) slightly higher than those of Westerners. His report indicates no substantial cultural differences appear in logical thinking competence. Hence, the source of the differences in style of thinking between Westerners and Easterners is in inherited genes related to IQ. Studies have suggested that Africans' IQ scores are lower than those of Europeans and Asians, according to the summary of data (Lynn, 2003). One suggestion is that this is because of the non-rich educational environment in the region of Africa to the south of the Sahara Desert (see Nisbett, 2009).

However, introducing the dual process theories, we face a problem: the cultural definitions of analytic and holistic styles (Nisbett et al., 2001) appear to parallel the properties of the two distinct systems of dual process theories. According to dual process theorists, the properties of the evolutionarily old heuristic system are implicit, automatic, fast, intuitive, contextual, associative, and so forth, whereas the properties of the evolutionarily recent analytic system are explicit, controlled, slow, reflective, abstract, rule-based, and so on. Although the term *dialectical* does not characterize the evolutionarily old heuristic system, the term *rule-based* does characterize the evolutionarily current analytic system. Does this mean that Westerners use the evolutionarily recent system while Easterners use the evolutionarily old system?

Yama, Nishioka, Horishita, Kawasaki, and Taniguchi (2007) proposed that cultural differences might be due to how people use the two kinds of systems. We applied the dual process model of Stanovich and West (2003) to explain the cultural differences in cognition, and appealed to its distinction between gene-installed goals and meme-acquired goals in each of the two systems. A meme is a piece of knowledge that reproduces itself and spreads through the culture, by analogy with genes that replicate and spread through plant and animal populations through breeding. We argued (Yama et al., 2007) that the distinction between the two systems (systems 1 and 2) indicates differences in hardware, whereas the distinction between the gene-installed goals and the meme-installed goals shows differences in software. Therefore, the gene-installed goals are culturally universal, whereas the meme-acquired goals vary with culture and they indicate how humans use both systems to be culturally adaptive. The cognitive capacity IQ tests measure corresponds to the gene-installed goals in the evolutionarily recent analytic system. In contrast, the cultural differences between rule-based thinking and dialectical thinking can be in the meme-installed goals in the evolutionarily recent analytic system. Depending on what a meme-installed goal requires of humans, they may take a single rule (rule-based thinking) or plural rules (dialectical thinking) into consideration. Their idea is compatible with one of the latest models of dual process theory (Stanovich, 2009). It consists of three kinds of minds: the reflective, algorithmic, and autonomous minds. The evolutionarily old heuristic system corresponds to the autonomous mind, and it is culturally universal. The evolutionarily recent system is divided into the algorithmic mind and the reflective mind. The algorithmic mind corresponds to the cognitive capacity that makes it possible for humans to think logically and is strongly related to what IQ tests measure. The reflective mind supervises the algorithmic mind and indicates how to use the capacity. The source of the cultural effects on cognition is located in the process of the reflective mind.

Differences between Chinese and Japanese

Focusing on the differences between Japanese and Chinese (Zhang et al., 2015), I propose another explanation for cultural differences. Zhang and colleagues (2015) and Yama (2016), although we do not reject all the explanations given earlier, have pointed out another possible explanation for the cultural differences in cognition. We invoke the distinction between Westerners' low-context culture and Easterners' high-context culture (Hall, 1976). Context is background knowledge – like common sense – that people implicitly share when communicating. People can utilize context more in a high-context culture than in a low-context culture. In a high-context culture, people pay more attention to context, and they give resolution of contradiction by implicit assumption. For instance, when they try to understand a proverb such as "Too humble is half proud," they may infer that the person who pretends to be humble wants to show that he or she is very modest, and thus is proud of his or her modest personality. The important point here is that Japanese culture is higher-context than Chinese culture (e.g., Würtz, 2006). Linguistic components such as subjects are more often omitted in Japanese sentences than in Chinese sentences. The omitted components are recoverable by context in the conversation. This means that Japanese are expected to be more sensitive to context and to use it than Chinese are. This may explain the differences in the Dialectical Self Scale score and the wisdom judgment score between Japanese and Chinese (Zhang et al., 2015).

Conclusion

My provisional conclusion is that Easterners may be dialectical on how they view the world including themselves, but they do not actually do dialectical inference when they face opposite opinions. The dialectical thinking is not related to general intelligence, which IQ tests measure.

Easterners' dialecticism may be explained by the cultural tradition of Taoism, Confucianism, and Buddhism. Easterners' folk belief is rooted in the cultural concept of *yin* and *yang*. Furthermore, I added another explanation based on the distinction between Westerners' low-context culture and Easterners' high-context culture.

The provisional theories are based on the results of cross-cultural studies comparing Easterners and Westerners. I do not give a clear definition of Easterners, but I am referring here to the peoples influenced by Chinese culture: Chinese, Koreans, and Japanese (East Asian). Researchers need to gather more data to investigate if other peoples do dialectical thinking, and if they do, whether their dialecticism is qualitatively different from Easterners'.

Note

1 Sāi raised horses for a living. One day he lost a horse and his neighbor felt sorry for him, but Sāi didn't care about the horse, because he thought it wasn't a bad thing to lose a horse. After a while the horse returned with another beautiful horse, and the neighbor congratulated him on his good luck. But Sāi thought that maybe it wasn't a good thing to have this new horse. His son liked the new horse and often took it riding. One day his son fell off the horse and broke his leg. Because of his broken leg, he couldn't go off to the war, as was expected of all the young men in the area. Most of them died, but his son could survive.

References

Benedict, R. F. (1934). *Patterns of culture*. New York: Houghton Mifflin.

Boas, F. (1911). *The mind of primitive man*. New York: Macmillan.

Choi, I., & Nisbett, R. E. (2000). Cultural psychology of surprise: Holistic theories and recognition of contradiction. *Journal of Personality and Social Psychology, 79*, 890–905.

Evans, J. St. B. T., & Over, D. E. (1996). *Rationality and reasoning*. Hove, UK: Psychology Press.

Friedman, M., Chen, H. C., & Vaid, J. (2006). Proverb preferences across cultures: Dialecticality or poeticality?. *Psychonomic Bulletin & Review, 13*(2), 353–359.

Hall, E. T. (1976). *Beyond culture*. Garden City, NJ: Anchor Books/Doubleday.

Ji, L.-J., Nisbett, R. E., & Su, Y. (2001). Culture, change, and prediction. *Psychological Science, 12*, 450–456.

Kühnen, U., Hannover, B., & Schubert, B. (2001). The semantic-procedural interface model of the self: The role of self-knowledge for context-dependent versus context-independent modes of thinking. *Journal of Personality and Social Psychology, 80*, 397–409.

Lynn, R. (2003). The geography of intelligence. In H. Nyborg (Ed.), *The scientific study of general intelligence: Tribute to Arthur R. Jensen*. Oxford, UK: Elsevier Science.

Ma-Kellams, C., Spencer-Rodgers, J., & Peng, K. (2011). I am against us? Unpacking cultural differences in ingroup favoritism via dialecticism. *Personality and Social Psychology Bulletin, 37,* 15–27.

Markus, H. R., & Kitayama, S. (1991). Culture and the self: Implications for cognition, emotion, and motivation. *Psychological Review, 98,* 224–253.

Masuda, T., & Nisbett, R. E. (2001). Attending holistically versus analytically: Comparing the context sensitivity of Japanese and Americans. *Journal of Personality and Social Psychology, 81,* 922–934.

Mercier, H., Yama, H., Kawasaki, Y., Adachi, K., & Van der Henst, J.-B. (2012). Is the use of averaging in advice taking modulated by culture? *Journal of Cognition and Culture, 12,* 1–16.

Mercier, H., Zhang, J., Qu, Y., & Lu, P., & Van der Henst, J.-B. (2015). Do Easterners and Westerners treat contradiction differently? *Journal of Cognition and Culture, 15,* 45–63.

Morris, W. M., & Peng, K. (1994). Culture and cause: American and Chinese attributions for social and physical events. *Journal of Personality and Social Psychology, 67,* 949–971.

Nakamura, H. (1985). *Ways of thinking of Eastern peoples: India, China, Tibet, Japan.* Honolulu: University of Hawaii Press.

Nisbett, R. E. (2003). *The geography of thought: How Asians and Westerners think differently . . . and why.* New York: Free Press.

Nisbett, R. E. (2009). *Intelligence and how to get it: Why schools and cultures count.* Philadelphia, PA: W. W. Norton & Company.

Nisbett, R. E., Peng, K., Choi, I., & Norenzayan, A. (2001). Culture and system of thought: Holistic versus analytic cognition. *Psychological Review, 108,* 291–310.

Norenzayan, A., Smith, E. E., Kim, B. J., & Nisbett, R. E. (2002). Cultural preferences for formal versus intuitive reasoning. *Cognitive Science, 26,* 653–684.

Peng, K., & Nisbett, R. E. (1999). Culture, dialectics, and reasoning about contradiction. *American Psychologist, 54,* 741–754.

Piaget, J. (1980). *Les formes élémentaires de la dialectique.* Paris: Gallimard.

Riegel, K. F. (1973). Dialectic operations: The final period of cognitive development. *Human Development, 16,* 346–370.

Said, E. W. (1978). *Orientalism.* New York: Pantheon.

Spencer-Rodgers, J., Boucher, H. C., Mori, S. C., Wang, L., & Peng, K. (2009). The dialectical self-concept: Contradiction, change, and holism in East Asian cultures. *Personality and Social Psychology Bulletin, 35,* 29–44.

Spencer-Rodgers, J., Peng, K., Wang, L., & Hou, Y. (2004). Dialectical self-esteem and East–West differences in psychological well-being. *Personality and Social Psychology Bulletin, 30,* 1416–1432.

Spencer-Rodgers, J., Williams, M., & Peng, K. (2010). Cultural differences in expectations of change and tolerance for contradiction: A decade of empirical research. *Personality and Social Psychology Review, 14,* 296–312.

Stanovich, K. E. (1999). *Who is rational?: Studies of individual differences in reasoning.* Mahwah, NJ: Erlbaum.

Stanovich, K. E. (2004). *The robot's rebellion: Finding meaning in the age of Darwin.* Chicago: University of Chicago Press.

Stanovich, K. E. (2009), Distinguishing the reflective, algorithmic, and autonomous minds: Is it time for a tri-process theory? In J. St. B. T. Evans & K. Frankish (Eds.), *In two minds: Dual processes and beyond* (pp. 55–88). Oxford: Oxford University Press.

Stanovich, K. E., & West, R. F. (1998a). Cognitive ability and variation in selection task performance. *Thinking & Reasoning, 4*, 193–230.

Stanovich, K. E., & West, R. F. (1998b). Individual differences in rational thought. *Journal of Experimental Psychology: General, 127*, 161–188.

Stanovich, K. E., & West, R. F. (2003). Evolutionary versus instrumental goals: How evolutionary psychology misconceives human rationality. In D. E. Over (Ed.), *Evolution and the psychology of thinking* (pp. 171–230). Hove, UK: Psychology Press.

Triandis, H. C. (1995). *Individual and collectivism.* Boulder, CO: Westview Press.

Van der Henst, J.-B., Mercier, H., Yama, H., Kawasaki, Y., & Adachi, K. (2006). Dealing with contradiction in a communicative context: A cross-cultural study. *Intercultural Pragmatics, 3*, 487–502.

Varnum, M. E. W., Grossman, I., Kitayama, S., & Nisbett, R. E. (2010). The origin of cultural differences in cognition: The social orientation hypothesis. *Psychological Science. 19*, 9–13.

Würtz, E. (2006). Intercultural communication on web sites: A cross-cultural analysis of web sites from high-context cultures and low-context cultures. *Journal of Computer-Mediated Communication, 11*, 274–299.

Yama, H. (2016). A perspective of cross-cultural psychological studies for global business. In N. Zakaria, A.-N. Abdul-Talib, & N. Osman (Eds.), *Handbook of research on impacts of international business and political affairs on the global economy.* Hove, UK: IGI Global.

Yama, H., Manktelow, K. I., Mercier, H., Van der Henst, J.-B., Do, K. S., Kawasaki, Y., & Adachi, K. (2010). A cross-cultural study of hindsight bias and conditional probabilistic reasoning. *Thinking and Reasoning, 16*, 346–371.

Yama, H., Nishioka, M., Horishita, T., Kawasaki, Y., & Taniguchi, J. (2007). A dual process model for cultural differences in thought. *Mind and Society, 6*, 143–172.

Zhang, B., Galbraith, N., Yama, H., Wang, L., & Manktelow, K. I. (2015). Dialectical thinking: A cross-cultural study of Japanese, Chinese, and British students. *Journal of Cognitive Psychology, 27*, 771–779.

14

FROM REASONING AND INTELLIGENCE RESEARCH TO INFORMATION DESIGN

Understanding and optimising the usability and acceptability of schematic transit maps

Maxwell J. Roberts

Any travel by public transport, anywhere in the world, will almost certainly result in an encounter with some sort of schematic map for planning a journey, assisting in locating the correct departure point, or confirming the status of a journey en route. This method of information presentation can be amongst the most complex that members of the public are likely to use in everyday life. Indeed, with ever-increasing network complexity worldwide, a recent mathematical analysis (Gallotti, Porter, & Barthelemy, 2016) suggests that there is a cognitive limit to the under-standability of complex transport networks, and a number of these worldwide have already exceeded this.

Typically, schematic maps are highly stylised, with routes shown as straight lines – horizontal, vertical, or 45° diagonals – joined by tightly radiused corners. Mathematically, this is known as an *octolinear* design. Topography may be considerably distorted, and most, if not all, surface details omitted, so that the focus of such designs is on the routes, stations, and interconnections between lines. Famously, Henry Beck's diagrammatic London Underground map, first published in 1933, adopted these principles, and they have been applied to almost every London design since (Garland, 1994; Roberts, 2005). With time, schematic maps have become particularly associated with urban rail networks worldwide (Ovenden, 2015).

For transport undertakings that publish a schematic network map, the belief is clearly that this will offer a simplified version of reality, improving usability compared with a fully detailed topographic map drawn to scale. Hence, the use of public transport is facilitated and encouraged. However, few cities have managed to emulate the success of the London version, which has been asserted to be a design classic, and voted one of Britain's most iconic creations (BBC Television, 1987, 2006). Indeed, public responses to some international works indicate that the creation of a genuinely successful design is not easily achieved. One of the most famous failures is the Vignelli New York subway diagram. Introduced in 1972 to critical acclaim (a copy is held in the collection of the New York Museum of Modern Art), it became the victim of campaigners who claimed that its abstractedness disconnected New Yorkers from their city. It lasted just 7 years, and was withdrawn in 1979, replaced by a map that sought to show topographical reality more accurately, along with more surface features (Lloyd, 2012). In Madrid, a controversial design introduced in 2007 generated considerable debate (e.g., Engel, 2007). It was intended to be compact, but depicted the network as a severe grid using just horizontal and vertical lines (technically, a *tetralinear design*), along with considerable topographical distortion and crushed suburbs. In both these cases, users judged that the supposed benefits of the schematic depiction were outweighed by the topographical distortion and abstractedness of the designs. The London Underground map ran into a similar problem in 2009 when, in an attempt to simplify it still further, the River Thames was removed. This made news and television headlines (e.g., *Daily Mail*, 2009), and the river was reinstated soon afterwards.

The Paris Metro is another example of a schematic map that does not fulfill its potential. The system is a challenge to show clearly, with a dense network of interconnected lines that follow complex twisting trajectories. Network expansion from the 1960s onwards put the established design under considerable pressure, and the rapidity with which new routes were constructed caused unprecedented design instability, with numerous different solutions attempted (Ovenden, 2009). The current official version, first released in 2000, adopted conventional octolinearity, but here the problem is different. Roberts, Newton, Lagattolla, Hughes, and Hasler (2013) argue that the complex line trajectories of the schematic do little to simplify the depiction of the network compared with topographical reality, merely converting twisting, turning lines into zigzags instead, so that the map changes the shape of the complexity rather than reduces it. They compared the official map with a novel curvilinear design, and found that this had considerably improved times for planning journeys between pairs of stations, compared with the official version.

The contrasting situations in London, New York, Madrid, and Paris highlight that the design of an effective schematic map that is genuinely easy to use, and is accepted by the general public, is not simple to achieve. Usability issues have to be addressed, and users have expectations that should be satisfied, within reason. Furthermore, different cities have gravitated towards different solutions (schematic versus topographical) and different degrees of topographical distortion for their schematic maps (high for London, low for Paris). It is noteworthy that users tend to object to certain adverse aspects of design (abstractedness, topographical distortion) but others tend to go unnoticed (e.g., failure to simplify line trajectories). This can be demonstrated strikingly in usability studies, where objective measures of planning times are recorded along with subjective measures (either questionnaire ratings of map usability or choice tasks where users are asked to select a preferred design). The subjective measures are correlated (e.g., Roberts et al., 2013), but the correlation between subjective and objective measures is effectively zero. Hence, people often choose maps that they find difficult to use, and reject maps that they find easy to use.

Psychologists will not be surprised by a dissociation between objective measures of design effectiveness and subjective evaluations of this. Such metacognitive failures have been observed for decades (e.g., Chabris & Simons, 2010; Kruger & Dunning, 1999). Often, the problem is that there are limited cues to whether performance is successful. Provided this is reasonably competent, and errors are few, then subtle cues, such as a tendency for a persistent difference between tasks of a few seconds, will simply be insufficiently salient, especially as self-monitoring is itself a task that demands cognitive resources (e.g., Dierckx & Vandierendonck, 2005). Without salient performance cues, and given that most users will not be experts at visual information design, it is inevitable that maps will be evaluated according to their superficial surface properties (e.g., *Are there significant topographical distortions?*) rather than the more subtle aspects of design that contribute more directly to usability – this tendency by novices has been observed for decades (e.g., Chi, Feltovich, & Glaser, 1981). Roberts (2014b) reports a preliminary analysis of an Internet-administered map rating task. People were asked to look at nine different versions of the London Underground map, and rate the usability of each one. One important finding was a massive *octolinearity bias* in ratings, even for designs deliberately intended to be difficult to use. All octolinear maps were given ratings which were considerably inflated relative to matched versions using different design rules; favourable ratings that were not warranted given either actual or predicted usability data. This bias is not surprising considering the ubiquitousness of octolinearity worldwide. As per the fluency framework (e.g., Alter & Oppenheimer, 2009), experience can result in a more positive evaluation for maps designed in this way, compared with less conventional ones. With repeated exposure, people therefore will develop opinions about the correct way to design a schematic map, and these expectations and prejudices will dominate their subjective evaluations. Objective measures and subjective evaluations will only be correlated if performance differences between designs are sufficiently large and salient to override expectations. Alternatively, the illusion of a correlation can be created in a case where a disliked aspect, such as noticeable topographical distortion, is by chance correlated with a more fundamental design weakness, such as complex line trajectories.

Of course, user acceptance is an important aspect of design. An impeccably effective map will have failed if people nonetheless reject it. The problem is that considerable individual differences exist in subjective evaluations – presumably the designers of the Madrid, New York, and Paris maps were pleased with the results, and the London officials responsible for removing the River Thames thought that this would be a useful change. Looking at actual data, the curvilinear Paris Metro map (Roberts et al., 2013) is a more effective design than the official octolinear version, but only around half the sample chooses it in usability studies, even when all people have experienced both maps. This figure reflects not only a failure of metacognitive monitoring, with expectations and prejudices overruling usability observations, but also considerable individual differences in map preference, with half of the sample prepared to put a conventional design to one side, preferring a radical alternative instead.

Conjectures, prescriptions, and frameworks for effective design

The dissociation between subjective evaluations and objectively measured performance means that the selection of new designs should always be based, at least in part, on usability testing, especially where departures from convention are being proposed. The general public cannot be blamed for their octolinearity bias, this is a natural consequence of their cognitive make-up. However, a more explicit bias; amongst graphic designers, transport officials, researchers, and commentators – the *octolinearity as a gold standard conjecture* – is less defensible. This is the widespread assertion that applying *octolinearity* will result in the best schematic map possible, no matter what the structure of the network (e.g., Ovenden, 2005). For example, until recently, this dictated the objectives of researchers attempting to automate schematic map design, so that Nöllenburg and Wolff (2011) described octolinearity as a *hard constraint* (i.e., it should never be broken) and suggested that "the main benefit of octolinear layouts is that they potentially consume less space and use fewer bends while still having a tidy and schematic appearance" (p. 626) and that "we believe that octolinearity, which is strictly followed by most real metro maps, is an essential ingredient for tidy and easy-to-read metro map layouts" (p. 627). It is also worth noting that, irrespective of technology through the ages, an octolinear design has always been easier to create than alternatives, so that ease of implementation may be partly responsible for this design bias.

Roberts et al. (2013) criticise the *octolinearity as a gold standard conjecture* from a number of different viewpoints. First, they note that very little in the psychological literature predicts or corroborates it. Second, a belief in this conjecture discourages consideration of the possibility that networks with different structures may require different design solutions, and also deflects from analysing maps from the perspective of the quality of implementation within the design rules adopted: many designers appear to believe, as evidenced in their products, that simply creating an octolinear diagram is a pathway to outstanding usability. This is not the case, and a poorly executed creation can easily result. Third, the superiority of the curvilinear map versus the official octolinear design demonstrated by Roberts et al. (2013) conclusively disproves the *strong* version of the conjecture (octolinearity will *always* result in the most effective design) although weaker versions are left intact (e.g., octolinearity will *usually* result in the most effective design, but not in instances where this is incompatible with network structure).

Roberts (2012) notes that octolinearity is just one of numerous angle-sets that could be used for schematic maps. In other words, the *level of linearity* can be varied. Hence, a design might use just two perpendicular angles (tetralinear), three angles at 60° to each other (hexalinear), four angles (octolinear), five angles (decalinear), and so on. A systematic and exhaustive exploration of these is suggested for any city whose network is to be mapped, and Roberts (2012) implements this for Berlin and London. The aim of this procedure is for the designer to specify the objectives for a design in advance, and then identify the level of linearity that best enables these to be met. However, precise guidance on design objectives is remarkably rare (Roberts, 2014b). Nöllenburg (2014) gives a substantial set (e.g., keep line trajectories as straight as possible, space stations evenly, station labels should not occlude lines, and relative positions of stations should be preserved). Ovenden (2009) provides a collection that is broadly compatible, but includes more subtle prescriptions (e.g., do not bend a line twice between a pair of stations, keep station labels horizontal) that may be more likely to affect aesthetic judgement than actual usability. Many of these prescriptions seem reasonable, and can be shown to be compatible with theories of human cognition (see later), but there is surprisingly little empirical evidence to demonstrate their efficacy (Roberts, 2014a). They form a somewhat disparate set of principles, not necessarily compatible with each other, and Roberts (2012, 2014b) therefore attempted to organise these into a broad framework of five categories.

Simplicity

The key requirement for a schematic map is that it converts the complex trajectories of routes into simple line trajectories on the diagram. Many designers appear to neglect or misunderstand this criterion, and in the process convert the complex line trajectories of reality into numerous short zig-zagging segments, despite the questionable utility in terms of information value.

Coherence

The *simplicity* criterion refers to individual line trajectories. The way these relate together to give the design organisation and *good shape* is also important, but harder to define and measure. Objectives can be specified that will contribute to coherence, such as maximising parallel lines, symmetrical divergence of branches, and aligning stations and termini. Coherence might also be achieved by emphasising regular, easily identified shapes, such as circles, equilateral triangles, horizons (grounding the design using horizontal lines), and/or grids.

Balance

Ideally, there should be an even density of stations across a map, or at least gentle density gradients, so that congested areas and empty spaces are not directly adjacent. The natural consequence of attempting to create a balanced design for an extensive network with a clear central region is that the centre will be enlarged and the suburbs compacted. An over-enlarged centre with over-compressed suburbs, however, can lead to a diffuse design without a clear attentional focus.

Harmony

Roberts (2012, 2014b) suggests a placeholder category for design aspects that are likely to influence aesthetics, but are unlikely to have any measurable impact on usability. There will be individual differences in this respect, but research does suggest that certain shapes and patterns tend to be rated as more pleasing than others (e.g., Lindell & Mueller, 2011). For example, line crossings at 90° might be preferred to non-perpendicular ones, and equilateral triangles preferred to narrow pointed isosceles ones.

Topographicity

In order to optimise a design according to these criteria, topographical distortion is inevitable to at least some extent. A schematic with poor topographicity is one in which distortion is sufficiently extreme that it adversely affects user confidence – as a result of significant conflicts with mental models of a city – or worse, leads to the planning of inefficient routes. For example, Guo (2011) looked at actual journeys taken on the London Underground, and found that for one region of the map, with poor topographicity, inefficient journeys were taken 30% of the time. Vertesi (2008) describes how Londoners' understanding of the structure of the city has been distorted by their knowledge of the London Underground map. One consequence of this is that users may take unnecessary journeys owing to exaggerated distances between stations implied by the current official design.

There are two key aspects to note about this framework. First, it is neutral in terms of the actual design rules. As long as the framework criteria are satisfied, the rules do not matter, so that a requirement for octolinearity is not specified. The second aspect is that the criteria are often in conflict with each other. For example, using many more angles than the four octolinearity ones allow will permit simpler, straighter line trajectories, but at the expense of the coherence of the design. Alternatively, straightening octolinear line trajectories may damage topographicity. Therefore, empirical testing is important not just to demonstrate the necessity of each of these criteria, but also to prioritise them. However, in lieu of this, showing that these components are compatible with the literature on reasoning and intelligence at least gives them a plausible initial foundation.

Embedding map design prescriptions in theories of reasoning and intelligence

For a reasoning researcher attempting to come to grips with a problem from the real world, there is a considerable body of established theories and findings to draw upon, derived from a variety of domains and tasks. The circumstances in which people succeed or fail in their attempts to make inferences are well documented and understood, and researchers can easily manipulate task structure with predictable consequences for individual item difficulty (e.g., Evans, Newstead, & Byrne, 1993; Manktelow, 2012). Underlying these effects is usually the working memory load of a task. The more mental steps necessary for completion, the harder any task will be (e.g., Birney & Halford, 2002; Roberts & Sykes, 2005). The effects of task format on performance can also be considerable: manipulations can be easily performed that hinder or facilitate identifying and representing the underlying logic of a task, with an imperfect representation increasing the working memory load (e.g., Meo, Roberts, & Marucci, 2007; Roberts, Welfare, Livermore, & Theadom, 2000). Mitigating against these manipulations, to at least some extent, are the effects of individual differences in intelligence and expertise, the former influencing the extent to which high working memory demands degrade performance (e.g., Carpenter, Just, & Shell, 1990; Stanovich & West, 1998), the latter whether efficient problem representations can be developed even when camouflaged by the surface structure of a problem (e.g., Chi et al., 1981).

For schematic maps, their most salient feature is the presentation of logical relationships (the structure of the network) in visual form. The findings from the literature on solving non-verbal intelligence test problems (such as Raven's progressive matrices, Raven, Raven, & Court, 1993) show that simple changes to the visual appearance of a problem, without changing the underlying logic, can have dramatic effects on item difficulty (Meo, Roberts, & Marucci, 2007; Primi, 2002; Roberts, Livermore, Welfare, & Theadom, 2000; Vodegel Matzen, Van der Molen, & Dudink, 1994). Difficulty is affected not only by the *quantity* of rules and elements, but also by their *quality*, so that if the shapes used are particularly complex, difficult to name, or overlapped, then individual item elements and their relationships will be harder to identify, with a profound knock-on effect for identifying the underlying logic of an item (see Figure 14.1). It is hard for people to reason if they cannot identify what they are reasoning about. Hence, the *simplicity* and *coherence* criteria can easily be mapped onto current research findings in intelligence.

Deductive reasoning research has been informative about the sorts of logical relationships people find difficult to process (e.g., Evans et al., 1993; Manktelow, 2012). This can have implications, for example, in understanding service patterns. The New York subway is famously difficult to map, but the task of understanding the network is made harder because some services operate as *exclusive disjunctions*. For example, along the Grand Concourse Line in the Bronx, many stations are served either by the B train, or by the D train, but *never by the B and D train together*. If services are difficult to comprehend, then the map will be likewise, irrespective of its configuration.

The provision of supplementary information on a map (e.g., concerning restrictions, exceptions, and opportunities for forward travel) is also of interest to reasoning researchers. Working memory capacity is challenged not only by the sheer quantity of such information, but also by its *quality*, with much of this incomplete, ambiguous, or incongruent with expectations. For example (taken from a London Underground map from 2008), if certain stations are flagged as having no late evening service, then it is reasonable to expect unflagged stations to have no late restrictions, but this inference is valid only for the London Underground stations, not the London Overground stations on the same map (Roberts, 2008, 2012). The successors to Wason's (1972) incomprehensible social security claim forms, full of double negatives, that led to his research into sentence-picture verification, are today's numerous ambiguous incomprehensible attempts to give people assistance via poorly designed or inconsistently used information graphics. Better intentioned, but no less pernicious.

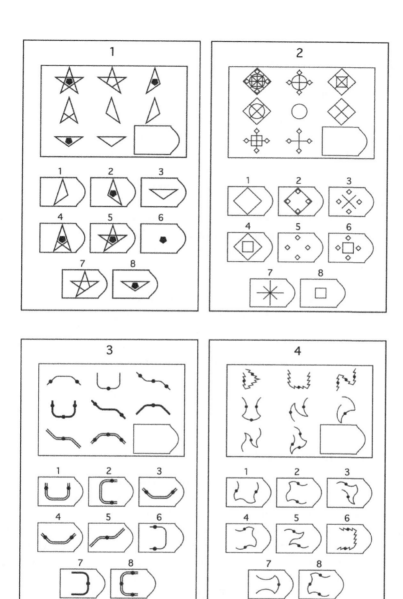

FIGURE 14.1 Four matrix items typical of the sort used in intelligence tests. Items 1 and 2 both have a rule that is straightforward to identify and apply, but Item 2 has more elements (six, as opposed to four for Item 1), making these harder to discern, and in turn the rule harder to identify. Item 2 should be the harder of the pair because of its higher cognitive load. Items 3 and 4 also have a straightforward rule, but the line trajectories in Item 4 are more complicated, making their relationships harder to identify, and therefore the rule harder to discover. Item 4 should be harder to solve than Item 3, despite being otherwise logically identical. Image © Maxwell J. Roberts, 2014. Reproduced with permission.

The benefits of effective design

What might be expected from a design that satisfies all of these framework criteria? A simple, coherent, balanced schematic map will have high *structural salience*, revealing the elements and their relatedness, and making the underlying network configuration easier to identify, facilitating both journey planning and learning, so that a virtuous circle is set up, with performance getting better as more is learnt. For such a design, we would expect fast journey planning, few errors, better remembered plans, and more easily reconstructed plans in the event of a failure to remember.

The design should also have good harmony, so that users like its appearance and accept it, and good topographicity, so that there will be no serious conflicts with users' mental models of the city, which might result in the map being rejected for lack of trustworthiness. Together, these will result in people electing to use the map rather than to rely on asking for assistance or using computerised journey planners, also facilitating learning and boosting future performance.

In comparison, a poorly designed schematic will struggle to offer any of these benefits. A lack of simplicity and coherence can bury the underlying structure of the network. Such a map may even have little to offer compared with a topographical version, other than the simplification entailed in removing street details and most other landmarks. With gross neglect of the framework criteria (especially for poor harmony and topographicity), users will reject it outright and the design will be short-lived.

Conclusions: back to Beck

Henry Beck's work is often misunderstood. Many commentators herald him as the inventor of schematic maps, which is clearly not the case. Transport cartography and information design had been evolving in this direction long before Beck had even considered experimenting with this approach (Dow, 2005; Roberts, 2012). Beck's use of octolinearity is also often given too much emphasis. Again, he is sometimes mistakenly asserted to have been the first to use this, and many designers revere it as a cartographic gold standard. We have already seen that this position is indefensible. The reality is that different networks have different topographical and geometric properties, and some may have poor compatibility with octolinearity (Roberts, 2012). Such misconceptions and preoccupations divert attention away from the possibility that some schematic maps might be more effective than others: optimising the various criteria within a set of design rules is at least as important as the choice of design rules itself. Beck's real achievement is that he chose the design rules (octolinearity) and then, within this constraint and with little precedent, produced an exceptional design: a textbook case of his adherence to the framework for effective design, and implying a better-than-usual understanding of the cognitive psychology of the user. Figure 14.2 shows the topographical reality of the Paddington area (1), in comparison with Beck's first attempt at this

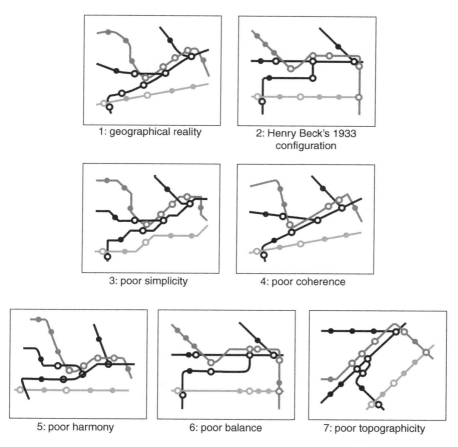

1: geographical reality   2: Henry Beck's 1933 configuration

3: poor simplicity   4: poor coherence

5: poor harmony   6: poor balance   7: poor topographicity

FIGURE 14.2   Sections of maps showing the line trajectories of an area of central London around Paddington. (1) represents topographical reality, as shown in maps immediately prior to Henry Beck. (2) shows Henry Beck's schematic depiction of reality. (3) demonstrates poor simplicity, with many corners, (4) has poor coherence, the trajectories are simple, but there are many different angles, and no pairs of lines are parallel. (5) has few angles and straight, parallel lines, but these do not cross at 90° and hence the harmony is poor. Such a design might be easy to use, but rejected by users. (6) has uneven station distribution and therefore poor balance, and (7) distorts topography considerably, hence *poor topographicity*. Image © Maxwell J. Roberts, 2014. Reproduced with permission.

configuration (2), and also what can go wrong if the framework is neglected. Hence, if Beck had used octolinear angles, but had not addressed the requirement for simplicity (3) – perhaps attempting to match topographical reality too closely – then a far less effective design would have resulted. Beck's early work was not special because it used straight lines, but because it had so few corners.

Of course, Beck could have chosen other angles for straightening the line trajectories (4), but the risk of poor coherence would have been considerable, for example with many non-parallel lines. However, even if he had attempted a non-octolinear design and maintained parallel lines, he could have chosen angles with poor harmony because of, for example, lack of perpendicular line crossings (5). Octolinear angles have a natural advantage in terms of this. Beck could have created an unbalanced design (6) or one with poor topographicity (7), in which the distortion conflicted too much with people's mental models of London. By avoiding this problem, users were more likely to appreciate the improved usability of the schematic map, and less likely to reject this new design for other reasons, hence ensuring the longevity of this approach for London and paving the way for this method of visual communication to become widespread in the future. Today, it is easy to find schematic maps worldwide which fail to address adequately one or more of the five categories of criteria for effective design from the proposed framework. A better appreciation of Beck's early success, as well as the psychological factors that underpin effective design, should lead to this happening less often in the future.

References

Alter, A. L., & Oppenheimer, D. M. (2009). Uniting the tribes of fluency to form a metacognitive nation. *Personality and Social Psychology Review, 13*, 219–235.

BBC Television (1987). *Design classics*. First broadcast 29 June.

BBC Television (2006). *The culture show*. First broadcast 16 March.

Birney, D. P., & Halford, G. S. (2002). Cognitive complexity of suppositional reasoning: An application of the relational complexity metric to the knight-knave task. *Thinking & Reasoning, 8*, 109–134.

Carpenter, P. A., Just, M. A., & Shell, P. (1990). What one intelligence test measures: A theoretical account of the processing in the Raven Progressive Matrices test. *Psychological Review, 97*, 404–431.

Chabris, C., & Simons, D. (2010). *The invisible gorilla*. New York: Crown Publishing.

Chi, M. T. H., Feltovich, P. J., & Glaser, R. (1981). Categorization and representation of physics problems by experts and novices. *Cognitive Science, 5*, 121–152.

Daily Mail (2009, 18 September). Boris Johnson puts Thames back on London Underground map after outrage over redesign. www.dailymail.co.uk/news/article-1213932 [accessed 1 July 2015].

Dierckx, V., & Vandierendonck, A. (2005). Adaptive strategy application in linear reasoning. In M. J. Roberts & E. J. Newton (Eds.), *Methods of thought: Individual differences in reasoning strategies* (pp. 107–128). Hove, UK: Psychology Press.

Dow, A. (2005). *Telling the passenger where to get off*. Harrow Weald, UK: Capital Transport Publishing.

Engel, M. (2007, 20 October). Tubular hell. *Financial Times*. www.ft.com/cms/s/0/b1b69118–7b7b-11dc-8c53–0000779fd2ac.html [accessed 1 July 2015].

Evans, J. St. B. T., Newstead, S. E., & Byrne, R. M. J. (1993). *Human reasoning: The psychology of deduction*. Hove, UK: Erlbaum.

Gallotti, R., Porter, M. A., & Barthelemy, M. (2016). Lost in transportation: Information measures and cognitive limits in multilayer navigation. *Science Advances, 2*, e1500445.

Garland, K. (1994). *Mr Beck's Underground map*. Harrow Weald, UK: Capital Transport Publishing.

Guo, Z. (2011). Mind the map! The impact of transit maps on travel decisions in public transit. *Transportation Research Part A, 45*, 625–639.

Kruger, J., & Dunning, D. (1999). Unskilled and unaware of it. *Journal of Personality & Social Psychology, 77*, 1121–1134.

Lindell, A. K., & Mueller, J. (2011). Can science account for taste? Psychological insights into art appreciation. *Journal of Cognitive Psychology, 23*, 453–475.

Lloyd, P. B. (2012). *Vignelli: Transit maps*. Rochester, NY: RIT Cary Graphic Art Press.

Manktelow, K. I. (2012). *Thinking and reasoning: An introduction to the psychology of reason, judgment and decision making*. Hove, UK: Psychology Press.

Meo, M., Roberts, M. J., & Marucci, F. S. (2007). Element salience as a predictor of item difficulty for Raven's Progressive Matrices. *Intelligence, 35*, 359–368.

Nöllenburg, M. (2014). A survey on automated metro map layout methods. Schematic Mapping Workshop 2014, University of Essex, April. https://sites.google.com/site/schematicmapping/Nöllenburg_survey.pdf [accessed 29 May 2015].

Nöllenburg, M., & Wolff, A. (2011). Drawing and labeling high-quality metro maps by mixed-integer programming. *IEEE Transactions on Visualization and Computer Graphics, 17*, 626–641.

Ovenden, M. (2005). *Metro maps of the world* (2nd ed). Harrow Weald, UK: Capital Transport Publishing.

Ovenden, M. (2009). *Paris underground: The maps, stations, and design of the Métro*. New York: Penguin Books.

Ovenden, M. (2015). *Transit maps of the world* (Second edition). New York: Penguin.

Primi, R. (2002). Complexity of geometric inductive reasoning tasks, contribution to the understanding of fluid intelligence. *Intelligence, 30*, 41–70.

Raven, J., Raven, J. C., & Court, J. H. (1993). *Manual for Raven's progressive matrices and Mill Hill vocabulary scales*. Oxford: Oxford Psychologists Press.

Roberts, M. J. (2005). *Underground maps after Beck*. Harrow Weald, UK: Capital Transport Publishing.

Roberts, M. J. (2008). Information pollution on the Underground map. http://privatewww.essex.ac.uk/~mjr/underground/information_pollution/ip.html [accessed 29 May 2015].

Roberts, M. J. (2012). *Underground maps unravelled, explorations in information design*. Wivenhoe, UK: Published by the author.

Roberts, M. J. (2014a). Schematic maps in the laboratory. Schematic Mapping Workshop 2014, University of Essex, April. https://sites.google.com/site/schematicmapping/Roberts-Empirical.pdf [accessed 29 May 2015].

Roberts, M. J. (2014b). What's your theory of effective schematic map design? Schematic Mapping Workshop 2014, University of Essex, April. https://sites.google.com/site/schematicmapping/Roberts-Theoretical.pdf [accessed 29 May 2015].

Roberts, M. J., Newton, E. J., Lagattolla, F. D., Hughes, S., & Hasler, M. C. (2013). Objective versus subjective measures of Paris Metro map usability: Investigating traditional octolinear versus all-curves schematic maps. *International Journal of Human Computer Studies, 71*, 363–386.

Roberts, M. J., & Sykes, E. D. A. (2005). Categorical reasoning from multiple diagrams. *Quarterly Journal of Experimental Psychology, 58A*, 333–376.

Roberts, M. J., Welfare, H., Livermore, D. P., & Theadom, A. M. (2000). Context, visual salience, and inductive reasoning, *Thinking and Reasoning, 6*, 349–374.

Stanovich, K. E., & West, R. F. (1998). Individual differences in rational thought. *Journal of Experimental Psychology: General, 127,* 161–188.

Vertesi, J. (2008). Mind the gap: The London Underground map and users' representations of urban space. *Social Studies of Science 38,* 7–33.

Vodegel Matzen, L. B., Van der Molen, M. W., & Dudink, A. C. (1994). Error analysis of Raven test performance. *Personality and Individual Differences, 16,* 433–445.

Wason, P. C. (1972). In real life negatives are false. *Logique et Analyse, 57–58,* 17–38.

15

HOW MOOD AFFECTS REASONING

Nick Perham

The ability to reason may not be the sole domain of human beings (Blaisdell, Sawa, Leising & Waldmann, 2006), but it is likely to be an ability that we use more than other animals. A key influence on reasoning behaviour is that of emotion. We all are familiar with phrases such as "seeing things through rose-coloured glasses" and being unable to think straight when the "red mist descends". However, this link between emotion and reasoning has not always been accepted and only in the past half a century or so has this association been explored in detail. This association is known to occur in two ways – either through the emotion or mood people are in or through the material they reason about. This chapter focuses on how cognition and emotion have (eventually) been explored together, how people's moods and emotions affect their reasoning abilities and some possible mechanisms that may underpin these phenomena.

Before we begin, I should point out that I will be using the terms *mood* and *emotion* interchangeably. Technically, *emotion* refers to an intense but brief reaction that relates to a specific target whereas *mood* is weaker in intensity than emotion but lasts longer and is unrelated to a specific target (Power & Dalgleish, 2008).

Despite what we might feel is an obvious connection between reasoning and emotion, it has not always been this way. Plato felt human beings comprised an earthly body inhabited by a divine soul (this idea exerted its influence on religious scholars, both Christian and Muslim, who held considerable sway during Western mediaeval history). This dualist account placed the position of emotions in the soul, and Plato felt they were irrepressible forces that interfered with and impaired our powers of reason (Power & Dalgleish, 2008). This separation of emotion and reason remained an influential point of view for a long period of time.

Eminent psychologists over the past 100 years have addressed the issue of emotions. William James, like the philosopher Rene Descartes before him, emphasised the physiological aspects of emotions, how they preceded an individual's actual emotional state and their propensity for objective measurement and investigation. In his collaborative work with Carl Lange, he argued that each emotion elicited a unique physiology yet did not reside in specialised brain regions (Hjelle & Ziegler, 1992). Indeed, debate still rages regarding whether there is just one, generalised physiological level of arousal (Ekman, 1982) or whether there are distinct ones relating to each emotion (e.g. Schachter & Singer, 1962).

A dispositional approach to personality emphasised an individual's predisposition to personality and thus certain emotional traits such as anxiety. Within this framework, Hans Eysenck initially identified two basic type dimensions, namely extraversion-introversion and neuroticism-stability. Scores on both of these dimensions gave rise to four groups; stable introverts (calm, reliable, careful), neurotic introverts (moody, anxious, unsociable), stable extraverts (carefree, talkative, outgoing) and neurotic extraverts (touchy, excitable, aggressive). However, Eysenck found that these two dimensions were unable to differentiate between individuals diagnosed with schizophrenia and those who were not. Thus, he introduced a psychoticism-superego dimension (Eysenck, 1965). Those who scored high in this were impulsive and insensitive to others whereas those who scored low were warm and socialised.

Psychiatrist Aaron Beck developed cognitive therapy whilst focusing on individuals with depression. Original versions were rather simplistic by stating that cognition caused emotion; however, over the years, and with many collaborators, cognitive therapy extended beyond depression to, for example, anxiety and schizophrenia (Beck & Emery, 1985; Beck & Rector, 2005). Borrowing from Bartlett (1932) and Piaget (1953), Beck and colleagues proposed that schemata were the structures that organised our memory, thinking and perception units. For example, presenting a picture of a house would activate a 'house schema' which would likely include a number of default items such as chimney or bedroom, even though they may not have been shown in the initial picture. Schemas also existed that related to interpersonal matters, roles and goals, and problems arose when these were dysfunctional. Typically they lay dormant until congruent stressors triggered them. Depression-related schema could cause individuals with depression to view themselves and their environment in a negative way. This meant that the individuals misinterpreted facts in the wrong (negative) way or blamed themselves for any misfortune that occurred rather than attributing such problems to a more probable, external source. Consequently these individuals saw the world as much worse than it actually was.

The idea that emotions could spread via a network of associations has a long history (e.g. Aristotle) and was initially used within cognitive science to explain the relationship between linguistic concepts (Quillian, 1968). Gordon Bower proposed arguably the most influential network theory of emotion (Bower, 1981). Emotions, along with concepts and events, were represented as nodes within a network. How something was activated within that network depended on a number of things such as how close the nodes were to each other, how strong the initial activation was and how much time had passed since that initial activation. For example, if someone experienced a reaction of fear when encountering a dog, previous experiences of encounters with other dogs were likely to be brought to mind as well as innate and learnt autonomic responses. This spreading activation was supported by studies showing a mood-state-dependent memory whereby participants induced into a happy or sad mood recalled more pleasant and unpleasant, respectively, childhood memories (Bower, 1981).

Network theories presupposed that emotions preceded any kind of cognitive processing. However, appraisal theories suggested the opposite. Schachter and Singer's (1962) theory suggested that there was one type of arousal common to all emotions, both positive and negative, and once this occurred, a cognitive appraisal took place to determine which emotion was to be elicited. This cognitive appraisal could be based on previous experience in which the person had encountered a similar situation or, if they were unsure why they were aroused, it could be provided by external cues in their environment such as another person. Recent research, however, indicates that one arousal shared by all emotions is incorrect as there are detectable physiological and bodily features between emotions (Ekman, 1982).

Research into reasoning and emotion advanced rapidly in the 1980s with such researchers as Michael Eysenck, Colin MacLeod, Andrew Mathews, Jon May, Karin Mogg, Anne Richards, Fraser Watts and Mark Williams. Their systematic approach garnered impressive publications that informed clinical psychologists regarding the development and maintenance of emotional disorders, via cognitive biases, as well psychologists with an interest in how information was processed.

Underpinning these cognitive biases were two stages of processing – priming and elaboration (Graf & Mandler, 1984). The former was an automatic, capacity-unlimited stage of processing whereby a stimulus was associated with its representation in long-term memory. Elaboration was argued to be explicit, strategic and capacity-limited. Williams and colleagues' work generally focused on how attention and memory manifested itself in the disorders of anxiety and depression. They argued that anxiety was characterised by automatic priming processes whereby anxious individuals were hyper-vigilant towards the detection of threat-related material. However, the lack of a general memory bias for threat-related information (e.g. Harvey, Watkins, Mansell & Shafran, 2004) led the authors to conclude that anxiety was also characterised by a shift in elaborative processing away from said threat material.

In contrast, individuals with depression showed a different pattern of performance which was due to elaborative processes underpinning their disposition. In general, there has been little evidence of attentional biases in depression (e.g. MacLeod, Mathews & Tata, 1986), which may indicate a failure to account for high levels of anxiety which could have obfuscated any effects (e.g. Gotlib & McCann, 1984). However, there is much evidence to show that individuals with depression have a bias when recalling emotionally valent words in such tasks as free recall, cued recall and autobiographical memory (e.g. Blaney, 1986).

This difference between anxiety and depression may well represent fundamental processing systems but, as Power and Dalgleish (2008) propose, it may also partly reflect the methodologies employed. They argued that elaborative processing could be a feature of anxiety but asking about the prevalence of threat-related information, rather than how well it is recalled, was a better way to investigate it. With regard to depression, the lack of attentional biases may be due to the words used in the task – the words may not be personal enough to the participants. For attentional biases in anxiety, the words were often matched to the anxiety concerns of the participants, for example, spider-related words for individuals with spider phobia. In contrast, exploration of attentional biases in individuals with depression tended to use generic sad words.

Power and Dalgleish (2008) proposed the SPAARS approach (Schematic, Propositional, Analogical and Associative Representation Systems), which incorporated elements of appraisal and cognitive biases. Emotions were deemed appraisal-based and a function of one's goals, and when these emotions were activated they elicited cognitive biases whereby information that was congruent to that emotion was favoured (e.g. recalled or attended to more often). The emotion process could occur in one of two ways. The first was a schematic route, in which appraisals were made in reaction to the interpretation of an event. This led to an action potential, physiological change and, finally, conscious awareness of that emotion. The second route was automatic and driven by associations based on interpretations about events that were not currently happening but had happened in the past. In this way, previously learnt reactions to events are triggered later on in life.

Most of these theories focused on the cognitive processes of memory and attention with much less mentioned about reasoning. Although memory and attentional processes may be part of the reasoning experience, they certainly are not always necessary. For example, there is little reason to remember the information in a reasoning task as it is usually present (e.g. conditionals, selection tasks).

Eysenck (1979) and Ellis and Ashbrook (1988) proposed the notion that anxiety and depression impaired reasoning performance by virtue of depleting working memory resources. Working memory gained most popularity from the multicomponent model proposed by Alan Baddeley and Graham Hitch (1974). It is a model that describes how transitory information is manipulated and retrieved, and their model posited a central executive component that was served by two slave systems, the phonological loop and the visuo-spatial sketchpad. The former was argued to be responsible for directing attention towards relevant information, inhibiting inappropriate responses, and coordinating cognitive processes when more than one was required to complete a task or more than one task must be done synchronously. The phonological loop stored the phonological information and prevented its decay by the activity of rehearsal and the visuo-spatial sketchpad stored both visual and spatial information. A fourth component, the episodic buffer, was introduced by Baddeley (2000) and was argued to be responsible for the integration of spatial, visual and phonological information.

With regard to reasoning performance, when a person was anxious or depressed, their preoccupation with these irrelevant thoughts meant fewer resources were available to process and manipulate information. For example, Channon and colleagues showed that individuals with depression evinced impaired syllogistic reasoning (Channon & Baker, 1994), Wisconsin Card Sorting Test (Channon, 1996) and discrimination learning (Baker & Channon, 1995) performance with the deficit attributed to working memory capacity limitations, in particular central executive functioning.

This impairment has also been observed in those suffering from anxiety. Darke (1988) asked high- and low-anxious undergraduates to verify the truth of a series of statements. In some of these statements, inferences needed to be made to perform the task correctly. For example, given the two sentences 'The woman drove the car' and 'She was happy,' it was necessary to recognise that the 'the woman' and 'she' referred to the same person. This integration was argued to occur automatically and thus not reduce working memory capacity and no difference was observed in the performance of high- and low-anxious individuals. However, in a second experiment, when the inferences had to be made explicitly, high-anxious individuals took significantly longer than low-anxious individuals as it made greater demands on their working memory resources.

Similar impairments have been shown with participants not suffering from anxiety or depression but with an induced negative mood (Oaksford, Morris, Grainger & Williams, 1996). Experiment 1 showed decreased performance on a deontic version of Wason's selection task (1968; see later in this chapter for more detail) and Experiment 2 showed that this deficit was exhibited by participants in a neutral mood who had to concurrently perform a central executive task (monitoring a luggage handling device) whilst completing Cheng and Holyoak's (1985) immigration deontic selection task.

It is not just current emotions and moods that are known to alter people's reasoning abilities. The mood someone anticipates they will be in following a decision can have a major influence on whether they make that decision. The expectation of events is the basis of almost all behaviour (Olsen, Roese & Zanna, 1996). When the outcome is worse than what we expected, we can experience the negative emotions of regret and disappointment. The former occurs when the outcome chosen is less favourable than the other available options. People regret that they chose a particular course of action when they see the results and compare them with the results of the other possible actions (Bell, 1982). Disappointment results from situations where the outcome of an action is worse than expected (Loomes & Sugden, 1982).

Although regret and disappointment theories were primarily used to understand consumers' choices in the marketplace, other human decision-making researchers have adopted the concept of anticipating the emotional outcome of a decision. Zeelenberg, van Dijk, Manstead and van der Pligt (2000) incorporated this emotional attribute into their decision-theoretic account. In this account the expected utility of an action was modified by the anticipated regret of an outcome. When regret was anticipated, the utility of that action decreased. Conversely, it was possible to anticipate positive regret (termed *rejoicing*), which had the opposite effect of increasing the utility of that action. One study that applied this to selection task performance was by Perham and Oaksford (2005).

In their study participants were given three deontic selection tasks from one of two perspectives. Deontic selection tasks are a variant of Wason's abstract selection task in which participants are asked to test the truth or falsity of a given hypothesis such as 'if there is a Z on one side of the card, then there is an 8 on the other.' Participants are then given four example cards of which they can only see one side. The cards show 'Z' (the p card), 'X' (the not-p card), '8' (the q card) and '1' (the not-q card), and participants are then asked which card or cards they need to turn over to decide whether the conditional is being violated. Typically, correct performance is around 10%. Deontic reasoning differs from abstract reasoning in that it requires people to consider social conventions and norms. As such, the utilities associated with each card turn are evoked and these costs and benefits focus participants on particular card responses, which leads to around 80% correct response rate. Information in the task can modify people's responses such that they choose particular cards in particular circumstances. One such example is the perspective that the participant is told to adopt. Using the scenario of a mother telling her son to tidy his room, Manktelow and Over (1991) showed that when participants adopted the mother's perspective, they chose the cards indicating that the son had gone out to play without tidying his room. In contrast, from the son's perspective, participants selected the cards showing that the son had tidied his room but was not allowed to go out to play.

In Perham and Oaksford (2005), from one perspective (the manager's task), the 'correct' response was not-p and q, and from the other perspective (the referee's task), the 'correct' response was p and not-q. Further, participants were given either a high- or low-threat (rated in a pilot study) version of each set of three tasks. For the high-threat version a highly threatening word was placed on the p card, and for the low-threat version a much less threatening word was placed on the p card. Using the high-threat sport (the low-threat version replaced the word 'blood' with the word 'head') task as an example, participants were told about a situation in which their team had reached the final of the cup and the referee was following the rule 'if there is a blood injury, then the player must leave the pitch.' Participants were then given the four cards which showed the words 'blood' (or 'head'), 'ankle', 'leave' and 'stay'. From the manager's perspective, the participants should have sought instances when their team had been cheated by a player leaving the pitch when they did not have a blood injury (ankle injury), the not-p and q cards. In contrast, from the referee's perspective, the participants should have sought instances when the match referee was failing to follow the rule by someone with a blood injury not leaving the pitch (stay), the p and not-q cards.

Results showed that in the manager's task, the high-threat card (not-p) was chosen significantly less often than the low-threat card (not-p). Further, this pattern was also observed for the q card. In contrast, in the referee's task, the high-threat card (p) was chosen significantly more often than the low-threat card (p), and this pattern also extended to the not-q card. Perham and Oaksford (2005) argued that the findings delineated between an evolutionary and a decision-theoretic account of decision making by supporting the latter – only this account predicted that the threat value would mediate card selections depending on the perspective the participants adopted whereas the evolutionary account predicted that, due to the supposed innate module of hazard detection, one should always avoid high threat. Perham and Oaksford, and Perham (2003), also suggested that participants could anticipate their future emotional responses to making these decisions.

Let us look at the manager's task first. As the manager of the team, you should be looking for situations when a player did not have a blood injury (not-p) but was made to leave the pitch (q) as this would weaken your team unfairly. However, it also means that you should not select cards related to the situation in which a player has a blood injury (or head injury in the low-threat condition) who leaves the pitch. Being unable to not select this serious situation could induce feelings of regret and you might experience more regret in the more serious situation, the blood injury, than the head injury. To avoid this regret we argued that participants selected the high-threat p card less often. In the referee's task, you should be seeking instances where the referee made a player with a blood (or head: p) injury leave the pitch (not-q) to discover whether the referee was following the rules. As the threat (blood or head) is now part of the situation which you should select, it is an opportunity for rejoicing (positive regret in Zeelenberg et al.'s, 2000, parlance), and consequently participants select the blood card more often than the head card. Furthermore, it is not just on the p card that these differences were observed, they also occurred on the not-q card. Given that this card was identical in the high- and low-threat conditions (stay), it suggests that participants reacted to the reverse side of the card, which was blood in the high-threat condition and head in the low-threat condition, in the same way as they reacted to the front side of the card which contained the threat words.

Research elsewhere suggests that it may not necessarily be mood that causes the impairment to reasoning performance, but just any irrelevant thoughts. I mentioned that Oaksford and colleagues (1996) showed poorer performance on a deontic selection task by participants induced into a negative mood state. What I did not disclose then was that the authors found the same effect for those induced into a positive mood state.

In my PhD thesis (Perham, 2003) I explored how people in an anxious mood state performed on the manager's deontic selection tasks. From the notion of working memory depletion, I predicted that the anticipated regret effect would be negated, compared to the neutral, mood condition. Participants in both conditions were shown a series of physically threatening or neutral words and Spielberger State Anxiety Inventory (Spielberger, Gorsuch & Lushene, 1970) scores indicated that those who saw the former were significantly more anxious than those who saw the latter. However, when looking at the performance data no difference appeared between the two groups. As predicted, the anxious group did not show the anticipated regret effect (Perham & Oaksford, 2006), but this was also the case for the neutral group. I hypothesised that the explanation might lie with the mood induction procedure. Both groups underwent the same procedure – watch a series of words, think about them and talk about them – which, arguably, could give rise to irrelevant thoughts. It was just that in one group these thoughts were physically threatening in nature and induced anxiety, and in the other group they were neutral and elicited no increase in anxiety.

Perham and Rosser (2012) tested this hypothesis using a similar mood induction procedure but with a task that was a more pure test of reasoning, namely syllogistic reasoning. Three groups' performance on syllogistic reasoning were compared – a control group, who just completed syllogisms, and two mood induction groups (using negative or neutral words) who completed the induction first. Only the mood induction group, who had to consider negative words, showed a significant increase in anxiety, yet both mood induction groups showed a decrease in syllogistic reasoning performance compared to the control group. We suggested that this drop in performance was not, therefore, due to anxiety, but due to irrelevant thoughts regardless of their content.

The use of irrelevant thoughts, or rumination, has been identified as a key mediating psychological process, amongst others such as self-blame and lack of adaptive coping, in the development of mental health problems (Kinderman, Schwannauer, Pontin & Tai, 2013). A propensity to dwell on the symptoms of one's distress and blaming oneself for negative events strongly determines how influential factors such as a family history of mental illness, life events/traumas and social deprivation are with regard to depression and anxiety. As such, how biological, social and circumstantial factors affect our mental health and well-being is mediated by how we process and perceive information in the world around us.

A possible mechanism by which these irrelevant thoughts might exert their influence lies with research exploring auditory distraction. The irrelevant sound effect (ISE) is possibly the most common form of auditory distraction and is arguably the most explored example in the laboratory (Colle & Welsh, 1976). It is the poorer performance (short-term memory task of serial recall in which a list of seven to nine items is recalled in the order in which they were presented) in a background sound condition compared to quiet. A successful explanation of it, the interference-by-process account (order information in the irrelevant sound conflicts with the retention of order information required for task performance; Jones & Tremblay, 2000), proposes two key prerequisites that need to be present for the ISE to be observed. Firstly, the sound must contain what is called changing-state information. For example, sound that contains the items 'n, r, p. . .' is significantly more disruptive to serial recall performance than a steady-state sequence such as 'c, c, c. . .' (see Perham, Banbury & Jones, 2007a; Perham & Sykora, 2012, for related studies). The second prerequisite, and important for current purposes, is that the task must require the use of seriation – it must require the retention and retrieval of item information in order. Participants do this via the language mechanism of rehearsal and when the task does not require seriation (Perham & Banbury, 2012; Perham, Banbury & Jones, 2007b), the ISE is not seen. Given that syllogistic reasoning involves being able to integrate information from both premises within the syllogism as well as evaluate whether a conclusion logically follows from those premises, it is likely that rehearsal is employed to retain and retrieve this information in its correct order (indeed a similar finding is noted with mental arithmetic performance but not with reading comprehension, Perham & Currie, 2014; Perham, Hodgetts & Banbury, 2013; Perham & Macpherson, 2012) and that this will be disrupted by changing-state irrelevant sound.

Further support for the influence of irrelevant thoughts on reasoning performance comes from elsewhere within the auditory distraction literature. Ball, Marsh, Litchfield, Cook and Booth (2015) gave participants insight problem solving in the presence of background speech (digits), articulatory suppression (speaking aloud a sequence of digits), thinking aloud about the task or quiet. Insight problem-solving tasks are those that, as you might expect, are suddenly solved by having insight into it – a so-called 'A-ha!' moment. An example is the Triangle Problem where participants have to change the direction of a series of circles arranged into a triangle, by just moving three circles. One of the features of these tasks is the use of speech-based processing, which, according to the special-process theory (e.g. Bowden, Jung-Beeman, Fleck & Kounios, 2005) can constrain productive thinking. The authors found that irrelevant sound and articulatory suppression relaxed thinking constraints produced by the participants' inner speech and consequently improved performance compared to the thinking aloud or quiet conditions.

In sum, although emotion and cognition, and more specifically mood and reasoning, has a long history, only quite recently have researchers been interested in how one impacts the other. This interest has been primarily advanced by those from a clinical perspective as well as those from a more cognitive viewpoint. How emotion and mood affects cognitive performance seems to depend on what particular emotion or mood is being experienced as well as the type of cognitive process being performed. In some situations this promotes an attentional or memory bias for particular information, and in other situations it reduces available resources that can impair reasoning performance. These resources may be the result of rumination or task-irrelevant processing and have little to do with emotion at all.

References

Baddeley, A. D. (2000). The episodic buffer: A new component of working memory? *Trends in Cognitive Sciences, 4*, 417–423.

Baddeley, A. D., & Hitch, G. J. (1974). Working memory. In G. A. Bower (ed.), *Recent advances in learning and motivation* (Vol. 8, pp. 47–89). New York: Academic Press.

Baker, J. E., & Channon, S. (1995). Reasoning in depression: Impairment on a concept discrimination learning task. *Cognition and Emotion, 9*(6), 579–597.

Ball, L. J., Marsh, J., Litchfield, D., Cook, R., & Booth, N. (2015). When distraction helps: Evidence that concurrent articulation and irrelevant speech can facilitate insight problem solving. *Thinking & Reasoning, 21*(1), 76–96.

Bartlett, F. C. (1932). *Remembering: A study in experimental and social psychology*. Cambridge, UK: Cambridge University Press.

Beck, A. T., & Emery, G. (1985). *Anxiety disorders and phobias: A cognitive perspective*. New York: Basic Books.

Beck, A., & Rector, N. (2005). Cognitive approaches to schizophrenia: Theory and therapy. *Annual Review of Clinical Psychology, 1*, 577–606.

Bell, D. E. (1982). Regret in decision making under uncertainty. *Operations Research, 30,* 961–981.

Blaisdell, A. P., Sawa, K., Leising, K. J., & Waldmann, M. R. (2006). Causal reasoning in rats. *Science, 311*(5763), 1020–1022.

Blaney, P. H. (1986). Affect and memory: A review. *Psychological Bulletin, 99,* 229–246.

Bowden, E. M., Jung-Beeman, M., Fleck, J., & Kounios, J. (2005). New approaches to demystifying insight. *Trends in Cognitive Sciences, 9,* 322–328.

Bower, G. H. (1981). Mood and memory. *American Psychologist, 36,* 129–148.

Channon, S. (1996). Executive dysfunction in depression: The Wisconsin card sorting test. *Journal of Affective Disorders, 39,* 107–114.

Channon, S., & Baker, J. (1994). Reasoning strategies in depression – Effects of depressed mood on a syllogism task. *Personality and Individual Differences, 17*(5), 707–711.

Cheng, P. W., & Holyoak, K. J. (1985). Pragmatic reasoning schemas. *Cognitive Psychology, 17,* 391–416.

Colle, H. A., & Welsh, A. (1976). Acoustic masking in primary memory. *Journal of Verbal Learning and Verbal Behavior, 15,* 17–32.

Darke, S. (1988). Effects of anxiety on inferential reasoning task performance. *Journal of Personality and Social Psychology, 55*(3), 499–505.

Ekman, P. (1982). Methods for measuring facial action. In K. R. Scherer & P. Ekman (Eds.), *Handbook of methods in nonverbal behavior research* (pp. 45–90). New York: Cambridge University Press.

Ellis, H. C., & Ashbrook, P. W. (1988). Resource allocation model of the effects of depressed mood states. In K. Fiedler & J. Forgas (Eds.), *Affect, cognition and social behaviours.* Toronto, Ontario, Canada: Hogrefe.

Eysenck, H. J. (1965). *Fact and fiction in psychology.* Baltimore, MD: Penguin.

Eysenck, M. W. (1979). Anxiety, learning, and memory: A reconceptualization. *Journal of Research in Personality, 13,* 363–385.

Gotlib, I. H., & McCann, C. D. (1984). Construct accessibility and depression: An examination of cognitive and affective factors. *Journal of Personality and Social Psychology, 47*(2), 427–439.

Graf, P., & Mandler, G. (1984). Activation makes words more accessible but not necessarily more retrievable. *Journal of Verbal Learning and Verbal Behavior, 23,* 553–568.

Harvey, A., Watkins, E., Mansell, W., & Shafran, R. (2004). *Cognitive behavioural processes across psychological disorders.* New York: Oxford University Press.

Hjelle, L. A., & Ziegler, D. J. (1992). *Personality theories: Basic assumptions, research, and applications.* New York: McGraw-Hill.

Jones, D. M., & Tremblay, S. (2000). Interference by process or content? A reply to Neath (2000). *Psychonomic Bulletin and Review, 7,* 550–558.

Kinderman, P., Schwannauer, M., Pontin, E., & Tai, S. (2013). Psychological processes mediate the impact of familial risk, social circumstances and life events on mental health. *PLoS One, 8*(10), e78564.

Loomes, G., & Sugden, R. (1982). Regret theory: An alternative of rational choice under uncertainty. *Economic Journal, 92,* 805–824.

Macken, W. J., & Jones, D. M. (1995). Functional characteristics of the inner voice and the inner ear. *Journal of Experimental Psychology: Learning, Memory, and Cognition, 21,* 436–448.

MacLeod, C., Mathews, A., & Tata, P. (1986). Attentional bias in emotional disorders. *Journal of Abnormal Psychology, 95,* 15–20.

Manktelow, K. I., & Over, D. E. (1991). Social roles and utilities in reasoning with deontic conditionals. *Cognition, 39,* 85–105.

Oaksford, M., Morris, F., Grainger, B., & Williams, J. M. G. (1996). Mood, reasoning, and central executive processes. *Journal of Experimental Psychology: Learning, Memory and Cognition, 22*(2), 476–492.

Olsen, J. M., Roese, N. J., & Zanna, M. P. (1996). Expectancies. In E. T. Higgins & A. W. Kruglanski (Eds.), *Social psychology: Handbook of basic principles* (pp. 211–238). New York: Guildford Press.

Perham, N. (2003). Anticipated and experienced emotion on deontic reasoning. Unpublished PhD thesis, Cardiff University.

Perham, N., & Banbury, S. P. (2012). The role of rehearsal in a novel call-centre type task. *Noise and Health, 14*(56), 1–5.

Perham, N., Banbury, S., & Jones, D. M. (2007a). Do realistic reverberation levels reduce auditory distraction? *Applied Cognitive Psychology, 21*(7), 839–847.

Perham, N., Banbury, S., & Jones, D. M. (2007b). Reduction in auditory distraction by retrieval strategy. *Memory, 15*, 465–473.

Perham, N., & Currie, H. (2014). Does listening to preferred music improve reading comprehension performance? *Applied Cognitive Psychology, 28*, 279–284.

Perham, N., Hodgetts, H. M., & Banbury, S. P. (2013). Mental arithmetic and non-speech office noise: An exploration of interference-by-content. *Noise and Health, 15*(62), 73–78.

Perham, N., & Macpherson, S. (2012). Mental arithmetic and irrelevant auditory number similarity disruption. *Irish Journal of Psychology, 33*(4), 181–192.

Perham, N., & Oaksford, M. (2005). Deontic reasoning with emotional content: Evolutionary psychology or decision theory? *Cognitive Science, 29*, 681–718.

Perham, N., & Oaksford, M. (2006). Experienced and anticipated emotion in deontic reasoning. *Proceedings of the 28th Cognitive Science Annual Conference,* Vancouver, Canada.

Perham, N., & Rosser, J. (2012). 'Not thinking' helps reasoning. *Current Psychology, 31*(2), 160–167.

Perham, N., & Sykora, M. (2012). Disliked music can be better for performance than liked music. *Applied Cognitive Psychology, 26*(4), 550–555.

Piaget, J. (1953). *The origin of intelligence in the child*. New Fetter Lane, New York: Routledge & Kegan Paul.

Power, M., & Dalgleish, T. (2008). *Cognition and emotion: From order to disorder*. Hove, UK: Psychology Press.

Quillian, M. R. (1968). Semantic memory. In M. Minsky (Ed.), *Semantic information processing*. Cambridge, MA: MIT Press.

Schachter, S., & Singer, J. (1962). Cognitive, social, and physiological determinants of emotional state. *Psychological Review, 69*, 379–399.

Spielberger, C. D., Gorsuch, R., & Lushene, R. (1970). *The State Trait Anxiety Inventory (STAI) test manual*. Palo Alto, CA: Consulting Psychologists Press.

Wason, P. C. (1968). Reasoning about a rule. *Quarterly Journal of Experimental Psychology, 20*, 273–281.

Williams, J. M. G., Watts, F. N., MacLeod, C., & Mathews, A. (1997). *Cognitive psychology and emotional disorders*. Chichester, UK: Wiley.

Zeelenberg, M., van Dijk, W. W., Manstead, A. S. R., & van der Pligt, J. (2000). On bad decisions and disconfirmed expectancies: The psychology of regret and disappointment. *Cognition and Emotion, 14*, 521–541.

16

TOWARD A RATIONALITY QUOTIENT (RQ)

The Comprehensive Assessment of Rational Thinking (CART)

Keith E. Stanovich, Richard F. West, and Maggie E. Toplak

Because we have been admirers of Ken Manktelow's work for some time, we are especially glad to participate in this volume honoring his work. In fact, Ken was one of the first to personally welcome us to the field of reasoning. This happened relatively recently because, although we are from Ken's cohort, our reasoning work did not begin until after we had made contributions to an entirely different research area. Although Richard and Keith had been admirers of the heuristics and biases tradition from its inception in the early 1970s, their first research contributions were in the psychology of reading, and this occupied them for 15 years (see Stanovich, 2000; Stanovich, Cunningham, & West, 1998). By the 1990s though, we had decided to make a contribution to the literature on thinking and reasoning that we had admired so much for so long.

Our earliest work garnered a very generous invitation from Jonathan Evans to address the Fourth International Thinking Conference in Durham in the summer of 2000. We say generous because we had just begun to contribute to the literature when we received the invitation. In terms of major publications, we had published our 1998 *Journal of Experimental Psychology: General* multiple experiment piece and we had summarized similar work in the book *Who Is Rational? Individual Differences in Reasoning* that had just come out (our *Behavioral and Brain Sciences* piece did not come out until 2001, even though it had a publication date of 2000). In short, we had only begun publishing in the field, and most of the main speakers at the conference had spent decades studying areas, tasks, and paradigms that we had only recently mastered.

As a result, we were excited about the conference but also relatively nervous when we arrived in Durham. We were meeting all the people who had studied in depth all of the tasks that we had put together in our individual differences studies. As Keith said to the Durham audience, our studies of individual differences were structured so that we had to look at associations and relationships across a wide variety of tasks. That put us in danger of being a kind of "Jack of all trades but master of none".We dreaded being grilled on a particular task by its inventor, when it was in fact just 1 of 20 or so that we had studied, and we of course were not experts on all of them.Well, we should not have worried.The attendees at that conference were quite gracious and fair. But most of all we remember running into Ken Manktelow early in the conference. Of course we knew not only of all his previous work, but we had been immensely influenced by his book *Reasoning and Thinking* that had just come out in 1999. Both Richard and Keith ended up teaching out of that book, but at the time we used it as a tremendous resource to get ourselves up to speed on the field. It is easy to imagine our relief when one of the first things Ken said to us was that *Who Is Rational?* had come out too late for him to comment on it in *Reasoning and Thinking*, as he would have done.We could not have been more reassured at the time, given that Ken's work on the selection task, deontic reasoning, causal reasoning, conditional reasoning, utility issues and reasoning tasks, and the distinction between epistemic and instrumental rationality had become essential tools in our research program.Thank you, Ken.

In the present chapter, we intend to give a sketch of where we have taken our work on individual differences in rational thought since that Durham conference. Our early empirical work on individual differences in rational thought (Stanovich & West, 1997, 1998c, 1999) was first cashed out in terms of theoretical insights concerning dual process theory and evolutionary psychology that were relevant to the Great Rational Debate in cognitive science (Stanovich, 1999, 2004; Stanovich & West, 2000).The next phase of our empirical work (see Stanovich & West, 2008b) led to the book *What Intelligence Tests Miss* (Stanovich, 2009). From that book, it was clear that the next logical step was following through on our claim that there was nothing preventing the construction of a rational thinking test.We outlined an early version of our framework for assessing rational thinking, along with suggested tasks, in Stanovich (2011, Chapter 10) and in Stanovich,West, and Toplak (2011). Building on this work, we have recently completed the construction of the first comprehensive assessment of rational thinking.We will describe the background of this effort in this chapter.

Conceptual background of the CART

Psychology has a long and storied history (more than 100 years old) of measuring the intelligence trait.Although, there has been psychological work on rational thinking, this research started much later and it was not focused on individual differences. Our research group has conducted one of the longest extant investigations of individual differences in rational thinking processes.We are near to completing (Stanovich,West, & Toplak, 2016) our work on the first prototype of a comprehensive test of rational thought (the Comprehensive Assessment of Rational Thinking, CART), and we will describe the background of our test and the nature of our progress in this chapter.

A novice psychology student might be a bit confused at this point – thinking that somewhere along the line they have heard definitions of intelligence that included rationality. Many people – students and nonstudents alike – think that intelligence means acting rationally, more or less. Indeed, it is true that even in academic discourse many theoretical definitions of intelligence incorporate rationality by alluding to judgment and decision making in the definition (see Stanovich, 2009, for a fuller discussion). Other definitions emphasize behavioral adaptiveness and thus also fold rationality into intelligence. The problem here is that *none* of these components of rationality – adaptive responding, good judgment, and decision-making – is assessed on *actual tests* of intelligence.

Publishers of IQ tests and their proponents have encouraged the view that you get everything you need in cognitive assessment from such tests. But in fact, by giving an intelligence test, one does not automatically get a measure of rational thinking. To get the latter, we need to actually construct a test of rational thinking. That is why we embarked upon creating the CART. Our premise was that because we now have conceptually grounded theories of rationality and because we have a prodigious number of tasks that measure the components of rationality (Baron, 2008; Evans, 1989, 2014; Kahneman, 2011; Stanovich, 1999, 2011), it is now possible to see what would happen if we began from the ground up to construct a rationality test around that concept only.

Synthesizing theoretical work and empirical research that began more than two decades ago (Stanovich, 1993; Stanovich & West, 1997, 1998c), we now have a prototype of such a test (Stanovich et al., 2016). We have proceeded with our eyes on the empirical literature on the nature of human judgment and decision making (Kahneman, 2011; Manktelow, 2012) and theoretical discussions of rationality in cognitive science (Evans, 2014; Stanovich, 2011, 2012). For years, we have been examining how one would go about constructing the best rational thinking test if the focus was solely on that construct (as opposed to viewing its study as somehow ancillary to investigations of intelligence). Finally, there is one further historical/contextual feature of the CART that deserves to be noted.

In 2002, cognitive scientist Daniel Kahneman won the Nobel Prize in Economics for work done with his longtime collaborator Amos Tversky (who died in 1996). The press release for the award from the Royal Swedish Academy of Sciences drew attention to the roots of the award-winning work in "the analysis of human judgment and decision-making by cognitive psychologists". Kahneman was cited for discovering "how human judgment may take heuristic shortcuts that systematically depart from basic principles of probability".

In short, Kahneman and Tversky's work was about how humans make choices and assess probabilities, and they uncovered very basic errors that are typical in decision making. Their work includes some of the most influential and highly cited studies in all of psychology, and it deserved to be honoured with the Nobel Prize. One reason this work was so influential was that it addressed deep issues concerning human rationality. Being rational means acting to achieve one's own life goals using the best means possible. To violate the thinking rules Kahneman and Tversky examined thus has the practical consequence that we are less satisfied with our lives than we might be.

Our research group has found systematic differences among individuals in the tendency to make errors of judgment and decision making (Stanovich & West, 1998c, 1999, 2000, 2008b; Toplak, West, & Stanovich, 2011, 2014a). The fact that there are systematic individual differences in the judgment and decision-making situations Kahneman and Tversky studied means that there are variations in important attributes of human cognition related to rationality – how efficient we are in achieving our goals. It is a curious fact that none of these critical attributes of human thinking is assessed on IQ tests (or their proxies such as the SAT test). This fact is curious for two related reasons. First, most laypeople are prone to think that IQ tests are tests of, to put it colloquially, good thinking. Scientists and laypeople alike would tend to agree that "good thinking" encompasses good judgment and decision making – the type of thinking that helps us achieve our goals. In fact, the type of "good thinking" that Kahneman and Tversky studied was deemed so important that research on it was awarded the Nobel Prize. Yet assessments of such good thinking are nowhere to be found on IQ tests. It is perhaps the most profound historical irony of the behavioral sciences that the Nobel Prize was awarded for studies of cognitive characteristics that are entirely missing from the most well-known mental assessment device in psychology – the intelligence test.

Critics of intelligence tests are eager to point out that the tests ignore important parts of mental life – many largely noncognitive domains such as socioemotional abilities, empathy, and interpersonal skills, for example. However, a tacit assumption in such critiques is that although intelligence tests miss certain key noncognitive areas, they do encompass most of what is important in the cognitive domain. It is just this assumption that we wish to challenge with the construction of the CART. Our test will operationalize an important cognitive domain not assessed by intelligence tests: the skills of judgment and decision making that are the foundation of rational thought and action.

Rationality in cognitive science

We follow many cognitive science theorists in recognizing two types of rationality: instrumental and epistemic (Manktelow, 2004; Over, 2004). The simplest definition of instrumental rationality, the one that emphasizes most that it is grounded in the practical world, is: Behaving in the world so that you get exactly what you most want, given the resources (physical and mental) available to you. Somewhat more technically, we could characterize instrumental rationality as the optimization of the individual's goal fulfillment. Economists and cognitive scientists have refined the notion of optimization of goal fulfillment into the technical notion of expected utility. Epistemic rationality concerns how well beliefs map onto the actual structure of the world. The two types of rationality are related. In order to take actions that fulfill our goals, we need to base those actions on beliefs that are properly matched to the world.

Manktelow (2004) has emphasized the practicality of both types of rationality by noting that they concern two critical things: what is true and what to do. Epistemic rationality is about what is true and instrumental rationality is about what to do. For our beliefs to be rational they must correspond to the way the world is – they must be true. For our actions to be rational, they must be the best means toward our goals – they must be the best things to do. Nothing could be more practical or useful for a person's life than the thinking processes that help them find out what is true and what is best to do.

More formally, economists and cognitive scientists define instrumental rationality as the maximization of expected utility. To be instrumentally rational, a person must choose among options based on which option has the largest expected utility. Decision situations can be broken down into three components: 1) possible actions; 2) possible states of the world; 3) evaluations of the consequences of possible actions in each possible state of the world. Expected utility is calculated by taking the utility of each outcome and multiplying it by the probability of that outcome and then summing those products over all of the possible outcomes.

In practice, assessing rationality in this manner can be difficult because eliciting personal probabilities can be tricky. Also, getting measurements of the utilities of various consequences can be experimentally difficult. Fortunately, there is another useful way to measure the rationality of decisions and deviations from rationality. It has been proven through several formal analyses that if people's preferences follow certain consistent patterns (the so-called axioms of choice: independence of irrelevant alternatives, transitivity, independence, and reduction of compound lotteries, etc.), then they are behaving as if they are maximizing utility (Dawes, 1998; Edwards, 1954; Jeffrey, 1983; Luce & Raiffa, 1957; Savage, 1954; von Neumann & Morgenstern, 1944). This is the so-called axiomatic approach to whether people are maximizing utility. It is what makes people's degrees of rationality more easily measurable by the experimental methods of cognitive science. The deviation from the optimal choice pattern according to the axioms is an (inverse) measure of the degree of rationality.

An axiomatic approach can be applied to assessing epistemic rationality as well. Recall that the expected utility of an action involves multiplying the probability of an outcome by its utility (and summing across possible outcomes). Thus, determining the best action involves estimating the probabilities of various outcomes. These probabilities are not conscious calculations of course – they are one's confidence estimates about states of the world. They are one's beliefs and the confidence that one has in them. If our probabilistic judgments about the states of the world are wrong, decision making will not maximize one's utility – our actions will not result in our getting what we most want. Thus, instrumental and epistemic rationality become intertwined. If we are to determine what to do, we need to make sure that our actions are based on what is true. It is in this sense that rationality of belief – epistemic rationality – is one of the foundations for rationality of action.

Rationality of belief is assessed by looking at a variety of probabilistic reasoning skills, evidence evaluation skills, and hypothesis testing skills. In order for a person to be epistemically rational, their probability estimates must follow the rules of objective probabilities – their estimates must follow the so-called probability calculus.

Mathematically, probability values follow certain rules. These rules form one of the most important normative models for subjective probability estimates.

The heuristics and biases literature

In the construction of our rational thinking assessment instrument, we have drawn on the vast literature that has demonstrated that people sometimes violate the normative rules of instrumental and epistemic rationality (Baron, 2008, 2014; Evans, 2014; Kahneman, 2011; Kahneman & Tversky, 2000; Koehler & Harvey, 2004; Manktelow, 2012). We have drawn heavily on this research, especially that of the so-called heuristics and biases tradition Kahneman and Tversky inaugurated in the early 1970s (Kahneman & Tversky, 1972, 1973; Tversky & Kahneman, 1974). The term *biases* refers to the systematic errors people make in choosing actions and in estimating probabilities, and the term *heuristics* refers to *why* people often make these errors – because they use mental shortcuts (heuristics) to solve many problems. Table 16.1 lists some of the tasks, effects, and biases from this literature that we have studied in our lab and from which we selected in order to construct the CART. Because much of the operationalization of our framework of rational thinking comes from the heuristics and biases tradition, it is important to explicate the logic of such tasks.

TABLE 16.1 Heuristics, biases, and effects studied in the Stanovich/West/Toplak lab

Tasks, effects, and biases	Individual differences citation from the work of our lab
Baserate neglect	Kokis, Macpherson, Toplak, West, & Stanovich, 2002; Stanovich & West, 1998c, 1998d, 1999, 2008b; West, Toplak, & Stanovich, 2008
Conjunction fallacy	Stanovich & West, 1998b; Toplak et al., 2011; West et al., 2008
Framing effects	Stanovich & West, 1998b, 1999, 2008b; Toplak et al., 2014a, Toplak, West, & Stanovich, 2014b
Anchoring effect	Stanovich & West, 2008b
Sample size awareness	Toplak et al., 2011; West et al., 2008
Regression to the mean	Toplak, Liu, Macpherson, Toneatto, & Stanovich, 2007; Toplak et al., 2011; West et al., 2008
Control group reasoning	Stanovich & West, 1998c; Toplak et al., 2011; West et al., 2008
Disjunctive reasoning	Toplak & Stanovich, 2002; West et al., 2008
Temporal discounting	Toplak et al., 2014a
Gambler's fallacy	Toplak et al., 2007; Toplak et al., 2011; West et al., 2008
Probability matching	Stanovich & West, 2008b; Toplak et al., 2007; Toplak et al., 2011; West & Stanovich, 2003
Overconfidence effect	Stanovich & West, 1998c
Outcome bias	Stanovich & West, 1998c, 2008b; Toplak et al., 2007; Toplak et al., 2011
Ratio bias	Kokis et al., 2002; Stanovich & West, 2008b; Toplak et al., 2014a, 2014b; West et al., 2008

(*Continued*)

TABLE 16.1 (Continued)

Tasks, effects, and biases	Individual differences citation from the work of our lab
Four-card selection task	Stanovich & West, 1998a, 2008b; Toplak & Stanovich, 2002; Toplak et al., 2014a; West et al., 2008
Ignoring P(D/~H)	Stanovich & West, 1998d, 1999; West et al., 2008
Sunk cost effect	Stanovich & West, 2008b; Toplak et al., 2011
Risk/benefit confounding	Stanovich & West, 2008b
Covariation detection	Stanovich & West, 1998c, 1998d; Sá, West, & Stanovich, 1999; Toplak et al., 2011; West et al., 2008
Belief bias in syllogistic reasoning	Macpherson & Stanovich, 2007; Stanovich & West, 1998c, 2008b; Toplak et al., 2014a, 2014b
Omission bias	Stanovich & West, 2008b
Informal argument evaluation	Stanovich & West, 1997, 2008b; Sá et al., 1999
Unconfounded hypothesis testing	Stanovich & West, 1998c; Toplak et al., 2011
Myside bias	Sá, Kelley, Ho, & Stanovich, 2005; Stanovich & West, 2007, 2008a, 2008b; Toplak & Stanovich, 2003; Toplak et al., 2014a, 2014b
Expected value maximization	Stanovich, Grunewald, & West, 2003; Toplak et al., 2007
Bias blind spot	West, Meserve, & Stanovich, 2012; Toplak et al., 2014a
Newcomb's problem	Stanovich & West, 1999; Toplak & Stanovich, 2002
Prisoner's dilemma	Stanovich & West, 1999; Toplak & Stanovich, 2002
Hindsight bias	Stanovich & West, 1998c
One-Side bias	Stanovich & West, 2008a
Certainty effect	Stanovich & West, 2008b
Willingness to pay/ willingness to accept	Stanovich & West, 2008b
Evaluability: less is more effect	Stanovich & West, 2008b
Proportion dominance effect	Stanovich & West, 2008b

Heuristics and biases tasks were designed for human brains, not animal brains. What we mean by this is that heuristics and biases tasks were designed for brains that could at least *potentially* experience mental conflict. This is why Kahneman (2000) stressed that "Tversky and I always thought of the heuristics and biases approach as a two-process theory" (p. 682). All multiple-process models of mind, including the currently popular dual process theories (Evans & Stanovich, 2013), capture a phenomenal aspect of human decision making that is of profound importance – that humans often feel alienated from their choices. We display what both folk psychology and philosophers term *weakness of will*. For example, we continue to smoke when we know that it is a harmful habit; or we order a sweet after a large meal, merely an hour after pledging to ourselves that we would not. However, we display alienation from our responses even in situations that do not involve weakness of will.

Discussion of heuristics and biases tasks often leads to a conceptualization within a dual-process framework, because most of the tasks in the heuristics and biases literature were deliberately designed to pit an automatically triggered response against a normative response generated by more controlled types of processing (Kahneman, 2011). Since Kahneman and Tversky launched the heuristics and biases approach in the 1970s, a wealth of evidence has accumulated in support of the dual-process framework (Evans & Stanovich, 2013). In many such theories, the defining feature of Type 1 processing is its autonomy – the execution of Type 1 processes is mandatory when their triggering stimuli are encountered, and they are not dependent on input from high-level control systems. Autonomous processes have other correlated features – their execution tends to be rapid, they do not put a heavy load on central processing capacity, they tend to be associative – but these other correlated features are not defining (Stanovich & Toplak, 2012). The category of autonomous processes would include: processes of emotional regulation; the encapsulated modules for solving specific adaptive problems that evolutionary psychologists have posited; processes of implicit learning; and the automatic firing of overlearned associations.

In contrast with Type 1 processing, Type 2 processing is nonautonomous. It is relatively slow and computationally expensive. Many Type 1 processes can operate in parallel, but Type 2 processing is largely serial. One of the most critical functions of Type 2 processing is to override Type 1 processing. This is sometimes necessary because autonomous processing has heuristic qualities. It is designed to get the response into the right ballpark when solving a problem or making a decision, but it is not designed for the type of fine-grained analysis called for in situations of unusual importance (financial decisions, fairness judgments, employment decisions, legal judgments, etc.). Type 1 processing heuristics depend on benign environments. In hostile environments, they can be costly (see Hilton, 2003; Over, 2000; Stanovich, 2004).

In order to override Type 1 processing, Type 2 processing must display at least two related capabilities. One is the capability of interrupting Type 1 processing and suppressing its response tendencies. But suppressing the Type 1 response is not helpful unless a better response is available to substitute for it. Where do these better responses come from? One answer is that they come from processes of hypothetical reasoning and cognitive simulation that are a unique aspect of Type 2 processing (Evans, 2010; Evans & Stanovich, 2013; Stanovich, 2004, 2011). Humans alone appear to be able to represent a model of an idealized (i.e., hypothesized) response, while still maintaining a first-order model of current response tendencies.

When we said that heuristics and biases tasks were designed for human brains, not animal brains, we did not mean to say that rationality cannot be assessed in nonhuman animals. To the contrary, the axiomatic approach to rationality assessment mentioned previously allows the rationality of nonhuman animals to be assessed as well as that of humans, because it defines instrumental rationality as adherence to certain types of consistency and coherence relationships (see Kacelnik, 2006; Luce & Raiffa, 1957; Savage, 1954). In fact, many animals appear to have a reasonable degree of instrumental rationality (Hurley & Nudds, 2006). The adaptively shaped behavior of nonhuman animals can, in theory, deviate from the axioms of rational choice because it is possible for the optimization of fitness at the genetic level to dissociate from optimization at the level of the organism (Stanovich, 2004).

So although the assessment of nonhuman rationality and irrationality is possible, the really interesting issues of rationality arise when we have an organism with the possibility of different types of processing (Type 1 and Type 2) priming different responses. In such a situation (the situation that spawns dual-process conceptualizations), assessing which of the minds wins out becomes of immense interest (and diagnostic of degrees of rationality). It is just this situation that heuristics and biases tasks put under the microscope. These tasks, interpreted within a dual-process framework (Kahneman, 2011), end up being diagnostic of the dominance of Type 1 versus Type 2 processing in determining the final response.

For a person who defaults often to Type 1 processing, environments can be either benign or hostile. A benign environment is an environment that contains useful cues that, via practice or evolutionary history, have been well represented in Type 1 subsystems. Additionally, for an environment to be classified as benign, it must not contain other individuals who will adjust their behavior to exploit those relying only on Type 1 processing. We would argue (Stanovich, 2004; Stanovich & West, 2000) that the modern world is somewhat hostile to Type 1 processing in critical ways, thus making it important to assess rational thinking tendencies via the logic of heuristics and biases tasks.

It is appropriate here to emphasize another way in which intelligence tests fail to tap important aspects of rational thinking. The novice reader might have thought at this point that it seems that intelligence tests clearly measure Type 2 reasoning – that is, conscious, serial simulation of imaginary worlds in order to solve problems. This is all true, but there is a critical difference. Intelligence tests contain salient warnings that Type 2 reasoning is necessary. It is clear to someone taking an intelligence test that fast, automatic, intuitive processing will not lead to superior performance. Most tests of rational thinking do not strongly cue the subject in this manner. Instead, many heuristics and biases tasks suggest a compelling intuitive response that happens to be wrong.

In heuristics and biases tasks, unlike the case for intelligence tests, the subject must detect the inadequacy of the Type 1 response and then must use Type 2 processing to both suppress the Type 1 response and to simulate a better alternative. To illustrate this difference, we might imagine asking a subject if larger or smaller sample sizes were better, as we might in a university statistics course. This would be a much easier question than a traditional heuristics and biases item, because no issue of recognition is involved – the respondent would not have to detect the *relevance* of sample size. He/she would be *focused* on its relevance by being asked directly about it. This of course makes for a much easier problem. As statistics instructors ourselves, we have commonly seen that a student may answer a direct question about sample size correctly in a multiple choice format, but then when given something like Kahneman and Tversky's hospital problem, does not perceive the relevance of sample size and answers incorrectly.

In short, most of the tasks in the heuristics and biases literature were deliberately designed to pit an intuitive but incorrect response against a normative response. This means that such tasks have both processing and knowledge requirements. From a processing standpoint, the necessity of overriding Type 1 processing must be detected. Then, the intuitive response primed by Type 1 processing must be inhibited and the normative response must be retrieved or synthesized and then substituted by Type 2 processing.

In addition to these processing requirements, successful performance on heuristics and biases tasks requires the presence of several important knowledge bases. The knowledge, rules, and strategies that can be retrieved and used to replace a Type 1 intuitive response have been referred to as *mindware* (see Stanovich et al., 2011), a term David Perkins coined in a 1995 book (Clark, 2001, uses the term in a slightly different way from Perkins' original coinage). The mindware available for use during cognitive simulation is in part the product of past learning experiences. This means that individual differences will appear in the ability to simulate better alternatives to a Type 1 response based on variation available in the mindware. The mindware that allows the computation of more rational responses needs to be available and accessible during simulation activities.

The framework and composition of the CART

It is important to stress that knowledge and process are intertwined in most heuristics and biases tasks, but that it is not the case that the dependence on knowledge and the dependence on process are the same for each and every task. Some heuristics and biases tasks are more process dependent than knowledge dependent. Others are more knowledge dependent than process dependent. Still others seem to stress both knowledge and process quite strongly.

Table 16.2 presents the overall framework for the CART, as well as some indication of the tasks used for assessment and the assessment domains. The left column of Table 16.2 serves to represent tasks saturated with processing requirements. The second column from the left represents tasks relatively saturated with knowledge from specific rational thinking domains. The first two domains of rational thinking represented in the upper left – probabilistic and statistical reasoning and scientific reasoning – have process and knowledge so intertwined that they span both columns in Table 16.2 to emphasize this point.

Working down the left column, Table 16.2 next identifies some tasks that have heavy processing requirements. The first set of tasks are indicators of the tendency to avoid miserly information processing. That humans are cognitive misers has been a major theme throughout the past 40 years of research in psychology and cognitive science (see Dawes, 1976; Evans, 1984, 1989; Kahneman, 2011; Simon, 1955, 1956; Tversky & Kahneman, 1974; for the evolutionary reasons, see Stanovich, 2004, 2009). When approaching any problem, our brains have available various computational mechanisms for dealing with the situation. These mechanisms embody a tradeoff, however. The tradeoff is between power and expense. Some mechanisms

TABLE 16.2 Framework for classifying the types of rational thinking tasks and subtests on the CART

Tasks saturated with processing requirements (detection, sustained override, hypothetical thinking)	Rational thinking tasks saturated with knowledge	Avoidance of contaminated mindware	Thinking dispositions that foster thorough and prudent thought, unbiased thought, and knowledge acquisition
Probabilistic and Statistical Reasoning Subtest		Superstitious Thinking Subtest	Actively Openminded Thinking Scale
Scientific Reasoning Subtest		Anti-Science Attitudes Subtest	Deliberative Thinking Scale
Avoidance of Miserly Information Processing Subtests: - Reflection versus Intuition - Belief Bias Syllogisms - Ratio Bias - Disjunctive Reasoning	Probabilistic Numeracy Subtest	Conspiracy Beliefs Subtest	Future Orientation Scale
Absence of Irrelevant Context Effects in Decision Making Subtests: - Framing - Anchoring - Preference Anomalies	Financial Literacy and Economic Knowledge Subtest	Dysfunctional Personal Beliefs Subtest	Differentiation of Emotions Scale
Avoidance of Myside Bias: - Argument Evaluation Subtest	Sensitivity to Expected Value Subtest		
Avoiding Overconfidence: - Knowledge Calibration Subtest	Risk Knowledge Subtest		
Rational Temporal Discounting Subtest			

have great computational power – they can solve a large number of novel problems with great accuracy. However, this power comes with a cost. These mechanisms take up a great deal of attention, tend to be slow, tend to interfere with other thoughts and actions we are carrying out, and require great concentration that is often experienced as aversive (the Type 2 processing discussed earlier in this chapter). Humans are cognitive misers because their basic tendency is to default to other less-accurate processing mechanisms of low computational expense (the Type 1 processing discussed earlier in this chapter). The CART contains several subtests that assess a person's ability to avoid miserly information processing.

Continuing down the left column of Table 16.2 are some other tasks that are best viewed as indirect measures of the avoidance of miserly processing. All are heavy in their processing requirements. All of these tasks and their associated effects, although involving miserly processing, are still quite complex tasks. More than miserly processing is going on when someone answers suboptimally in all of them. Our only theoretical claim is quite minimal – it is only that, whatever else is responsible for task performance, they are all likely to have miserly processing somewhat involved. In any case, they are all important measures of rational thinking in their own right, whether or not they are due to miserly information processing. Our focus with the CART is not on resolving the theoretical disputes surrounding every one of these effects. For example, the measurement of overconfidence would be part of our rational thinking assessment battery regardless of what the explanation for the effect turns out to be. With that caveat in mind, the left-hand column of Table 16.2 shows several other important additional categories of our assessment battery: the absence of irrelevant context effects in decision making; the avoidance of myside bias; the avoidance of overconfidence in knowledge calibration; and rational temporal discounting of future rewards.

In the second column from the left in Table 16.2 are four components of the CART that represent components that are particularly heavily dependent on knowledge bases. This is not to say that these components are completely independent of the degree of miserly processing, just that variation on them is considerably less dependent on processing considerations and much more dependent on the presence of certain specific types of declarative knowledge than other tasks. These subtests of the CART tap the following: probabilistic numeracy; financial literacy and economic knowledge; sensitivity to expected value; and risk knowledge.

The third column in Table 16.2 reflects the fact that irrational thinking is potentially caused by two different types of mindware problems. Missing mindware, or mindware gaps, reflect the most common type – where a person does not have access to adequately compiled declarative knowledge from which to synthesize a normative response to use in the override of Type 1 processing. However, Stanovich (2004, 2009, 2011) has discussed how not all mindware is helpful or useful in fostering rationality. Indeed, the presence of certain kinds of mindware is often precisely the problem. We coined the category label *contaminated mindware* for the presence of declarative knowledge bases that foster irrational rather than rational thinking, which is represented in the third column of this table.

There are probably dozens of different kinds of contaminated mindware if one looks very specifically at narrow domains of knowledge. It would obviously be impossible for a test of rational thinking to encompass all of these. Instead, we have focused on just a few of the broader categories of contaminated mindware that might have more general implications and might have some domain generality in their effects. Of course, rational thinking as indicated by CART performance is defined as the *avoidance* or *rejection* of these domains of contaminated mindware. The third column from the left in Table 16.2 lists the four categories of contaminated mindware that the CART assesses: the rejection of superstitious thinking; the rejection of anti-scientific attitudes; the rejection of conspiracy beliefs; and the avoidance of dysfunctional personal beliefs.

Finally, the far right column of Table 16.2 shows a set of supplementary measures that are included in the CART, but are not part of the overall rational thinking score on the test itself. Column four lists some thinking dispositions that we measure by self-report questionnaires. Psychology studies many different thinking dispositions. However, we have chosen those specifically relevant to rational thinking. For example, we have focused on thinking dispositions that foster prudent thought, and those that foster unbiased thought and unbiased knowledge acquisition. The four thinking dispositions that we assess are: actively open-minded thinking; deliberative thinking; future orientation; and the differentiation of emotions. These self-report measures are different from the other performance measures on the CART, which is why they are not part of the overall score on the test, but instead provide supplementary information. They are not part of the total score on the test because, among other things, the maximum score on a thinking disposition measure should not be equated with maximal rationality. Optimal functioning on these measures is traced instead by an inverted U-shaped function. Maximizing these dispositions is not the criterion of rational thought itself. Thinking dispositions such as these are a means to rationality, not ends in themselves. For this reason, the thinking dispositions subscales are segregated in the CART and not treated as direct measures of rational thinking themselves.

Overall, the CART assesses both epistemic rationality and instrumental rationality. Aspects of epistemic rationality that are assessed on our instrument include: the tendency to show incoherent probability assessments; the tendency toward overconfidence in knowledge judgments; the tendency to ignore base rates; the tendency not to seek to falsify hypotheses; the tendency to try to explain chance events; the tendency to evaluate evidence with a myside bias; and the tendency to ignore the alternative hypothesis.

Additionally, the CART assesses aspects of instrumental rationality and irrationality, such as: the ability to display disjunctive reasoning in decision making; the tendency to show inconsistent preferences because of framing effects; the tendency to substitute affect for difficult evaluations; the tendency to over-weight short-term rewards at the expense of long-term well-being; the tendency to have choices affected by vivid stimuli; and the tendency for decisions to be affected by irrelevant context.

Complications and context of rational thinking assessment

For many years, we have argued (see Stanovich, 2009) that professional inertia and psychologists' investment in IQ testing have prevented us from realizing that our science had developed enough to allow us to develop a parallel RQ test. With the development of the CART, our research group has turned this prediction into reality. Although our initial effort should be viewed more as a prototype, it accomplishes the task of showing that there is nothing conceptually or theoretically preventing us from developing such a test. We know the types of thinking processes that such an instrument would assess, and we have in hand prototypes of the kinds of tasks that would be used in the domains of both instrumental rationality and epistemic rationality – both of which are represented on the CART.

Unlike many such lists of thinking skills in textbooks, the conceptual components of the CART are each grounded in a task or paradigm in the literature of cognitive science. In fact, many (e.g., context effects in decision making; probabilistic reasoning) have generated enormous empirical literatures. For example, many paradigms have been used to measure the avoidance of miserly information processing (left column of Table 16.2, third row). The study of belief bias – that people have difficulty processing data pointing toward conclusions that conflict with what they think they know about the world – has yielded several such paradigms (e.g., Evans, Barston, & Pollard, 1983; Evans & Curtis-Holmes, 2005; Markovits & Nantel, 1989).

Another part of the CART that is richly populated by work in cognitive science is a set of tasks that collectively define the mental tendency to not be affected by irrelevant context in decision making (left column of Table 16.2, fourth row). All three paradigms that assess the latter tendency have generated enormous literatures. Resistance to framing has been measured with countless tasks (e.g., Levin, Gaeth, Schreiber, & Lauriola, 2002; Maule & Villejoubert, 2007), as has the resistance to irrelevant anchoring in decisions (e.g., Epley & Gilovich, 2004, 2006; Jacowitz & Kahneman, 1995). Lichtenstein and Slovic (2006) summarized several decades worth of work on preference anomalies that followed their seminal research in the 1970s (Lichtenstein & Slovic, 1971, 1973).

The existence of the CART is our attempt to follow through on a claim made years ago (Stanovich, 2009) – that there is no *conceptual* barrier to creating a prototype of a test of rational thinking. This does not of course mean that there is not substantial work to be done in turning the prototype into an easily usable test. We have given a book-length treatment (Stanovich et al., 2016) of the 20 years of work on individual differences in rational thinking that went into the development of our prototype.

We are exploring the full psychometric structure of our instrument in the ongoing study. Regarding the psychometrics of our instrument, many pairs of relationships have been explored already (see Stanovich et al., 2016), but the full structure remains to be investigated. It is important, though, to understand what various psychometric structures would – and most important – would not tell us. For example, if several components or measurement paradigms turn out to be highly correlated, that will make assessment more efficient and logistically easier, but it will not enhance or diminish the status of these components as aspects of rational thought. Conversely, finding that many of the components or measurement paradigms are separable in individual difference analyses in no way detracts from the importance of any component. In short, the point is that psychometric findings do not trump what cognitive scientists have found are the conceptually essential features of rational thought and action.

All of this is not to deny that it would obviously be useful to really know the structure of rational thinking skills from a psychometric point of view. Our past research has contributed substantially to clarifying that structure. We have found that certain rational thinking tasks consistently correlate with each other even after cognitive ability has been partialled out. For example, we have found that the ability to avoid belief bias in syllogistic reasoning is related to the ability to reason statistically in the face of conflicting case evidence – and that this relationship is maintained after intelligence is partialled out (Stanovich & West, 1998c; West et al., 2008). Additionally, our group has consistently found rational thinking tasks that are predicted by thinking dispositions after cognitive ability has been partialled – particularly tasks involving statistical reasoning and informal argumentation (Kokis et al., 2002; Stanovich & West, 1997, 1998c; Toplak et al., 2011, 2014a; West et al., 2008).

Rationality is a multifarious concept. It is unlikely to yield as substantial a g-factor as is the case with intelligence (Deary, 2013; Hunt, 2011). Thus, assessment might be logistically difficult and reporting outcomes from a rational thinking test might be complex. However, we should not shirk from measuring something just because it is logistically difficult – particularly if the domain is important.

Integrating rational thinking assessment into psychological science

When a layperson thinks of individual differences in reasoning, they think of IQ tests. It is quite natural that this is their primary association, because IQ tests are among the most publicized products of psychological research. This association is not entirely inaccurate either, because intelligence is correlated with performance on a host of reasoning tasks (Carroll, 1993; Deary, 2000; Hunt, 2011). Nonetheless, certain very important classes of individual differences in thinking are ignored if only intelligence-related variance is the primary focus. A number of these ignored classes of individual differences are those relating to rational thought.

We tend not to notice the mental processes missing from IQ tests because many theorists have adopted a *permissive* conceptualization of what intelligence is rather than a grounded conceptualization. Permissive theories include aspects of functioning that are captured by the *vernacular* term *intelligence* (adaptation to the environment, showing wisdom, creativity, etc.) whether or not existing tests of intelligence actually measure these aspects. *Grounded* theories, in contrast, confine the concept of intelligence to the set of mental abilities actually tested on extant IQ tests. Adopting permissive definitions of the concept of intelligence serves to obscure what is missing from extant IQ tests. Instead, in order to highlight the missing elements in IQ tests, my research group has adopted a more scientifically justified (see Stanovich, 2009) grounded notion of the intelligence concept.

Grounded theories adopt the operationalization of the term that is used in both psychometric studies of intelligence and neurophysiological studies. This definition involves a statistical abstraction from performance on established tests and cognitive ability indicators. The grounded view of intelligence then takes the operationally defined construct and validates it in studies of educational attainment, cognitive neuroscience, developmental trends, and information processing.

The operationalization of rationality is different from that of intelligence and thus, as every introductory psychology student is taught, the concepts must be treated as different. Our comprehensive test of rational thinking will go a long way toward grounding the rationality concept – a concept that captures aspects of thought that have heretofore gone unmeasured in assessment devices.

In summary, we have coherent and well-operationalized concepts of rational action and belief formation. We have a coherent and well-operationalized concept of intelligence. No scientific purpose is served by fusing these concepts, because they are very different. To the contrary, scientific progress is made by differentiating concepts. We have a century-long history of measuring the intelligence concept. It is high time we put equal energy, as a discipline, into the measurement of a mental quality that is just as important – rationality.

Author note

Preparation of this chapter was supported by a grant from the John Templeton Foundation. The opinions expressed in this publication are those of the authors and do not necessarily reflect the views of the John Templeton Foundation.

References

Baron, J. (2008). *Thinking and deciding* (Fourth edition). Cambridge, MA: Cambridge University Press.

Baron, J. (2014). Heuristics and biases. In E. Zamir & D. Teichman (Eds.), *The Oxford handbook of behavioral economics and the law* (pp. 3–27). Oxford: Oxford University Press.

Carroll, J. B. (1993). *Human cognitive abilities: A survey of factor-analytic studies*. Cambridge: Cambridge University Press.

Clark, A. (2001). *Mindware: An introduction to the philosophy of cognitive science*. New York: Oxford University Press.

Dawes, R. M. (1976). Shallow psychology. In J. S. Carroll & J. W. Payne (Eds.), *Cognition and social behavior* (pp. 3–11). Hillsdale, NJ: Erlbaum.

Dawes, R. M. (1998). Behavioral decision making and judgment. In D. T. Gilbert, S. T. Fiske, & G. Lindzey (Eds.), *The handbook of social psychology* (Vol. 1, pp. 497–548). Boston: McGraw-Hill.

Deary, I. J. (2000). *Looking down on human intelligence: From psychometrics to the brain*. Oxford: Oxford University Press.

Deary, I. J. (2013). Intelligence. *Current Biology, 23*, R673–R676.

Edwards, W. (1954). The theory of decision making. *Psychological Bulletin, 51*, 380–417.

Epley, N., & Gilovich, T. (2004). Are adjustments insufficient? *Personality and Social Psychology Bulletin, 30*, 447–460.

Epley, N., & Gilovich, T. (2006). The anchoring-and-adjustment heuristic: Why the adjustments are insufficient. *Psychological Science, 17*, 311–318.

Evans, J. St. B. T. (1984). Heuristic and analytic processes in reasoning. *British Journal of Psychology, 75*, 451–468.

Evans, J. St. B. T. (1989). *Bias in human reasoning: Causes and consequences*. Hove, UK: Erlbaum.

Evans, J. St. B. T. (2010). *Thinking twice: Two minds in one brain*. Oxford: Oxford University Press.

Evans, J. St. B. T. (2014). *Reasoning, rationality and dual processes*. London: Psychology Press.

Evans, J. St. B. T., Barston, J., & Pollard, P. (1983). On the conflict between logic and belief in syllogistic reasoning. *Memory & Cognition, 11*, 295–306.

Evans, J. St. B. T., & Curtis-Holmes, J. (2005). Rapid responding increases belief bias: Evidence for the dual-process theory of reasoning. *Thinking and Reasoning, 11*, 382–389.

Evans, J. St. B. T., & Stanovich, K. E. (2013). Dual-process theories of higher cognition: Advancing the debate. *Perspectives on Psychological Science, 8*, 223–241.

Hilton, D. J. (2003). Psychology and the financial markets: Applications to understanding and remedying irrational decision-making. In I. Brocas & J. D. Carrillo (Eds.), *The psychology of economic decisions (Vol. 1): Rationality and well-being* (pp. 273–297). Oxford: Oxford University Press.

Hunt, E. (2011). *Human intelligence*. Cambridge, MA: Cambridge University Press.

Hurley, S., & Nudds, M. (2006). The questions of animal rationality: Theory and evidence. In S. Hurley & M. Nudds (Eds.), *Rational animals?* (pp. 1–83). Oxford: Oxford University Press.

Jacowitz, K. E., & Kahneman, D. (1995). Measures of anchoring in estimation tasks. *Personality and Social Psychology Bulletin, 21*, 1161–1167.

Jeffrey, R. C. (1983). *The logic of decision* (Second Edition). Chicago: University of Chicago Press.

Kacelnik, A. (2006). Meanings of rationality. In S. Hurley & M. Nudds (Eds.), *Rational animals?* (pp. 87–106). Oxford: Oxford University Press.

Kahneman, D. (2000). A psychological point of view: Violations of rational rules as a diagnostic of mental processes. *Behavioral and Brain Sciences, 23*, 681–683.

Kahneman, D. (2011). *Thinking, fast and slow*. New York: Farrar, Straus & Giroux.

Kahneman, D., & Tversky, A. (1972). Subjective probability: A judgment of representativeness. *Cognitive Psychology, 3*, 430–454.

Kahneman, D., & Tversky, A. (1973). On the psychology of prediction. *Psychological Review, 80*, 237–251.

Kahneman, D., & Tversky, A. (Eds.). (2000). *Choices, values, and frames*. Cambridge: Cambridge University Press.

Koehler, D. J., & Harvey, N. (Eds.). (2004). *Blackwell handbook of judgment and decision making*. Oxford, England: Blackwell.

Kokis, J., Macpherson, R., Toplak, M., West, R. F., & Stanovich, K. E. (2002). Heuristic and analytic processing: Age trends and associations with cognitive ability and cognitive styles. *Journal of Experimental Child Psychology, 83*, 26–52.

Levin, I. P., Gaeth, G. J., Schreiber, J., & Lauriola, M. (2002). A new look at framing effects: Distribution of effect sizes, individual differences, and independence of types of effects. *Organizational Behavior and Human Decision Processes, 88*, 411–429.

Lichtenstein, S., & Slovic, P. (1971). Reversal of preferences between bids and choices in gambling decisions. *Journal of Experimental Psychology, 89*, 46–55.

Lichtenstein, S., & Slovic, P. (1973). Response-induced reversals of preference in gambling: An extended replication in Las Vegas. *Journal of Experimental Psychology, 101*, 16–20.

Lichtenstein, S., & Slovic, P. (Eds.). (2006). *The construction of preference.* Cambridge: Cambridge University Press.

Luce, R. D., & Raiffa, H. (1957). *Games and decisions.* New York: Wiley.

Macpherson, R., & Stanovich, K. E. (2007). Cognitive ability, thinking dispositions, and instructional set as predictors of critical thinking. *Learning and Individual Differences, 17*, 115–127.

Manktelow, K. I. (2004). Reasoning and rationality: The pure and the practical. In K. I. Manktelow & M. C. Chung (Eds.), *Psychology of reasoning: Theoretical and historical perspectives* (pp. 157–177). Hove, UK: Psychology Press.

Manktelow, K. I. (2012). *Thinking and reasoning.* Hove, UK: Psychology Press.

Markovits, H., & Nantel, G. (1989). The belief-bias effect in the production and evaluation of logical conclusions. *Memory & Cognition, 17*, 11–17.

Maule, J., & Villejoubert, G. (2007). What lies beneath: Reframing framing effects. *Thinking and Reasoning, 13*, 25–44.

Over, D. E. (2000). Ecological rationality and its heuristics. *Thinking and Reasoning, 6*, 182–192.

Over, D. E. (2004). Rationality and the normative/descriptive distinction. In D. J. Koehler & N. Harvey (Eds.), *Blackwell handbook of judgment and decision making* (pp. 3–18). Malden, MA: Blackwell Publishing.

Perkins, D. N. (1995). *Outsmarting IQ: The emerging science of learnable intelligence.* New York: Free Press.

Sá, W., Kelley, C., Ho, C., & Stanovich, K. E. (2005). Thinking about personal theories: Individual differences in the coordination of theory and evidence. *Personality and Individual Differences, 38*, 1149–1161.

Sá, W., West, R. F., & Stanovich, K. E. (1999). The domain specificity and generality of belief bias: Searching for a generalizable critical thinking skill. *Journal of Educational Psychology, 91*, 497–510.

Savage, L. J. (1954). *The foundations of statistics.* New York: Wiley.

Simon, H. A. (1955). A behavioral model of rational choice. *The Quarterly Journal of Economics, 69*, 99–118.

Simon, H. A. (1956). Rational choice and the structure of the environment. *Psychological Review, 63*, 129–138.

Stanovich, K. E. (1993). Dysrationalia: A new specific learning disability. *Journal of Learning Disabilities, 26*, 501–515.

Stanovich, K. E. (1999). *Who is rational? Studies of individual differences in reasoning.* Mahwah, NJ: Erlbaum.

Stanovich, K. E. (2000). *Progress in understanding reading: Scientific foundations and new frontiers.* New York: Guilford Press.

Stanovich, K. E. (2004). *The robot's rebellion: Finding meaning in the age of Darwin.* Chicago: University of Chicago Press.

Stanovich, K. E. (2009). *What intelligence tests miss: The psychology of rational thought.* New Haven, CT: Yale University Press.

Stanovich, K. E. (2011). *Rationality and the reflective mind.* New York: Oxford University Press.

Stanovich, K. E. (2012). On the distinction between rationality and intelligence: Implications for understanding individual differences in reasoning. In K. Holyoak & R. Morrison (Eds.), *The Oxford handbook of thinking and reasoning* (pp. 343–365). New York: Oxford University Press.

Stanovich, K. E., Cunningham, A. E., & West, R. F. (1998). Literacy experiences and the shaping of cognition. In S. Paris & H. Wellman (Eds.), *Global prospects for education* (pp. 253–288). Washington, DC: American Psychological Association.

Stanovich, K. E., Grunewald, M., & West, R. F. (2003). Cost-benefit reasoning in students with multiple secondary school suspensions. *Personality and Individual Differences, 35,* 1061–1072.

Stanovich, K. E., & Toplak, M. E. (2012). Defining features versus incidental correlates of Type 1 and Type 2 processing. *Mind & Society, 11,* 3–13.

Stanovich, K. E., & West, R. F. (1997). Reasoning independently of prior belief and individual differences in actively open-minded thinking. *Journal of Educational Psychology, 89,* 342–357.

Stanovich, K. E., & West, R. F. (1998a). Cognitive ability and variation in selection task performance. *Thinking and Reasoning, 4,* 193–230.

Stanovich, K. E., & West, R. F. (1998b). Individual differences in framing and conjunction effects. *Thinking and Reasoning, 4,* 289–317.

Stanovich, K. E., & West, R. F. (1998c). Individual differences in rational thought. *Journal of Experimental Psychology: General, 127,* 161–188.

Stanovich, K. E., & West, R. F. (1998d). Who uses base rates and P(D/~H)? An analysis of individual differences. *Memory & Cognition, 26,* 161–179.

Stanovich, K. E., & West, R. F. (1999). Discrepancies between normative and descriptive models of decision making and the understanding/acceptance principle. *Cognitive Psychology, 38,* 349–385.

Stanovich, K. E., & West, R. F. (2000). Individual differences in reasoning: Implications for the rationality debate? *Behavioral and Brain Sciences, 23,* 645–726.

Stanovich, K. E., & West, R. F. (2007). Natural myside bias is independent of cognitive ability. *Thinking & Reasoning, 13,* 225–247.

Stanovich, K. E., & West, R. F. (2008a). On the failure of intelligence to predict myside bias and one-sided bias. *Thinking & Reasoning, 14,* 129–167.

Stanovich, K. E., & West, R. F. (2008b). On the relative independence of thinking biases and cognitive ability. *Journal of Personality and Social Psychology, 94,* 672–695.

Stanovich, K. E., West, R. F., & Toplak, M. E. (2011). Intelligence and rationality. In R. J. Sternberg & S. B. Kaufman (Eds.), *Cambridge handbook of intelligence* (pp. 784–826). New York: Cambridge University Press.

Stanovich, K. E., West, R. F., & Toplak, M. E. (2016). *The Rationality Quotient (RQ): Toward a test of rational thinking.* Cambridge, MA: MIT Press.

Toplak, M., Liu, E., Macpherson, R., Toneatto, T., & Stanovich, K. E. (2007). The reasoning skills and thinking dispositions of problem gamblers: A dual-process taxonomy. *Journal of Behavioral Decision Making, 20,* 103–124.

Toplak, M. E., & Stanovich, K. E. (2002). The domain specificity and generality of disjunctive reasoning: Searching for a generalizable critical thinking skill. *Journal of Educational Psychology, 94,* 197–209.

Toplak, M. E., & Stanovich, K. E. (2003). Associations between myside bias on an informal reasoning task and amount of post-secondary education. *Applied Cognitive Psychology, 17,* 851–860.

Toplak, M. E., West, R. F., & Stanovich, K. E. (2011). The Cognitive Reflection Test as a predictor of performance on heuristics and biases tasks. *Memory & Cognition, 39,* 1275–1289.

Toplak, M. E., West, R. F., & Stanovich, K. E. (2014a). Assessing miserly processing: An expansion of the Cognitive Reflection Test. *Thinking & Reasoning, 20,* 147–168.

Toplak, M. E., West, R. F., & Stanovich, K. E. (2014b). Rational thinking and cognitive sophistication: Development, cognitive abilities, and thinking dispositions. *Developmental Psychology, 50,* 1037–1048.

Tversky, A., & Kahneman, D. (1974). Judgment under uncertainty: Heuristics and biases. *Science, 185,* 1124–1131.

von Neumann, J., & Morgenstern, O. (1944). *The theory of games and economic behavior.* Princeton, NJ: Princeton University Press.

West, R. F., Meserve, R. J., & Stanovich, K. E. (2012). Cognitive sophistication does not attenuate the bias blind spot. *Journal of Personality and Social Psychology, 103,* 506–513.

West, R. F., & Stanovich, K. E. (2003). Is probability matching smart? Associations between probabilistic choices and cognitive ability. *Memory & Cognition, 31,* 243–251.

West, R. F., Toplak, M. E., & Stanovich, K. E. (2008). Heuristics and biases as measures of critical thinking: Associations with cognitive ability and thinking dispositions. *Journal of Educational Psychology, 100,* 930–941.

INDEX

Page numbers in italics indicate tables and figures.

2–4-6 examplar: production, belief 34; proprieties 35; relevance, dilution 36; relevance, overemphasis 33
2–4-6 paradigm, difficulties (pragmatic origin) 33
2–4-6 task (Wason) 40–3; failure, confirmation bias (cause) 31–2; observations/claims 31–2; performance, determination 30; performance, facilitation (cognitive/pragmatic factors) 32–4; pragmatic factors 29; pragmatic factors, impact (Van der Henst replication) 34–6
2–4-6 triple, random generation 35
2x2 contingency table *100*
3x3 de Finetti table *18*
10–12–14 testing 31
10–12–23 testing 31

abduction 156–7
absolute calculation error, positive predictor 47
acceptability requirement 25
accessibility model, updated version (proposal) 76
accumulated bets, impact *155, 157*
action 66
action problems, inference problems (contrast) 44
Actively Open-minded Test (AOT) 48; differences, absence 48–9
adaptive coping, absence 198
additive algebraic structures 129

affect-driven cues 78
affirmation, negation (asymmetry) 104–5
agent-environment system (productivity), interactivity (usage) 46–7
aggression, motive 134–5
aggressor: motive, extenuating circumstances 135; victim, proximity 130
A-ha moment 199
algebraic structures, observation 129
Alzheimer's disease (AD), blame judgement (comparison) 131
Alzheimer's patients, moral judgement 131–2
analytic cognition 170–1
Anderson, Elijah (social information integration theory) 128–9
animals problem 48
answers, changing (probability) *68*
anterior cingulate cortex (ACC), activation 89
anxiety, depression (difference) 193–4
arithmetic problem 48
artificial frequency distributions, absence 23
artificial intelligence (AI) studies 110
ascendingness, relevance 33
asymmetry: focalisation/negation 102–4; usage 104–9
Attentional frame (A-frame) 98, 100–1; B-frame, distinction 101; biases, relationship 109–10; causal induction, representation 100; trade-offs/frame-switching 109–10

attentional resources 89
attributes, asymmetry (usage) 106–8
Aumann, Robert 143
Autism Spectrum Disorder (ASD),
	teenagers 132–4
awkwardness, degree (rating) 119–20
axiomatic approach 206
axioms of choice 206

background knowledge 174
backward induction 139; locus classicus
	146–7; reasoning, usage 145; usage
	145–7
backward induction argument 140–1;
	initiation 144; validity 142–5
Baddeley, Alan 194
Balanced frame (B-frame) 98; A-frame,
	distinction 101; expression 101;
	intervention/commitment 101–2; usage,
	aim 102
Ball, Linden J. 29
Baratgin, Jean 15, 98
base-rate conflict problem 89
Base-Rate Neglect and Moral Judgment 88
base-rate problems, usage 90
base rates 83; evidence, re-evaluation
	88–92; information 90; probability 77
bat-and-ball problem, usage 89
Bayesian approach 61–2; implications 62–3
Bayesian model, usage 106
Bayes's Theorem, likelihood ratio 43
Beck, Aaron 192
Beck, Henry 186–8
belief-based responses: availability 90; DI
	account assumptions 89–90
belief bias 83, 87; avoidance 216; evidence,
	re-evaluation 88–92
Belief-Bias Effect 88
belief, rationality (assessment): 206–7
belief-related biases 109
belonging, base-rate probability 77
benefits, people's judgements (study) 58
bias 73; belief bias 83; confirmation bias
	31–2; matching bias 116; outcome bias,
	susceptibility 161–2
biases: A-frame, relationship 109–10;
	cognitive biases 193; literature 207–11;
	Stanovich/West/Toplak lab 207–8
biconditional interpretation, defect 22
biconditional response, defect 22
bipolar causality 102
bivalence, principle 15–16
blame, judgement 128–30; comparison 131;
	issuance, ability 131
body, mind (relationship) 120–3

brain, thinking/deciding 40–6
Buddhism, tradition 172
Burn story 131–2

candidate cause/target effect, covariation
	information (representation) 100
cards, vowel/even number (appearance)
	55–6
care orientation 128
casava root (eating), face tattoo (presence)
	59–61
causal induction, studies 99
causality: bipolar causality 102; factors 99;
	monopolar causality 100–1
causal reasoning: dual frames 98; two
	frames, characteristics 99
causes, rarity 100
centering (inference form) 24
Centipede game 139; backward induction
	reasoning, usage 145; exponential
	Centipede game, game tree (Aumann)
	142; game tree (Rosenthal) 140;
	infinite-horizon version 147; linear
	Centipede game 140; payoffs 142
centipede games: experimental evidence
	145; rationality/backward induction 139
central London, line trajectories (map
	sections) 187
certainty 66; cognitive resources, allocation
	67–9; fluency 77–8; goal state 69–70;
	rationality 77–8; resource allocation,
	relationship 69
chances 159
change: likelihood 118; perception 172;
	principle 168
changing answers, probability (linear
	relationship) 68
children, moral algebra 133
Chinese, Japanese (differences) 174–5
cognitive biases 193
cognitive capacity, support 173
cognitive default 103
cognitive economy 100
cognitive efforts, deployment 119
cognitive load 121–2
cognitive processes, monitoring/control 66
Cognitive Reflection Task: bat-and-ball
	problem 89; usage 87
cognitive resources, allocation 67–9
cognitive science, rationality (impact)
	205–7
cognitive style/ability 88
cognitive therapy, development 192
collectivism, individualism (distinction)
	171–2

Colman, Andrew M. 139
commitment (B-frame) 101–2
common knowledge assumption 141, 143
communication, utterances (performative function) 30
competitive models, likelihood (comparison) 106
Comprehensive Assessment of Rational Thinking (CART) 202; conceptual background 203–5; construction 207; existence 215; framework/composition 211–14; performance measures 214; subtests, classification framework *212*
computer-based jackpot machine, development 33–4
concept learning, Wason study 29
concurrent outputs, availability 88
conditional assertion 16
conditional event 21, 106
conditional probability hypothesis 21; confirmation 21–2
confidence: action, basis 69; aspirational level, meeting 70; bias 73; calibration 70–3; cues 74–8; discrimination 71–3; familiarity, cue 75–6; fluency, cue 75; judgements 74; memory, positive relationship 71–2; misplaced confidence, consequences 72; relative accuracy 71–2; threshold 70
Confidence, signals 67
confirmation, asymmetry 105
confirmation bias 31–2, 116
conflict base-rate problems, processing 88–9
conflict detection 88–9
Confucianism, tradition 172
conjunction fallacy, lottery tickets (betting odds) *154*
conjunction probability *154*
conjunctive sufficiency 24
conjunct, probability *154*
consequentialist principles, basis 84–5
contaminated mindwave 213–14; domains, avoidance/rejection 214
context 174
context-dependent judgements 128
contradiction, principle 168
contrast-class cues, provision 33
control 66–7
converse Czech book theorem 158
converse Dutch book theorem 155
converse scam theorem 161
conversion steps 156
core (step) 156
costs, people's judgements (study) 58

counterfactual strategy, usage 32
covariation information (representation), 2x2 contingency table (usage) *100*
credences 159
critical thinking, improvement 45–6
cross-cultural experiments 168
cultural differences 173
cultural priming, results 171
cultural relativists, criticisms 166
curse of knowledge 108–9
Czech book theorem 157–8

Darwinian algorithms 10
datum, diagnosticity 43
DAX (complementary rule) 32; ascendingness, relevance 33
DAX hypothesis, negative tests 32–3
DAX-MED version 110
D-cell: disregard 100–1; infinite divergence, implications 100
deciding 40–6
decision making: conflict 87; errors 205
decisions, personal taste basis 61–2
decision-theoretic account 61
decision-theoretic approaches 10
deduction, asymmetry (usage) 104–6
deductive reasoning, research 184
Default Interventionist (DI): accounts 86–8; accounts, assumptions 89–90; DPT, description 86; dual process account, re-evaluation 83; dual process, experimental evidence 83–4
"defective" 2x2 de Finetti table *17*
defective biconditional interpretation 22
defective biconditional response 22
defective truth table 16
"defective" truth table 15
de Finetti table: "defective" 2x2 de Finetti table *17*; many-valued extension 23; 3x3 de Finetti table *18*; usage 21
deflationary use 20
deliberative processing, requirement (absence) 91
deontic conditional: indicative conditional, contrast 57; usage 60
deontic logic, characteristics 56
deontic modals 58, 60
deontic reasoning 54, 123; Bayesian approach 61–2; historical sketch 55–7; occurrence 62; reliance 133; understanding 130
deontic rules, costs/benefits 59–61
deontic selection task 59; indicative selection task, contrast 56
deontic statements, generation 61

deontic tasks: indicative tasks, differences 59–60; reduction, impossibility 57
deontological (non-utilitarian) processing, increase 91
depression: anxiety, difference 193–4; performance pattern, differences 193
depression-related schema 192
Descartes, Rene 191
diagnostic probability 100–1
diagnostic search choices 44
dialectical reasoning 167–70
Dialectical Self Scale 169–70, 172
dialectical thinking, rule-based thinking (contrast) 170
dialecticism 167–8; explanation 170–5
differentiation mode 99
Disappointment theories 195
discrepancy reduction model 69–70
discrimination 71–3
dog's tail, pull/bite 58–9
domains: domain-specific module, Darwinian algorithm 60; self-assessments, objective assessments (relationship) 72–3
dual-factor heuristic (DFH) 100; criticism 101; output, monopolar characteristic 101
dual frames 98
dual-goal (DG) facilitation effect, impact 32–3
dual-goal (DG) instructions 32
dual process (DP): account, re-evaluation 83; conceptualizations 210; examination, paradigms (usage) 85; paradigms 84–6, 88; theories 173
dual processing, evidence 87–8
dual process theory (DPT) 83; claims 84
Dutch book arguments 151–7; bridging process 156–8; upside-down analogue 158
Dutch books 153–6; bets, set 155; creation 154; psychological plausibility 159–62
Dutch book theorem 155, 158; converse Dutch book theorem 155

Easterners: dialectical reasoning 167–70; dialecticism, explanation 170–1; holistic cognition 170–1; illogical reasoning, meaning 166
Easterners, dialecticism (explanation) 170–5; cultural tradition, basis 171–2
economic knowledge 213
effects: rarity 100; Stanovich/West/Toplak lab 207–8
egocentrism: decline 126–7; impact 109
Ekbom, Lennart 147–8
Elqayam, Shira 151

embrained bodies, world interactions 46–9
emotion: process, occurrence 194; reference 191
enumerative (positive) tests, pursuit 31
epistemic rationality 205–6; assessment, axiomatic approach (usage) 206
Evans, Jonathan St. B.T. 1, 115, 202
events, probability (overestimation) 117
expected value, sensitivity 213
expense, power (tradeoff) 211, 213
experience, benefit 120
exponential Centipede game, game tree (Aumann) 142
extended mind 151
extenuating circumstances, moral judgement 134–6
Eysenck, Hans 192
Eysenck, Michael 193

face tattoo, presence 59–61
fallacies 18–20; usage 117
familiarity, cue 75–6
feedback, interest 42–3
Feeling of Error (FOE) 89
Feeling of Knowing 67, 71; judgements, increase 76
Feeling of Rightness (FOR) 11, 67; cues 78; linear relationship 68
female psychology, male psychology (differences) 127–8
Festschrift 152
figure confirmation 105
financial literacy 213
finite-horizon Prisoner's Dilemma 147
fluency 77–8; cue 75; misleading cue 74–5
focalisation, asymmetry 102–4
Footbridge problem 84–5, 87
formal classical reasoning 115–16
formal operations, non-contradictory thinking 168
FOR signals 77–8
fourfold correlation coefficient, limit 100
Fourth International Thinking Conference (Durham) 202
frames 98
frame-switching 109–10
Frosch, Caren 139
Functional Magnetic Resonance Imaging (fMRI), usage 89

Games and Economic Behavior (von Neumann/Morgenstern) 139
game theory (history), backward induction (usage) 145–7
game tree 140

gender, moral reasoning (relationship)
127–8
gene-installed goals 174
Gilligan, Carol 127–8, 129
Gimenes, Guillaume 115
Great Rational Debate 203
ground confirmation 105
grounded cognition: examination 120–1;
    influence 121–2; studies 123
grounded rationality 162
grounded theories 216–17
group goals 171

handedness, flexibility 121–2
Handley, Simon 83
Hattori, Ikuko 98
Hattori, Masasi 98
heuristics: literature 207–11; processes 75;
    Stanovich/West/Toplak lab study 207–8
high-functioning autism (HFA) 133
Hitch, Graham 194
holism, principle 168
holistic cognition 170–1
Howarth, Stephanie 83
human reasoning, architecture 62–3
hypotheses: datum, diagnosticity 43;
    oppositional types, construction/
    testing 32
hypothesis testing 106
hypothesis testing behaviour: determination
    43; transformation 41

if not-q, then not-p 106
if p, then necessarily q (modal operator) 22
if p, then probably q (modal operator) 22
if p, then q (form) 55, 57
if p, then q (probability) 18, 21, 24
if p, then q (violators) 60
illogical reasoning, meaning 166
illusion of foresight 103
incorrectness, gut feeling (implication) 89
indicative conditional: "defective" 2x2 de
    Finetti table 17; deontic conditional,
    contrast 57; speech act 58–9; usage,
    perspective 17
indicative reasoning, historical sketch
    55–7
indicative selection task, deontic selection
    task (contrast) 56
indicative tasks, deontic tasks (differences)
    59–60
individualism, collectivism (distinction)
    171–2
inductive reasoning: relevance, role 30;
    Wason study 29
inference form 24

inference problems, action problems
    (contrast) 44
inferences, normative premises 54
inference ticket 15; strength/ticket 21
Inference to the Best Explanation (IBE)
    156–7
inferentialism 25
inferior frontal cortex (IFC), activation
    (enhancement) 87
infinite-horizon game version 147
information design 178; balance
    182; benefits 186; coherence 182;
    conjectures/prescriptions/frameworks
    181–3; harmony 182–3; simplicity 182;
    topographicity 183
information processing, avoidance 215
insight problem solving 48–9
instructional manipulations 46
instrumental ought 153
instrumental rationality 206; CART
    assessment 214; defining 209–10
intelligence: permissive conceptualization
    216–17; reasoning 178; theories, map
    design prescription (embedding) 183–4;
    vernacular term 216–17
intelligence quotient (IQ): difference
    173–4; extant tests 217; testing,
    investment 215; tests 204
intelligence tests: criticism 205; matrix
    items, usage 185
interactivity: impact 49; usage 46–7
interdependence, attitude 171
intervention (B-frame) 101–2
interventionist dual process account,
    re-evaluation 83
intuitive thinking, rule-based thinking
    (contrast) 170
irrationality: assessment 210; CART
    assessment 214
irrational thinking 213
irrelevant sound effect (ISE) 198
irrelevant thoughts/rumination: support
    199; usage 198

jackpot conditions 35–6; initial rule
    announcement 35
jackpot machine, development 34–5
James, William 191
Japanese, Chinese (differences) 174–5
Jeffrey table 23; example 24
Johnson-Laird, Philip 115
judgement: errors 205; making 84; problem,
    normative/logical structure (basis)
    91–2; tasks (responses), T2 processing
    (involvement) 92
Judgements of Learning 67

Judgements of Learning (Metcalfe/Finn) 69
Judgements of Solvability 67
justice orientation 128

Kahneman, Daniel 204
knowledge: assumption 141; background
    knowledge 174; common knowledge
    assumption 141; increase 120; levels *24*;
    limits 118
Kohlberg, Lawrence 127
Krockow, Eva M. 139

laboratory work, importance 45
Lange, Carl 192
Lepeltier, Sandra 126
letter (sealing), 5d stamp 56–7
Letter-number rules, usage 6
license, irrelevance 17
likelihood ratio 43
linear Centipede game 140
linearity, level 181–2
linguistic concepts, relationship 192–3
logical relationships, presentation 184
logical structure, intuitive sensitivity
    89–92
logic, wisdom (contrast) 118–20
London Underground map: knowledge
    183; problems 179
loss aversion 152
lottery tickets: betting odds *154*; outcome
    155, 157; winning, chances 155
love-hate relationship, possibility 20

MacLeod, Colin 193
male psychology, female psychology
    (differences) 127–8
Manktelow, Ken 1, 5–6, 115, 152, 202–3
many-valued extension 23
maps: design effectiveness/subjective
    evaluations, objective measures
    (dissociation) 180; design prescriptions,
    embedding 183–4; implementation
    181; layouts, readability 181; line
    trajectories *187*; octolinear maps, ratings
    180; schematic transit maps, usability/
    acceptability (understanding/optimising)
    178; supplementary information,
    provision 184
matching bias 116
material conditional (material implication)
    15; equivalence 17; true value 20
material conditional, truth table *16*
Mathews, Andrew 193
May, Jon 193
meaning, context (contribution process) 30
MED (complementary rule) 32

MED hypothesis, positive tests 32–3
MED rule, descendingness (relevance) 33
meme-acquired goals 174
meme-installed goals 174
memory, confidence (positive relationship)
    71–2
mental arithmetic 47
mental health problems 198
mental representation 57
Mercer, Tom 115
mere exposure condition 36
mere-exposure effect 180
metacognition 66–7
metacognitive measures, impact 68–9
metamemory: literature, findings 76;
    research 71
metaphors, usage 123
meta-representation, asymmetry (usage)
    108–9
mind, body relationship 120–3
mindwave 211; contaminated mindwave
    213–14
misplaced confidence, consequences 72
missing-link conditional 25
modal, explicit/implicit use 19–20
modal fallacy 19
modal operators 22
Mogg, Karin 193
monitoring 66–7
mono-factorial algebraic structures 129
monopolar causality 100–1
mood: impact, process 191; induction
    procedure 198; weakness 191
moral algebra 133–4
moral decision making, temporal dynamics
    (examination) 91
moral development, social interaction
    (relationship) 126–8
moral dilemma, performance
    (developmental patterns) 87
moral judgement 83, 128–36; Alzheimer's
    patients 131–2; deontic reasoning,
    involvement 132; evidence, re-evaluation
    88–92; extenuating circumstances 134–6;
    factors 129–30; perspective-taking ability,
    involvement 132; premoral judgement
    126–7; structure 130–1
Moral Judgment 88
moral reasoning 126; development,
    classification 127; gender, relationship
    127–8
moral rules, basis 84–5
moral subjectivism 126–7
multi-attribute utility theory (MAUT)
    151–3, 160
multiplicative algebraic structures 129

naïve dialecticism, measurement 169–70
naïve theory 166–7
natural language conditionals, scope
    ambiguity (presence) 19
natural language indicative conditional,
    example 16
natural selection, impact 60
negation: affirmation, asymmetry 104–5;
    asymmetry 102–4; logic 15–16
network theories 193
new information, diagnostic value 44–5
non-dialectical proverbs 169
nonhuman rationality, assessment 210
non-occurrence 102
non-occurrence, occurrence: asymmetry
    100; complementary relationship 102–3;
    non-symmetrical relationship 103
non-prominent pair 107
normative generalisation 156
normative ought 153
normative rationality, violation 152
normative theory 160
normativism 153
norm enforcement, emergence 62
not-p cells, conditional 23
not-p or not-q (supposition) 20
not-p or q (supposition) 15–16
not-p & q (material conditional) 20
number sequences, manipulation 41–2

occurrence, non-occurrence: asymmetry
    100; complementary relationship 102–3;
    non-symmetrical relationship 103
octolinear angles, usage 187–8
octolinear design 178
octolinearity: gold standard conjecture 181;
    ubiquity 180
octolinear maps, ratings 180
one-off decisions 160
one-shot Prisoner's Dilemma 147
ought 162; inference 57–9; instrumental
    ought 153; normative ought 153
outcome bias, susceptibility 161–2
overconfidence, presence 72
Over, David E. 7, 15, 54, 98
Over, Harriet 54

Paris Metro, schematic map (example)
    179
payoffs 139–40
p cards 196–7
Pennequin, Valérie 115
Penney, Krüsi 35
people, naïve theory 166–7
perfect information, competitive games
    145–6

performance (determination) 74; pragmatic
    factors, role 30
Perham, Nick 191
Perkins, David 211
personality, dispositional approach 192
perspective taking 130–1; ability,
    reliance 133
petrol consumption, determination 44
physical balance 122–3
Piaget, Jean (theory) 126–7
P(if p, then q), identity 21
P(if p, then q), natural language
    conditional 20
plague condition 42
player rationality 143
player vertex, rationality 144
pleonastic use 20
P(not-p or q), probability 20
positive consequences, testing 42
positive test strategy, application 31–2
postal task, real life activity 56
power, expense (tradeoff) 211, 213
p & q (material conditional) 20
pragmatic factors: impact, Van der
    Henst replication 34–6; importance 8;
    role 30
pragmatic generalisation 156, 160–1;
    damage 161
pragmatic rationality 155
pragmatic reasoning schemas 57
pragmatic relevance 10
precondition, meeting 8
prediction flexibility 118
pre-exposure triples, composition 34
premoral judgement 126–7
principal principle 159
principle of bivalence 15–16
Prisoner's Dilemma: finite-horizon
    Prisoner's Dilemma game 147; game,
    conventional payoffs *146*; one-shot
    Prisoner's Dilemma game 147
prisoner's fallacious reasoning, exposure
    148
probabilistic numeracy 213
probability calculus 206–7
probability conditional 106
problems: everyday life usage 116–18;
    non-conflict version 77; physical
    presentation 46
prominent pair 107
pseudodiagnostic reasoning 43–5
psychological science, rational thinking
    assessment (integration) 216–17
Psychology of Reasoning (Wason/
    Johnson-Laird) 5
Pulford, Briony D. 139

Punch story 135
Push story 131, 135

Ramsey test 20–1; usage 21
random process condition 36
rationality 77–8, 139; assessment 206;
    assumption 141, 143; Dutch book
    arguments, bridging process 156–8;
    epistemic rationality 205–6; grounded
    rationality 162; impact 205–7;
    instrumental rationality 206; irrationality,
    assessment 210; nonhuman rationality,
    assessment 210; normative rationality,
    violation 152; operationalization 217;
    player rationality 143; player vertex
    144; pragmatic rationality 155; scams,
    relationship 151; types 205–6
rationality of belief, assessment 206–7
rationality quotient (RQ) 202
rational thinking 210; skills, structure 216;
    test 215
rational thinking, assessment:
    complications/context 215–16;
    psychological science, integration
    216–17
rational thinking, types (classification
    framework) 212
realistic conditionals, experiments 23
real-world hypothesis testing 29
reasoning 115, 178; biases 74–5, 77;
    conflict 87; context 41, 45–6; deductive
    reasoning, research 184; dual process
    examination, paradigms (usage) 85;
    everyday life usage 116–18; formal
    classical reasoning 115–16; grounded
    cognition, influence 121; illogical
    reasoning, meaning 167; mood, impact
    (process) 191; moral reasoning 123;
    performance 194–5; performance,
    irrelevant thoughts (influence) 199;
    problems, solving (training) 73; schemas
    10; theories, map design prescriptions
    (embedding) 183–4
reductionist position 152–3
Regret theories 195
Rejoicing 195
relative accuracy 71–2, 74
relevance, communicative principle 30
resource allocation, certainty
    (relationship) 69
rethinking time, linear relationship 68
Richards, Anne 193
risk knowledge 213
Roberts, Maxwell J. 178
Rubin's vase 103, 104

rule-based inference 167
rule-based reasoning 167
rule-based thinking: intuitive/dialectical
    thinking, contrast 170; preference 167
rumination, usage 198

Salvano-Pardieu, Véronique 126
scams, rationality (relationship) 151
scam theorem 161
schematic maps 178; examples 178–9;
    logical relationships, presentation 184;
    usage 181–2
Schematic, Propositional, Analogical, and
    Associative Representation Systems
    (SPAARS) approach 194
schematic transit maps, usability/
    acceptability (understanding/
    optimising) 178
scope ambiguity, presence 19
sealed letter, 5d stamp 56–7
selection task: continuation 58; deontic
    nature, recognition 57; distribution 4;
    early work 4–7; recent work 10–11
self-assessments: basis 74; objective
    assessments, relationship 72–3
self-blame 198
self-defeating prophecy 148
self-evaluations, responses 169
Shapiro, Diana 5
Shot story 132
similarity models, construction 107
skin conductance responses (SCRs),
    usage 89
sociability, attitude 171
social Darwinism, impact 166
social exchanges/cheating, benefits/
    costs 61
social information integration theory
    (Anderson) 128–9
social interaction, moral development
    (relationship) 126–8
social norms 54; creation 58
social psychological research, connections
    54–5
space considerations 30–1
Spielberger State Anxiety Inventory
    197–8
standard control condition 36
Stanovich, Keith E. 202
Stanovich/West/Toplak lab, study
    207–8
structural salience 186
subprime perfect Nash equilibrium
    141–2
supraliminal priming 123

sure loss *155*
sure win *157*
syllogistic reasoning, belief bias
    (avoidance) 216
symbolic reasoning 122

T1 processes, concurrent outputs
    (availability) 88
T1-T2 conflict, identification 88
T2 processes, concurrent outputs
    (availability) 88
T2 processing 88; involvement 92; system,
    engagement 91
tablet group/condition 48
Takahashi, Tatsuji 98
Taoism, tradition 172
teenagers, Autism Spectrum Disorder
    (ASD) 132–4
terminal nodes, payoffs 140
thematic facilitation effect 5
Theory of Mind (ToM) problem 109
thinking 40–6; essence 45–6; irrational
    thinking 213; product 46; quality,
    improvement 45–6; rational thinking
    210; rule-based thinking, preference
    167; transformation 49; types, dual
    frames 98
Thompson, Valerie A. 11, 66
ticket, irrelevance 17
time, rethinking (linear relationship) *68*
Tip of the Tongue phenomenon 71
Toplak, Maggie E. 202
topographical distortions 180
topographicity: damage 183; problems 186
transformation problem 47
triples: assignation 110; examples 34–5;
    generation 33–5; pre-exposure triples,
    composition 34; relevance 36
triple tests 33
true, pleonastic/deflationary use 23
truth functional 15
truth table 15; defect 16; examples *16*;
    future 23–5; past 15–18; present 20–3
truth values 15
Tversky, Amos 204
two frames, characteristics *99*
two-response paradigm, usage 70
Type 1 processing 209–11, 213
Type 2 processing 209–11, 213

uncertainty, recognition 118
unexpected hanging 147–8
utilitarian moral judgements, intuitive basis
    90–1
utilitarian principles, basis 84–5
utility conditional, classification 58
utility, independent ratings 45
utterances, performative function 30

Vaccine condition, participants 42–3
Vallée-Tourangeau, Frédéric/Gaëlle
    35, 40
Van der Henst, pragmatic factors replication
    34–6
ventromedial prefrontal cortex (VMPC),
    damage 87
Vignelli New York subway diagram, failure
    178–9

Wade, Caroline N. 29
Wason, Peter 115; citations, distribution *3*;
    impact 2–4; papers, distribution *4*; 2–4–6
    task, factors 29
Wason selection task: features, seminal
    theoretical papers *4*; history 1; usage
    115
Watts, Fraser 193
weakness of will 208
Web of Science (WoS) 2
Westerners, analytic cognition 170–1
West, Richard F. 202
What Intelligence Tests Miss (Stanovich) 203
white supremacy, impact 166
Who Is Rational? (Evans) 202–3
Williams, Mark 193
will, weakness 208
Wisconsin Card Sorting Test 195
wisdom, logic (contrast) 118–20
working memory (WM) 88; limitations,
    impact 33; measures 91–2; reliance 86;
    resources (availability), limitation (effect)
    86; span scores, prediction 48–9
working memory capacity (WMC) 87;
    utilitarian judgement, relationship 92

Yama, Hiroshi 166
yin/yang 172

zero-end modification 142

For Product Safety Concerns and Information please contact our EU representative GPSR@taylorandfrancis.com Taylor & Francis Verlag GmbH, Kaufingerstraße 24, 80331 München, Germany

Printed and bound by CPI Group (UK) Ltd, Croydon, CR0 4YY

08/05/2025

01864331-0002